# Good Housekeeping's

## Complete book of

# NEEDLECRAFT

# Good Housekeeping's

## Complete book of

# NEEDLECRAFT

## by Vera P. Guild

**Good Housekeeping**
*Book Department*
**250 West 55 Street**
**New York 19, N.Y.**

# Introduction

Skill in the needle arts remains one of the most useful, rewarding, and enjoyable accomplishments a woman can possess. Although it is no longer necessary for you, today's woman, to make all your clothes and furnishings by hand, the needle crafts can still afford you hours of productive leisure activity and bring you unlimited pleasure.

GOOD HOUSEKEEPING'S COMPLETE BOOK OF NEEDLECRAFT was written to help you enjoy the rich satisfaction that can be found in these arts today. The book shows you how to take advantage of modern advances and apply them in the execution of traditional and contemporary designs. It suggests the latest methods that ensure more professional results, and short cuts that leave more time for the interesting details. In short, it takes the basic skills that have been practiced by centuries of women and adapts them especially for you and your world.

Each chapter offers a thorough and independent discussion of one of the hand arts. From an easy-to-follow introduction to materials and equipment, you are led step-by-step through all the fundamentals until you are able to execute the beautiful and intricate designs offered at the end of every section. More than 1,100 illustrations make all the directions clear and quickly understood. If you are a beginner, you can learn to master a new skill; if you are more advanced, you can perfect your technique; and if you are an expert, you can discover new and exciting ways to apply your knowledge.

While each topic is explained in such a way as to help you regardless of the degree of skill you possess, the book itself is designed to increase your interest in all the crafts. You will discover that needlecraft has infinite facets. Besides the more widely practiced arts of sewing, knitting, and crochet, it encompasses tatting, quilting, netting, rug making, and needlepoint. It is possible for you not only to learn to create a dress or sweater, but also to work beautiful Irish lace, do English smocking, and make braided rugs, patchwork quilts, embroidered trimmings, and countless other articles.

With these new skills at your fingertips you will find hundreds of ways to brighten your home and delight your family. You will know how to make skirts, suits, and dresses and to knit sweaters that fit more perfectly than ready-made garments, you will be able to finish clothes to the exact taste of the wearer, and you will never again be disappointed by the discovery that the color and style you prefer is not carried in your size. In addition, the savings you will enjoy will let you buy all the little extras you would like to add to your wardrobe.

To your home you will bring new ideas and abilities which will allow you to personalize your decor and redecorate at minimum cost. You will find that new slipcovers can add life to your family room and that a handmade rug can bring warmth to your guest room, while needlepoint seat covers will lend an air of dignity and luxury to living or dining room. By making or trimming many of your furnishings yourself, you find your whole house beginning to reflect your own particular taste and charm.

While needlecraft makes a very practical contribution to your home and wardrobe, it makes an even greater contribution to your personal satisfaction. Few activities are as rewarding as those that use your creative talents and few achievements give as great a sense of accomplishment as those that require both manual skill and imagination. I sincerely hope that this book will help you find the real pleasure that can be derived from these arts.

V.P.G.

# Acknowledgments

For their gracious cooperation and assistance in the preparation of the technical material in this book, grateful acknowledgment is made to the following authorities in the sewing and allied fields: Coats and Clark Inc., Lily Mills, American Thread Co., Simplicity Pattern Co., Singer Sewing Machine Co., Necchi Sewing Machine Sales Co., Pfaff Sewing Machine Co., Paragon Art and Linen Co., Emile Bernat and Sons, Columbia–Minerva Corp., Bernhard Ulmann Co., Consolidated Trimming Corp., Waverly Fabrics, Kate's Trade Shop.

Special thanks are offered to Janette Householder, designer of the Color Plate Rug; Berta Fry, weaving consultant, for editorial assistance; and to Mildred Spaeth, weaving instructor, for the loan of handwoven articles.

V.P.G.

# Contents

How to plan a sewing room • Equipment needed • Advice on buying and handling fabrics • Step-by-step dressmaking guide for the beginner • Pattern adjustment • How to cut, fit, tailor, and finish a garment • Hints on marking and pressing • Directions for all the basic stitches, seams, hems, tucks, darts, ruffles, pleats, fastenings, and many other sewing details • Help with unusual sewing problems.

Guide to threads and fabrics • Over forty basic embroidery stitches and their variations • How to combine stitches to form interesting designs • Embroidery stitches of more intricacy • A complete pattern for a sampler.

Choosing designs and fabrics • How to put a quilt together, do the quilting stitch, make stuffed quilting • Directions for pieced, appliqué, bisquit, and piece- and quilt-as-you-go quilts with complete patterns for the different types • Hints on caring for quilts.

How to do real English smocking: choosing fabrics and threads, preparing material, gathering or gauging, and smocking stitches • How to do mock and "box pleat" smocking • Four pattern designs for English smocking.

# COLOR PLATES

Good Housekeeping's

Complete book of

# NEEDLECRAFT

CHAPTER 1 # *Sewing*

Almost all women do some kind of sewing. They sew for the most part because they like to. They have found that it is fun and that it satisfies the urge to create. Furthermore there are many advantages in making your own clothes: they fit better, they are styled for your figure, and you can use the fabric of your choice. And who can resist the lovely fabrics offered to the home sewer today? In addition to all of this you can save money, or for the same money you can have more clothes.

Even if you prefer buying your own clothes it is sometimes great fun to make something for someone else, an appropriate gift or an extra surprise for a favorite grandchild or niece. Many women who have never sewed in their lives feel the urge to do so when the first grandchild comes along.

Sewing is a satisfying occupation and makes a wonderful hobby. The basic techniques are given here to start you on your way or to serve as a reference when you come up against a problem.

## IN-A-WALL SEWING ROOM

You may be fortunate enough to have a room to devote exclusively to sewing. How-ever, with today's limited living space you may have only a section of a wall you can utilize for it.

Actually a fully equipped sewing room can be planned in a rather small space as shown on the Color Plate. This is an in-a-wall Sewing Room built in the *Good Housekeeping* Sewing Center.

On the upper shelves you will see storage boxes for fabrics. These are in reality blanket boxes which come ready-covered in attractive glazed chintz. The front panels drop down, which makes it easy to get at the fabrics. One of the boxes can be reserved for work-in-process.

The pattern box on the shelf below is simply a shoe box turned sideways, making four perfect compartments for patterns. On the next shelf you will see a row of transparent plastic refrigerator boxes serving as containers for all kinds of notions, such as snaps, buttons, elastic, zippers, etc.

The sewing machine rests on a pull-out table which is on casters and slides in and out easily. A swivel lamp behind the machine casts a direct light on your sewing.

The two drawers below can be used for storage of attachments, etc., or for extra thread. There is also a roomy storage cabinet beneath the sewing machine large enough to hold a mending basket or other sewing equipment.

A scissors-and-spool board pulls out at the right of the sewing machine. This can hold thread, scissors and pinking shears, bobbins, pin cushion, gauges, and all the small things needed as you work at the machine.

The large space at the right holds a dress form, sleeve board, and ironing board. Also there is room to hang partly finished garments.

The folding doors have two full-length mirrors on the inside. When the mirrors are set at an angle they will give you front, side, and rear views of your garment. With the doors shut the unit is closed off out of sight.

The plans for this unit are available. Send 25¢ for In-A-Wall Sewing Room to Good Housekeeping Bulletin Service, 959 Eighth Avenue, New York 19, New York.

## SEWING EQUIPMENT

### You Will Need

**Sewing Machine.** Many improvements have been made on sewing machines in recent years. Investigate thoroughly a number of good machines before you buy, and purchase one that suits your needs. Keep it clean and in good running order.

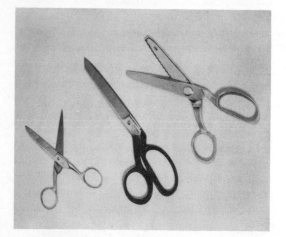

**Scissors and Shears.** Buy dressmaking shears of good quality and keep them for this purpose only. Pinking shears are a time saver, and a pair of small scissors is useful for many small jobs.

**Needles.** Save time by keeping assorted sizes of both hand and machine needles on hand. Hand needles come in several types: Sharps, Betweens, and Crewel. Sharps are of medium length and are most commonly used. Betweens are extra short and are especially good for doing fine stitching on heavy fabric. Crewel or embroidery needles have large eyes and can also be used for regular sewing. An emery bag for cleaning rusty needles is useful.

**Thread.** Also have available an assortment of threads in colors and black and white. Mercerized thread, both regular size and heavy duty, basting cotton, silk, and a heavy thread for sewing on buttons—all should be on hand. Nylon and Dacron threads are good for synthetics and wools, especially those materials with elasticity such as jersey. When matching thread to fabric choose a slightly darker color since it works up lighter.

**Pins.** Use good quality dressmaker pins and a pin cushion.

**Press Cloths.** You can use an old sheet or a length of cotton drill. It should be free of starch and lint. Chemically treated cloths and a new see-through cloth are also available. You will need both heavy and light weight press cloths.

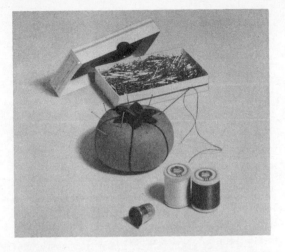

**Thimble.** This should comfortably fit the middle finger. Never try to sew without a thimble.

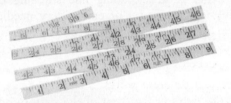

**Tape Measure.** Select a 60″ length of sturdy type. Replace when worn.

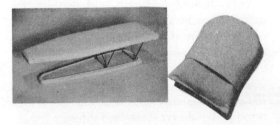

**Rulers and Yard Stick.** A 6″ ruler, a 12″ or 18″ ruler, and a yard stick are all very much needed.

**Iron and Ironing Board.** Have a well-padded ironing board and a good iron. Investigate new types of boards and covers. Also try out steam irons to learn if they fit your needs.

**Tailor's Chalk.** Keep both light and dark chalk for marking various colored fabrics.

**Additional Equipment to Aid You**

Sleeve board

4

Tailor's ham, press mitt, and wooden clapper (see section on pressing)

Velvet board (a stiff but pliable "board" covered with needles over which velvet can be pressed) or a piece of plush 6″ by 12″

Dressmaker's carbon paper, light and dark colors

Tracing wheel

Loop turner

Small sharp awl

Bodkin

Ripper

Hem gauge

Skirt marker

Cutting table

Full-length mirror

Dress form

Inquire at notions counters for the above, and look occasionally thereafter for new and useful sewing aids which appear from time to time.

## IF YOU ARE A BEGINNER

It *is* possible to *jump right in* and make something to wear. If you have never done much sewing and would like to learn to make your own clothes, *then learn by doing.* This is possible *if you can follow directions.* There are many industries in existence today because women like to sew, and they are doing everything in their power to help make sewing easy. This includes making available all kinds of sewing aids, such as sewing machines which do everything but talk, notions and gadgets to save time, thread, zippers, beautiful fabrics, and patterns for things to make for the whole family. Many of these same companies distribute instruction leaflets designed to teach even the least experienced; magazines do their share to assist and inspire; and the patterns themselves include easy to follow directions with step-by-step diagrams to lead the way.

Assuming that you have a *place to sew* and have assembled at least a minimum of equipment necessary for this fascinating craft, here is a list of suggestions offered to help you on your way.

### Step-by-Step Procedure

**1.** Take these measurements of your figure, jot them down, and take them with you to the store.

    *a.* Bust, over the fullest part—do not let tape measure drop at the back.

    *b.* Hips, over the largest part, which is usually about 7″ below the waist.

    *c.* Waist, around smallest part of the waistline.

**2.** Select your fabric, learn the width, but do not buy it. Select something easy to handle. Do not start with a sheer or slippery fabric, a plaid, or one with a nap or pile such as velvet or corduroy.

**3.** Select your pattern. Choose a simple design. To choose your correct pattern size you will first have to forget all about your ready-to-wear size. It has no meaning here—this is a different world. Study the measurement charts in the front of the pattern book and decide (according to your measurements) which *type* you are—misses, women's, junior (a size, not an age), half-size, etc. Then look for a pattern under that category. Buy a dress or blouse pattern by bust measurement, with this exception: when buying a dress pattern, if the hip measurement is unusually large and out of proportion to the bust, then buy according to hip measurement. Since this may necessitate a great deal of alteration on the blouse pattern, it might pay to buy two patterns, one for bust measurement and one for hip. Buy skirt patterns by waist measure. Always buy the pattern size nearest your actual measurements.

**4.** Look on the pattern envelope to determine how much fabric to buy for your size in the width fabric you have selected.

**5.** Ask if the fabric has been pre-shrunk. If not, buy a few inches more than the pattern calls for. Also learn the fiber content of the fabric. Is it all wool, silk, cotton, linen (natural fibers); or is it a synthetic or man-made fiber like rayon, nylon, Dacron, Acrilan,

Orlon, etc.? It may be a blend of two or more of any of these fibers. In any case this knowledge is necessary for proper handling and care of the fabric. If there are any special instructions on care of the fabric try to find this out when purchasing. Buy fabric and "findings" (thread, zipper, etc.).

**6.** If the fabric was not pre-shrunk, do this before cutting (see special instructions on shrinking fabrics).

**7.** Remove the instruction sheet from the pattern envelope and read it carefully. This will save time and errors.

**8.** If your pattern needs alterations, *make them now*. If this is properly done there will be little fitting to do. See "Pattern Alteration."

**9.** Assemble your sewing equipment. Study cutting guide of pattern and circle proper one for your size and the width of fabric. Cut the garment watching the grain line and observing other precautions (see cutting tips).

**10.** Mark, pin, and baste, following instructions as given on sheet. Fit garment.

**11.** Stitch and press as you go. (See hints on pressing.)

**12.** Fit again.

**13.** Finish details, hang skirt, and give final pressing.

This is the general procedure. The following pages give methods and techniques in more detail.

## PUTTING A GARMENT TOGETHER

There are two general methods:

### Custom Method

Alter the pattern carefully before cutting. After cutting garment, mark all pieces at one time. Then remove pattern from blouse parts and stay-stitch all curved or slanted edges. If there are no center seams, baste a guide line down center front and back. Make a row of machine basting between notches at top of sleeve.

Sew darts on front, back, and sleeves. Press. Join blouse front and back at shoulder and underarm seams, leaving opening for placket. Press. Stitch sleeve seam and press. Baste sleeve in armhole, easing in fulness between notches by pulling one thread of machine basting. Press seam toward sleeve.

Remove pattern from skirt, stay-stitch curved edges, and baste guide line down center front and back. Pin and baste side seams starting from bottom or hem edge, leaving left side open for placket. Try on, adjust, stitch, and press.

Baste bodice and skirt together at waistline and fit garment.

Pin in shoulder pads if called for. Make necessary adjustments. Stitch waistline seam and put in zipper. Finish neckline. Press. Try on, mark and put in hem.

### Quick Construction Method

There are short cuts which can be taken when fit is not as important as speed. Children's clothes and some types of house

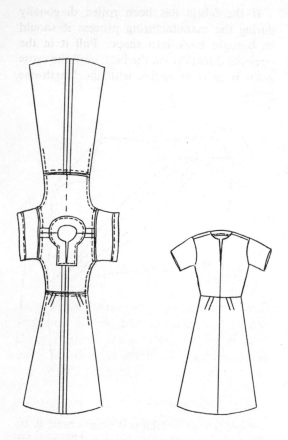

dresses and work clothes can be made in this way when time is limited. Proceed as follows: Alter pattern before cutting the garment. Stay-stitch all curved edges. Do all flat work, such as darts in bodice front and back and skirt front and back. Finish front of bodice if seamed or faced. Face back of neck (if no collar). Join shoulder seams of bodice and facings in one operation. Press and turn facing to inside. Adjust waist length if necessary. Join front and back seams of skirt if any. Press seams open. Make the sleeves but do not sew up underarm seam. Join front bodice to front skirt and back bodice to back skirt. Press seams open. Sew sleeves to armhole. The garment at this stage should still be flat. Try on and adjust at side seams if necessary. Now join side seams and underarm sleeve seam in one operation. Stitch, starting at bottom or hem edge and leave side seam open for placket. Press seams, finish placket, and put in hem.

## FABRICS

### Fibers

The natural fibers are as follows:

*Silk,* which comes from the cocoon of the silk worm. Silk is very strong. It is lustrous, soft and absorbent, and drapes well. It takes dye well and beautiful rich colors can be obtained. These can be (but are not always) fast to light and washing.

*Cotton,* which is obtained from the seed pod of the cotton plant. Cotton is a versatile fiber, very absorbent, strong, and light weight. It can be dyed fast to light and washing and takes well to special finishes.

*Linen,* which comes from the stem of the flax plant. Linen is one of the strongest fibers and very absorbent. It creases easily unless treated. It is cool, has a high luster, and can be dyed color fast.

*Wool,* which comes from sheep. Wool is inherently warm, is absorbent, and wears well. It can be dyed fast to light and washing and is fairly strong.

And other fibers such as camel's-hair, cashmere, mohair, and vicuna, which come from various animals.

**Man-made Fibers.** The synthetic fibers are made from various materials and by many chemical processes. Their number is growing. Some of the better known ones are rayon, nylon, acetate, Dacron, Orlon, Acrilan, Dynel, Vicara, Fiberglas, and plastic.

These also have their own distinctive properties. Some of the qualities of the new fibers to look for are quick drying, wrinkle resistance, water repellence, moth and mildew resistance, permanent shape retention (pleats), and low absorption.

**Blends.** There are many blends of natural and synthetic fibers giving fabric some of the qualities of each. Many fabrics contain several fibers, and new combinations are continually being devised.

When buying fabric learn its fiber content, what can be expected of it, and the special care it will need.

## Fabric Terms

The two outside edges of fabric are known as the *Selvage*. It is usually a woven edge and will not fray. Knit fabrics have no selvage; they may or may not be woven as a tube. The selvage is often woven more tightly than the rest of the fabric and therefore should either be trimmed off or clipped at intervals to prevent drawing.

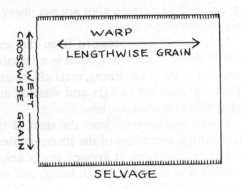

The *Grain* of the fabric runs lengthwise and crosswise. Lengthwise threads are called warp and crosswise threads are called weft. The lengthwise grain is especially important when cutting a garment. *The grain line of the fabric must match the grain line on the pattern.*

## Fabric Preparation

The ends of the fabric may not have been cut exactly with the cross grain when purchased and will need to be straightened. If fabric can be torn, clip selvage and tear across. If not, pull a crosswise thread and cut along the line it leaves.

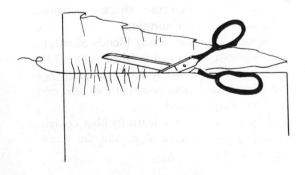

If the fabric has been rolled diagonally during the manufacturing process it should be brought back into shape. Pull it in the opposite direction, on the bias, until the cross grain is at right angles with the lengthwise grain.

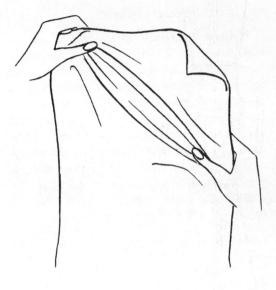

Press out all wrinkles. Woolens need to be pre-shrunk unless marked "Thoroughly sponged and ready for the needle." See section on "Pressing" for instructions on shrinking.

## How to Handle Special Fabrics

**A Word About Plaids.** Plaids present a problem in cutting because they must be matched. There are two kinds of plaids, even and uneven. Matching an even plaid is not very difficult. The matching notches must be laid on corresponding stripes of the plaid. The pattern pieces can, however, be placed facing either way.

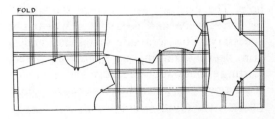

An uneven plaid is more difficult. It must be treated as a one-way fabric with all pattern pieces laid in the same direction. Here again matching notches must be placed on corresponding horizontal and vertical stripes.

## Other Special Fabrics

**Napped Fabrics.** Fabrics with a pile or nap, such as velvet, velveteen, corduroy, wool broadcloth, etc., take some care in cutting. All pattern pieces must be laid in the same direction so that the nap throughout the garment will run in the same direction and thus avoid a light and dark appearance. You will notice that when the nap runs up, the fabric looks darker and richer; when it runs down, it appears lighter and shiny. By running the hand over the fabric you can easily tell which way the nap lies.

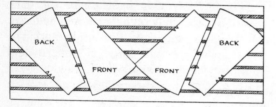

**Stripes.** Matching stripes for a chevron effect on a skirt is not difficult. Use a four-piece skirt pattern. Fold fabric crosswise with stripes matching. Lay front and back skirt pieces diagonally on the fabric placing corresponding notches on matching stripes.

## FITTING AND FINISHING HINTS

1. Buy the correct pattern for your type and size.

2. Alter your pattern before cutting. Check your measurements with the pattern allowing for "ease" and make necessary adjustments. See section on Pattern Adjustment. This will save much fitting later.

3. Run a basting line the full length of center front and back of garment to show if lengthwise threads ("grain") are perfectly straight. Crosswise threads likewise should be perfectly horizontal and should be marked with basting.

4. Retain the lines of the design by keeping the picture before you when you fit. Try dress on right side out.

5. Wear suitable undergarments when trying on dress. Also wear heels of proper height. Try on a suit jacket over a blouse and skirt and a coat over a dress. Stand in a natural manner before a long mirror.

6. Try on the belt if called for; this helps to locate the normal waistline. Pin in shoulder pads if called for; add a little more padding if one shoulder is low.

7. Do not fit too tightly. Ease is necessary for movement and for appearance. Avoid wrinkles. The customary allowance for ease at bust is about 4½″, and 2½″ at upper arm. Also avoid tightness across the back, as the sleeves will pull out. A skirt will slip up if too tight around the hips.

8. In plain set-in sleeves the seam at the armhole should be perfectly smooth.

9. Baggy shorts or slacks may need a shorter crotch.

10. Underarm bodice seams should be perfectly straight up and down and shoulder seams should be directly on top of the shoulder.

11. Side and lower darts in blouse should point to the crown of the bust and end about an inch from it. In case of a low, heavy bust they may end further from the crown.

12. If collar stands away from the neck at the back, remove it and take darts at top of blouse back. Pin collar to blouse. If it is too long, trim shorter at front ends following the line of the pattern.

13. If there are wrinkles across top back of blouse it is probably too long in the center. Trim at neckline and top of shoulder.

14. If skirt wrinkles at top across the

back, it may either be too tight around the hips or too long between waistline and hips. Adjust.

15. Waistline seam should not show above or below the belt.

16. Be sure the zipper is entirely covered with the lap.

17. There should be no ridge at top of hemline. If so, the stitches may be too tight or the pressing not done well.

18. Do not omit interfacings when called for; they make a big difference in the finished appearance of a garment.

## CUTTING

### General Hints

Allow yourself *plenty of space* for cutting. Use the floor if you have no table large enough. Accurate cutting is difficult in cramped quarters.

Look over your pattern carefully. Study especially the enclosed instruction sheet. A cutting diagram will be given. Select the one for your size and width of fabric and circle it.

*Alter your pattern* before cutting. Patterns have to be made in standard measurements but almost every figure varies somewhat from standard proportions. See section on Pattern Adjustment for altering the pattern to fit your figure.

*Grain line* is so important that we mention it again, as it must be kept in mind while cutting. Most patterns have a long printed line which is to be laid parallel with the selvage. Check with ruler as you pin on the pattern. Pin carefully on seam line keeping pattern and fabric flat and smooth.

Cut each piece accurately. Notches may be cut in or out or marked later with chalk.

### To Cut a True Bias

Fold fabric so the cross grain threads run parallel to the selvage or lengthwise grain. The diagonal line formed is the true bias.

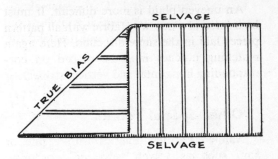

Cut on the fold; then measure and cut strips the width desired.

## MARKING

There are several ways of marking the notches, darts, etc., which serve as guides when putting the garment together.

*With Chalk.* Use light chalk on dark material, dark chalk on light colored material. Mark notches on edges. For inside markings, insert pins straight through pattern and fabric at intervals along lines. Fold pattern back to pins, mark both sides and remove pins.

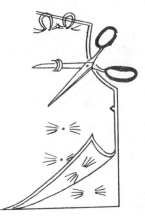

*With Tailor's Tacks.* Use an unknotted double thread in a contrasting color. Take two short stitches through pattern and the layers of fabric. Cut top loops and clip threads between layers leaving tufts on both pieces of fabric.

*With Tracing Wheel.* Use dressmaker's carbon paper in a color which will show on your fabric. This method is not practical for

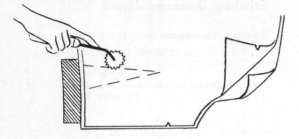

loosely woven or very sheer fabrics. Also, it will spot in pressing on certain fabrics, so a test should be made. Cut paper in strips and lay one piece face up under fabric layers and another face down on top layer under pattern. (This method assumes that fabric has been laid wrong side out for cutting.) Trace straight lines with ruler and others free hand. Diagram shows one layer of fabric only.

## PRESSING

Pressing is very important to good sewing. Have your equipment handy and press each seam or dart before joining to another seam. Press with the grain of the fabric. Lift the iron from place to place instead of pushing it along as in ironing.

### Equipment

A well-padded ironing board and a good iron of suitable weight. Steam irons are preferred by many.

A sleeve board. If necessary a rolled magazine covered with a towel can be used.

Press mitt for armholes, etc. This can be made.

Press cloths: one heavy cotton drill and one of lighter weight muslin.

Tailor's cushion. This can be made.

Sponge.

Clapper.

Needle board or piece of plush.

## Shrinking the Fabric

To prevent disappointment after washing or dry cleaning, shrink the fabric before cutting. Many fabrics are now pre-shrunk; it is well to make sure when buying the fabric.

A tailor will shrink woolen fabric for you, but you can do it yourself. Start the day before you want to do the cutting. Wet a bed sheet and lay it on a flat surface. Snip the selvages of your fabric if they appear tightly woven. Leave the fabric folded lengthwise and lay it on the wet sheet. Roll up the sheet and fabric and leave overnight. Remove and smooth out to dry. The fabric may require some pressing and, if so, do this while slightly damp. Linen and cotton may be soaked in cold water several hours to shrink. Hang evenly and drip dry.

### Pressing Darts

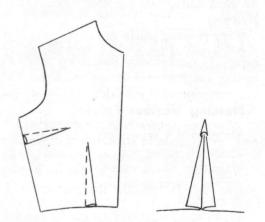

Waistline and shoulder darts are pressed toward the center of the garment. Underarm and sleeve darts are pressed downward. If the fabric is heavy, slash darts and press open.

### Pressing Seams

Plain seams are pressed open before being joined to the next one. Edge-stitched seams are pressed flat.

Use a tailor's cushion or press mitt when pressing curved seams to keep the rounded

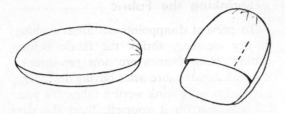

lines of the garment. A press mitt is very useful for armholes. Finish off by turning right side out, using heavy cloth on top and press mitt inside.

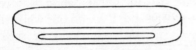

A tailor's wooden clapper is used on woolens to sharpen edges of the collar, lapels, etc. Beat during pressing while fabric is full of steam.

When pressing pleats, press only to within 5 or 6 inches of lower edge. After hemming, finish pressing.

## Pressing Various Fabrics

Always use a press cloth over wool and press on the wrong side. It can be pressed from the right side if necessary (pockets, etc.) by placing a piece of the woolen fabric under the press cloth.

Rayon and silk should always be pressed on the wrong side using a warm iron only. All synthetics are very sensitive to heat. It is well to test a piece of the fabric to learn how warm to have the iron. If there is much sizing, use tissue paper as a press cloth.

Cotton can be pressed from the right side. Dampen to remove wrinkles.

Linen can be pressed from either side.

Embroidered fabrics should be pressed from the wrong side over a thick soft pad or towel.

A needle board is used for velvet, but a piece of plush or velveteen may answer. To steam velvet, place damp cloth over standing iron and hold velvet lightly over steam.

# BASIC SEWING

## Stitches Done by Hand

**Basting.** Basting is temporary and is used to hold the fabric in place until it is stitched.

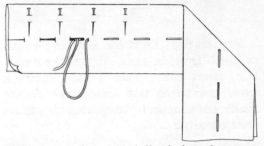

Basting may be even (all stitches the same length) or uneven (long and short stitches).

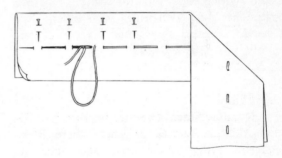

Do not pull too tightly or stretch fabric as you work.

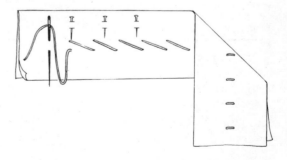

**Diagonal Basting.** Used for holding several thicknesses of fabric together on collars, front interfacings, etc. Keep the needle straight up and down; this makes a slanted stitch.

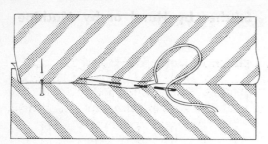

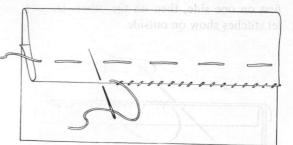

**Slip Basting.** Used for matching stripes or plaids from the right side and for alterations when fitting. Take a short stitch on lower layer; then take a stitch by slipping needle inside upper layer. Stitches should not show on outside.

**Hemming.** Hide knot under hem edge. Take a small stitch picking up a thread or two of the fabric, then catching into very edge of hem as shown. Used for many types of hems but not on skirts, as it will show on the outside.

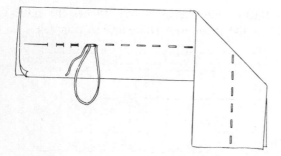

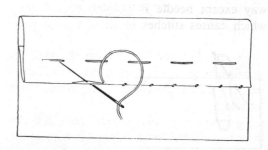

**Running Stitch.** Used for handsewn seams on delicate fabrics or where there is no strain. Hold fabric taut and take up smallest possible amount on the needle. Make all stitches an even length. With practice several stitches may be taken on the needle at one time.

**Blind-Hemming.** This is done the same as plain hemming but the stitches are farther apart. The stitches should not show on the right side. It is sometimes used for hems of skirts.

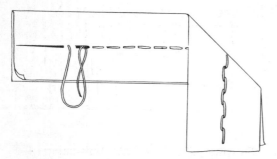

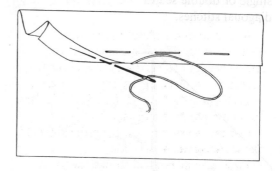

**Back-Stitch.** Bring needle out on the seam line and insert it one stitch back. Bring out one stitch ahead. Insert needle where it last came out and bring out one stitch ahead. Repeat. If done evenly this looks much like machine stitching and can take the place of it.

**Slip-Stitch.** This should be invisible on both sides. Pick up a thread or two of the fabric; then run needle inside hem edge about ¼". Often used for hemming skirts.

*Note:* Two folded edges can be slip-stitched together by catching into inside fold first on one side, then on the other. Do not let stitches show on outside.

## Stitches by Hand or by Machine

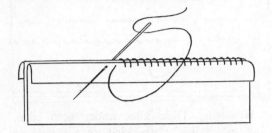

**Whipping.** Used to join two folded or hemmed edges. If needle is slanted as shown, stitches will be slanted. Work on very edge.

*Note:* Overhanding is done in the same way except needle is pointed toward you, which causes stitches to lie straight across.

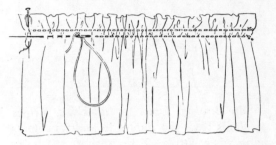

**Gathering.** This is running stitch drawn up to make gathers.

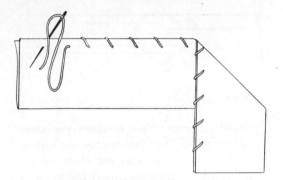

**Overcasting.** Usually done on raw edges and made deep enough to prevent fraying on single or double seams. Slant needle to make diagonal stitches.

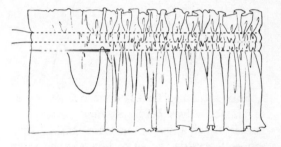

**Shirring.** This is several rows of gathers at even distances apart.

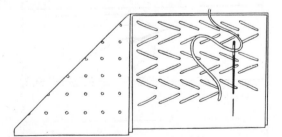

**Padding Stitch.** Work from left to right. Similar to slanted basting. Take a short stitch holding needle in vertical position. Barely catch into lowest layer as stitch should be invisible on outside.

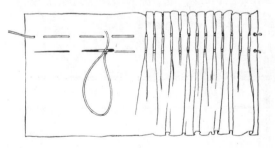

**Gauging.** This is the foundation for smocking. The stitch is a little longer on the right side than underneath but must be done evenly. The rows should be spaced evenly and the stitches directly under each other. When drawn up it will make even folds or pleats. Allow about three times the width for fulness.

## Stitches by Machine

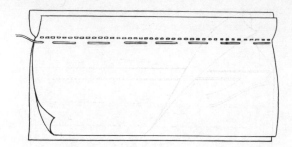

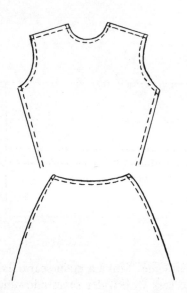

**Plain Seam.** With edges even, pin and baste right sides together. Stitch and press open. No finishing is needed when seam will be covered or the garment lined. On sheer fabrics stitch again just outside first stitching and trim close to the second stitching.

**Stay-stitching.** This is done on all curved or slanted edges before sewing garment together. Stitch a line of regular machine stitching just outside the seam line (in the seam allowance). Stitch from the widest part to the narrowest. This acts as a stay and will help prevent stretching and keep the shape of the garment.

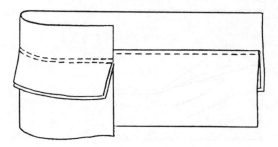

**Top-stitched Plain Seam.** Make a plain seam and press edges to one side. Top-stitch near seam line on right side.

## Kinds of Seams

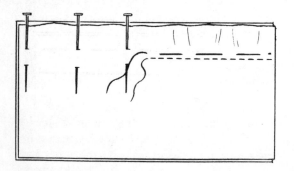

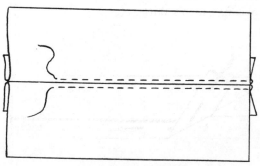

**Easing Fulness.** Keep full side toward you. Pin at close intervals matching ends or notches. Baste and stitch. Allow no tiny pleats to form.

**Double Top-stitched Seam.** Make a plain seam and press open. On outside, stitch close to the seam line on both sides. This gives a tailored-looking finish.

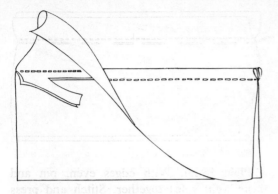

**French Seam.** Make a plain seam on the right side and trim close to the stitching. Turn, crease and stitch again deep enough to cover raw edges on inside. Used on fine fabrics and children's wear.

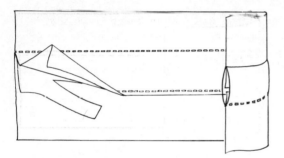

**Flat Felled Seam.** This may be done on the inside or outside of the garment. Stitch a plain seam and press to one side. Trim the under seam allowance. Turn under the raw edge of top seam allowance; baste and stitch close to edge. Used on tailored garments, pyjamas, men's shirts, etc.

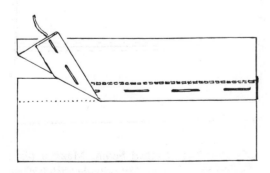

**Lapped Seam.** This is done on the right side of the garment. Turn under one seam

allowance and lap over the other. Stitch along folded edge. If stitching is done about ¼″ from the edge, the seam will look like a tuck.

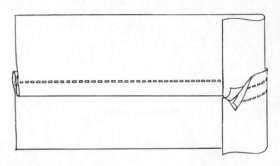

**Welt Seam.** Make a plain seam. Trim one edge. Press with wider seam allowance over narrow one. Stitch on outside ¼″ from seam line. A second stitching may be done near the seam line for a double-stitched welt seam. Very useful on heavy fabrics.

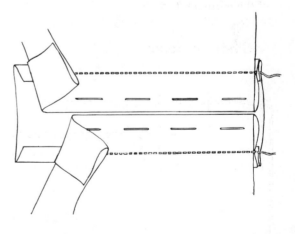

**Slot Seam.** Press under seam allowance on both edges. Center a strip of self fabric underneath. Baste and top-stitch both sides ¼″ or more away from center.

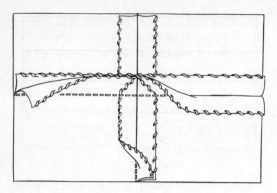

**Crossed Seams.** Stitch and press open first seam. Match and stitch crossing seam. Clip corners as shown.

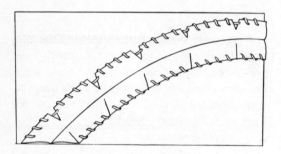

**Curved Seam.** Curved seams must be clipped in order to lie flat. They may be pressed open or to one side and edges overcast.

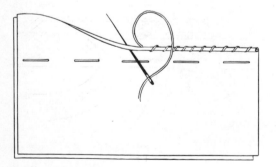

**Rolled Seam.** Suitable for sheer fabrics. Make a plain seam. Roll edges together and whip while rolling. Do not pull tight.

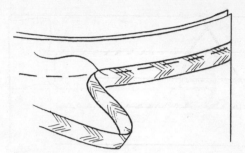

**Stayed Seam.** Certain places in tailored garments require taped seams. Apply the tape as the seam is basted. Stitch through all thicknesses, or whip tape on by hand after seam is stitched.

**Piped and Corded Seam.** Fold a strip of bias through the center. Place between edges of seam with the fold extending beyond the seam line on right side. Baste and stitch.

To make a corded seam insert cording inside bias fold, and baste before placing in seam.

## Seam Finishes

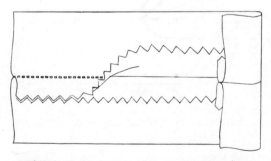

**Pinked Seam.** Use only on firmly woven fabrics. Stitch and press open or to one side and pink edges.

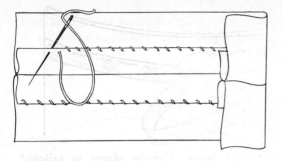

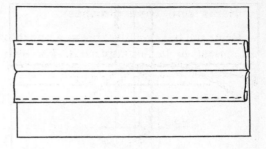

**Overcast Seam.** Edges of a plain seam may be overcast after pressing open. If edges are pressed to one side, overcast together.

**Seam with Stitched Edges.** Make seams and press open. Turn edges under and stitch close to edge. They can be stitched before being pressed open.

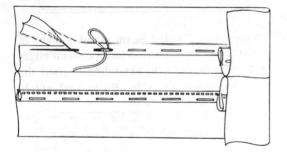

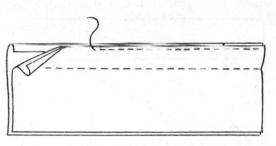

**Bound Seam.** Used on unlined jackets or coats. Stitch seam and press open. Bind edges with seam binding or bias fold.

**Seam with Edges Stitched Together.** Make a plain seam. Turn edges toward each other and stitch together.

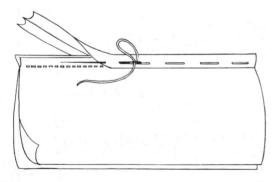

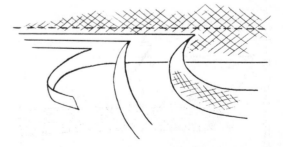

**Double-bound Seam.** Stitch seam, trim and bind both edges together with seam binding or bias fold.

**Beveled Seam.** Used on seams with interfacing or on thick fabrics. After seam is stitched, the layers are trimmed to different widths. This avoids a ridge on edge of seam.

## Hems and Hem Finishes

Hems can be decorative, but as a rule they are meant to be inconspicuous. For skirt

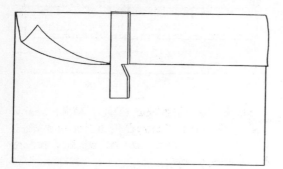

hems, after marking, turn on the hem line and pin and baste on the fold. Use a gauge to mark the width of hem and trim. Use the finish best suited to fabric and garment.

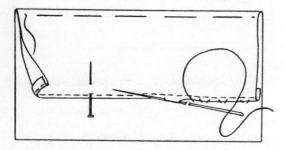

**Hem with Stitched Edge.** Use on cotton or firmly woven silk or synthetic fabrics. Turn under raw edge and stitch. Pin in place and slip-stitch.

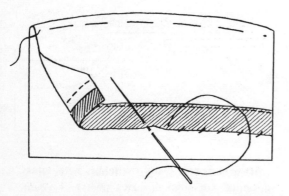

**Taped Hem.** Especially good for fabrics which ravel easily. After turning and trim-

ming, stitch seam binding to edge of hem, easing slightly. Pin and blind-hem edge of tape to skirt.

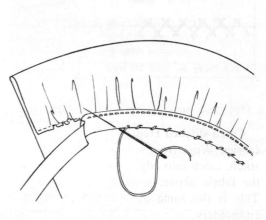

**Circular Hem.** To get rid of fulness in hem, run a row of machine-basting (long stitches) at top of hem. Pull up to fit and distribute fulness evenly. Using a damp cloth, press to shrink out fulness. Stitch seam binding to edge and blind-hem to position.

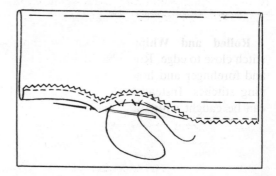

**Tailor's Invisible Hem.** Stitch and pink the raw edge. Baste hem ½″ away from stitching. Turn the pinked edge back and slip-stitch, catching into hem and then picking up only a thread or two of skirt fabric. Press edge flat. There is little pull on this type of hem and it is practically invisible on the outside.

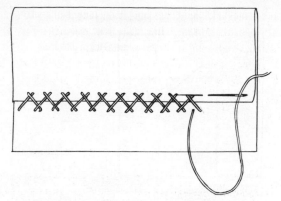

edge toward you ¼″ or less. Hide the knot under the fold and take a tiny stitch in the fabric below the fold and a little forward. Take a tiny stitch in edge of fold and a little forward. Repeat for an inch or so. The effect will be zigzag stitches. Draw up and the hem will roll. Repeat.

**Catch-stitched Hem.** Very good for heavy fabrics. Work from left to right. With back-stitch, catch into edge of hem and then into the fabric above, working back and forth. This is the same as herringbone stitch in embroidery.

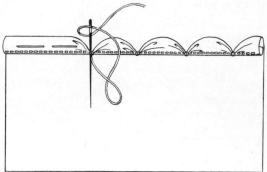

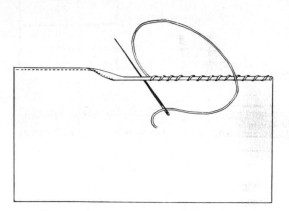

**Shell Hem.** This is a decorative finish. Baste a narrow hem (about ½″ or less). Make running stitches along turned edge of hem for ¼″ to ½″. Take 2 stitches over the edge, drawing up tightly. Repeat, spacing evenly. This can also be used on tucks.

**Rolled and Whipped Hem.** Machine-stitch close to edge. Roll edge between thumb and forefinger and hold in place with whipping stitches. Instead of whipping, the roll can be caught with slip-stitching.

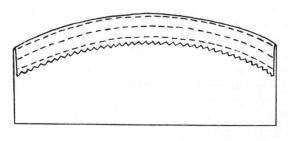

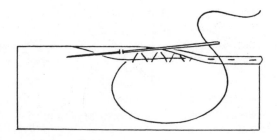

**Jiffy Hand-rolled Hem.** This is a quick way to make a narrow rolled hem. Fold the

**Hem with Decorative Stitches.** After pinking edge, turn a narrow hem and press. Do several rows of machine-stitching spacing evenly. Suitable for a circular hem.

## Corners

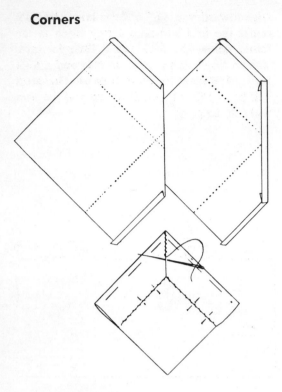

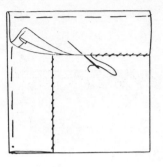

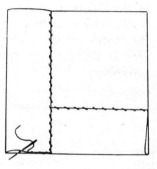

**Trimmed Corner.** Used on pockets, etc. Turn hems the desired width and crease. Turn edges on seam line and press. Fold corner diagonally exactly on creased corner point and trim to within ¼″. Turn hem on creased lines, baste edges, press, and hem.

cut away fabric where it overlaps, leaving seam width. Put in hems and slip-stitch lower edge.

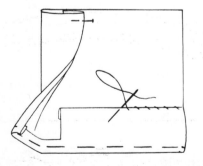

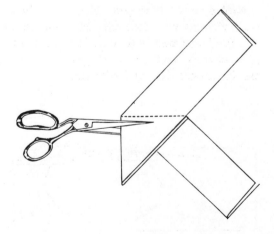

**Overlapping Corner.** Turn up hem on one side and baste. Before turning second hem,

**Mitered Corner.** Turn hem to the outside and fold the corner so it lies flat. Stitch

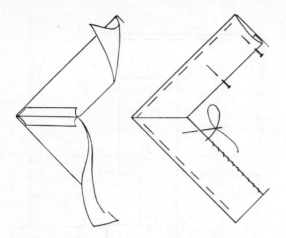

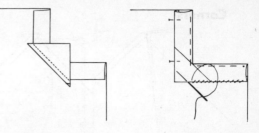

diagonally on the folded line ending exactly at the corner. Trim seam and press open. Turn to inside and finish hem.

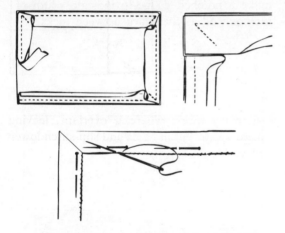

**Turning Corner with Trimming Band.** Right sides together, pin band to edge of fabric. Turn corner by making a fold in band. Crease fold. Unpin and stitch on crease. Trim and press seam open. Turn band to reverse side of fabric, and hem by hand.

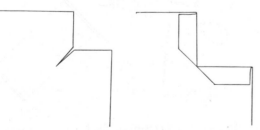

**Corner with Extension.** Cut diagonally into corner the desired width. Fold hem to

wrong side and stitch bias edge of a triangle across corner. Turn under edges and hem.

### Darts

The primary purpose of darts is to fit or mold the garment to the curves of the figure at the bust, hips, shoulders, etc. They are usually done on the inside of the garment. Darts should be basted for a first fitting and adjusted if necessary.

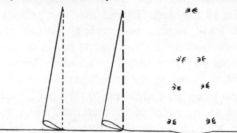

**Simple Dart.** After marking, fold fabric so markings match. Pin, baste, and stitch. Last few stitches at point should taper off very close to edge. In heavy fabrics, slash and press open.

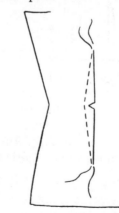

**Waistline Dart.** These darts come to a point at both ends and are clipped at the waistline to prevent drawing.

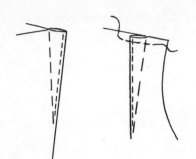

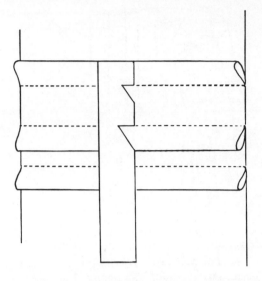

**Edge-stitched Dart.** Mark, pin, and baste. Stitch on the folded edge only. Turn dart and baste to garment across top. After seaming, remove basting.

**To Stitch a Dart with No Thread Ends.** Darts are sometimes made on the outside as functional trimming. When used in this way, there is a method of stitching with one thread so there are no thread ends at the point of the dart. Thread machine as usual but leave needle unthreaded. Thread the needle with the bobbin thread but in reverse of the way it is usually threaded. Tie the bobbin thread to the spool thread and wind spool until the knot is up to the spool. Now start at the point of the dart and stitch the dart with this continuous thread.

make a notched gauge to indicate width of tuck as well as the space between tucks.

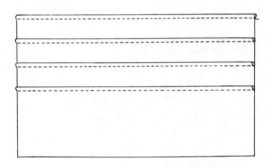

**Pin Tucks.** These can be run by hand or by machine. Measure and crease the fabric on the grain. Stitch close to the crease.

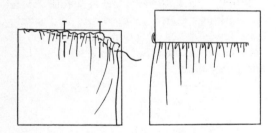

**Gathered or Pleated Dart.** The lower edge of the slash is wider than the top, as indicated by the pattern. Gather or pleat the lower edge to fit the upper. Seam together, tapering to the end of the slash. The slash may be stayed with a piece of fabric before gathering.

## Tucks

Tucks are usually used for decoration and may be all of even width or they may be graduated in width. To insure even spacing,

**Decorative Trimming Tucks.** Draw a wavy or scalloped line. Use tiny overhand stitches following the line.

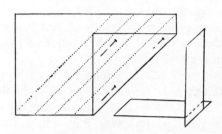

## Bias Bindings and Facings

**Grouped Tucks.** Arrange tucks in groups, spacing as desired.

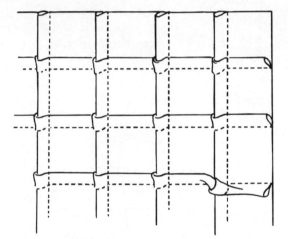

**Cutting Bias Binding.** Use a square or rectangular piece of fabric; fold so the crosswise grain, or weft meets, or is parallel to the selvage edge or lengthwise grain. The diagonal edge is the true bias. Pin on fold and mark rows of bias the desired width. Cut.

Lap ends of 2 strips so threads are parallel. Stitch, trim, and press open.

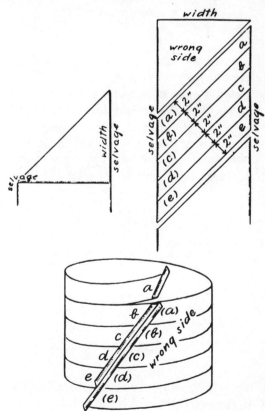

**Cross Tucks.** Measure, mark, and stitch tucks in one direction. Mark and stitch tucks in opposite direction crossing the first group. Use on light weight fabrics only.

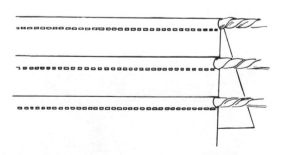

**Corded Tucks.** Measure for tucks. Encase cord at marking and stitch using cording foot.

**Cutting a Continuous Strip of Bias.** Use a rectangular piece of fabric which has been cut on the grain.

24

On the wrong side of the fabric mark a true bias line from the upper corner to the opposite side. (The easiest way to do this is to crease and fold as explained above.)

Measure down the width of bias wanted and draw a second line. Measure and mark remaining space.

With right sides together, fold lengthwise (markings will be crosswise). Match the first line to the second line allowing for a ¼″ seam. The following lines will match. Stitch seam, press open, and cut a continuous strip.

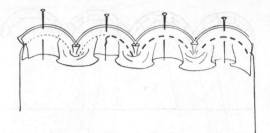

**Binding Scallops.** With bias toward you and edges even, baste binding to scalloped edge, easing it over curves and stretching at corners. Stitch and trim seam to ⅛ inch.

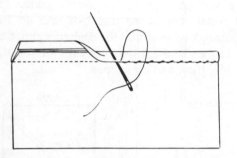

**Using Single Binding.** Use bias tape or cut a bias strip. With right sides together and edges even, stitch seam. Turn binding over seam to wrong side. Hem to seam. Edge may also be encased in bias fold tape in one operation. Baste and stitch catching all thicknesses.

Turn under on wrong side and hem to stitching, mitering corners.

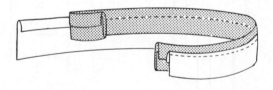

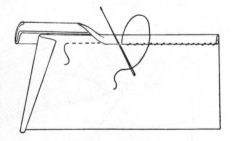

**Piped Facing.** Press the edges on a true bias strip so the fold is twice as wide on one side as on the other. Wrong sides together, place piping so it extends beyond fold. Baste and stitch on outside edge.

**French Binding.** Used on sheer fabrics. Cut binding 6 times the finished width and press double lengthwise. Raw edges together, stitch seam. Turn folded edge over and hem to seam line. Most attractive when very narrow.

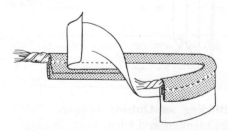

*Note:* Cording may be encased in bias before application.

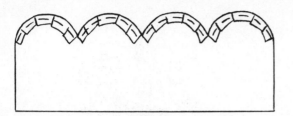

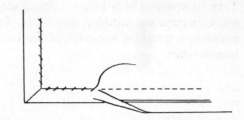

**Scallops with Piping.** Turn and baste the edges of the scallops to the wrong side, clipping them so that they will lie flat. Baste a

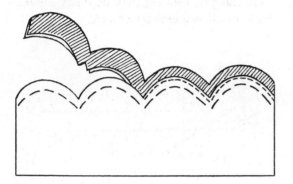

folded bias piping under edges letting a little extend beyond edge. Top-stitch on edge of scallops.

raising needle over fold at corner. Turn to wrong side and hem.

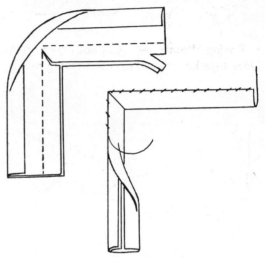

**Binding Inside Corner.** With right sides together and edges even, pin and baste bias binding to corner. Stretch binding at corner, and when stitching pivot the needle. Turn to wrong side and hem.

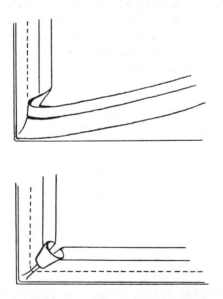

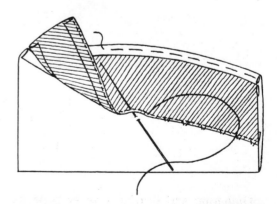

**Binding an Outside Corner.** With right sides together and edges even, pin and baste bias binding to corner. Allow fabric to make a perfect miter at corner. Stitch around,

**Facing a Hem.** Cut a true bias about 2″ wide for facing or use ready-made facing in cotton or acetate. Lay right sides together with edges even and stitch. Press seam open.

Turn to wrong side making the fold a seam-width beyond the stitching and baste. Turn under and stitch the raw edge of the facing. Hem to skirt.

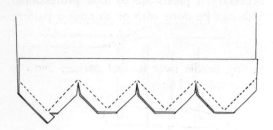

**Facing Points or Scallops.** With right sides together, baste and stitch facing to fab-

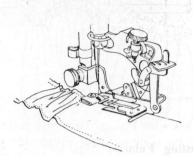

Ruffling or pleating may be quickly done with sewing machine attachments.

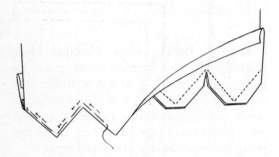

ric. Trim seam, clip corner, and cut off points. Turn to right side and baste along fold.

### Gathering, Shirring, Ruffles

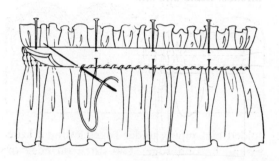

**Stayed Shirring.** Cut a piece of fabric for a stay the size of shirred area plus seam all around. Turn under edges of a stay so it is the width of the shirring. Pin and baste to wrong side and hem invisibly.

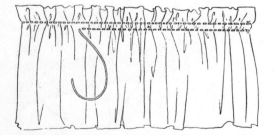

Gathering and shirring may be done by hand or machine. See Stitches under Basic Sewing for gathering by hand. To gather by machine, set for longest stitch. Pull up the bobbin thread.

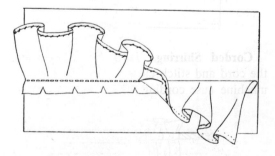

**Circular Ruffle.** Finish the edge of the ruffle. Stay-stitch near the seam line on inside curve and clip almost to the stitching. With right sides together, pin and stitch ruffle in position.

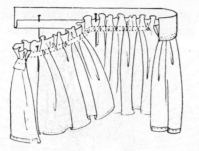

**Adjusting Fulness.** Measure and mark ruffle and the space it is to fit into 4 equal parts (or more if it is a long space). Draw up and match markings and adjust fulness evenly in the spaces. Fasten gathering threads. Baste and stitch.

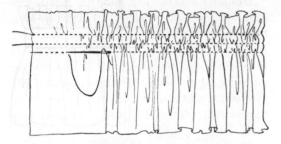

**Ruffle with Heading.** Turn edge the width of the heading plus seam allowance. Make 2 or 3 rows of gathers by hand or machine. Baste in place, adjusting fulness, and stitch.

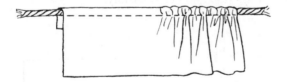

**Corded Shirring.** Turn fabric encasing the cord and stitch close to cord by hand or machine (use cording foot). Make as many

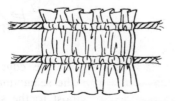

rows as desired. Draw gathers up on the cord to the required fulness.

## Pleating

Pleats may be pressed or, for a softer effect, be left unpressed. Careful marking is necessary if pleats are to look professional. This can be done with or without a pattern.

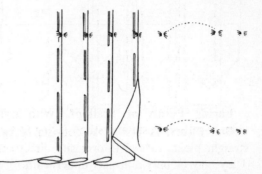

**Using a Pattern when Pleating.** Mark carefully the pattern indications given for pleats. Bring markings of a fold to the next line of markings. Pin, baste, and press. In small areas it is possible to pin on pattern and pleat pattern and fabric together. Baste and press. Remove pattern, stitch, and press.

**Pleating without a Pattern.** For a full pleated skirt (edges of pleats meeting) the fabric allowance is 3 times the hip measurement at the widest part. Join seams leaving placket opening at top of one seam. Measure length and hem the skirt. Lay in the pleats, pin and baste, tapering and lapping to fit waistline. Keep pleats uniform. Try on. Press and stitch.

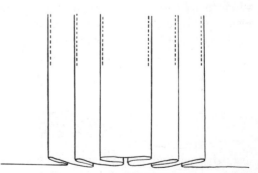

**Stitching Pleats.** To prevent stretching fabric, stitch yoke pleats in place from the bottom up.

**One-way Knife Pleats.** Lap pleat from right to left and arrange so a pleat will cover the placket.

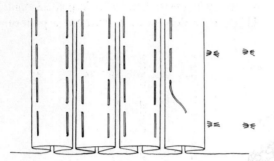

**Box Pleats.** A box pleat consists of two straight pleats turned in opposite directions. They may or may not meet underneath.

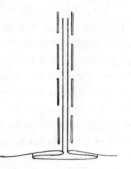

**Inverted Pleat.** An inverted pleat consists of two straight pleats turned toward each other and meeting.

**Edge-stitching Pleats.** Pleats may be edge-stitched (on the fold) if desired. This keeps the pleats in. After skirt is hemmed and pleats are basted, start at the bottom and stitch to waistline or to the point where the pleats are to be stitched in place. Edge-stitching is often used on sunburst pleats.

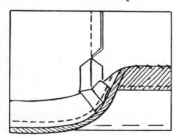

**Hemming Pleat with a Seam.** Press seam open inside of hem.

Turn up hem and clip seam at top if fab-

ric is firmly woven. In thin fabrics turn the edge gradually. Finish hem and press pleat.

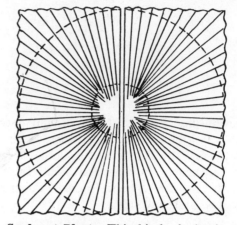

**Sunburst Pleats.** This kind of pleating is done by machine. Prepare fabric by sewing together pieces to form a large square. Have it pleated. Cut out center circle a little less than the waist measurement. Stay-stitch the cut edge. Make placket on line of a pleat. Attach waistband to the cut edge clipping curves. Edge-stitch pleats if desired. Try on and mark hem.

**Machine Pleating.** There are many kinds to choose from. If you are near a good pleating establishment, consult them to learn how much width to allow and how to prepare fabric. It may differ for different pleating designs. After pleating, baste around top edge catching each pleat.

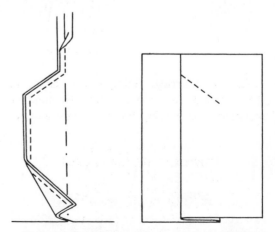

**Extension Pleat.** Stitch seam and extension seam. Fold pleat on seam line. Clip and press open the seam above pleat. On right side stitch top of extension to skirt to hold in place.

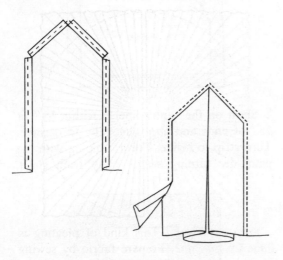

**Inverted Box Pleat, Set In.** Clip corners of opening the width of seam. Lay pleated section under opening, centers matching. Baste and stitch around opening.

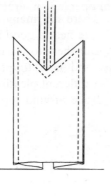

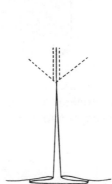

**Set-in Pleat at Seam.** Stitch seam above extension and press open. Fold extension to inside and press. Pin and stitch the underlay piece, matching sides and top edges. Stitch slant-wise on outside to hold in place.

## Buttonholes

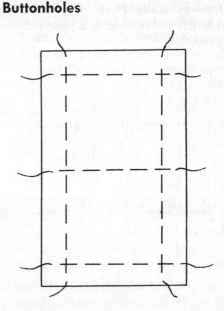

**Marking for Buttonholes.** Buttonholes should be ⅛″ longer than the buttons (larger for ball buttons). For one or more buttonholes, mark the width with vertical basting lines. Mark for each buttonhole with horizontal basting. Follow grain of fabric in both bastings.

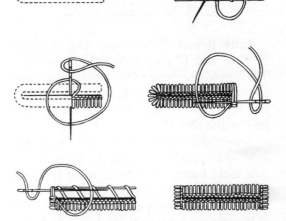

**Worked Buttonholes.** After garment is completed mark position of buttonhole. Baste marking following a thread of the fabric. Machine-stitch around. Cut on basting and overcast edges.

Work from right to left fanning stitches at end nearest edge of fabric. Finish with bar at other end. Buttonholes are worked vertically on shirt bands, fly fronts, and other narrow strips. In this case both ends have bar tacks.

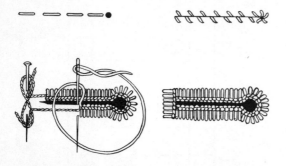

**Tailored Buttonholes.** Punch the end near edge of fabric with a stiletto. Baste and stitch as above. Cut on marked line and overcast edges. For a corded edge, work over a strand of buttonhole twist held taut with a pin. Work a bar tack at end of buttonhole.

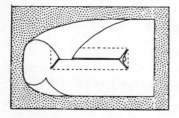

**Patch-Bound Buttonholes.** Cut a patch 2″ wide and 1″ longer than the buttonhole. The lengthwise grain of the fabric should run lengthwise of the buttonhole. The fabric can be cut on the true bias. This is often done on checks and plaids.

*Note:* The patch can be cut in one long strip and basted over all buttonholes at one time if the buttonholes are 2″ apart or more. After stitching around buttonholes the strip is cut half-way between each buttonhole.

If separate pieces are used, crease fabric patch through center lengthwise. Open out and, with right sides together, center and baste with the crease over the marked basting line. Stitch ⅛″ each side of basting and across ends making square corners.

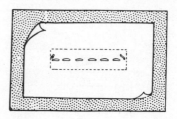

Slash on the center line to within ¼″ or ⅜″ of ends and clip diagonally to corners. Turn strip to inside. Form a piping with the patch by turning seams away from slash.

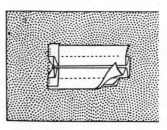

Make tiny box pleat at each end. Baste around. Also take a few short overhand stitches at each end of opening on wrong side to reinforce pleat.

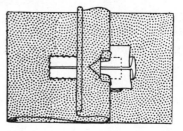

*To face buttonhole,* slash facing through buttonhole opening, clipping corners. Turn in edges and hem.

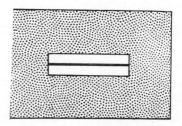

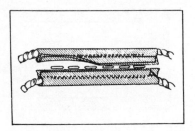

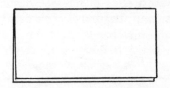

**Corded or Two-Piece Buttonholes.** For each buttonhole you will need a strip twice its length plus two inches. Prepare enough for all buttonholes at one time. Cut a strip ¾″ wide on the bias or straight of fabric. Fold lengthwise right side out and stitch with or without encased cord ⅛″ from fold.

**One-Piece Fold Buttonholes.** Cut a strip 1″ wide and 1″ longer than finished buttonhole. Right side out, fold piece lengthwise down center and press lightly.

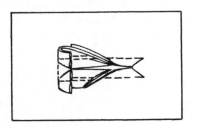

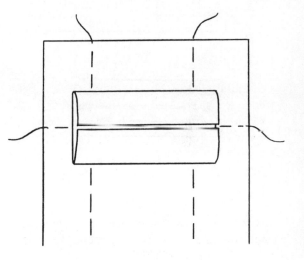

On right side baste the two strips with raw edges meeting on the line of marking for buttonhole. Stitch both sides but not across ends. Slash and clip to corners. Turn strips to wrong side.

Fold with raw edges meeting at creased line. With raw edges up baste to right side of fabric centering over marking.

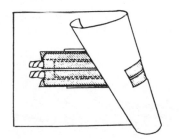

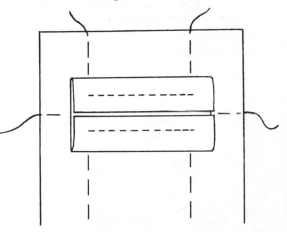

Stitch the triangular ends to the piping. This can be done by hand. Press and face same as Patch-Bound Buttonhole.

Baste and stitch ⅛″ each side of raw edges the length of buttonhole but not across ends.

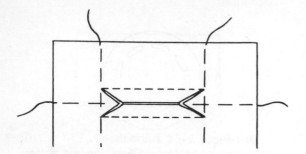

Slash center line and diagonally to corners.

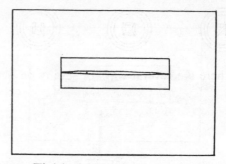

corners. Finished buttonhole should be true and square at corners and follow grain of fabric.

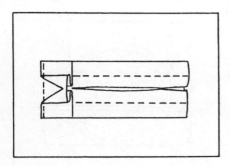

Turn patch to wrong side and stitch the small triangles to the patch by hand, keeping

## Fastenings

**Sewing on Buttons.** HOW TO MARK: Lap garment properly and mark position of button centering it at outer end of buttonhole.

Set button in place with pin on top. Starting on right side, conceal knot under button.

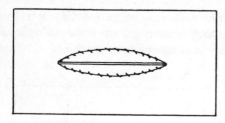

Sew through button and over the pin taking care that the stitches on wrong side are short and almost invisible. Remove pin and wind thread under button to form shank.

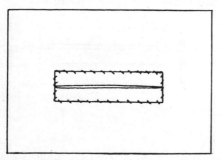

corners square. Press. If facing is called for, slash facing and hem by hand. Facing may be finished with square corners by slashing

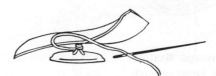

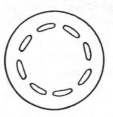

There are several ways of sewing on buttons.

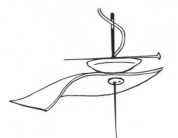

On coats and jackets where there is much strain, a small stay button may be used on the wrong side for reinforcement.

PERFORATED DISK: Disks or rings are covered in the same way as wooden mold. Using matching buttonhole twist take stitches one at a time around edge through disk and fabric. Back-stitches or more decorative stitches may also be used.

**Link Buttons.** These can be made by sewing buttons to the ends of a finished narrow fabric strip. The link can also be made like a French tack. Run thread several times between buttons, then work over the thread with close blanket stitch as shown.

On both mold and disk the back may be finished off neatly by cutting a small square or circle of the fabric and applying to the back of the button. Turn in edges and hem. This covers raw edges and serves as a shank for sewing on.

**Shank Buttons.** Place the shank so stitches will be parallel to edge of garment. This relieves strain. For removable buttons make eyelets. (See Embroidery Section.)

## Loops and Tubing Fasteners

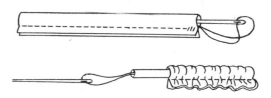

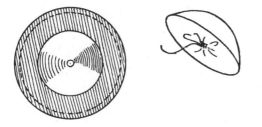

**Covered Buttons.** WOODEN MOLD: Cut a circle large enough to almost meet at back of mold. Run gathering stitches close to edge, insert mold and draw up. Sew over and over to fasten.

**To Make Fabric Tubing.** Fold lengthwise a bias strip of the desired width then stitch and trim seam  Turn inside out with thread and bodkin or tubing turner. Or at-

tach cord at one end of the bias strip, stitch with cording foot and pull cord through tube to turn bias inside out.

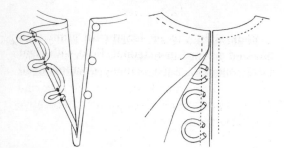

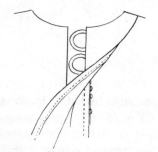

**Applying Loops.** Make as above or use purchased cord. Measure and mark spaces. Pin cord to inside of opening extending loops beyond the edge. Sew loops in place with overhand stitches. Loops may also be cut to fit buttons and sewed on separately. If facing is used place loops on right side with facing on top. Stitch and turn facing.

**Buttonhole-Stitch Loops.** Sew back and forth leaving thread the right length to fit

over buttons. Cover with buttonhole stitch using needle with the eye as the point.

**Frogs.** Use fabric or purchased cord. Twist cord into desired shape keeping seam underneath. Sew in place on wrong side. Attach to garment leaving one loop free to slip over button.

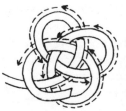

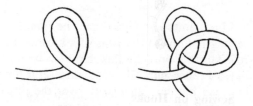

**Chinese Buttons.** Make a fabric cord 6 to 8 inches long, or longer if cord is thick. Follow carefully the steps given in the diagrams. Keep the loops open and rather loose while working; then ease them into a rather tight ball button. Tack the ends and clip.

## Metal Fastenings

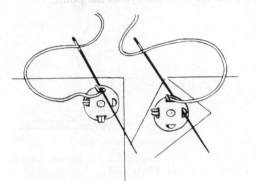

**Sewing on Snaps.** The socket must be exactly opposite the ball. Sew in place with overhand stitches taking several stitches in each hole.

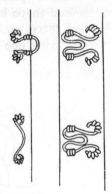

**Sewing on Hooks and Eyes.** When using on edges, place eye slightly back from the edge and leave the hook extending a little. Sew over and over in each ring and under the end of the hook. Thread eyelets may be made in place of the eyes. Make same as buttonhole-stitch loops, only smaller.

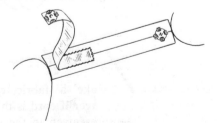

**Lingerie Strap.** Use tape or ribbon and attach on shoulder seam of garment as shown, using snap fastener.

## Belts

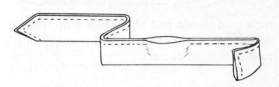

**Plain Belt.** Cut on lengthwise grain with one end pointed or diagonal. Fold with right sides together, stitch, leaving opening, trim

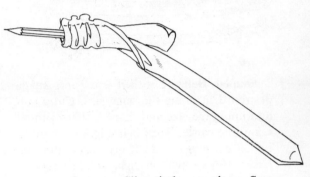

seam and turn. Slip-stitch opening. Sew buckle on straight end. Make eyelets if needed.

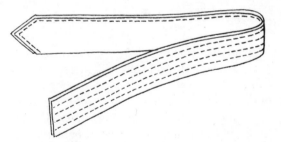

**Interfaced Belt.** Cut interfacing of pre-shrunk cotton and stitch to one half of belt on wrong side before folding and stitching. Make several rows of stitching to hold facing in place. Finish as for plain belt.

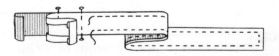

**Belt with Stiffening.** Use belting ribbon which serves as back and facing. Cut fabric ¾″ wider and longer than backing for turn-

## Pockets

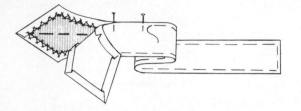

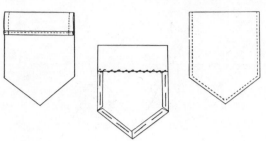

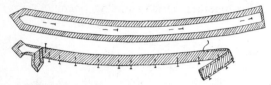

ing under. Pin and baste in place. Edge-stitch on right side. Sew on buckle.

**Shaped Belts.** Cut belt size and shape desired. Cut lining the same size. Cut a stiff interlining the size and shape of belt without seam allowance. Turn belt edges over interlining, clipping curves if necessary. Pin and baste. Edge-stitch on right side if desired. Hem lining edges to belt.

**Patch Pockets Plain.** May be pointed at bottom or not, as desired. Turn in seam allowance at top to wrong side and press. Turn hem to right side and stitch seam at sides. Turn hem to wrong side. Turn and press side seams. If pocket is pointed at bottom, turn up point first, then turn remaining seams. Slip-stitch hem. Baste pocket in place on garment and top-stitch close to edge. On children's garments a small piece of tape may be used at corners on inside of garment for reinforcement.

## Carriers

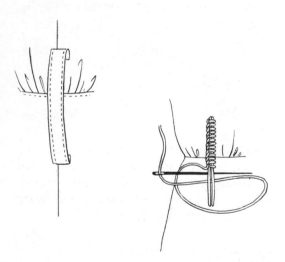

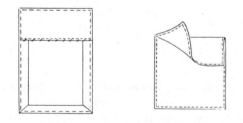

**Flap Pocket.** A loose flap may be made using same procedure as above, but the hem is cut wide enough to include flap. The extra width is later turned to the outside.

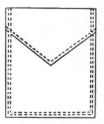

**Fabric.** Use a narrow strip of fabric, folded and stitched (about ¼″ wide when finished). Attach to dress, turning in ends.

**Worked.** Make like a French tack, the proper size to hold belt.

A stitched-down flap is turned to the outside and stitched.

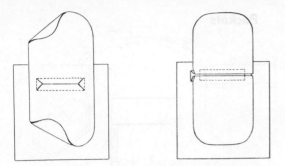

**Bound Pocket.** Made very much like a bound buttonhole. The pocket piece must be 1″ wider than the opening and twice the depth of pocket plus 1″.

On the pocket piece mark or press a line 1″ below center.

Right sides together, this line is centered over the pocket line. Baste on the line. Stitch ¼″ each side of basting and across ends. Slash on center line and diagonally to corners. Turn pocket to wrong side through slash.

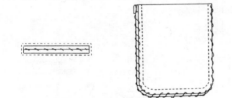

Turn seams back from opening and form a pleat at each end. Baste and press. If desired, pocket may be edge-stitched around on outside. On inside, fold together, baste and stitch around. Trim edges if necessary. Overcast raw edges.

**Welt Pocket.** Cut pieces for welt 1″ longer than pocket opening and twice as wide as finished width plus ½″. Cut pocket piece same as for bound pocket. With right sides together, fold welt lengthwise and stitch ends taking ½″ seams. Trim, turn, and press. (a) On right side of garment lay welt with raw edges just below pocket line.

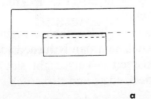

Fold pocket piece 1″ below center. Right sides together, center the fold over opening. Open out, baste and stitch ¼″ each side of marking and across ends (see Bound Pocket) catching welt below marking but not across ends. Slash down center and diagonally to corners. (b) Push pocket through and seam together. (c) Turn welt up and press. Slip-stitch welt ends to position.

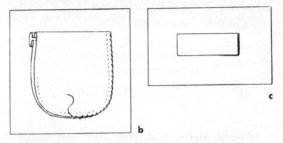

*Flap pocket* is made the same way, except flap is made and placed *above* marking with raw edges on line.

## Collars

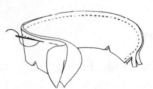

**Applying with Bias Band.** Face the collar leaving neckline side open. Trim seam, turn, baste on folded edge and press. Pin and baste collar to neckline with back centers matched. Turn edge of front opening ¼″ to wrong side and stitch.

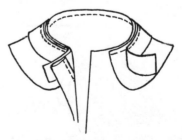

Hem front opening. Baste 1½″-wide bias at edge of collar and overlapping hem. Stitch around neck.

Trim seam, clip on curve, and press. Turn edge of bias to wrong side and blind hem.

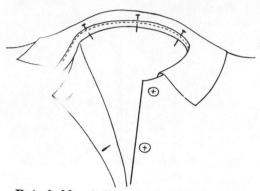

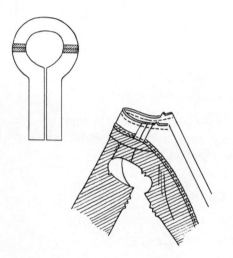

**Detachable Collar.** Face collar leaving neck edge open. Trim, turn, and baste on folded edge. Press. Bind edge of collar with 1″-wide bias strip turning in ends.

Matching center backs, pin collar to neckline. Slip-stitch in place. Snaps may be used to hold collar in place.

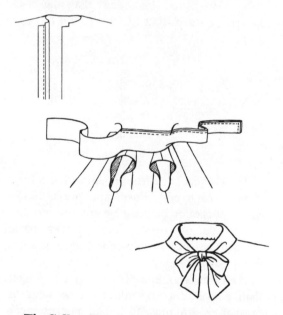

**Applying with Facing.** Face the collar leaving neckline open. Trim seam, turn, baste on folded edge, and press. Pin and baste collar to neckline with back centers matched.

Seam back facing to front facings at shoulder line and press seams open. Pin and baste facings to neckline. Baste and stitch neck seam. Trim, clip curve. Turn facing edges ¼″ to wrong side and stitch.

**Tie Collar.** This is used on a plain lapped closing. Cut tie the width desired. Turn front hems of blouse to right side and stitch at neckline. Clip where stitching ends. Turn to wrong side.

Right sides together and center backs matched, baste tie collar to neckline. Stitch as far as the clip.

Fold tie in half lengthwise, right sides together. Stitch ends and sides as far as the clip. Trim seams. Turn right side out, turn under at neck edge, and slip-stitch.

Turn facings to inside and press. Tack at shoulder seam.

## Necklines

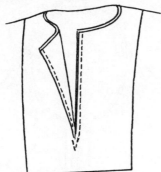

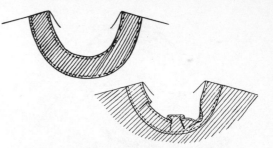

**Slashed Neckline with facing.** Baste facing to garment right sides together, down center of slash. Stitch ¼″ each side of basting graduating to nothing at point. Stitch again around point. Slash to point and turn to wrong side, baste on fold, and press.

under seam allowance and stitch. Hold facing away from bodice and top-stitch on facing near the seam line. Turn to wrong side and press. Tack at shoulders.

## Sleeves

**Types of Sleeves.**
**Long**

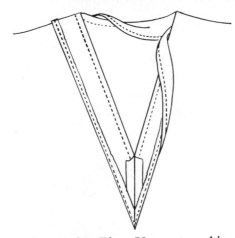

**V-Neck with Bias.** Use a true bias cut 1½″ wide. Right sides together, baste to neckline, mitering at point. Press seam open. Stitch around, trim seam, clipping on curves and at point. Turn and slip-stitch invisibly.

**Shaped Facing.** Cut and sew facing together at shoulder seam. Press seams open. With right sides together baste and stitch to neckline. Trim and clip seam and press seam toward facing. On outer edges of facing turn

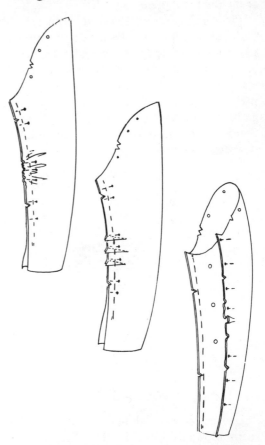

One-piece with gathers for ease at elbow.
One-piece with darts for ease at elbow. These may be left unstitched.
Two-piece shaped for ease.

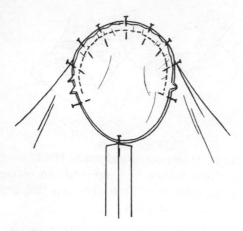

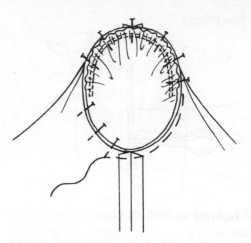

**Setting in a Plain Sleeve.** (In a two-piece sleeve join back seam first and press open.)

Machine-baste (use long stitch) between notches around sleeve top. Join underarm seam and press open.

Place right side of sleeve to right side of garment and hold so the inside of sleeve is toward you. Match and pin underarm seams and notches and the shoulder marking to the shoulder seam. Pull up machine-basting easing fulness to fit armhole avoiding pleats and gathers. Pin at close intervals and baste. Stitch around, starting at underarm and with sleeve side down.

**Gathered Sleeve.** Use two rows of gathering between notches.

With sleeve toward you and right sides together pin sleeve in armhole matching all markings. Baste, stitch, and press.

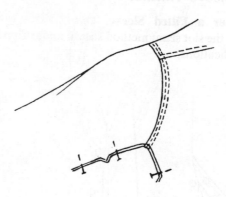

Use a tailor's cushion or mitt and press seam allowance toward sleeve, shrinking out any remaining ease. (On very closely woven fabrics remove sleeve after fitting to armhole and press around top of sleeve after drawing up machine-basting and before basting sleeve into armhole.)

**Shirt Sleeve.** Use a flat felled seam to join sleeve to shirt armhole before making underarm seam. The shirt seam may be turned over the sleeve seam (which is trimmed) or the shirt seam may be trimmed and the sleeve seam be turned over it.

**Gusset in Kimono Sleeve.** A gusset may be added if sleeve is too tight at underarm. On front and back of blouse at underarm mark for a slash about 3″ long pointing toward the shoulder. Stitch ½″ each side of marking to nothing at the point.

Slash between stitching. Stitch underarm seams. Cut a piece of fabric on grain 4″ square. Working from wrong side, pin and baste gusset to slashed edge with ½″ seams

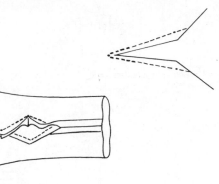

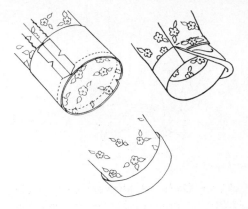

and tapering to nothing at points of slashes. Stitch.

*Hints:* For added strength gusset may be edge-stitched close to seam line on outside. For a fine tailored finish, gusset is sometimes lined with a square of lining fabric. Cut same size as gusset, turn under edges and hem.

### Sleeve Finishes

**For a Fitted Sleeve.** SLIDE FASTENER: Use the slot seam method shown under zipper applications.

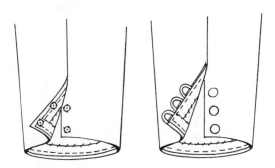

FACED WITH SEAM BINDING: Clip seam where opening ends; then baste and stitch seam binding to right side around edges, mitering corners. Turn to wrong side and hem edge of binding to sleeve invisibly. Lap and sew on snaps.

LOOP FASTENING: Sew fabric loops to front edge of seam. Apply seam binding as for faced sleeve. Lap and sew on buttons. Thread loops may be used and are applied after seam binding is put on.

A buttoned pleat may be used to fit sleeve to wrist. Try on, pin pleat. Sew on buttons and make thread loops.

**Turned-Back Cuffs.** PLAIN: Pin right side of cuff to wrong side of sleeve, matching seams. Stitch and turn to right side. Turn under raw edge and hem over seam. Press. Turn cuff back and tack at seam.

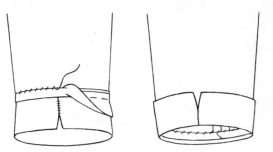

SHAPED: Make the cuff and pin to outside of sleeve. Baste bias strip on top. Join ends and stitch on seam line through all thicknesses. Turn under raw edge of bias and hem. Press. Whip cuff edges together. Turn back cuff.

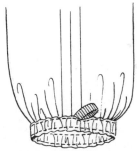

**Casing Hem for Elastic.** Face or hem lower edge of sleeve leaving opening for elastic. Edge-stitch on fold. Insert elastic and close opening.

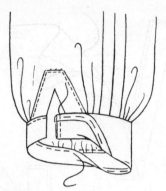

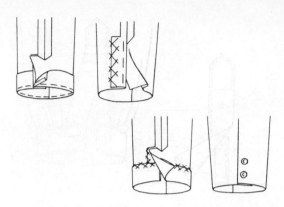

**Cuff on Gathered Sleeve.** Apply facing to slashed opening, turn to wrong side, and blind-hem. Gather sleeve edge and make cuff band. Baste right side of cuff to right side of sleeve adjusting gathers evenly. Stitch, turn to wrong side, turn under edge, and hem over seam.

**Vent with Buttons.** A two-piece sleeve sometimes calls for this finish. Join front seam and back seam above opening. Make buttonholes in upper sleeve section if called for. Clip seam at top end of opening on under sleeve and press seam open above clip. Turn up hem and catch-stitch. Turn extension on upper sleeve, face buttonholes, miter corner, and catch-stitch in place. Turn back extension, miter corner, and catch-stitch. Sew on buttons.

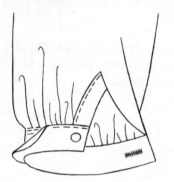

The slash may be bound instead of faced. Cut binding on straight grain and bind opening. Gather edge of sleeve and apply cuff.

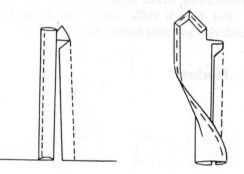

**Classic Shirt-Sleeve Cuff.** Stay-stitch each side of line for opening. Slash opening and diagonally to corners of seam allowance.

Two pieces are used to finish the opening: the underlap extension and the overlap band. Baste right side of underlap to wrong side of back edge. Stitch, taking 1/4" seam, and turn to right side. Turn edge over seam and stitch.

Baste right side of overlap to wrong side of front edge. Stitch, taking 1/4" seam. Turn to right side. Baste under 1/4" seam allowance on free edge and around point.

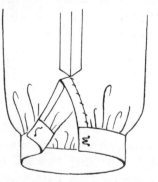

When sleeve opening is on a seam, clip seam at top end of opening and bind opening. Gather edge and apply cuff, turning under top binding.

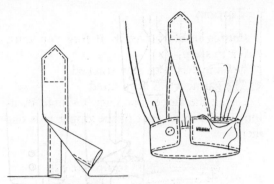

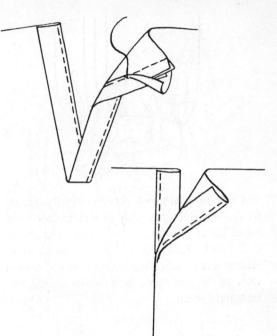

Fold and baste in position with the point in the center. Stitch across upper end, around point, and down side.

Cut interfacing for cuff minus seam allowance on inner edge. Baste interfacing to cuff facing. Right sides together, pin and stitch cuff to facing leaving open at inner edge. Trim seam, turn, and baste edges. Gather edge of sleeve.

With cuff facing to wrong side of sleeve, baste to gathered edge and stitch. Turn edge of outer cuff and baste over seam. Stitch all around cuff. Make worked buttonholes.

For French cuffs, which are wider, fold underlap to inside before putting on cuff.

Turn under edge and stitch. On delicate fabrics start from right side, turn to wrong side and hem by hand.

## Plackets

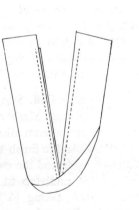

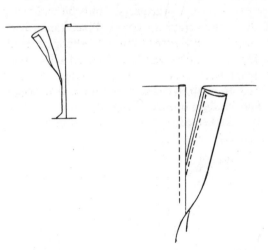

**Slashed Placket with Binding.** Use a strip twice as long as slash and at least 2″ wide. Baste right side of strip to wrong side of slash, tapering slash seam to nothing at point. Stitch and turn binding to right side.

**Placket with Pleat.** Cut a slash, then cut at right angles each side at base of slash ¼″. Turn edges ¼″; then turn left edge again ¼″ and stitch. Turn right edge ½″ and stitch. Lap to form pleat at bottom of slash. Stitch across at lower end through all thicknesses. For a wider pleat make diagonal slash longer.

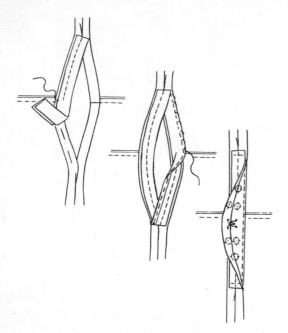

**Dress Placket, Two-piece.** Cut a bias strip for front of placket 1″ longer than opening and 1½″ wide. Cut back strip on straight grain the same length but 2″ wide. Turn under seam allowance on back opening, baste on fold, and press. Fold the wide strip down the center and press. Place under back opening, raw edges even, folded edge extending. Stitch on outside on basted edge. Face front with bias strip turning edge ⅛″ past the seam line. Press. Lap and sew on snaps with hook and eye at waistline.

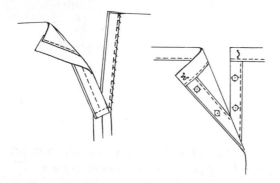

**Skirt Placket.** Use bias facing on front edge and straight piece on back as for dress placket. Stitch together at lower ends. Attach waistband. Sew snaps on placket and hooks and eyes on waistband.

## Zippers

**Putting in Skirt Zipper.** Before you start, check to see if—

Opening has been stay-stitched.

The garment has been fitted.

Check the zipper opening; it should be as long as the metal part of the zipper plus one inch.

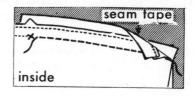

1. Machine-baste opening together (use longest stitch). Stitch seam tape to front seam allowance to widen it. Press seam open.

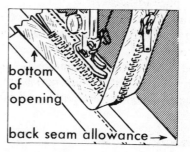

2. Working on the inside of the skirt throughout, put zipper in place face down. Match bottom of zipper to bottom of opening. Have the full width of the chain on the back seam allowance and edge of chain along seam line. Stitch with the edge of the foot against chain. Keep checking position of chain.

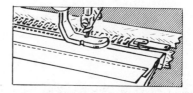

3. Change to zipper or cording foot. Turn the zipper right side up, folding seam allowance close to zipper chain. Stitch along the fold for the full length of tape as shown.

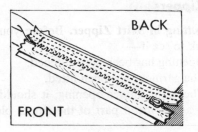

4. Open out garment, turn zipper face down over front seam allowance making a small pleat at lower end as shown. Stitch across tape just below the stop and up the other side close to the chain.

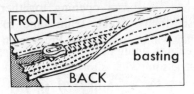

5. Press placket on wrong side. Remove machine basting (clip at intervals).

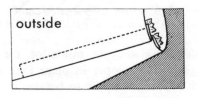

6. Press placket on right side using thick cloth to avoid shine. A tailor's ham is useful here.

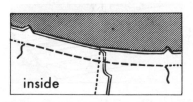

**Putting in Dress Zipper.** Check in same manner as for skirt zipper. Machine-baste and press seam open.

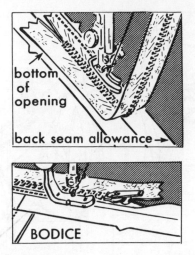

Steps 2 and 3 same as for skirt zipper.

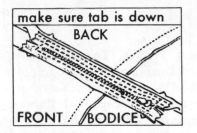

Open out garment, turn zipper face down over front seam allowance, making a small pleat at each end as shown. Stitch across tape just below stop and up the other side close to chain and across top.

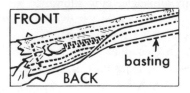

Press placket on wrong side and remove machine-basting.

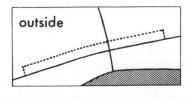

Press on right side using thick cloth to avoid shine.

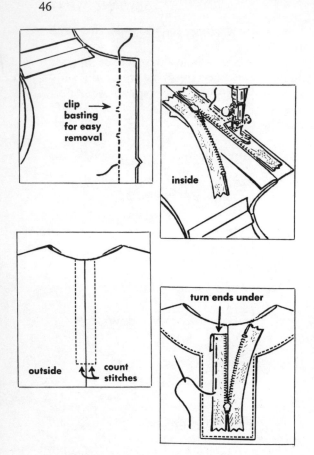

## Lining Skirts

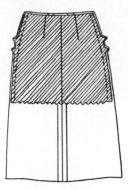

**Neck Zipper.** Check as for skirt zipper, and machine-baste opening. Press seam open. Clip basting.

Open zipper and place face down. Have one tape on single seam allowance with teeth against seam line. Stitch with edge of foot against teeth. Close the zipper.

Change to zipper foot. Turn garment to outside and, starting at neckline, stitch around zipper as shown making square corners at lower end. Press on wrong side and remove basting. Press on right side using thick cloth.

For slashed opening, slip-baste edges together. Baste gripper face down as shown. Close gripper and stitch on right side.

**For Faced Openings.** Apply facing and hold opening together on right side with overcasting. Lay the open zipper face down with teeth against the seam line. Baste along tape turning under top ends. Close zipper and follow step 2 under Neck Zipper.

**Lining a Skirt Back.** To prevent a bulge in the back of a skirt a half-lining may be used. Choose a firm fabric which will not stretch, such as rayon taffeta. Do not use crepes.

To cut the lining use the back skirt pattern but cut it somewhat shorter. It should come well below the widest part of the hips. Stay-stitch skirt and lining and pink the lower edge of lining. Make darts and seams same as in skirt and press. Wrong sides together, lay lining to skirt back and baste side seams. To take some of the strain from the skirt, the lining may be extended about 1/8″ each side on side seams when basting together. This makes it slightly narrower than the skirt back. Make up the skirt treating the lined back as one piece. Jersey and other knitted fabrics should be lined both front and back.

**Lining a Flared Skirt.** Use only fabrics which are pre-shrunk or do the pre-shrinking yourself. Choose a simple pattern with no more than four gores.

Cut skirt and lining from the same pattern following the grain line with care. Stay-stitch waist and top curve of seams.

Wrong sides together, baste lining pieces to outer skirt pieces smoothing together on a flat surface. Baste at side seams and several rows between. Stitch side seams treating fabric and lining as one. Let hang overnight to allow for stretching. Finish skirt and try on. Adjust length and trim lining to hem line. Turn hem and blind-hem to lining.

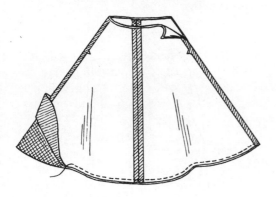

**Reversible Skirt.** Cut two skirts from the same pattern. Stitch seams on both, leaving plackets open. Let hang overnight to allow for stretching. Right sides together, baste together at waistline. Try on and adjust length. Stitch skirts together around lower edge and trim seam. Remove waistline basting and turn right side out. Finish placket and sew on belt. Tack the seams together with invisible stitches. Apply waistband.

# TAILORING

The classic jacket with notched collar presents some typical tailoring problems.

## Preparation

In tailoring, great care in preparing the fabric is essential:

**1.** Be sure the fabric and interfacing are pre-shrunk. Do it yourself if necessary.

**2.** Straighten ends of fabric.

**3.** Make alterations on pattern before cutting.

**4.** When cutting, follow grain line with precision.

**5.** If fabric is light weight, use a good quality hair canvas (or one that will withstand dry cleaning) of medium weight or lighter for interfacings.

## After Cutting

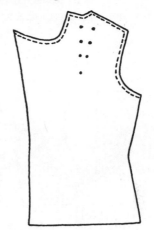

Stay-stitch all curved seams. Trace the grain with basting lines across the bust and top of back and sleeves and down center back and front. These will be a great help in fitting.

The weight of the jacket is supported at the shoulder line and in fitting the grain line must be kept vertical and horizontal.

## Preparation for Basted Fitting

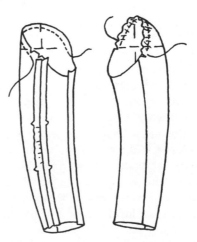

The first fitting should be a basted fitting. This permits adjustments to the figure in all areas, not just at the underarm.

Baste all darts on front and back. Baste shoulder, underarm, and sleeve seams. Press seams open lightly. Baste-stitch sleeve seams and tops of sleeves and draw up to fit armholes. Shrink-press and baste in place.

Baste interfacing to fronts of jacket. Baste undercollar pieces together and baste to neckline.

## Fitting

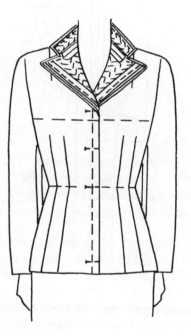

Try on jacket right side out over blouse and skirt. Lap and pin at center front.

Add shoulder pads if called for. Fit with enough ease to allow for lining. Distribute any needed fulness or take in equally on darts and seams. Check grain lines; do not pull these out of line when fitting.

If cross grain line sags, the shoulder may need raising. Adjust armhole seams for wide or narrow shoulders. Bend elbow and check strain at armhole.

Pin together at top buttonhole to find where roll of lapel begins. Mark the roll line with pins.

## Sewing

Balance up the adjustments, rebaste (if necessary), and stitch darts and seams. Slash darts, clip curved seams, press seams and darts open. When pressing, use tailor's ham and *mold* the garment on all curves. This is very important to a good fit. Certain places, such as points of darts, can be shrunk to smoothness with careful steam pressing.

## Interfacing

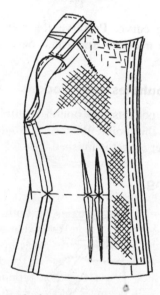

The interfacing is tacked to the front of the jacket with padding stitches which are invisible on the right side. Starting on the roll line, work padding stitches on lapel section rather close together. Work several rows more loosely up and down fronts below lapels.

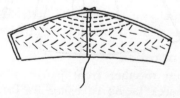

Lap, stitch, and trim collar interfacing and baste to undercollar around outer edges. Mark roll line and work rows of padding stitches outside of line, rolling and shaping in the hand. Inside of roll line stitch several rows by hand or by machine about 1/4″ apart

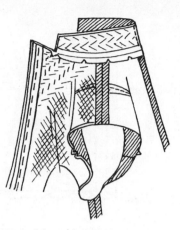

following curve. Preserve the roll. Rebaste collar to neckline and stitch only as far as seam line.

### Buttonholes and Pockets

Set-in pockets and bound buttonholes are made at this point. Worked buttonholes are done after jacket is finished.

### Facing

Seam together front jacket facings and back neck facing (if called for in pattern) at shoulder; then attach collar at neckline. If there is no back neck facing (patterns differ) attach collar to front facings at neckline. Clip on curves and press open. With right sides together, pin, baste, and stitch facing and collar to jacket. Match all seams

carefully at notch. Take a few stitches at notch by hand.

On soft fabrics the edge seam of lapel may need taping. Use a pre-shrunk tape, baste, and whip edge to seam line. The width of tape lies inside (on jacket area).

The back neckline seam may also be taped to prevent stretching.

### Beveling Seams and Turning

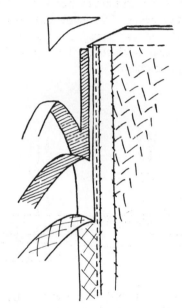

Thick seams must be trimmed to prevent ridges. Trim corners as shown. Bevel seams by trimming seam allowance of interfacing to seam line. Trim seams so that one is slightly wider than the other (¼″ and ⅜″). Trim neckline seam at notch. Cut away interfacing under neckline seam and press seam open.

For a sharper edge on seams, press them open before turning, using tip of iron. Turn facings, crease edges, and baste rolling edge of collar under slightly. Below lapel, roll seam slightly to the inside. All neckline seams, pressed open, should match perfectly. Tack seams together invisibly. Steam-press edges using clapper (back of hair brush will do).

## Sleeves

Rebaste sleeves in position. Fit again (with shoulder pads if called for) over skirt and blouse and make any further adjustments necessary. Mark sleeve and jacket length. Hem at bottom should not be less than 1".

## Finishing

Stitch in sleeves and steam-press to shrink any fulness at cap. (See "Setting in Plain Sleeve.") Turn and baste hems on fold in jacket and sleeves. Trim hem and press flat. Trim hem under facing to regular seam allowance and catch-stitch. Turn front facing same length as hem.

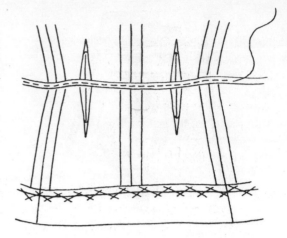

## Lining Jacket

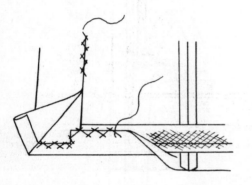

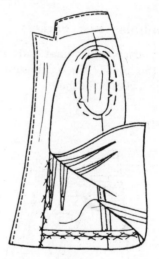

Reinforce hem line with interfacing using bias strip of light weight interfacing (muslin will do) cut ½" wider than hem plus seam width. Turn and press seam allowance along one side. Lay muslin inside hem with fold on hem line letting it overlap onto front facing. Slip-stitch along fold. Tack upper edge of interfacing to jacket with tailor's hem (see Hems and Hem Finishes). Catch-stitch edge of jacket hem to interfacing. Use same procedure in sleeve hems. Catch-stitch front facing to jacket easing over bust.

Clip collar at shoulder seam and catch to seam at back of neck. If using back neck facing, tack at seam line.

Give jacket a final pressing from inside. If waistline is to be accented, sew seam binding by hand around waistline on inside. Hand picking or machine-stitch trimming is done before lining.

Make same alterations on lining as on jacket. Pin, stitch, and press darts and lengthwise seams of lining but leave shoulder seams open. Lay in and pin pleat at center back. Lining must have enough ease to prevent drawing.

Turn jacket inside out; pin lining to jacket matching seams and center back. Tack underarm seams from inside. Baste around armholes, matching underarm seam and working up on each side, leaving 2 or 3 inches free at top on both front and back. Clip on curves. Turn under seam allowance on back shoulder and lap over front. Turn under seam at back of neck and down fronts, clipping on curves and easing slightly. Pin at frequent intervals and hem. Make a bar tack or catch-stitch

## Color Plate 1 — In-A-Wall Sewing Room

A fully equipped sewing room can be planned for a small space. In this wall unit there are shelves for storage boxes of all sizes, a roll-out table for sewing machine, and a large space for dress form, ironing board, etc. The folding doors have full-length mirrors on the inside and when closed the working unit is out of sight. Full description is given in Chapter 1, Sewing.

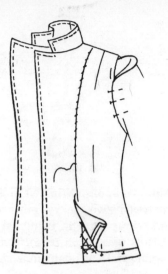

the pleat just below neck edge and at waist-line.

Finish lower edge of lining hem by catching to jacket hem with slip-stitching and allowing for ease to fold over. Edge of fold should come about ¾″ above lower edge of jacket.

Slip on sleeve lining, pin and hem, matching underarm seams. Turn under, pin and hem around armhole and at lower edge (allowing for ease as on hem of jacket).

Try on jacket, mark for buttons and sew on.

## Tailoring Hints

Press lining and jacket thoroughly before setting lining into jacket.

When setting in lining, baste lining to jacket around armhole seam. Allow ample length in sleeve lining to prevent drawing.

Lay a soft pleat at center back of lining. Make bar tacks at neck, waistline, and near lower edge to hold.

For a professional appearance, press each section thoroughly as you work. Do not leave for one final pressing.

For a good fit at the waistline on a tailored dress make an inside belt of belting ribbon. Stitch along center of belt to the waistline seam stopping 1″ from zipper and leaving ends loose. Finish with hooks and eyes to fit waistline.

On a kimono-type sleeve, before setting in gusset make a bar tack by hand at the point where slash ends at underarm. This will reinforce against strain.

After cutting a garment and before unpinning front and back pieces, run a basting down center front and back. Keep these lines vertical when fitting.

## UNUSUAL SEWING DETAILS

### Trimmings and Decorative Details

**Self-Fringe.** There are various ways of making fringe. Self-fringe can be made on many fabrics. Cut fabric on grain. Draw a thread (or two on fine fabric) where you want the fringe to end. Machine-stitch on this line. Pull threads to the stitching.

**Plain Fringe.** Make a gauge of heavy paper the desired width and length of the fringe. Fasten end of yarn and wrap around the gauge laying strands closely side by side. Stitch by machine about ½″ from the top. Cut loops at bottom and tear away paper. Turn under edge of fabric and stitch to fringe.

**Knotted Fringe.** Cut yarn twice the length of fringe plus allowance for knot. (This varies with size of yarn.) Take 2 or more strands, fold in middle. Insert crochet hook in edge of fabric or knitted piece. Pull loop through. Draw ends of yarn through the loop and pull up knot. Trim evenly when finished.

A more decorative knotting may be done. Pick up half the threads in each group and knot together. This may be repeated picking up alternate groups.

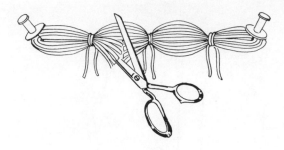

**Making Cord.** Cut yarn a little more than twice the length of finished cord. Use several strands for a heavy cord. Fold in half and catch the loop over something stationary, or work in the hand if cord is short. Keep taut and twist the strands until they are tight. Fold in half, slip off loop, and let the cord twist itself together. Tie ends.

**Making Pompons.** Wind yarn back and forth between two heavy push pins (see diagram). Wrap and tie tightly at intervals leaving ends of an inch or so. Cut between the wrappings. Trim pompons and fluff into balls.

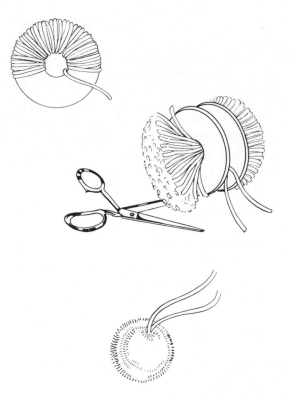

**Making Tassels.** Cut a gauge of cardboard the length the tassel is to be. Wrap yarn or thread around it to thickness desired. Tie a self-thread around top strands leaving long ends. Cut loops at bottom. Wind a thread around tassel near top and tie. Clip ends and slip the knot under the wrapping. Trim ends of tassel evenly.

Or cut 2 cardboard disks the desired size with ¼″ hole in center. Cover the disks with yarn, using a blunt needle. Slip scissors between discs and cut around edge. Wind and tie thread around center leaving ends for fastening.

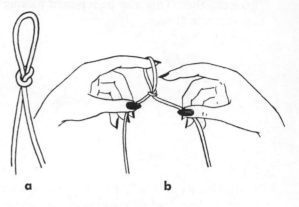

**Snow-Man Fringe.** Suitable for trimming a child's scarf.

Cut two pieces of cardboard, one 4″ wide and the other 2½″ wide.

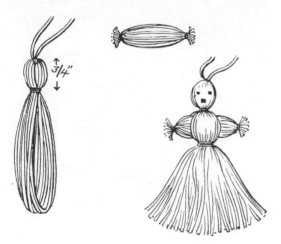

On the larger cardboard wind white knitting worsted around 40 times. Tie securely at top and slip off cardboard leaving long end. To form a "head" wind a piece of yarn ¾″ from top. Tie and clip ends.

For arms, wind yarn around smaller cardboard 20 times. Cut through ends and wind and tie ends.

Cut through end loops of body. Divide in two and slip arms between. Tie beneath arms for waistline. Take a couple of short stitches with red yarn for mouth and with black thread for eyes.

Make as many dolls as needed. Place dolls' arms end to end and tack them together catching into winding thread. Attach dolls

to scarf with ends left at top, leaving about ½″ free.

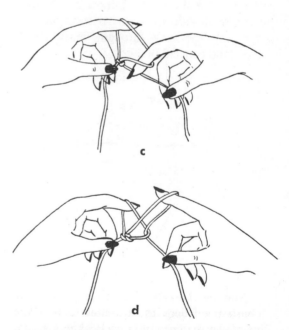

a               b

**Monk's Cord.** Calculate the length of cord desired and measure off 9 times this amount of heavy thread. (*a*) Fold in half and make a slip knot at the center. (*b*) Slip this loop over forefinger of left hand. The string that pulls easily should be in the left hand and the string that does not pull is in

c

d

the right hand.* (*c*) and (*d*) Through the loop on the left hand, using right forefinger, draw right strand through to make a loop. Slip out left forefinger and insert right thumb in the loop and draw up pulling left strand

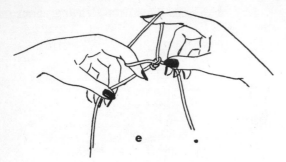

e

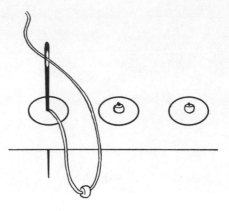

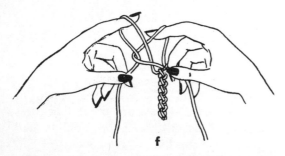

f

sequin, and into cloth near where needle came out. Fasten thread securely or bring needle out at next place if not too far apart.

tight. (*e*) and (*f*) The loop is on the right hand; insert left forefinger and draw left strand through, making a loop. Insert left thumb and pull up tight. Repeat from* alternating from side to side. To end, pull last strand all the way through. Thread with needle and conceal in cord.

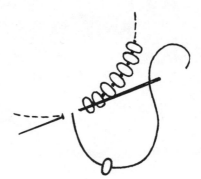

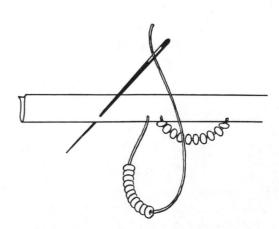

**Sewing on Sequins in a Line.** Follow the line of the design. Use a back-stitch and sew sequins on one at a time.

**Sewing Sequins Singly.** Use a very fine needle (a beading needle is best). Bring up from wrong side, thread through sequin, through small glass bead, back through

**Beading.** Beads are sewed on with back-stitch, usually in rows. They can also be applied in loops.

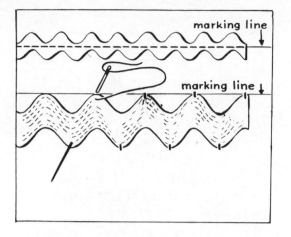

**Rickrack.** Rickrack can be sewed on by hand or by machine. Mark line for center of rickrack. Pin and baste. Sew with short stitches from point to point. If rickrack is very wide take a stitch between points. Narrow rickrack can be stitched down the center by machine.

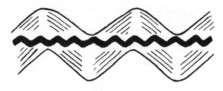

For interesting effect, sew baby rickrack down center of wide rickrack.

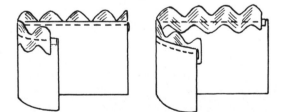

Place rickrack under folded edge of fabric with points showing and edge-stitch.

Or lay rickrack·on top of fabric near edge and stitch down the center.

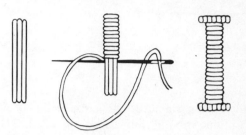

**Bar Tack.** Take several vertical stitches. Work over and over with satin stitch catching into the fabric. Work small bars at each end.

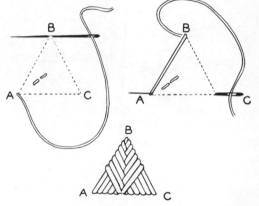

**Arrowhead Tack.** Mark a triangle. Bring needle out at left corner A. Take a short stitch from right to left at top of triangle B. Insert needle at right corner C and bring out slightly to the right of stitch at left corner A. Following line of triangle, take a stitch at top just below the first stitch. Insert needle at right corner just inside of first stitch. Repeat until triangle is filled.

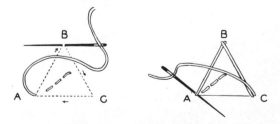

**Crow's-Foot Tack.** Mark a triangle. Bring needle out at lower left corner A. Take a short stitch from right to left at top of triangle B. Take a short stitch from right to left across point of triangle C. Take a short

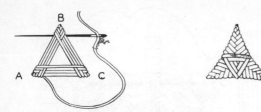

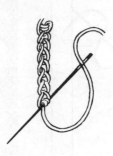

stitch from right to left across point at A. Continue around until triangle is filled. The sides of the triangle will draw in a little.

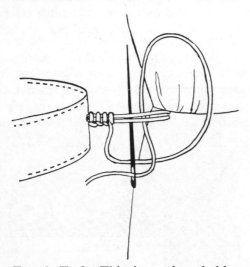

end, pull thread all the way through loop and sew to second piece of fabric.

## Working with Lace

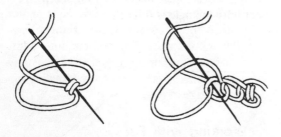

**French Tack.** This is used to hold two surfaces together loosely. For example, in tacking coat lining to coat at hem or belt to dress. Take several stitches back and forth between the two pieces. Work blanket stitch over them to cover. Use needle backward to avoid catching into stitches.

**Lace Application.** Use a fine needle and thread when working with lace. Some lace edgings (Val) can be gathered by pulling the edge thread. Otherwise they must be "fulled" while whipping on.

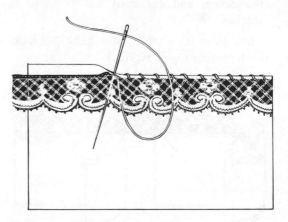

**Chain Tack.** Take several stitches in one place to form a short bar. Turn needle and push eye through the bar with thread over to form a loop. Pull up. Continue with eye of needle in each loop to form a chain. At the

**Lace on Rolled Edge.** Make a rolled hem and sew on lace in one operation.

**Lace on Hemmed Edge.** After hemming, with right sides together, overhand lace to fabric.

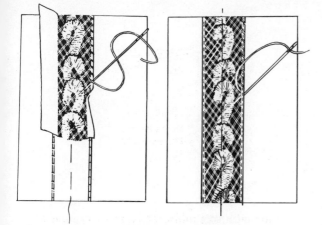

**Setting in Lace Insertion.** Baste insertion right side up to right side of fabric. Hem edges. Cut away fabric underneath leaving narrow edges. Roll edges and whip with fine stitches.

**Setting in Lace Medallions.** Baste motif on right side of fabric. Hold down edge with short over and over (satin) stitches and cut away fabric underneath close to stitches. Or sew edge with running stitches or backstitches. Cut fabric away underneath leaving enough to roll and whip catching lace.

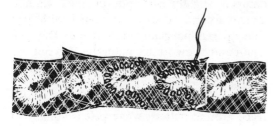

**Joining Lace Invisibly.** Overlap and match the pattern exactly and baste. Whip around the design and cut away excess close to stitches.

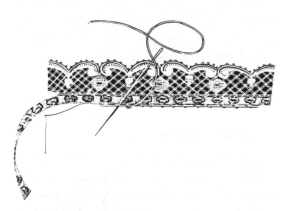

**Flat Lace Corner.** If possible have center of motif come at corner. Cut a triangle leaving the motif intact. Do not cut into edge. Lap corners and whip together. Lace may also be gathered at corner by drawing up thread in edge of lace.

## Working with Fur

**General Instructions.** If using a pattern cut away all but ⅛″ of seam allowance.

Lay the pattern on wrong side of fur (pelt side) and mark around. The hair of the fur should all go in the same direction.

**Joining Lace and Entre-deux.** Roll and whip edges of entre-deux to fabric and lace. If entre-deux has finished edges, simply whip together.

It may be necessary to cut the parts into sections to achieve this.

Cut the fur on the pelt side with a sharp razor blade, cutting only through the leather.

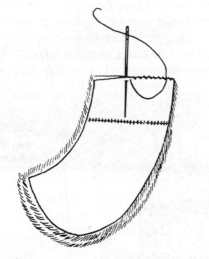

Sew the parts together, taking up the edge only, with small whipping stitches and using a waxed thread.

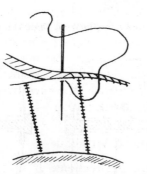

The edges of fur should be taped to provide something to sew to. Hold with pelt side toward you and sew edge of tape to edge of fur with whipping stitches.

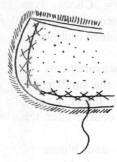

Line with soft fabric or lamb's wool cut a little smaller than the pelt. Turn the tape to the back and tack to the lining with herringbone stitch. The fur should roll slightly on the edge to give a soft effect.

If the fur you are using needs flattening, dampen slightly and pin or tack (thumb tacks) around edges to a board with pelt side up pulling gently into shape. Dampen again and allow to dry naturally. Do not use heat or sun to dry as this will cause leather to crack.

When dry, remove fur from board and trace around pattern while pelt is somewhat stiff. Before taping and finishing rub until soft, as you would after washing leather gloves.

**To Make a Fur Pompon.** Cut a circle of fur the desired size. Tape the edge. Gather edge of tape using strong thread. Cut short length of tape to be used as "shank." Catch in ends of tape as you work. Stuff with a wad of cotton and draw up.

## PATTERN ADJUSTMENT

### General Hints

Before buying your pattern take the following measurements over a simple dress of thin material and well-fitting foundation garments:

Bust. . . . . . . around the fullest part
Waist. . . fairly snug at natural waistline
Hip. . . around fullest part (about 7″ below waistline)

Compare these measurements with those

on the various charts in the front of the pattern catalog. Choose your type (Junior, Misses, Women's, Half-size, etc.) and then pick the size which is closest to your measurements.

If your measurements are between two sizes, choose the smaller if you like a snug fit. Choose the larger if you like a looser fit. You will of course alter the pattern where necessary.

Buy dress and blouse patterns by bust measurement and skirt and slack patterns by hip measurement.

For a figure which is very much out of proportion (for example, very large hips and a small bust), it saves time and trouble to buy two patterns, one for the bust measurement and one for the hip measurement.

One thing which must be taken into consideration when altering a pattern is "ease." For a simple fitted bodice, for example, the pattern may allow for about 4″ ease (patterns differ in amount of ease). For a bust which actually measures 32″ (and the pattern says 32″) the pattern with seams and darts subtracted will measure 36″ (or more). About 2″ ease is allowed on hip measurements and ½″ around the waistline. If this were not done a dress or skirt would be too tight to be comfortable. Do not lose this ease when altering your pattern.

Also remember that the fashion and the style of the garment influence ease. A shirtwaist dress with full bodice will have much more ease than the tailored type. And the same is true of skirts.

If you are hard to fit, it is advisable whenever possible, to make up a muslin of the garment (after making major adjustments in pattern) and fit it to the figure before cutting into the fabric.

You can also buy a basic pattern or a simple dress pattern with long sleeves; make it up in muslin and fit it to your figure; and keep it on hand for reference when fitting any garment.

A dress form exactly like your figure is also a tremendous help when altering and fitting.

## How to Alter Your Pattern

Most patterns indicate with printed lines where lengthening and shortening should be done.

**To Lengthen.** BODICE AND SKIRT: Cut across pattern and spread the necessary amount. Pin to a paper underlay.

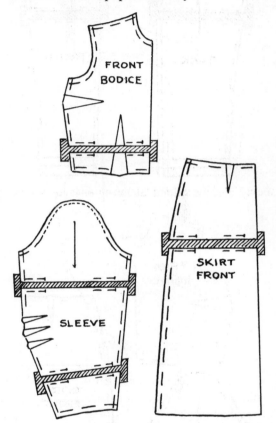

SLEEVE: Cut and spread above or below elbow, or both places if necessary.

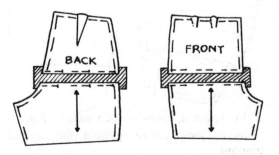

SLACKS AND SHORTS: Cut pattern and spread above and below crotch. Extra length

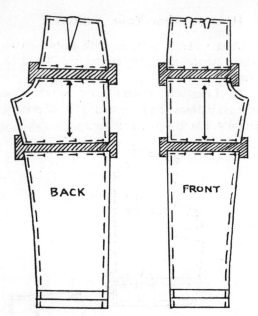

may also be added at lower edge of slacks.

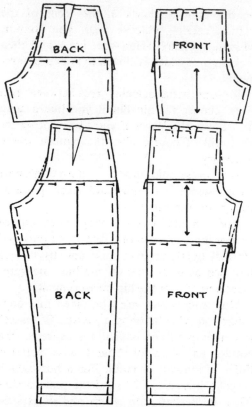

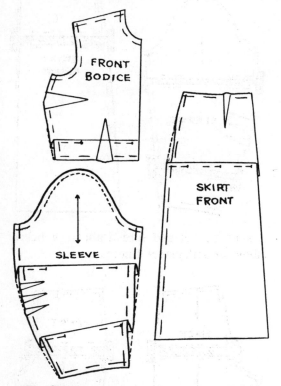

and below crotch. Additional shortening may be done at lower edge of slacks.

**To Shorten.** BODICE AND SKIRT: Fold a pleat or tuck across pattern the needed amount.

SLEEVE: Fold a tuck above or below elbow or both if necessary.

SLACKS AND SHORTS: Fold a tuck above

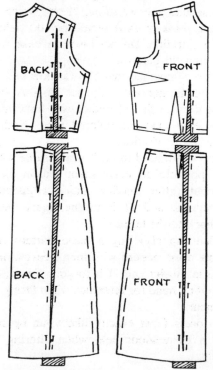

**Large Waistline.** Slash front bodice from waistline to crown of bust. Slash back bodice from waistline almost to shoulder. Spread correct amount and pin to paper underlay. Diagram page 60, lower right.

Slash skirt front and back directly below bodice slash, spread and pin to underlay.

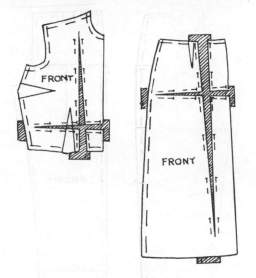

**Large Waistline and Abdomen.** Adjust as for large waistline. Also slash across front 3″ or so above waistline, tapering to nothing at underarm, and spread desired amount. Slash skirt across front and spread desired amount.

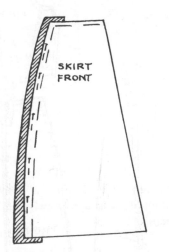

**Large Hips.** Determine how much needs to be added and add ¼ the amount to each side at front and back of skirt, tapering to nothing at the waistline.

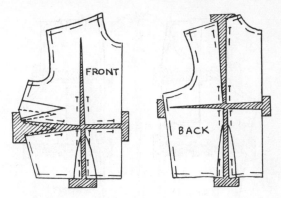

**Large Bust Line.** FRONT: Add to length as before. Slash from waistline and taper to shoulder. Spread desired amount. Adjust darts.

BACK: Add to length and spread desired amount adding dart at underarm if necessary. Slash from waistline and taper to shoulder.

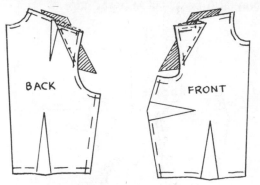

**Narrow Shoulders.** Make a slantwise slash from center of shoulder to armhole. Lap amount necessary and pin to underlay. Draw a new straight shoulder line.

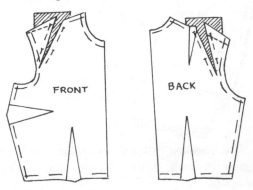

**Wide Shoulders.** Slash as for narrow shoulders and spread desired amount. Pin to underlay and draw new shoulder line.

For a thin arm make a fold lengthwise at center of sleeve. Take off an equal amount at underarm on front and back bodice.

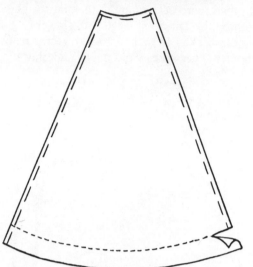

**Large Upper Arm.** Sleeve should allow "ease" of 1½″ to 2½″ around arm just below armhole. Slash lengthwise through center tapering to nothing at lower edge. Spread desired amount. To flatten pattern, bring together at top and fold in dart on each side. Retain curve at top of sleeve.

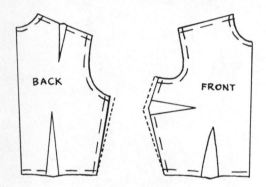

The same total amount must be added at underarm seam on front and back bodice.

**Shortening Circular Skirt.** Take off the necessary amount at lower edge. Or cut across on a circular line 8″ or 9″ below waistline and lap. Correct the side seam lines.

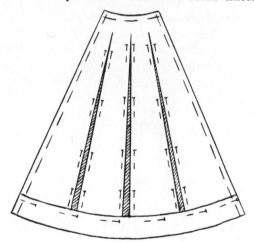

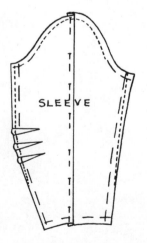

To preserve the width in shortening, slash from lower edge to waistline and spread apart enough to fit the original hem.

**Lengthening Circular Skirt.** Add to the hem line.

## THINGS TO SEW

Here follow a number of articles for you to sew, with step-by-step, easy-to-follow instructions and diagrams.

If you are a beginner, choose a simple item to start with—the man's tie, the bed jacket, the apron, or a simple toy. The hand-bag accessories, although smaller, are not necessarily easier, as they must be done accurately and neatly or they lose their charm.

The bassinet is a more complicated project, but if directions are carefully followed it should come out well.

### Man's Tie

**Materials.** ¼ yard 36"-wide lengthwise-striped heavy silk or cotton, for one tie, or ¾ yard 36"-wide crosswise-striped heavy silk or cotton for four ties. ¼ yard thin muslin. Smooth wrapping paper for pattern.

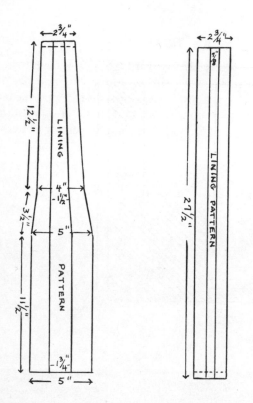

**Pattern.** Make a paper pattern, following diagram. Use outside lines for tie and inside lines for lining.

**Cutting.** ¼″ seams are allowed. No seam allowance is needed on lining, except at ends for piecing together. Pin tie pattern on fabric so stripes run crosswise on tie. Cut one narrow and one wide piece. Cut lining from muslin.

**Making.** Right sides together, join the two pieces at narrow ends where seam allowance is shown on pattern (this is center of tie). Press seam open. Lap and sew center seam of tie lining. Place lining down center on wrong side of tie. Turn ends of tie ¼″ to wrong side. Slip-stitch across ends, and press. Fold sides of tie (as far as lining) to the center, pin, baste, and press. Turn under one edge; pin, and slip-stitch the full length of tie.

## Bed Jacket

**Materials.** 1 yard 54″-wide white wool flannel. 1 yard 48″-wide silk or nylon pink or white sheer print, for lining. 7 yards baby gold rickrack. 3½ yards ½″-wide gold, pink, and white woven braid. 1 yard ½″-wide white ribbon.

**Cutting (½″ seams allowed).** To make pattern, follow cutting diagram, or mark directly on the flannel, and cut. Use flannel pieces as guides, and cut lining pieces for fronts, back, and sleeves.

**Making.** Find top center back, and mark 3″ each side. Sew fronts to back at shoulder up to markings. (This leaves 6″ open at center back and a 3″ lapel on each side of front.) Press seams open. Mark center on one long side of each sleeve. With this center point matching shoulder seam of jacket, pin and stitch sleeves to jacket. Press seam. Clip jacket seam at underarm. With jacket wrong side out and folded at shoulder line, pin and sew sleeve and underarm seams. Turn and press ½″ seam allowance to wrong side on all jacket edges except lapels, which are turned to right side 9″ from top edge. Make lining in same way as jacket. Press seams open.

TRIMMING: On right side of fronts and lower edge of jacket, pin and stitch one row of gold rickrack ½″ from folded edge, starting and stopping 8″ from top. Pin and stitch braid 1/16″ in from rickrack, starting and stopping 7½″ from top and mitering corners on lower fronts. Stitch braid on both edges. Pin and stitch another row of gold rickrack on other side of the braid starting and stopping 7″ from top. Trim lapels in same manner, mitering corners and ending lower ends of braids 1″ below turn of lapels. Trim sleeve edges in same manner. (The trimming of three rows of braid should be about 1″ wide when finished.)

LINING THE JACKET: Place lining and jacket wrong sides together. Pin along all seams. Turn under ½″ around sleeves, at back of neck, around lower edge, and up fronts to point where lapel begins. Cut away lining at lapel fold, leaving ¼″ for turning under. Turn under along fold, and pin. Blind-hem lining to jacket. Press carefully. Cut ribbon into two 16″ lengths, turn in ends, and sew to wrong side of fronts just below lapel.

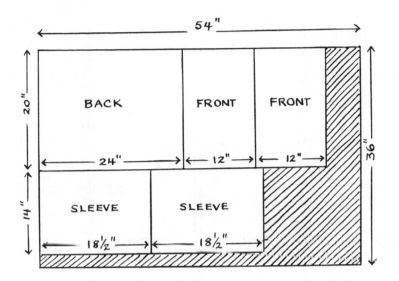

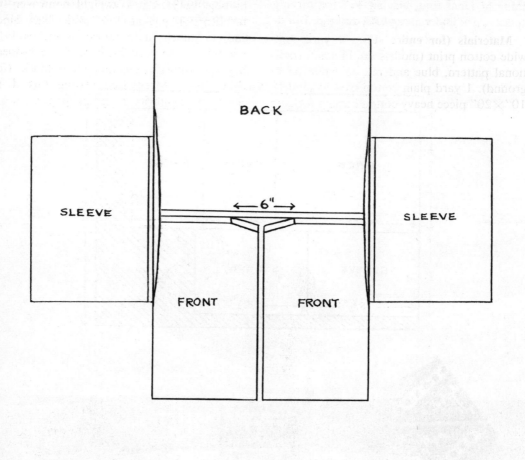

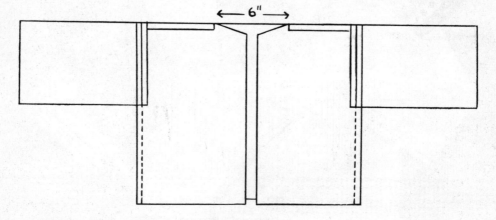

## Handbag Accessories

**Materials (for entire set).** ¾ yard 36″-wide cotton print (models are in small traditional pattern, blue and red on white background). 1 yard plain cotton (red in model). 10″×20″ piece heavy cotton batting for coin purse interlining. 30″×36″ piece single-sheet batting. ½ yard heavyweight nonwoven interfacing. 1 package ½″-wide bias binding, to match plain fabric. 4 inches ¼″-wide elastic. ½ yard fine cord. 8″ neck-opening-type zipper, to match plain fabric (for coin purse). Mercerized sewing thread, to match plain fabric. 1″ graph paper.

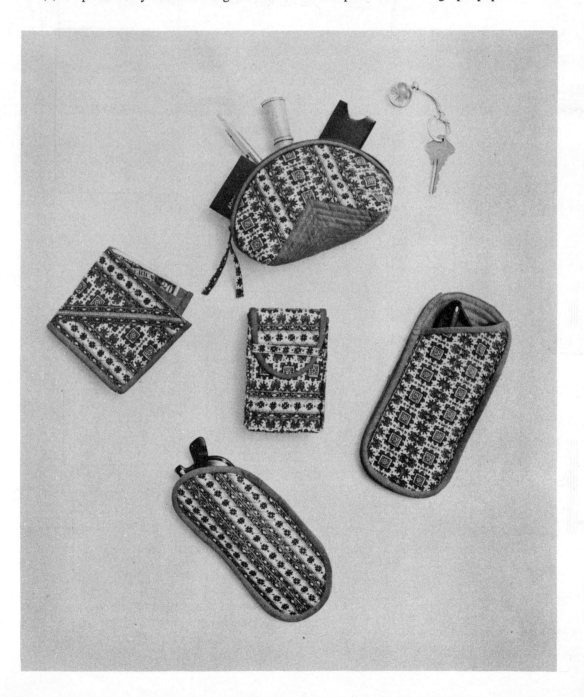

**Notes.** Quilting design for each accessory may be as simple or as elaborate as you wish. Machine-stitch lines diagonally across fabric, forming parallel lines, diamonds, zigzags, or any other pattern.

Where pattern is given on a graph, copy on 1″ graph paper, enlarging each square to 1″.

### Single Spectacles Case

Cut 4″×8″ pieces, as follows: two sections from print fabric, on lengthwise grain; two sections from plain fabric; two sections from interfacing; two sections from sheet batting. Place together in this order: one plain section; one interfacing; one batting; one printed section, right side up. Baste together, matching edges. Quilt as desired. Make two such pieces.

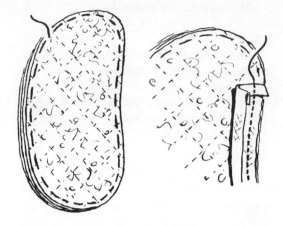

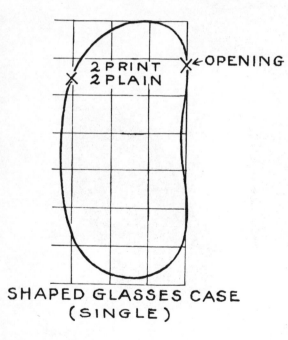

SHAPED GLASSES CASE
(SINGLE)

around, easing around curves. Let ends lap; cut. Turn to wrong side; hem down folded edge. Repeat on second section. Pin the two sections together, plain sides facing. Starting and ending at X points, stitch around through all thicknesses, just inside line of bias binding. Take a few backward stitches with machine at beginning and end of stitching line.

### Double Spectacles Case

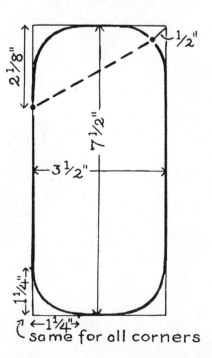

Copy and cut pattern. Cut out quilted pieces from pattern; be sure to have them facing, one right side up, one wrong side up. Press open one fold of bias tape. Starting at one X point and folding end over as sketched, pin this edge of tape to edge of one quilted section, on right side, edges even. Stitch

Prepare and cut pattern. Following it, cut two pieces of plain fabric and one piece of sheet batting, *adding ¼" seam allowance all around*. Place the three pieces together, with batting in center. Stitch all around, leaving one end open. Trim allowance to ⅛"; turn to right side through opening. Turn in raw edges; press and edge-stitch around. Quilt upper end as shown.

Cut pattern as shown. Place pattern on right side of quilted piece; cut out carefully. Mark fold lines on right side with lines of basting.

Press open one fold of bias tape. Starting at one corner of top, baste and stitch open edge to right side of top edge and around flap, easing over curve. Turn to wrong side; hem down.

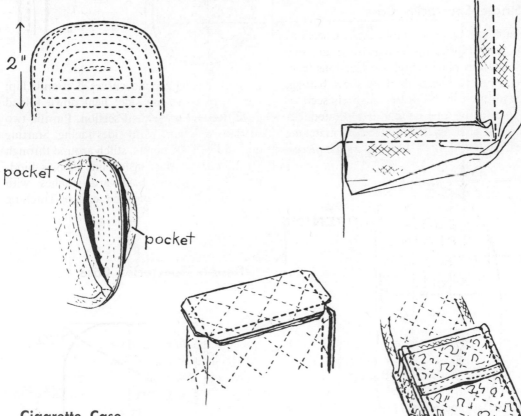

## Cigarette Case

Follow directions for single spectacles case, but using this pattern with top trimmed off at dotted line shown on sketch. Bind edges of the two outer pieces as instructed, finishing by hand at corners. Place the plain piece between the two printed ones before assembling.

Cut one 10"×11" square each of print fabric, plain fabric, and interfacing; two 10"×11" squares of sheet batting. Place together as follows: plain fabric; batting; interfacing; batting; print fabric, right side up. Baste together, and quilt as desired.

Stitch side hems together, wrong side out. Clip through seam allowance into the two corners. Notch other seam allowances as marked.

Fold bottom; match edges carefully to side bottom edges; pin, and baste. Stitch around, and trim seam allowance to less than ⅛". Turn case to right side.

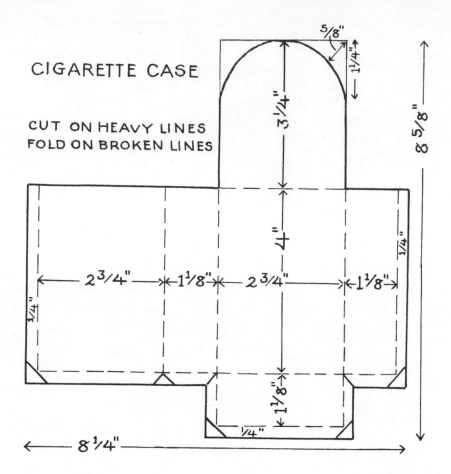

# CIGARETTE CASE

## CUT ON HEAVY LINES
## FOLD ON BROKEN LINES

Cut 1″×3¼″ strip of print fabric. Fold strip to about ¼″; stitch along two edges. Folding ends under, pin strip across front of case about 1″ below top edge, as shown.

Make a sharp crease at baste-marked corners; stitch along crease ⅛″ from edge. Do this along all four corners (treating seamed corners in the same manner) and around bottom.

## Wallet

Cut 5″×9″ pieces as follows: one each from print fabric, plain fabric, and interfacing; two of cotton batting. Place together, edges even, as follows: one layer batting; interfacing; batting; print fabric, right side up; plain fabric. Stitch together along 9″ edge ½″ from edge. Trim away seam allowance on batting and interfacing as close as possible to stitching line. Press seam open. Turn plain fabric to other side, as shown, covering batting, etc. Press seam. Make a line of top-stitching ⅛″ from seamline.

Baste all layers together, and quilt as desired. Cut this quilted piece down to 4″× 7½″. The diagonal band on the pictured wallet was made by cutting a 1″×7″ strip of print fabric, turning long edges ¼″ under and top-stitching to quilted piece. Trim ends even with wallet edges.

From plain fabric, cut one 6½″×7½″ piece; one 5½″×7½″ piece; two 5½″× 3½″ pieces.

Fold each of the last two pieces crosswise (to measure 2¾″×3½″). Press. Trace notch, shown here in actual size, on tissue paper. Transfer markings to one end of a

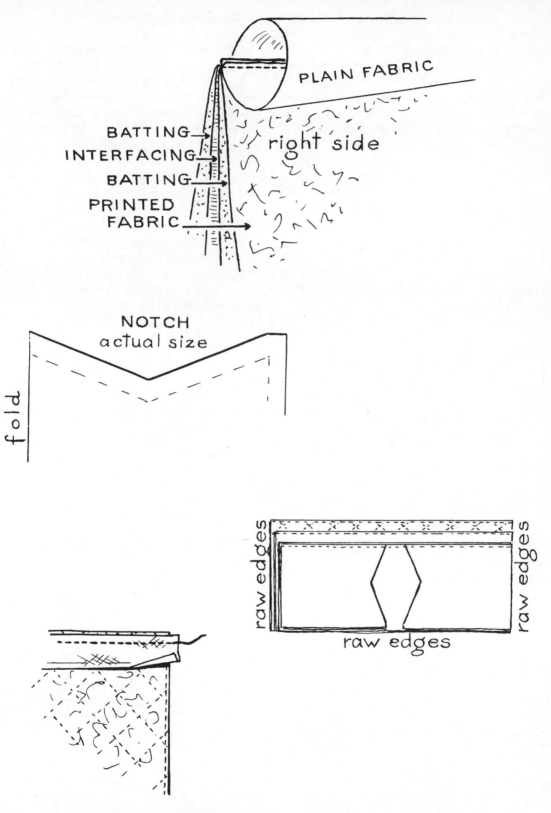

PLAIN FABRIC

right side

BATTING
INTERFACING
BATTING
PRINTED
FABRIC

NOTCH
actual size

fold

raw edges

raw edges

raw edges

folded piece; stitch along marked line. Trim seam allowance to ⅛"; clip into corner of notch. Turn to right side, and press.

Fold the 5½"×7½" piece in half lengthwise. Press. Place the two notched sections on it, matching folded edges, as shown. Make a line of top-stitching along folded edges. Fold remaining piece in half lengthwise. Topstitch along fold.

Place these two prepared sections on plain side of quilted section, matching all raw edges. Stitched edges are graded, as shown. Baste and stitch around the three raw edges.

Press open one fold of bias tape. Starting at one top corner of wallet, on right side and letting end of tape extend, as shown, stitch tape around three sides of wallet, easing at corners. Turn ends in; turn tape to inside of wallet, and sew down by hand.

## Zippered Coin Purse

**Patterns.** For purse, copy pattern on graph, enlarging each square to 1". Cut out.

For quilted patch, measure and mark pattern as given at lower left. Cut out.

**Quilting.** Cut one 10"×10" square each of print fabric, heavy batting, and interfacing. Baste together in that order, print right side up. Quilt as desired.

**Cutting.** From purse pattern, cut one section from quilted piece, one from plain fabric (lining); place pattern on folded fabric, as indicated.

From second pattern, cut one piece of plain fabric, on fold, as indicated.

From plain fabric, cut two 1"×11" bias strips (piece if necessary); one 2¾"×6" piece; one 2¾"×3½" piece.

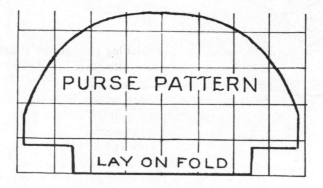

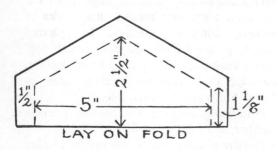

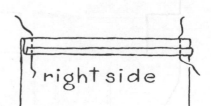

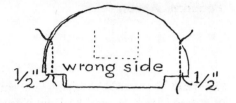

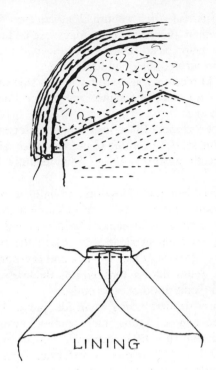

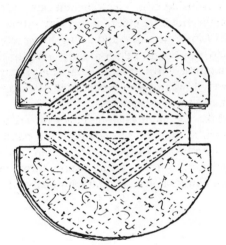

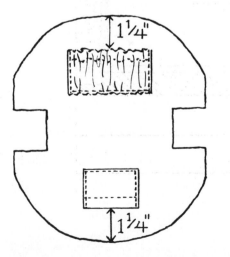

**Making (½″ seams allowed).** Turn under seam allowance on the two points of plain section cut from pattern. Press. Baste over quilted section as shown. Edge-stitch in place, and quilt as shown, using width of presser foot as a guide.

POCKETS: On both 2¾″-wide pieces, crease one long edge ¼″ to one side, and fold same edge ½″ to other side, as shown. Stitch side edges. Turn this hem to wrong side. Stitch hem on smaller piece. On longer piece, attach each end of a 3¼″ piece of elastic inside each side seam of pocket hem. Stretch elastic as you stitch hem. Turn under seam allowance around other sides of pockets, trimming corners. On shirred pocket, gather bottom edge to match top. Center each pocket on pocket-lining section, top edge 1¼″ from each curved edge, as shown. Stitch around three sides.

Fold lining section across bottom, pockets together, and stitch up sides as shown.

Prepare two lengths of welting by placing cord inside bias strips and stitching close to cord.

Baste and stitch welting along curved edge of quilted piece, all raw edges even. Turn welting up; baste down all seam allowances against wrong side of quilted piece.

Fold piece across bottom, wrong side out. Stitch up sides the same way as for lining (above).

Open zipper. Place inside quilted section, pinning tapes to welting seam allowance, zipper teeth against welting. Sew securely by hand.

Turn both quilted section and lining wrong side out. Fold one open end of lining section as shown, seam in center. Fold one end of quilted section in same way. Place the two sections together, back to back and raw edges even. Seam across through all thicknesses. Do the same at other open end.

Turn so that lining is inside purse. On curved edge of lining, turn seam allowance under, and slip-stitch edge over zipper tapes.

Cut ½″×3″ strip of print fabric. Turn in raw edges, and top-stitch together. Stitch across ends. Fold in half crosswise, and attach fold securely to zipper tab as a pull.

## Peasant Apron

**Materials.** ½ yard 36-inch-wide, solid-color cotton fabric. ¾ yard 36-inch-wide cotton print. 1 package double-fold bias tape in contrasting color. Mercerized sewing thread to match.

**Cutting.** Following cutting diagrams, cut print and plain fabric.

**Making.** Bind print fabric with bias tape around inside edge (see diagram next page).

Right sides together, join print fabric to plain fabric at sides and along lower edge.

Sew the bound edges at sides only to the plain fabric, and continue the stitching straight down to lower edge of apron. Also stitch down center to form two pockets.

Make ¼″ hem on long edges of ties and 1″ hem at one end of each tie. Fold band in half lengthwise. Pleat tie end; fit into end of waistband; stitch. Trim seam; turn, and press. Gather apron, and attach waistband.

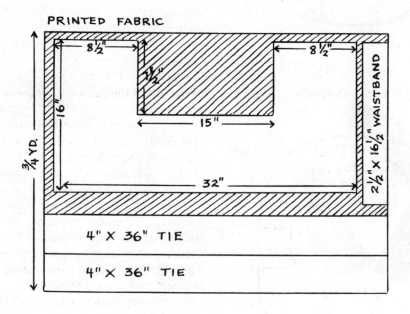

PRINTED FABRIC

¾ YD.

8½″  8½″

7½″

16″

15″

2½″ × 16½″ WAISTBAND

32″

4″ × 36″ TIE

4″ × 36″ TIE

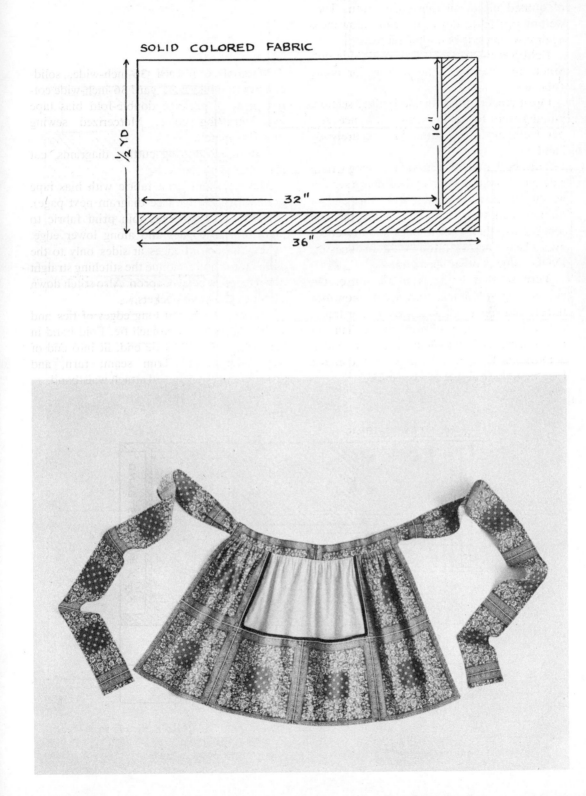

SOLID COLORED FABRIC

½ YD

16"

32"

36"

76

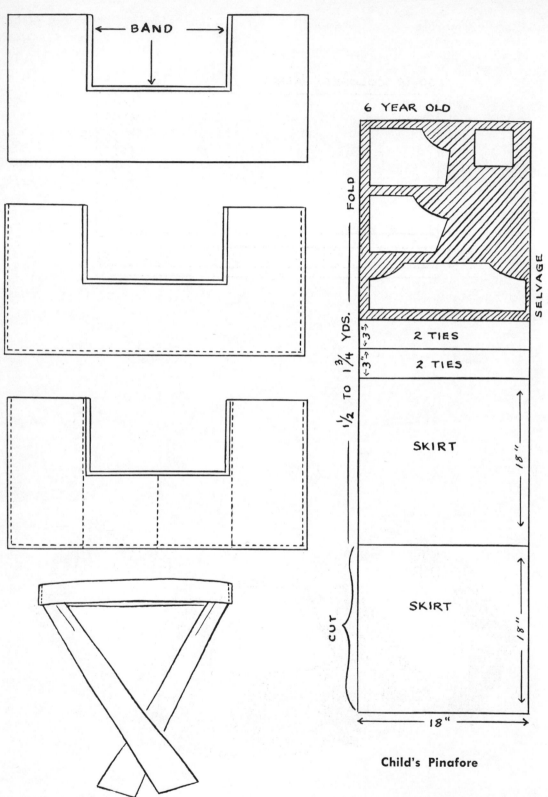

BAND

6 YEAR OLD

FOLD

SELVAGE

1½ TO 1¾ YDS.

2 TIES

←3"→ ←3"→

2 TIES

SKIRT

18"

CUT

SKIRT

18"

18"

**Child's Pinafore**

**Peasant Apron**

## Child's Pinafore

**Materials.** 1½ yards white cotton sateen, for size 2 and 4; 1¾ yards white cotton sateen, for size 6. Small pieces red, green, and gold cotton for appliqué. Mercerized sewing thread (white). Six-strand embroidery floss to match appliqué pieces. 1 yard white twill tape (½" seams are allowed).

**Pattern.** Trace desired size of bodice pattern, pages 78 and 79.

**Cutting.** Cut pinafore, following cutting diagram, shown opposite.

**Making.** 1. Right sides together, seam bodice front and back at underarm. Seam facing in same way. Press seams open. 2. Right sides together, join facing to front bodice, stitching at sides and along top. Trim seams, and turn right side out. 3. Join skirt sections. Pink seams, and press open. Make narrow hems at two ends, and gather across top. 4. Right sides together, join skirt to bodice, adjusting gathers. Turn under seam allowance on facing, and slip-stitch to skirt. 5. Make ¼" hems on long edges of shoulder ties. Pleat; cut ends; turn under, and hand-stitch to bodice as shown. 6. Attach twill tape in same manner to back of bodice. 7. Hem pinafore (3" hem allowed: adjust to child). 8. Pockets, page 80. Make ¼" hem at top of pockets. Trace design, and trace onto pockets, using dressmaker's carbon paper. Trace cherries, leaves, and flowerpot on various colors, as indicated. Cut out on line. Apply to pockets with blanket-stitch, using three strands of matching embroidery floss. Work stems in green outline stitch. 9. Sew pockets in place, back-stitching at top to hold securely.

# BODICE FRONT

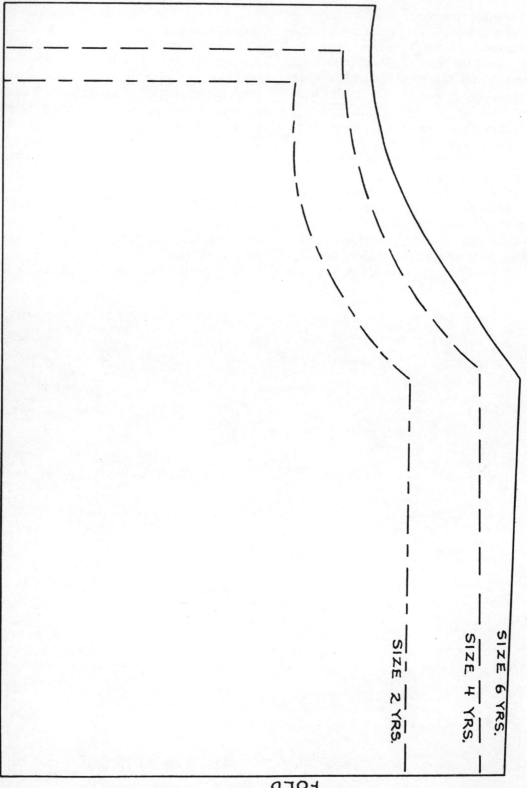

SIZE 6 YRS.

SIZE 4 YRS.

SIZE 2 YRS.

FOLD

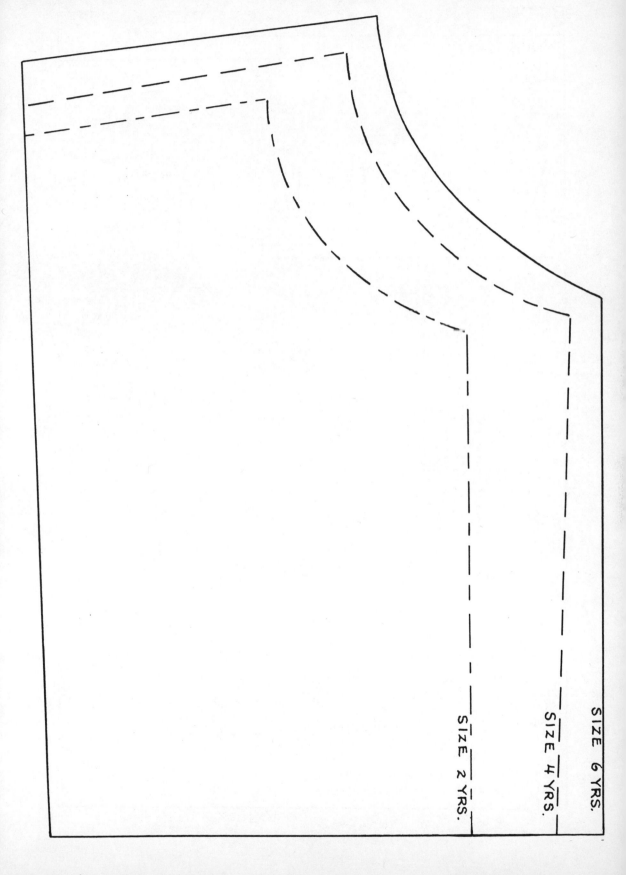

SIZE 2 YRS.

SIZE 4 YRS.

SIZE 6 YRS.

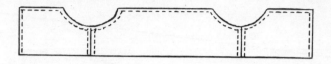

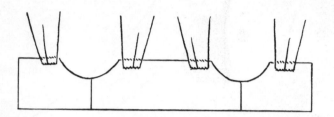

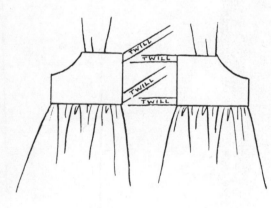

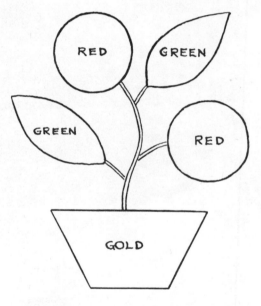

## Big and Little Sock Dolls with Patchwork Skirts

**Materials.** 1 pair size-13 medium-heavy white men's socks (over-all length, about 22″). Kapok or Dacron* fiber for stuffing. 1 ball brown rug yarn. ½ yard narrow red ribbon. 6″×7″ piece of black felt. Tiny scrap red felt. A few strands red, black, brown, white, pink six-strand floss. 10″ x 44″ medium-weight muslin (may be pieced). Bright print cotton: one piece about 15″ square; scraps of about a dozen different colors and with small patterns. Under ½ yard organdy. 2 yards ¼″ wide lace edging. 1 yard narrowest white elastic. Package bias-fold tape. 1 spool each peach and white; 2 spools red; 1 spool brown, to match rug yarn, mercerized sewing thread. Package peach or flesh-color dye.

*Registered trade mark.

82

**To Make Doll Bodies.** Tint socks peach or flesh color. Tint a piece of thin white string at the same time.

**Large Doll.** 1. Slip one sock over hand. Fold heel flat toward toe, and sew to sole. Measure 10″ as shown, and mark on sock front and back.

2. Stuff sock to this line, not too hard; cut sock on line. Fold in raw edges, and sew together.

3. About 6¼″ from tip of toe (top of head), push stuffing up and down, and tie off neck with tinted string. Knot will be in center back.

4. Place remaining sock piece flat, and cut through both side folds. Fold each piece lengthwise, wrong side out, and seam as shown, making narrow seams and rounding corner. Trim corner. Turn to right side, and stuff. Fold in raw edges, and sew up opening.

5. Form foot by sewing a fold 2″ from tip, as shown. Sew leg tops to doll body, seams turned to back.

6. Cut 8½″ from foot of second sock, as shown. Cut as shown for arms. Turn wrong side out, and seam tip and long edge. Turn right side out, and stuff. Sew ends with seam to one side.

7. Sew arms to sides of doll body 1¼″ below neck, seam side toward back.

8. Cut about ten 4″ pieces of rug yarn. Fold in half, and sew folded ends to top of head as shown, for bangs.

9. Cut about thirty-six 12″ lengths of rug yarn. Covering top ends of bangs, sew down over head as shown; stitches form hair parting. Cut red ribbon in half, and tie hair to each side as shown, forming bows.

10. From red felt, cut mouth as given here actual size. Whip to face 1¼″ above neck. With thread doubled, take a couple of stitches from corner to corner of mouth, running needle through stuffing and pulling slightly to form dimples.

11. Cut two eyes from black felt. Attach to face 1¾″ above mouth and 2¼″ apart. With black thread, make stitches to form eyelashes. Using all six strands of white floss, make a French knot a little off center in each eye. With brown floss, make a few ½″ stitches

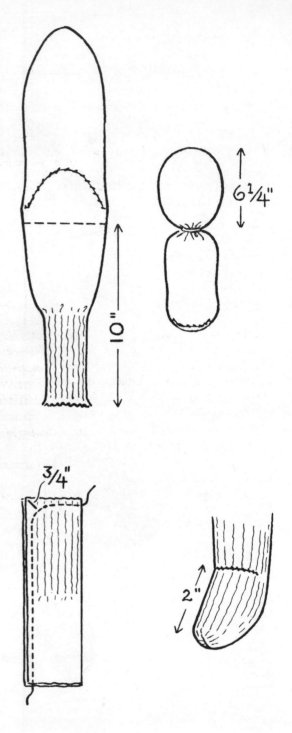

½″ above each eye for eyebrows. For nose, make a few stitches with pink floss ½″ above mouth, or attach a tiny circle of pink felt. Rouge cheeks with lipstick.

**Color Plate 2 — Embroidered Gingham Sampler**

Many of the stitches given in Chapter 2, Embroidery, are used in making this sampler on checked gingham. See that section for further instructions.

**Pocket Doll.** From remaining piece of sock, cut one 3″×3″ piece; one 1½″×7½″ strip on lengthwise grain.

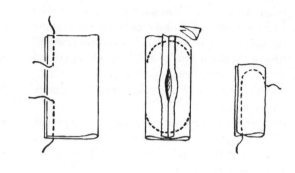

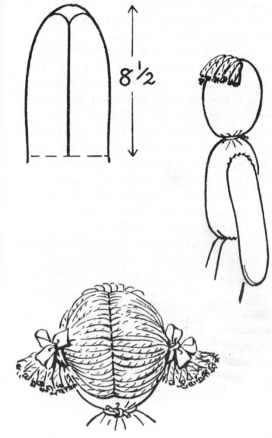

MOUTH
PATTERN

⊂⊃EYEBROW

EYE
PATTERN

12. Fold square in half on lengthwise grain, wrong side out. Seam as shown, leaving 1″ opening in center. Fold again with seam in center, and stitch around as shown. Trim off corners.

13. Turn through opening, and stuff. Sew opening. Tie off neck about 1¼″ from top.

14. Fold strip in half lengthwise, wrong side out. Stitch long edge. Cut strip into two 2″ and two 1¾″ pieces. Stitch one end of each piece as shown. Trim corners.

15. Turn to right side; stuff; sew ends, and attach to body—the long pieces for legs, the short pieces for arms.

16. Make a few stitches for each eye with black floss, and a few stitches with red floss for mouth. Rouge cheeks with lipstick.

17. Cut eight 2¾″ lengths of rug yarn. Sew four across head, front to back, the front ends forming bangs. Sew remaining four strands in opposite direction. Trim ends. Make two tiny bows from red floss, and attach to each side of head.

## To Make Clothes
## (make ¼″ seams)

**Large Doll.** PANTIES: Cut two pieces of organdy 6″×12″. On each piece, turn under one long edge ⅛″, and crease. Stitch a length of lace edging on top. Stitch a second row ½″ above. Make a line of stitching (long stitch) 1″ above edge; draw up slightly. Stitch elastic to this line, on wrong side, stretching elastic as you stitch.

18. Pin together short edges of the two pieces, right sides facing. Stitch down 4½″ as shown. Do this at both ends. Clip seam allowance at seam end; crease open.

19. Fold panties so seams are together in center. Seam leg ends as shown.

Make a ½″ hem at top edge for casing.

Open seam in casing, and draw a 9″ length of elastic through. Secure ends.

BLOUSE: From organdy, cut one 3″×10″ piece and two 3″×12″ pieces.

20. Seam together ends of 3″×10″ piece. Crease the two long edges ⅛″ to wrong side, and top-stitch. Fold piece so seam is in center. Mark a semicircle at this point as shown, using a spool end as guide. Cut out.

21. On other two strips, crease both long edges ⅛″ to one side. Make a line of machine-stitching along edges, using longest stitch and stopping short of strip end. Fold each strip in half; seam ends. Draw up stitching along edges, to form puffed sleeves.

22. Matching seam to center of "armhole," sew in one half of sleeve. Top half will form shoulder.

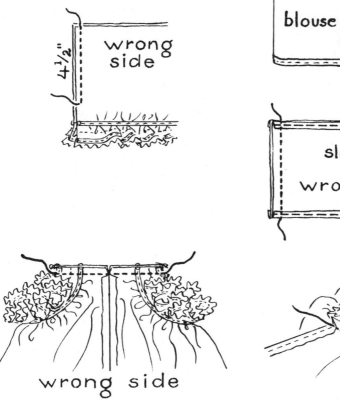

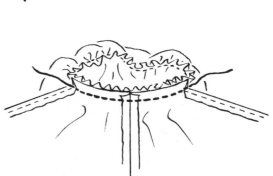

DRESS: Cut large piece of print on straight grain as follows: 1 strip 2″×11½″ (top). 2 strips 2″×6½″ (top). 1 piece 3½″×4″ (pocket).

1. Place 10″×44″ muslin strip flat on table. Cut print scraps into various squares, triangles, etc. Arrange on muslin strip so they overlap slightly. Pin or hand-baste in place. Using thread to match top and pocket fabric, stitch down all edges with zigzag stitch on sewing machine. Trim patches even with muslin edge.

2. Stitch one edge of bias binding over one long edge of piece.

3. Fold piece crosswise, wrong side out. Seam short edges together through bias binding and 7″ up. Press seam open.

4. For hem, turn up edge with bias binding, and slip-stitch to wrong side.

5. Make a ½″ hem on one 3½″ edge of pocket piece. Crease other edges ¼″ under. Pin pocket to dress to left of center front (seam of dress is at center back), bottom edge of pocket 2½″ from hem. Top-stitch around three sides, very close to edge.

6. Face each side of dress opening with bias binding.

7. Make a line of machine-stitching (longest stitch) ¼″ below top edge of dress. Draw up to 10″ distributing gathers evenly.

8. Fold 11½″ strip lengthwise, wrong side out. Seam one end across, as shown. Seam opposite end across and 1″ along edges. Trim seams. Turn to right side.

9. Baste one raw edge of strip to top of dress, right sides together, letting stitched end extend as shown. Stitch around.

10. Turn up; turn raw end in, and hem to inside over stitching line.

11. For shoulder straps, fold the two shorter strips in half lengthwise, wrong side out. Seam long edges. Turn to right side; crease edges.

12. Place dress on doll, opening in back, top edge under arms. Pin shoulder straps in place, ends to inside of dress. Sew in place at top and bottom of band, trimming ends as needed.

13. Attach snap or hook and eye at back.

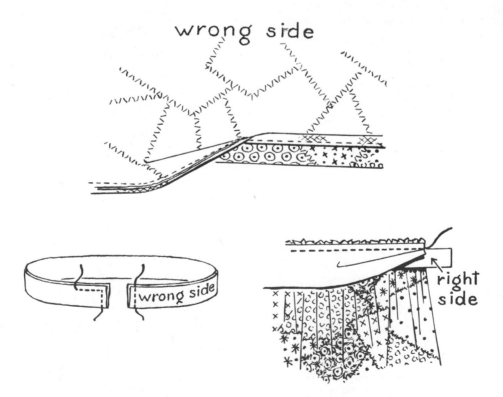

wrong side

wrong side

right side

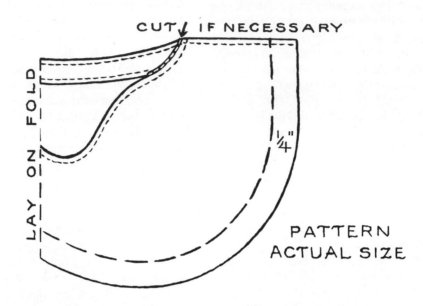

CUT IF NECESSARY

LAY ON FOLD

¼"

PATTERN
ACTUAL SIZE

SHOES: Half pattern is given actual size. Trace on tissue paper; fold, and cut out as whole pattern. Cut two of black felt, but only mark cutout with crayon or white pencil. Make a line of stitching along top edge, as shown, and around marked area. Cut out. Fold shoe in half; seam edges as marked. Trim seams. Turn shoe to right side. If it is loose on doll's foot, cut "strap" as marked (on outer side of foot), and attach a tiny black snap, tightening as necessary.

**Pocket Doll.** Cut organdy into one 2½"× 12" strip and three 1¼"×4" strips.

PANTIES: Stitch three rows of lace edging on one short piece as shown. Turn top edge under, and top-stitch. Fold strip crosswise, wrong side out; seam ends; turn right side out. Place on doll, seam at center back. Draw up line of stitching at top to form gathers. Tack back and front together between legs to form panties.

BLOUSE SLEEVES: On remaining small pieces, turn long edges under, and top-stitch with long stitch. Fold piece crosswise, and seam ends. Draw up edge-stitching to form gathers. Place puff sleeves on doll, and tack to body.

BIAS
BINDING

DRESS: Cut small patches of print, and arrange over large organdy strip. Attach and trim as before. Seam ends of strip together to within ½" of top. Finish dress edge with bias binding. Place on doll; secure opening with stitch in back.

TOP EDGE

ACTUAL SIZE

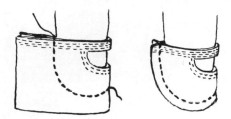

SHOES: Cut two strips of black felt ¾"× 2½". At center of each, mark an opening, given here actual size. Make lines of stitching along edge and around opening mark. Cut out opening. Place strip on "foot"; baste to fit snugly. Take off, and stitch. Trim seam; turn shoe to right side. Put on doll, and tack on.

## Twin Sock Dolls

The two dolls are identical except that one wears blue-check sleepers, the other pink-check sleepers and a hair ribbon.

**Materials.** 1 pair light-pink mercerized-lisle socks, foot size 7½", ankle length 5½". Cotton or kapok for stuffing. 6"×12" piece pink-check gingham. 6"×12" piece blue-check gingham. ½ yard ½"-wide lace edging.

1 yard 1"-wide, cotton fringe braid for hair. Scrap pink felt or flannel. Scrap red yarn. Pink, black, and white sewing thread. 13"× 16" piece of flannel or blanket fabric. 2 yards satin ribbon to match.

**Making.** DOLL BODY (make ¼" seams): Cut sock as shown. When opened, the leg piece should measure 2½"×2¾"; the arm pieces, 2¼"×2½".

Stuff head to 2½" from sock tip. Tie with a bit of fine white string or strong thread. Stuff body. Turn in bottom edges, and whip together.

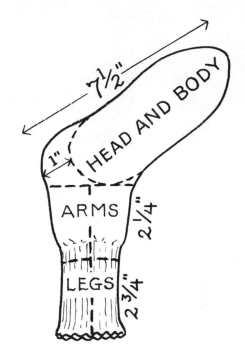

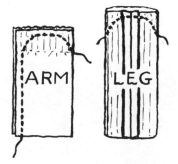

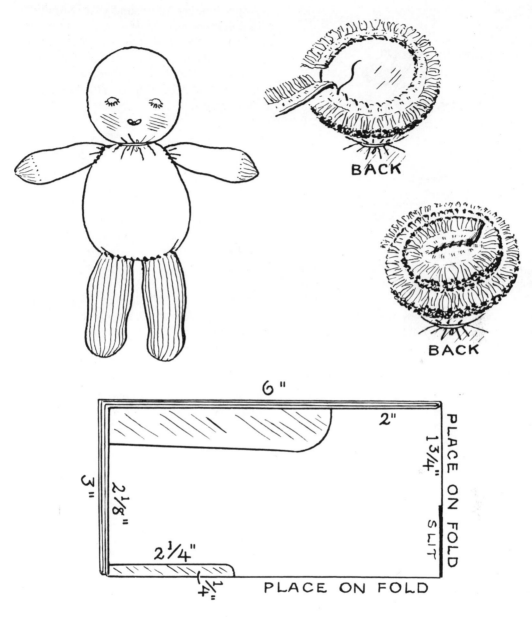

For arms and legs, fold pieces wrong side out; make side seams. Sew ends, folding leg sections with seam in center (back) as shown. Turn to right side. Stuff. Turn in open ends, and whip to doll body as shown.

For mouth, use scrap of red yarn. Take two ¼″ horizontal stitches about ¾″ up from neck. Pull down center, and hold in place with two small vertical stitches. For eyes, cut two half-circles ¼″ across, from pink felt or flannel. Using black thread to simulate lashes, whip curved edges of eyes to doll face about ½″ above mouth and 1″ apart. Rub a little lipstick on cheeks.

For hair, use half of yellow braid fringe for each doll. Tack braid end to one side of head as shown; bring across front of head, tacking down straight edge. Tack down in circles until top of head is covered. Trim end of braid as necessary.

SLEEPERS (make ¼″ seams): Make pattern as shown. Fold gingham in four; place

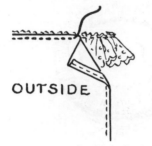

OUTSIDE

Apply binding all around case, turning in ends and mitering corners. Cut remaining ribbon in two. Sew one length to each side of case, on outside, at level of "pocket" edge. Cut a deep notch in free ribbon ends. When dolls are inside, bunting is folded as shown in photograph.

pattern on two folds as indicated. Cut. Slit neckline to 1¾″ from sleeve edge as shown. Make a 1¾″ slit down center back.

Make side and crotch seams. Turn under back opening edge with running stitch; run a gathering thread through top of embroidery or lace edging; draw up to match neck edge. Seam to neck edge, right side to inside of neck; turn in ends. Fold to outside; tack down. Turn under ¼″ at sleeve and leg edges; hold down with a gathering stitch. Draw up, leaving opening for arms and legs. Put sleepers on dolls; slip-stitch back opening together.

Make a bow with 4″ of ribbon from blanket binding, and tack to top of girl's head.

## Felt Blocks:

## Cube

**Materials.** 4″×24″ piece of bright-colored felt. Small piece of contrasting felt for letters. Shredded foam rubber for stuffing.

**Making.** Cut six 4″ squares of felt with pinking shears. Cut out six letters of contrasting felt, and appliqué one letter to each square. With your choice of embroidery stitch or plain stitching, sew squares together at edges, leaving small opening for stuffing. Stuff, and stitch opening.

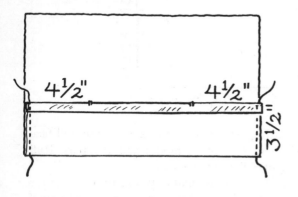

BUNTING: Apply ribbon binding to one 16″ edge of blanket piece. Turn up that edge 3½″. Stitch up sides, making narrow seams. Tack "pocket" securely 4½″ from sides, as shown.

## Drum

**Materials.** 4½″×22″ piece of bright-color felt. Small piece of contrasting felt for letters. Shredded foam rubber for stuffing.

**Making.** Cut two circles of felt 4½″ in diameter, and a rectangle 4½″×13″. Cut numbers 1 through 7 from contrasting felt. Appliqué number 1 to one circle and number 7 to the other circle, and numbers 2, 3, 4, 5, 6 spaced evenly on the rectangle.

With a zigzag stitch, or plain stitching sew long edges of rectangle to circumference of circles. Stuff, and sew open side seam by hand.

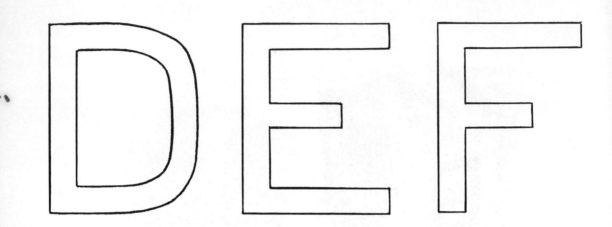

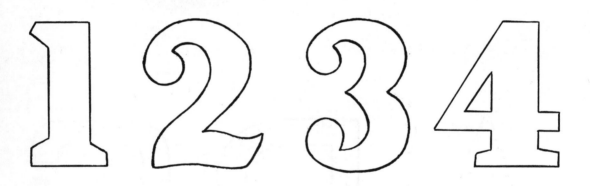

## Humpty Dumpty

**Materials.** ¼ yd red percale. ¼ yd unbleached muslin. 2″×36″ strip of printed cotton. Small pieces of red, white, and black felt. 1 yd red yarn for nose. Soft cotton for stuffing.

**Cutting.** Trace patterns given, and cut as follows:

4 triangles of muslin
4 triangles of red cotton
4 red legs
4 red arms
4 muslin hands

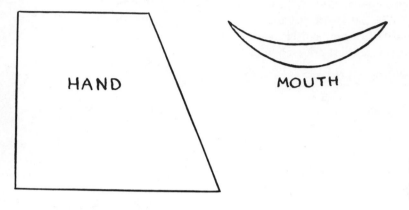

HAND

MOUTH

EYE

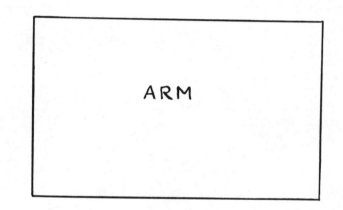

ARM

2 outside eyes of black felt
2 inside eyes of white felt
1 red felt mouth

**Making.** Seams allowed are ¼″. Pin and sew two leg pieces together, leaving open at top, and stuff. Repeat for other leg. Join hand piece to arm (make four). Right sides together, sew arms and hands around three sides, leaving open at top, and stuff. To one red triangular section, pin and baste top of legs 2″ from point. Pin and baste another red section to the first. Stitch. Continue with remaining sections to finish lower part of toy.

Sew muslin triangles together in same manner. Pin and baste tops of arms to center of side sections of red, with raw edges even.

With right sides together and seams matching, pin, baste, and stitch upper section to lower, leaving open across back section for stuffing. Stuff firmly, and sew opening.

For tie, fold print fabric in half lengthwise, wrong side out, and stitch along raw edges. Turn right side out, and press. Turn in ends, and slip-stitch. Place around toy just above arms, and tie a bow in front. Tack to prevent slipping.

Make a small pompon of the yarn for nose. Pin in place, following photograph, and tack. Tack on mouth and eyes (white felt on top of black). Draw on eyebrows with black crayon, and make a dot in each eye for pupil.

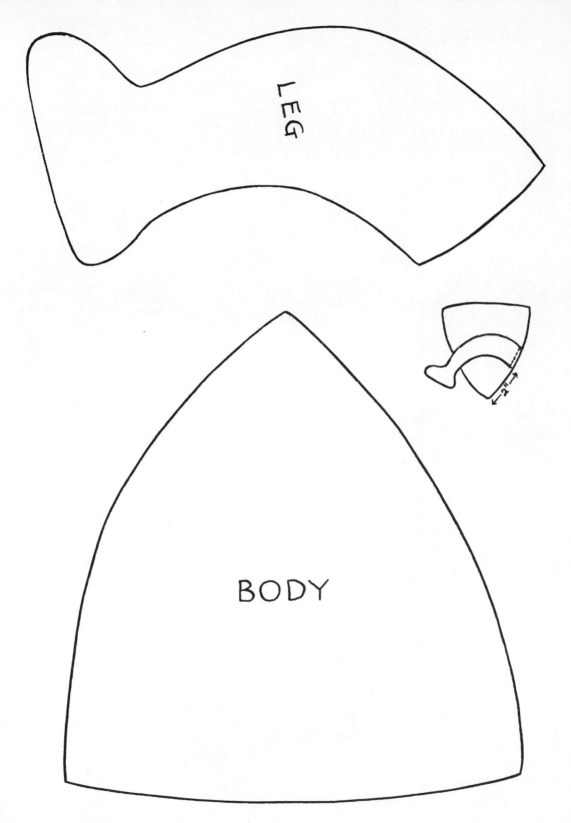

## Bassinet with Flounce

For those who want to make an elaborate bassinet, this is a practical answer. The flounce, hood ruffle, and lining, all separate, can be removed for quick drip-dry laundering (nylon fabric used throughout). Although it looks intricate, almost anyone could attempt it—if the directions are followed step by step. We made ours in pale yellow and white, but any baby shade may be used.

**Materials.** Large bassinet on wheels. At rim, our bassinet measures 41″ long and 21″ wide. Mattress to fit bassinet. 38½″×42″ purchased pillowcase in light yellow or yellow-and-white stripe. 1¾ yds pale-yellow quilted nylon, 44″ wide, for lining. 6½ yds matching yellow nylon taffeta, 44″ wide. 6 yds white flock-dot nylon, 48″wide. 5 yds lace-edged white nylon beading, 1¾″ wide. 11 yds embroidered white nylon edging, 2½″ wide. 7 yds pale-yellow nylon ribbon, ½″ wide. 4 yds pale-yellow nylon ribbon, 4″ wide. 3 yds snap-on tape. 1 ball pale-yellow yarn ("Orlon" or nylon). 1¼ yds elastic, ½″ wide.

**Lining.** In making this size bassinet, follow cutting diagram to cut lining and strips. (*Note:* If another size is used, measure both the inside of bassinet at the rim and the depth (from rim); add 4″ for top hem and 4″ at bottom.) Cut strips, 4″ wide, to attach lining to flounce.

With right sides together, sew the two lining pieces together at ends, tapering seam from ½″ at top to 2″ at bottom. Fig. 1. Press seam open.

Turn top edge ¼″ to wrong side, and stitch.

Place lining in bassinet, wrong side out, and fit by pinning a large dart at each side of end seams where bassinet curves. Remove lining and stitch darts. Fig. 2. Sew bias strips of nylon taffeta together (see cutting diagram for taffeta), and bind lower edge of lining. Place lining in bassinet.

Sew the two 4″ strips together, and trim to make a strip 64″ long, or length required to reach around top of bassinet (not including hood). Turn edges ¼″ to wrong side, and stitch.

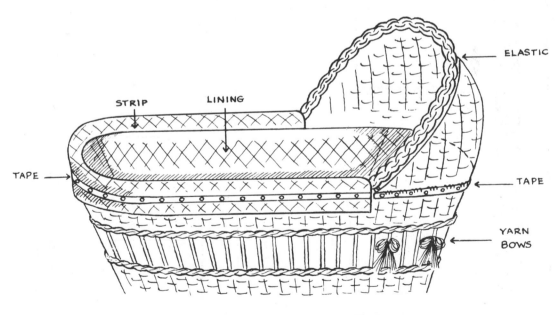

Fig. 3

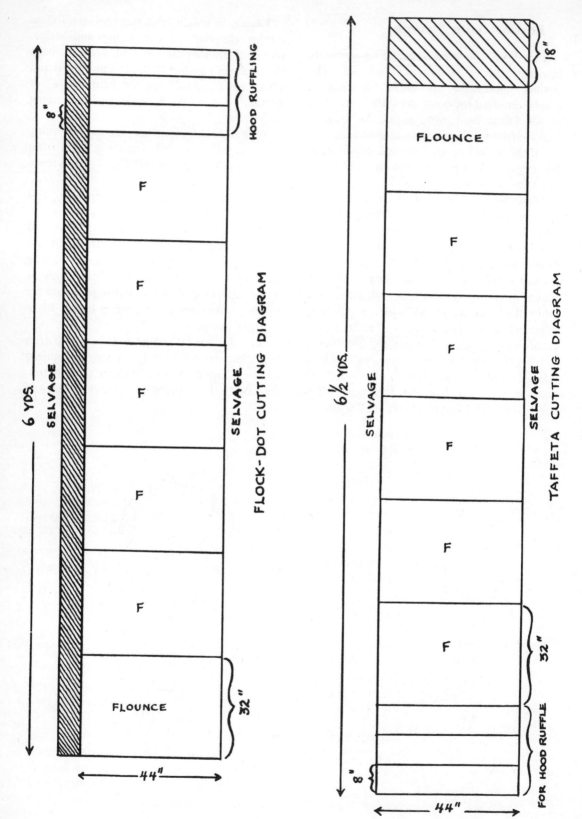

SELVAGE

6 YDS.

8"

HOOD RUFFLING

F

F

F

F

F

FLOUNCE

32"

SELVAGE

44"

FLOCK-DOT CUTTING DIAGRAM

18"

FLOUNCE

F

F

F

F

F

32"

6½ YDS.

SELVAGE

SELVAGE

8"

FOR HOOD RUFFLE

44"

TAFFETA CUTTING DIAGRAM

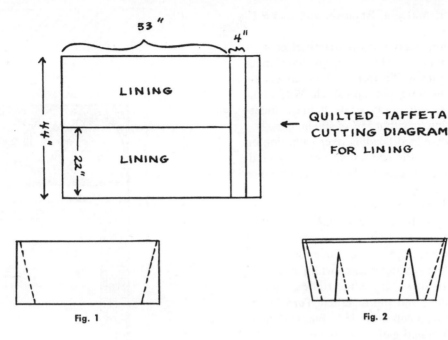

Fig. 1                    Fig. 2

Separate snap-on tape, and machine-stitch under part of tape along one edge of strip. Cut off remaining tape. Thread a thick needle with doubled heavy thread or crochet cotton. Whipstitch remainder of under part of snap-on tape to wicker around the base of the hood, in line with the rim of the bassinet. Start with first snap at the regular interval, and let end as it will at opposite side. Fig. 3. Turn 4″ at top of lining to wrong side. Slip strip under lining (with tape to outside), and pin around, adjusting so tape is in line with tape on hood of bassinet. Slipstitch strip to lining. Thread needle with doubled yarn. At three or four places at back of bassinet, just below hem of lining, insert needle through wicker from outside of bassinet, take a small stitch in lining, and bring needle out; cut off needle, and tie a bow on outside of bassinet—this holds lining in place. Fig. 3.

**Flounce.** Follow cutting diagrams for taffeta and flock dot. (*Note:* If another size bassinet is used, measure bassinet from just below rim to floor, and add 1″. Cut six pieces of nylon taffeta this length. Cut six pieces of white flock-dot nylon this length minus 1″.)

Sew nylon-taffeta lengths together on selvage edges (½″ seams) to make a continuous piece. Do the same with the flock-dot pieces. Turn pieces with seams inside. Place yellow flounce inside white flounce. Turn top edges toward each other ½″, pin around, and edge-stitch. Set machine at longest stitch, and stitch ¼″ from top. Stitch again ¼″ below this. Now pull up bobbin threads of long stitching, gathering to fit around bassinet (about 3 yds) as follows: clip bobbin threads at seams, and pull threads evenly at each side of each panel until panel measures about 18″. Leave ends of threads free, or wind over pins.

Match upper strip of snap-on tape to fit the tape on quilted strip and tape around back of bassinet; cut length required. Divide into six portions (about 18″), and mark with pins. Starting at a seam on the flounce, pin this tape to inside of top, ⅛″ below edge. Fit the 18″ sections of flounce to 18″ sections of tape. Pin carefully. Using zipper or cording foot on machine, stitch top edge of tape to flounce.

Snap flounce to bassinet. Turn up lower edge of under layer of flounce (taffeta) 1″

from floor, and pin. Remove, and make 1″ hem around.

Lay embroidered nylon edging at edge of flock-dot flounce so lower edge is same length as underflounce. Pin around. Turn under raw edge of trimming, pin, and stitch. With pinking shears, trim away white flounce underneath edging to within ½″ of stitching.

Lay lace-edged beading over gathering on top of flounce. Pin and sew securely, by hand, at top edge of beading band. Snap flounce to bassinet.

**Hood Ruffle.** Sew taffeta pieces together, and make a 1″ hem along one edge. Sew flock-dot ruffling same as taffeta. Sew embroidered edging on one edge (as was done for flounce) so that white ruffling is same width as yellow. With seams down, lay white ruffle on top of yellow ruffle, and pin together. Turn in top edges toward each other ½″, pin, and edge-stitch. Stitch and gather as for flounce. Draw up threads to fit over hood, meeting top of flounce at sides. Sew on beading as on flounce.

With hammer and small tacks, fasten end of elastic on one side of hood (under rim). Stretch it over hood just under rim so it will fit snugly, and tack to other side. Fig. 3. Cut off excess elastic. Fasten small safety pins at intervals to under side of gathered edge of ruffle. Then open each pin, and enclose elastic so pin will slide along elastic. Run narrow ribbon through beading over hood, and fasten at each end. Run ribbon through beading at top of flounce, beginning at one side near hood, and leaving long ends. Tie in bow with long loops. With wide ribbon, make a large bow with four loops and streamers, and tack by hand at foot of flounce (see photograph).

## Clothesbasket Bassinet

Here's an inexpensive and quickly made bassinet for the new baby.

**Materials.** Large wicker clothesbasket, measuring 22″ across and 28″ in length at top. 1 firm bed pillow and plastic zip-on

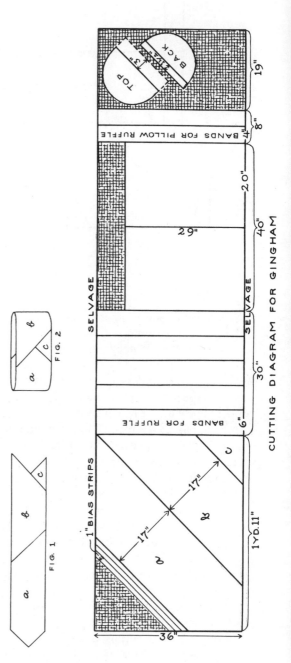

cover. 4 yds blue-and-white (or other baby color) checked gingham, 36″ wide with ⅛″ checks. 3 yds jumbo white rickrack. ½ yd muslin, 36″ wide. 6 oz "Dacron" filling. 8 small snap fasteners. One 20″ zipper, white or to match gingham.

**Cutting.** Following sketch, cut paper pattern for pillow. Fold muslin in half with selvage edges together. Lay pattern with lower edge on fold, and cut.

Following cutting diagram, cut gingham. *Note:* When cutting gingham pillow, add 3″ to lower edge of pattern for top. Fold lower edge of pattern up 1½″ for cutting pillow back.

**Lining.** Using a, b and c bias strips (Fig. 1), turn under edge of one strip about 3 squares of the gingham; lap to end of second strip, matching checks. Pin, and slip-stitch together (piecing should not show). Pin ends together, points matching, lap, and slipstitch as before to make a continuous bias piece. (Fig. 2). Make narrow hem along one raw edge (this is bottom edge). Sew together the five 6″-wide ruffle strips to make a continuous band. Make narrow machine-stitched hem along one edge of band. Set machine for longest stitch, and stitch around ruffle ½″ from other edge. Pull up gathers with bobbin thread to fit top edge of lining. Distribute gathers evenly. With right side of ruffle facing right side of lining—and with edges even—pin, and stitch. Press seam toward bias. Fig. 3. Lay rickrack on right side, covering seam; pin, and stitch down center of rickrack. Fit lining to basket, and cut a

slot at each end for handles. Bind slots with bias, and sew on snaps to hold slot together inside handle. Fig. 3. Press.

**Slip Cover for Pillow-Mattress.** Using the two 20″×29″ pieces, apply zipper to one end. Then stitch together around remaining edges.

## Decorative Pillow

**Pillow Form.** Stitch together around curved edge of muslin; leave opening for filling. Turn to right side. Stuff with "Dacron," and sew opening by hand.

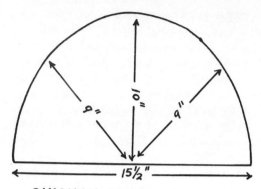

GINGHAM PILLOW PATTERN

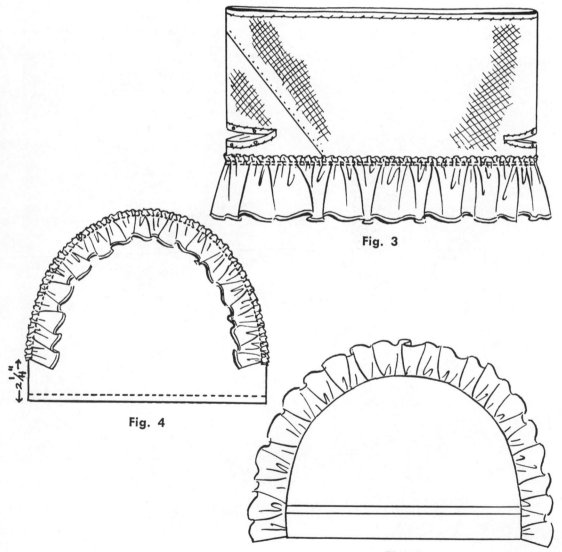

Fig. 3

Fig. 4

Fig. 5

**Gingham Cover.** Stitch together the two 4"-wide strips to form one long strip (ruffle). Make narrow machine-stitched hem along one edge and ends. With longest stitch on machine, stitch ½" from other edge, and gather. Make a ½" hem at lower edge of both top and back of gingham pillow pieces. With right sides together and edges even, pin ruffle to top to within 2¼" of lower edge on each side. Fig. 4.

Lay back of pillow on top of front piece (ruffle between); fold front extension to the back, lapping hems. Pin, and stitch around. Turn, and press. Sew snaps on hems. Fig. 5. Sew on rickrack where ruffle meets front.

## Carriage Cover 30"×38"

Washable corduroy makes a practical and handsome carriage cover for spring use.

**Materials.** 1⅜ yds corduroy, 36" wide, in aqua or any other light shade. 2½ yds embroidered nylon banding, 1" wide. 1⅜ yds batiste or lawn to match corduroy, for lining. 3 yds satin ribbon, ⅝" wide, to match corduroy.

**Directions.** Following cutting diagram, cut corduroy and lining. On corduroy, measure and mark with pins the two trimming lines indicated as banding on cutting diagram. Place banding over marking and pin, remov-

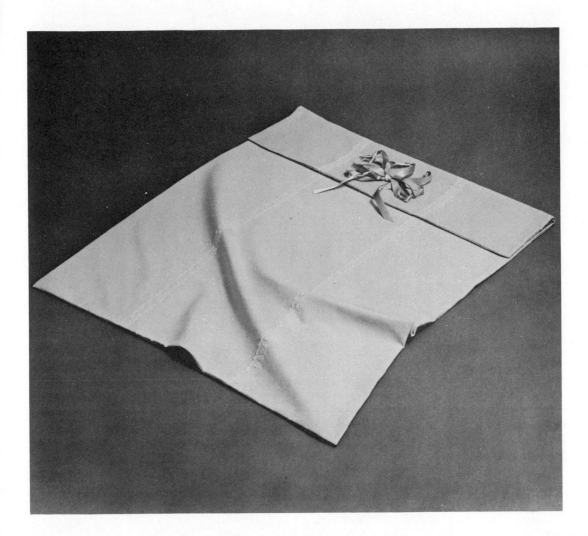

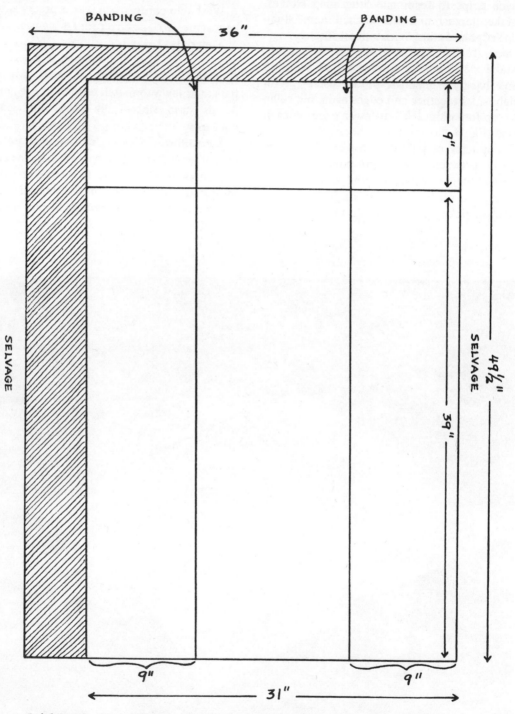

CUTTING DIAGRAM FOR CORDUROY CARRIAGE COVER

ing pins beneath. Stitch by machine close to each edge of banding. With right sides together, place lining over cover. Pin and stitch ½″ seams around 3 sides; leave one 31″ end open. Do the same with flap; leave one 31″ end open. Turn both pieces right side out. Crease edges, and press. Lay right side of flap to wrong side of cover, with raw edges even. Pin, and stitch across. Bind raw edge of seam. Turn flap over to right side, and press. Make a rosette-type bow out of ribbon, and tack to center of flap. (Remove bow when laundering.)

## White Ruffled Pillow

**Materials.** 1 baby pillow form 12″×15″. ½ yd crisp white lawn or batiste. 2½ yds embroidered edging of lawn or batiste, 2½″ wide.

**Directions.** Cut lawn as shown on diagram (back is in two pieces that lap in center of pillow). Make a ¾″ hem along width (13″) of both back pieces. Right sides together seam ends of embroidered edging together. Set machine for long stitches, and stitch ½″ from raw edge of embroidered edging. Pull up bobbin thread, and gather to fit around top of pillow. With right side of ruffling facing top of pillow—and with raw edges even —pin along gathering line. Arrange gathers evenly, and push a little extra fullness to each corner, so that ruffle will lie flat when opened. With right sides down, and hemmed edges lapping in center, lay back pieces on pillow front (over ruffle), outside edges even. Pin, and stitch around. Turn pillow inside out, and press. Slip in pillow form.

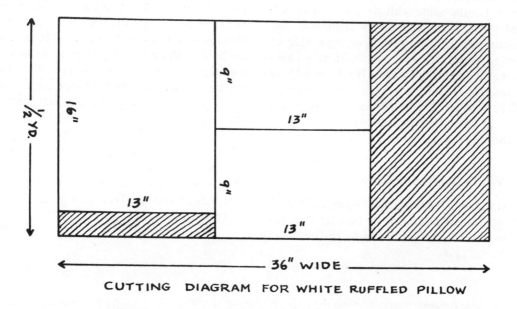

CUTTING DIAGRAM FOR WHITE RUFFLED PILLOW

## Cabana Coat

The popular cabana coat, long a seaside favorite of men, can be worn as robe or lounging jacket, at home or on business trips. And in summer it can go fashionably to the beach.

**Materials.** 2 yds striped cotton, 38" wide; 1⅛ yds black cotton, 38" wide.

**Directions.** Following Fig. 1, cut robe of striped cotton, centering a stripe through center front and back.

Following Fig. 2, cut belt and neckband of black cotton.

Seam sleeve pieces together as in Fig. 3 (top of sleeve).

Fold robe; mark top of shoulder (Fig. 4). Pin and stitch sleeve to robe, matching seam to shoulder marking (Fig. 5). Press this seam toward sleeve.

Stitch underarm and sleeve seam in one operation. Clip underarm (Fig. 6). At bottom of robe, make 2" hem.

Seam neckband pieces together; clip ¼" at neck corners of robe; with right sides together and seam at center back, stitch band to neck and front (Fig. 7). Starting at center back, fold band to wrong side down center; turn under raw edge and slip-stitch over seam. Turn in ends even with hem; slip-stitch.

Make a 2" hem at top of pocket; turn in ½" on remaining 3 sides; pin in position (on right or left side and at height desired). Edge-stitch (Fig. 8). Make a 1¼" hem at edge of sleeves.

Stitch belt pieces together to form one long strip; fold in half lengthwise and stitch leaving one end open; turn and slip-stitch open end. From leftover fabric, cut 2 pieces 3"× 1"; and make belt carriers. Stitch at waist-line.

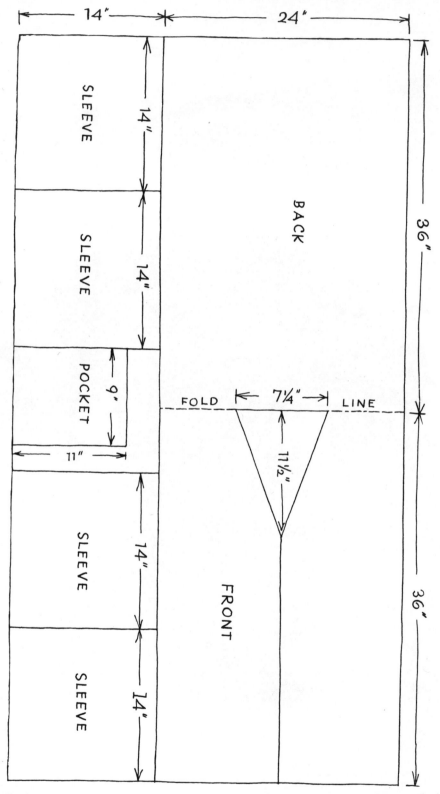

**Fig. 1**

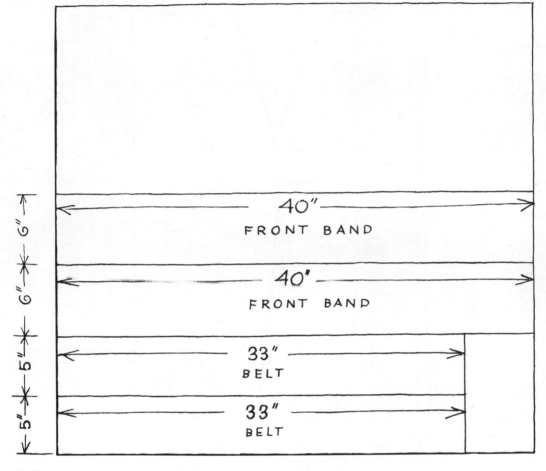

6"
6"
6"
6"
5"
5"
5"

40"
FRONT BAND

40"
FRONT BAND

33"
BELT

33"
BELT

**Fig. 2**

SLEEVE

**Fig. 3**

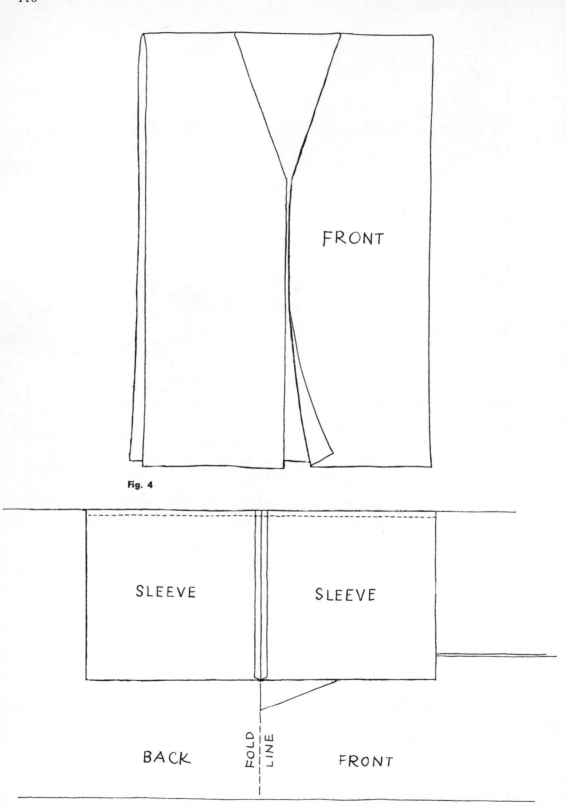

**Fig. 4**

SLEEVE

SLEEVE

BACK

FOLD LINE

FRONT

**Fig. 5**

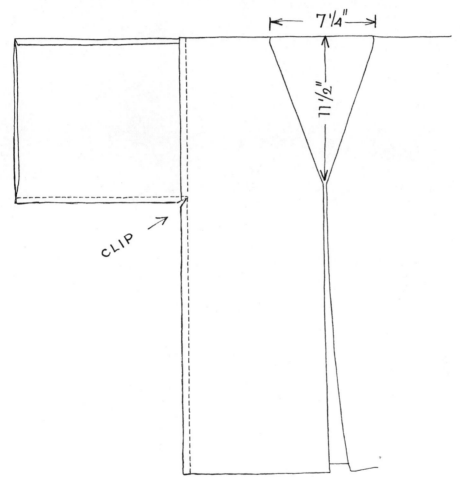

Fig. 6

**Fig. 7**

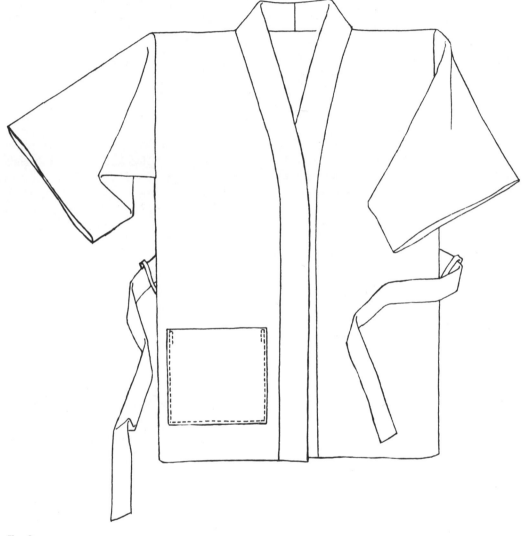

**Fig. 8**

CHAPTER 2 *Embroidery*

Needle and thread and a suitable fabric, plus a working knowledge of even a few embroidery stitches will give you the means of producing many beautiful things for your home or wardrobe.

The art of embroidery is very old and has been part of the cultural development of every nation. If one were to study the collections of old embroideries in museums and other places, it would be possible to assemble over 300 embroidery stitches.

All of the well-known stitches and some of the more unusual ones are given here in the hope that they will act as a spur to the imagination of those who enjoy or wish to learn this lovely craft.

The old custom of making a sampler was not a bad one, since working each stitch until it is perfected gives one confidence. Also the sampler itself can be decorative.

Suitable round thread linen with an even count is difficult to find and counting threads is something which few women will attempt in these modern times. However, since it is well to have some means of keeping stitches evenly spaced while learning, we suggest woven checked gingham or a similar fabric as a background for learning the basic stitches and starting one on the path of becoming a fine embroideress. (See color plate of gingham sampler.)

## THREADS

Many types of thread may be used for embroidery. The mercerized cotton threads such as six-strand floss and perle cotton in various sizes are the ones most commonly used and readily available.

It is interesting, however, to experiment with a variety of threads. Unusual effects can be obtained by using yarns or threads which were not originally intended for embroidery. For example, all types of wool yarns are very useful and the color ranges are magnificent. Cottons with a soft twist, linen, silk, rayon and other synthetics have great possibilities. Metallics are now made stronger and untarnishable and can be added for interesting glitter. Even jute, which is again available, will produce bold interesting effects suitable to contemporary interiors.

**Color Plate 3 — Horn-of-Plenty Quilt**

A lovely example of an appliqué quilt. This and many similar designs can be purchased stamped ready to make. See Chapter 3, Quilting.

# FABRICS

Fabrics offer an infinite variety of textures to be decorated and therefore are a challenge to the imagination. Suiting the stitch, the thread, and the design to the fabric calls for much thought and some practice, as well as good taste.

Linen has long been used for embroidery, and rightly so because of its suitability to many articles such as table linens, mats, towels, etc., which are so often decorated with stitches. Cotton is also widely used, especially for wearing apparel. Woolen fabrics with suitable decoration make lovely bed throws or afghans. Silk and rayon fabrics are rather difficult to handle, and, with some exceptions, are not as well adapted to this work as other fabrics. In general, use fine stitches and threads on fine fabrics, and bolder stitches and heavier threads on coarser fabrics.

Certain kinds of embroidery, such as Hardanger, can be done only on a suitable type of evenly woven fabric because of the necessity of counting threads. The most beautiful cross stitch work is also done by counting threads on round thread linen. These fabrics are not always available because the demand is not great enough to keep them on the market. These techniques are still practised by a relative few.

Many lovely designs can be purchased ready-stamped on linen. These are usually designed for cut work, cross stitch, or lazy daisy stitches and will answer the need of those who are not inclined to experiment on their own with stitches and fabric.

# STITCHES

## Running Stitch

Run the needle in and out of the fabric, making stitches of even length. This is a

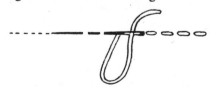

basic stitch in both sewing and embroidery. Stitches may be long or short as needed.

**Whipped Running Stitch.** Whip over each running stitch without picking up the fabric. A blunt needle or the eye of the needle instead of the point may be used to avoid splitting the thread of the running stitches.

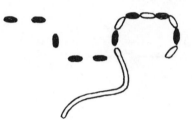

**Holbein or Double Running Stitch.** Work a simple running stitch with even spaces between. Turn and fill spaces left open. The stitch appears the same on both sides. Holbein designs are usually geometric, and often combined with cross stitches.

## Back-Stitch

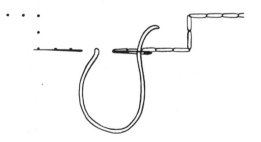

Work from right to left. Take a short stitch. Insert the needle at the beginning of this stitch and bring it out a stitch ahead. Repeat across. Result should resemble machine stitching and be neat and regular.

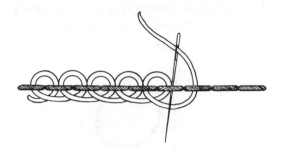

**Pekinese Stitch.** The foundation line is back-stitch. A second thread is interlaced as shown. This is frequently found in Chinese embroideries. If drawn tightly it gives a braided effect.

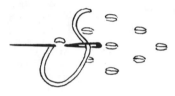

## Seed or Dot Stitch

Each stitch consists of 2 back-stitches worked into the same place. It may be used in regular rows or hit or miss as a filling stitch, known as seeding.

## Fern Stitch

Work three straight stitches of equal length all radiating from one point. If repeated along a curved line they give the effect of a fern-like leaf. It also may be used for veinings in large leaves.

## Bermuda Fagoting or Three-sided Stitch

Also known as Point Turc. When working on fine or sheer fabrics use a thick needle and fine thread to get a lacy or openwork effect.

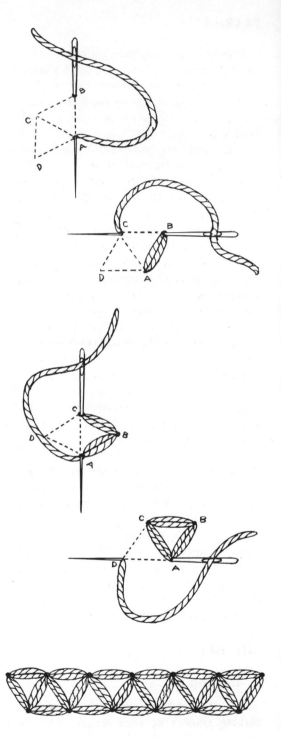

The stitch does not need to follow the thread of the fabric but can be used on curves, scallops, etc. It is often used to apply lace on fine lingerie, or for fine appliqué.

## Punch Stitch

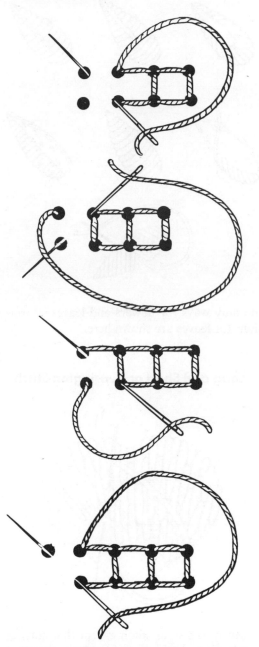

Similar to Bermuda Fagoting but with 4 sides. Follow the diagram making upright stitches all the same length or over the same number of threads. Pull threads taut. Work a similar row back again. Continue until the space is filled. Turn work and repeat the process completing the squares. Always work into holes made by previous stitch.

## Outline or Stem Stitch

Work from left to right, keeping thread always on same side of needle—either to left or right of it. Bring needle out where last stitch went in, following the line, which may be curved or straight.

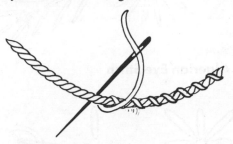

**Whipped Stem Stitch.** Work outline or stem stitch; then whip over it spacing stitches evenly. Needle should not enter fabric. Used for bold lines.

## Rambler Rose Stitch

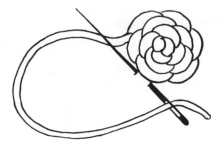

Begin the center with a single outline stitch, or with several satin stitches for a raised center. Work closely around the center with outline stitch keeping needle pointed to the left and the thread below the needle.

## Straight or Spoke Stitch

Single straight stitches of any desired length and worked in any direction. It may be used to form flowers, leaves, etc. Shown here combined with French knots and running stitch.

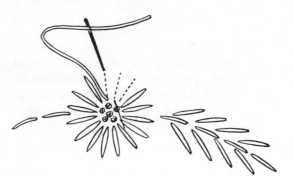

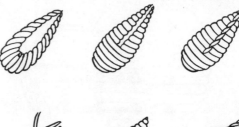

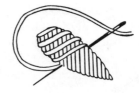

### Algerian Eye Stitch

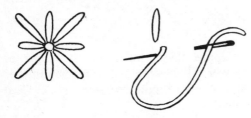

Each star or eye consists of eight stitches all taken into a central point. Arrange the stitches in a square. This can be done on canvas.

### Satin Stitch, Plain

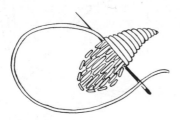

Stitches must be close enough together to cover the fabric; the edges should be very even and neat. This is not easily done and takes practice. The stitches may be worked in any direction but they should not be too long. Large spaces may be broken up. Before working, the area may be padded with rows of running, back, or outline stitches. Satin stitch, slanted or straight, may be used

in many ways for flowers and leaves. Variations for leaves are shown here.

### Long and Short or Kensington Stitch

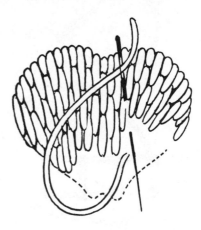

Much like satin stitch except that stitches are long and short. A nice way to blend colors because one row encroaches upon another. It is used in various-shaped designs for shading and filling in.

### Horizontal Flat Stitch

Take a short horizontal stitch across the top of the leaf and bring needle out to the left

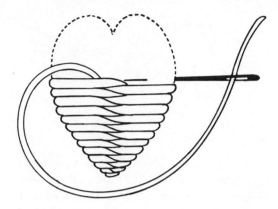

of the center. *Insert needle at right top edge and bring out to right of center. Insert at left top edge and bring out at left of center. Repeat from * until leaf is filled. The stitch can also be slanted, in which case the first stitch is done vertically.

## Dorondo Stitch or Raised Fishbone

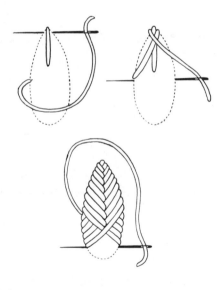

Make a long vertical stitch (halfway down from point of leaf). Bring needle out at left side opposite the end of this long stitch. Take a short stitch at top of leaf from right to left and insert needle on opposite side of where first stitch came out. Bring needle out below stitch on opposite side. Take another stitch at top just below the first, and so on until space is filled.

## Open Herringbone Stitch

Sometimes called catch-stitch. There are many variations. Work from left to right along 2 imaginary parallel lines. These may be drawn lightly or one can follow the weave. Bring needle out on line at lower left. Take a short back stitch on upper line a little to the right keeping thread under the needle. Take a back-stitch on lower line a little to the right with thread under the needle. Continue, keeping spaces even.

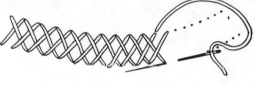

**Closed Herringbone Stitch.** Work herringbone with stitches touching so space is filled.

**Double Herringbone Stitch.** Work a row of open herringbone stitches with wide spaces. Work a second row using a contrasting color, placing stitches in spaces between and interlacing as you work.

**Laced Herringbone Stitch.** Work open herringbone stitch. Then lace a second thread around the crosses that have been formed. Make two complete circles around each upper cross and one and a half around each lower cross. Always interlace under and over the foundation stitches and under and over the thread being used.

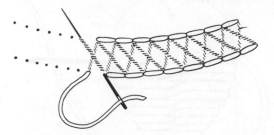

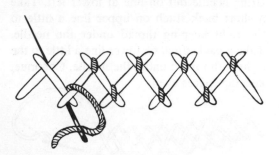

**Threaded Herringbone.** Work open herringbone and lace in manner shown. When lacing do not let needle and thread enter the fabric.

**Shadow Embroidery.** This is closed herringbone stitch worked "wrong side out." It is done on sheer fabric so the underneath stitches show through in shadow effect. It can be worked along parallel lines or to fill simple shapes such as leaves and petals. Take a back-stitch on upper line; then one on the lower line.

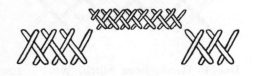

**Tacked Herringbone.** Work a row of open herringbone. Work a small single vertical or horizontal stitch over each place where stitches cross.

**Chevron Stitch**

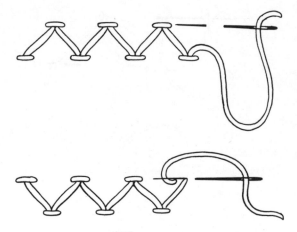

**Narrow and Wide Herringbone.** Without changing thread, an ornamental border may be made by changing the width of the stitches at regular intervals.

**Ornate Herringbone Stitch.** Work a large single chain stitch over each point where stitches cross on open herringbone stitch. Very effective in bold heavy thread or yarn in contrasting colors.

This stitch is also worked on parallel lines and is somewhat similar to herringbone. Take a short stitch on the top line, and bring needle out in the center of this stitch. Take a stitch half the length of the top stitch on line below. Insert needle to the right and bring needle out where the last stitch went in. Arrange stitches so the cross threads come from the center of stitch taken on the line. See diagram.

## Cross Stitch

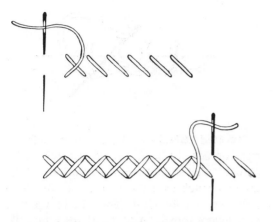

## Plain Blanket Stitch

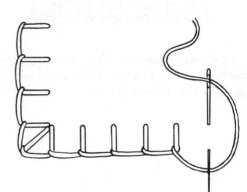

This can be started either at the right or the left. Make a row of slanted stitches of equal length and evenly spaced. Work back over them with the same stitch but slanting in the opposite direction. This makes a row of cross stitches. The reverse side will show a row of upright stitches.

Work from left to right. Bring needle out on line (or very close to hem edge). Take an upright stitch to the right with needle pointed down keeping thread under the needle, and come out on line or edge. Diagram also shows how to turn a corner with blanket stitch. Many variations of this stitch are possible.

**Double Cross Stitch.** This consists of a cross stitch done on the diagonal (as above) with another cross worked over it centered in spaces between.

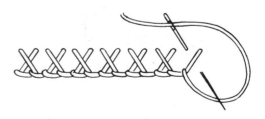

**Tent Blanket.** Slant stitches to form points (which resemble a row of tents).

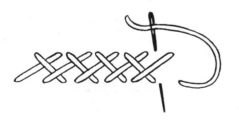

**Long-armed or Long-legged Cross Stitch.** The first stitch of the cross is longer and more slanted than in regular cross stitch. The second stitch of the cross is done immediately after the first and is the usual length and slant. This gives a plaited effect. May be worked on linen or canvas.

**Crossed Blanket.** Work a blanket stitch slanting needle from right to left. Work another over it slanting needle from left to right. Place it so stitches will cross.

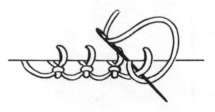

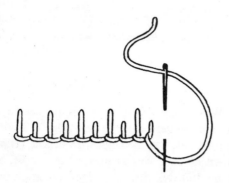

**Graduated Blanket.** Vary the length of stitches to make patterns. Great care must be taken to keep groups uniform.

**Long and Short Blanket.** Worked same as plain blanket stitch but with stitches of different lengths.

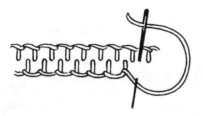

**Grouped Blanket.** Work stitches in groups of two or more with a wider space between each group. This makes a nice border on a narrow hem if not done too boldly.

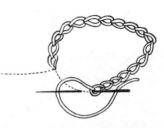

**Double Blanket.** Work a row of plain blanket stitch. Turn work and make another row taking stitches between those of the first row. Keep all stitches even and of equal length.

**Knotted Blanket.** Work from left to right on edge of hem. Take first stitch as for plain blanket stitch leaving a loose loop. Take another stitch over the loop as shown; then pull into a tight knot. This shows up best in a heavy thread. Additional rows may be added, being worked into the last row of loops to make wider decoration.

**Mille Fleur.** Draw a circle. Work blanket stitch around, inserting needle at or near center. Make all stitches the same length.

## Simple Chain Stitch

Bring thread out on the line. Insert needle where thread came out and take a short stitch on the line keeping thread under the needle. Draw up. This makes a loop which should lie flat. Insert needle where thread came out and take another stitch in same manner. Keep stitches the same length.

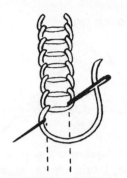

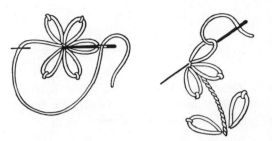

**Open Chain or Ladder Stitch.** This is worked on parallel lines. Bring needle out on left line and insert on right line. Bring needle out on left line below first stitch with thread under needle. Loop must be kept somewhat loose. Insert needle on right line with loop under it; bring needle out on left line and so on. Keep the spaces even. They may be any size desired.

**Detached Chain or Lazy Daisy Stitch.** Work as for chain stitch but insert needle just outside (or below) loop. Bring needle out wherever next stitch is wanted. The stitches may be placed to form daisy petals or spaced evenly for filling stitches.

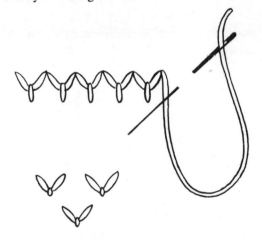

**Feathered Chain.** Work on parallel lines. Starting on one of the lines, work a slanted chain. Following the slant, insert needle a little *inside* of the second line. Bring needle out *on* the second line a little above where it went in. Make another slanted chain. Continue back and forth.

**Fly-Stitch or Y-Stitch.** This is a detached chain stitch worked open. Picture a V when inserting the needle. Hold the loop down at center below with a stitch as for detached chain or daisy stitch, but make it a little longer.

### Feather Stitch

With thread under slanted needle, make a blanket stitch to the right of a straight perpendicular line. With thread under needle make a blanket stitch to the left. Repeat. Fancy feather stitch is made by working several stitches on each side. They may be evenly spaced or grouped. A further variation is made by pointing the needle straight

**Zigzag Chain.** Worked the same as ordinary chain stitch, but the stitches are slanted in such a way as to make a zigzag line.

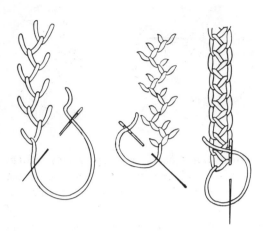

## Plain Couching

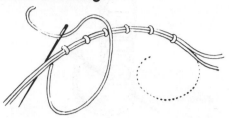

A heavy thread or a group of threads are laid on the fabric. With another thread (usually of contrasting color), hold the heavy thread down with short stitches across it at regular intervals. Do not allow the heavy thread to pucker. This can be done on curved or straight lines.

down so the outside stitches are parallel and closed.

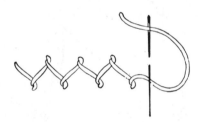

**Creton Stitch.** A variation of feather stitch. With thread under needle, work back and forth keeping needle pointing straight up or straight down.

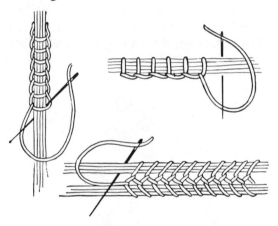

**Fancy Couching.** The couching stitch may be varied by slanting, grouping, or zigzagging. Stitches such as cross stitch, feather stitch, or blanket stitch may be used to hold down the heavy thread. Keep spaces even for the best effect.

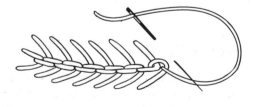

**Fish-Bone Stitch.** Another variation of feather stitch. Slant the needle more and take stitches longer than for regular feather stitch. Always bring needle out at center line.

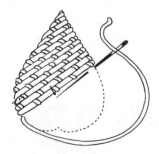

**Bokhara Couching.** Used for filling an enclosed space. The same thread is used for the laid thread as for holding it down. The thread to be couched is laid from left to right.

This is held down on return by small slanting stitches evenly spaced. Roumanian couching is very similar, the difference being that the return stitches are taken at a very long slant. When finished, it is difficult to distinguish the laid from the couching stitch.

### French Knot

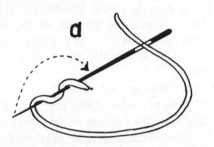

Bring needle to right side. (*a*) With left hand wind thread over needle 2 or 3 times or more (depending upon size of knot desired).

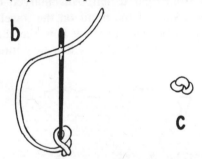

(*b*) Insert needle close to where it came out. (*c*) While adjusting tension with left hand, draw needle to wrong side forming knot.

### Bullion Stitch

Bring needle to right side. Take a short stitch (whatever length desired) and bring needle out at the same place as before. Wind thread over the needle several times—enough to fill space the length of the stitch taken. Hold the "wind" with left hand while pulling thread through so it will be smooth and even. This may be used to make a rambler rose, daisy, or other design.

### Coral Knot or Snail's Trail

Work from right to left. Take a short slanting stitch on the line. Allow the thread to lie over, then under, the needle. Draw up to make a knot. Take another stitch a little farther along and repeat.

### Armenian Edging

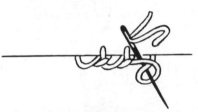

Work from left to right on the edge of a hem. Bring thread out on the very edge. Insert needle a little to the right, pointed up. Before pulling thread through, loop it around the needle as shown. Pull tight. This forms a knot on the edge. Effective in heavy thread. See also Armenian needlepoint lace.

### Swedish or Needle Weaving

Draw threads for a border of the desired width. Upper and lower edges of the border may be hand hemstitched to help group the stitches. Use no knot; bring needle out at edge of border leaving an end. Weave over and under 2 sets of threads as shown. Fill the space closely by pushing darning stitches to-

126

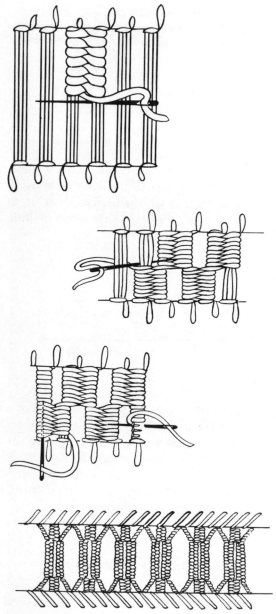

gether as you work. Finish bar and fasten thread by running down center of bar. Do same with next starting thread. Bars may be grouped to form varied patterns. Whenever

possible pass needle under stitches to get from one group to another.

To finish a raw edge of material, first overcast edge, then work overhand stitches to give appearance of a woven bar.

## Darning on Huck

This is a very old art and many lovely designs can be made with it. It is a simple but effective type of embroidery done on the surface of huckaback towelling. The raised thread of the fabric occurring at regular intervals forms the basis of the work, which is simply a darning stitch. Choose the side of the fabric where the threads of the raised dots run up and down and parallel with the selvage. This is actually the wrong side of the fabric.

Use a blunt-pointed needle and either 6-strand floss or perle cotton size 5 or 8, depending upon the fineness of the weave of the huck. Start with a strand of thread long enough to reach across the border (if making towels). Follow the chart. Start at the center of the design and the center of the fabric and work from right to left. An enlarged detail of the center of the motif on the towel pattern is given here to show how the threads cross. Pull the thread only half-way through,

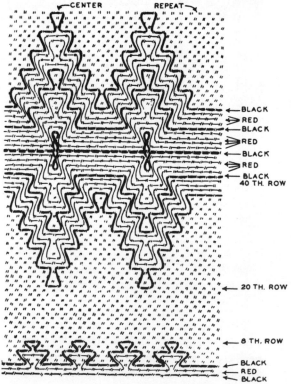

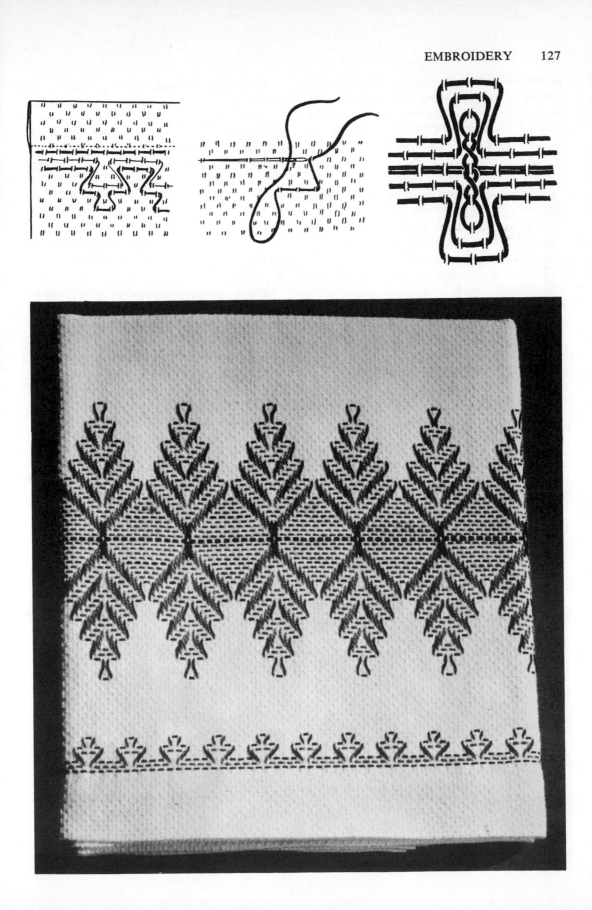

leaving an end long enough to work the other half of the design, so that you can later turn the towel up side down and work the other half of the border. Be careful not to go through the fabric to the wrong side. Fasten thread neatly by running back through a few stitches. Do not pull thread too tightly. Elaborate borders are traditional and varied, but simpler designs may also be made. Colored huck is now available and comes wider than formerly, giving greater scope to this fascinating technique.

The same principle may be applied on other fabrics, such as checked gingham or dotted Swiss, catching the squares or dots in place of the raised threads on the huck.

This work is sometimes done with wool on coarse huck for knitting bags, pillows, etc. It is also possible to work on the right side of the huck by inserting the needle from top and bottom of the raised threads instead of from the sides. A more squared-off pattern results.

## PILLOWS

### General Directions

Buy a foam-rubber pillow of the desired size. Measure the side edges, and cut fabric to the same size, plus ½″ all around. For example, for a 14″ by 14″ pillow, cut two 14½″ by 14½″ squares. Boxing strips, where needed, are cut 1″ wider than pillow sides. If welting is to be done with self-fabric, an extra ½ yard of fabric will be needed.

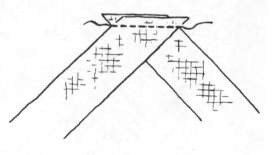

For self-welting, buy ⅜″ cotton cable cord, and cut 2″-wide fabric strips on the true bias. Piece bias as shown above. Press seams. Baste over cable cord, stretching bias slightly.

To apply welting, baste it around edge of pillow section on right side as shown at right, all raw edges even. At corners, clip through welting-seam allowance. Join ends by piecing bias as in Figure 1. Trim ends of cord so they meet; do not lap. On a knife-edged pillow, apply welting only around top section. On a boxed pillow, apply to both top and bottom sections. Stitch around, using cording foot.

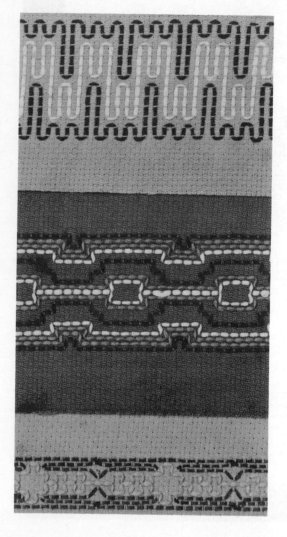

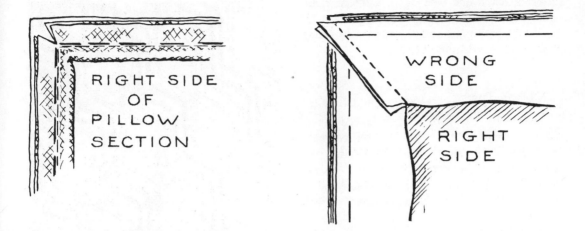

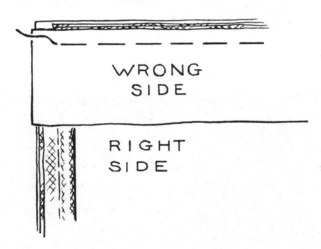

### Knife-Edged Pillow

Baste bottom section over prepared top section, right sides together, covering welting. Stitch around, using cording foot; leave one edge open. Turn to right side. Stuff pillow through opening. Turn in raw edge on bottom section, and hem by hand over welting stitching line.

### Boxed Pillow

Join boxing strips to go all the way around pillow. Starting at a corner on right side, baste boxing strip around top section of pillow, covering welting as shown at top right above. Seam ends, and trim, as shown above. Crease seam open. Stitch around, using cording foot. Matching edges of bottom section to raw edges of boxing strip, baste, and stitch around; leave one side open. Turn to right side. Stuff pillow through opening. Turn in raw edge on boxing strips, and hem by hand over welting stitching line.

### Oblong Pillow

**Materials.** ½ yard 36″-wide red huck (buy ½ yard extra if making self-welting). 6 skeins black and 9 skeins pearl-gray six-strand floss. Red mercerized sewing thread. 2 yards ready-made welting or cotton cable cord. 13″ by 17″ knife-edged foam-rubber pillow.

**Directions.** Cut a piece of fabric about 15″ by 18″. See general instructions for darning on huck. Because the design (shown at right) is entirely diagonal, start at one corner and proceed across entire surface. Follow general directions for making up pillow.

## Square Boxed Pillow

**Materials.** 1 yard 36″-wide dark-blue huck (add ½ yard if making self-welting). 6 skeins rose-red and 6 skeins lavender six-strand floss. Ready-made welting or cotton cable cord. Dark-blue mercerized sewing thread. 13″ by 13½″ square-edged foam-rubber pillow.

**Directions.** Cut a piece of fabric about 16″ square. Work design as shown on following page, following general instructions for darning on huck. Make up pillow.

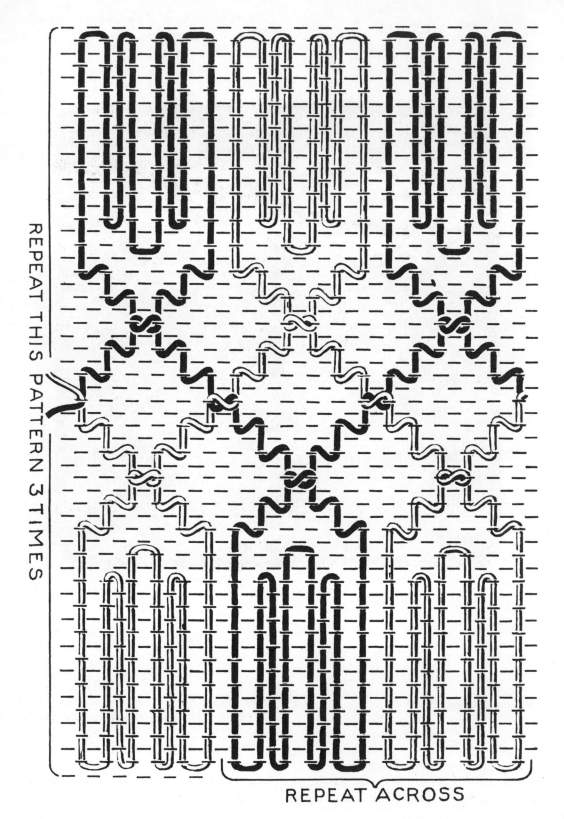

REPEAT THIS PATTERN 3 TIMES

REPEAT ACROSS

## Child's Pillow

**Materials.** 1 yard 36″-wide medium-green huck (add ½ yard if making self-welting). 10″ square pale-green huck. 1 skein white, 1 skein light-blue, 2 skeins China-blue, and 2 skeins red six-strand floss. 1 yard standard-width red rickrack. Green and red mercer-ized sewing threads. Four ¾″ red pompons. 15″ square, square-edged foam rubber pillow.

**Directions.** Work design, one half of which is shown on following page, in center of pale-green square. Turn edges under, and stitch over center of 16″ dark-green square. Stitch rickrack over edges of patch. Make up pillow as directed. Attach pompons where shown in photograph.

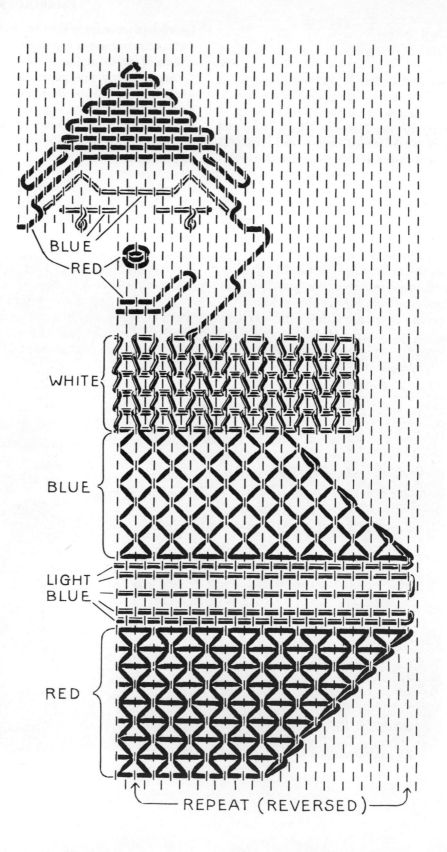

BLUE

RED

WHITE

BLUE

LIGHT
BLUE

RED

REPEAT (REVERSED)

# APRON

**Materials.** ¾ yard 36″-wide light-blue huck. ½ yard 36″-wide white huck. 3 skeins light-green and 4 skeins steel-blue six-strand floss. White and light-blue mercerized sewing threads.

**Directions.** Cut a 5″ by 18″ strip for waistband and a 7½″ square for pocket from the white huck.

Work band, as shown on following page, ½″ above one edge of waistband strip. First; work blue pattern then weave green floss back and forth across it, using 12 strands (two full thicknesses) of the green floss.

For pocket, stitch a ¾″ hem along one edge parallel with double threads (top of pocket). Work blue pattern over entire area.

Green (six strands) is then worked back and forth, each line extended all the way down to bottom of pocket and up to edge.

Cut a 24″ by 36″ piece from blue huck. Make narrow hems along selvage edges, a 3″ hem on one raw edge. Turn under edges of pocket, and stitch to blue section 4″ below top (raw) edge and 6½″ from right-hand edge. Make two lines of gathering stitches along top edge.

For ties, cut two 4½″ by 28″ strips from white huck. Make narrow hems along two long and one short edge. Gather the two raw ends, and attach to front part of waistband, as shown in diagram on following page, to the width of decorated band. Fold plain side over, and stitch both ends, as shown. Turn.

Gather top edge of apron to width of waistband. Stitch, right sides together. Turn waistband up. Turn raw edge in back; baste. Topstitch close to edge around all edges of waistband.

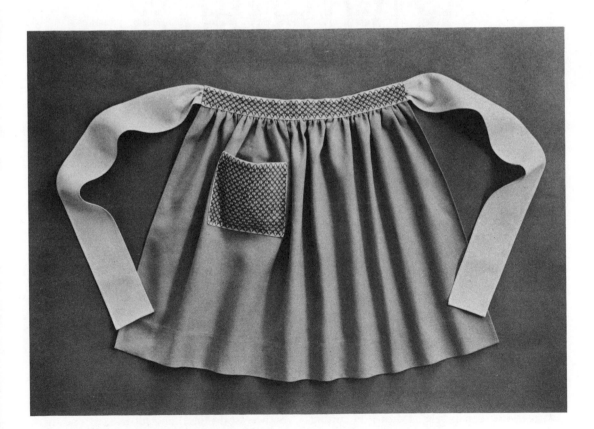

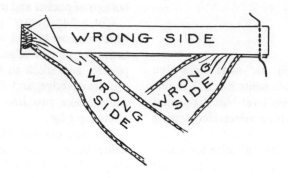

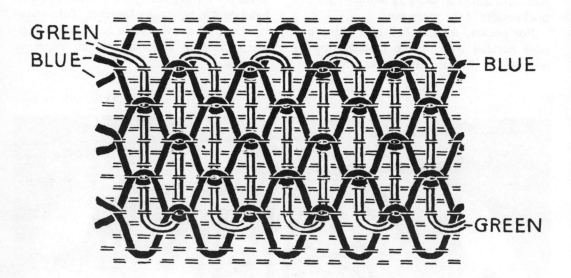

## CHILD'S PINAFORE (SIZE 6)

**Materials.** 1½ yards 36″-wide coral huck. 4 skeins yellow six-strand floss. Coral mercerized sewing thread. Three ⅝″ buttons.

**Directions.** Cut fabric as shown in cutting chart (Figure 11). Join the two skirt-back sections to the skirt-front section; press seams open.

Point A (Figure 12), where weaving starts, is 7″ above raw bottom edge and 3″ to right (facing the fabric) of right-hand seam. Follow entire outline of figure (mottled line in Figure 12), returning to A; then work outline of bodice (solid ļine), and fill in skirt ending at

B. Repeat across pinafore skirt to 3″ left of left-hand seam.

Work bib (chest-strap) design (see Figure 13) across bib section.

Fold shoulder straps and bib in half lengthwise; stitch one long and one short edge. Trim, turn, and press, bringing decorative strip on bib to center of band.

On skirt, turn back 2″ on the two side (selvaged) edges. Turn up 2″ hem at bottom edge, blind-stitching in place. At raw top edge, make two rows of gathering stitches.

Make narrow hems along two long and one short edge of each tie.

Pin open ends of shoulder straps to waistband, right sides together, 2¼″ from center, as shown in Figure 14. Draw up skirt gathers to match waistband, less ½″ at each end, as shown in Figure 15. Match wrong side to waistband edge, covering shoulder straps. Stitch. Turn in ends of waistband; fold to front; turn under front bottom edge of waistband; top-stitch over apron front and along two ends. Turn up shoulder straps; catch straps by hand to edge of waistband.

Turn in ends of bib strap; tack by hand to wrong side of shoulder straps, 1½″ above waistband, as shown in Figure 16.

Gather raw ends of ties to waistband width. Attach, right sides together, as shown in Figure 17, 1″ beyond each shoulder strap. Turn toward back; tack down on right side as shown in Figure 18.

Make a horizontal buttonhole on right-hand end of waistband; attach button to left-hand end. Make vertical buttonholes in waistband 3½″ from ends (see Figure 19). Attach buttons to ends of shoulder straps to match.

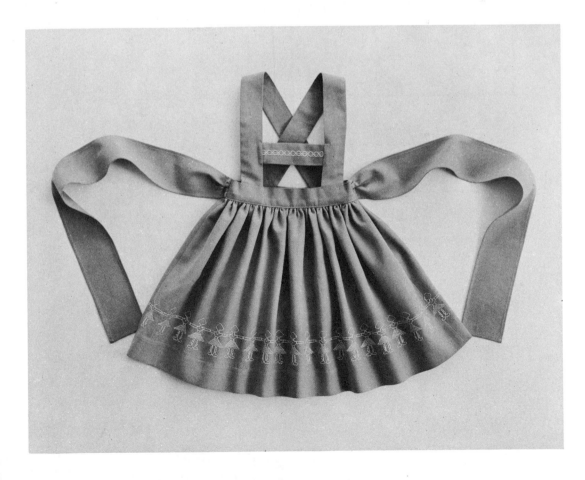

138

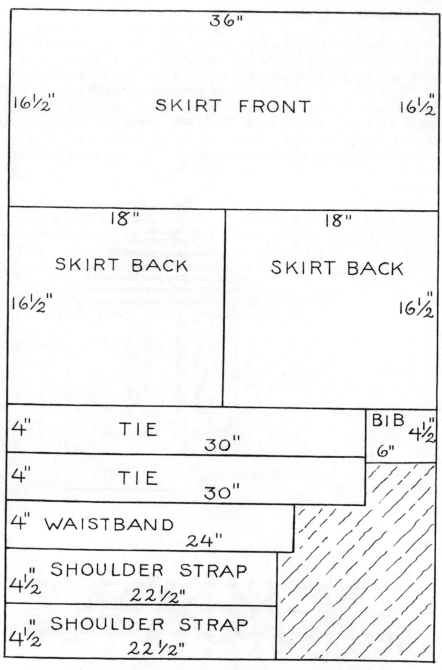

PINAFORE

**Fig. 11**

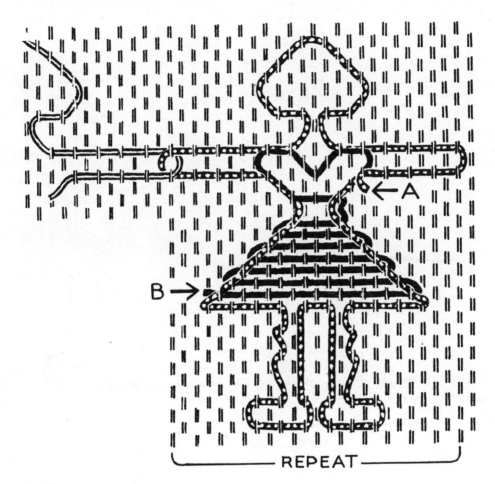

**Fig. 12**

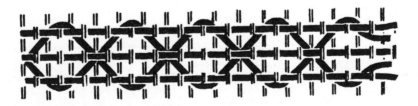

**Fig. 13**

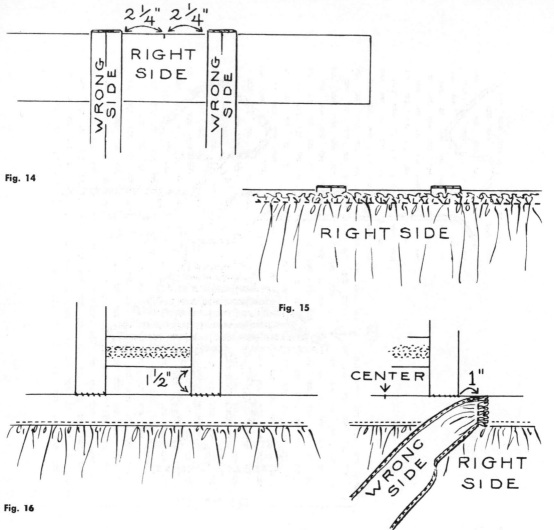

Fig. 14

Fig. 15

Fig. 16

Fig. 17

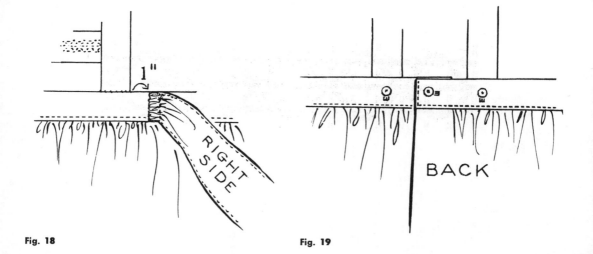

Fig. 18

Fig. 19

## ROUND POT HOLDER

**Materials.** ¼ yard 36″-wide tan huck. ¼ yard 36″-wide flannelette. 2 skeins deep-rose six-strand floss. Tan mercerized sewing thread.

**Directions.** Cut a 9″ square of huck. Draw a 9″ circle on it. Work design given on following page over entire circle. Cut out circle. Using this as pattern, cut out second circle from huck and four circles from flannelette.

Place flannelette circles together; stitch around. Place between the two huck circles; stitch around.

See cutting chart (on following page). Cut four 1¼″ strips of huck on true bias, one 1¼″ by 4½″ straight strip.

To make loop, fold in long edges of straight strip; fold in half lengthwise; top-stitch. Pin one end to top edge of circle on right side.

Join ends of bias strip. Press seams. Baste around circle, right sides together; lap ends. Stitch, taking ½″ seams. Turn strip to back; turn edge under, and hand-hem in place, folding free end of loop under edge of strip.

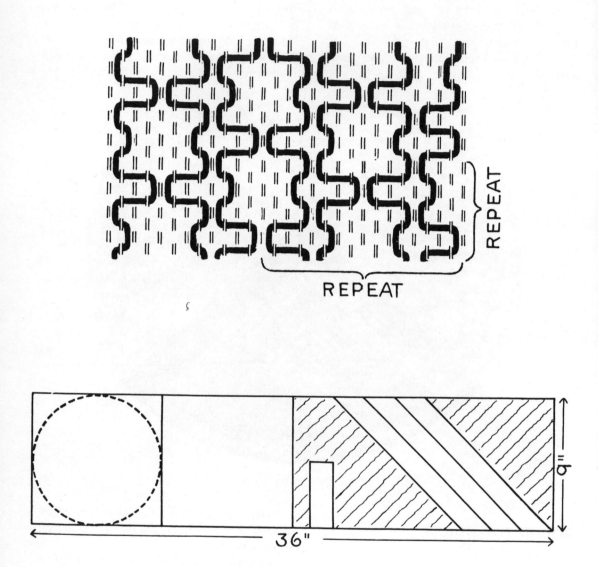

REPEAT

REPEAT

36"

9"

## SQUARE POT HOLDER

**Materials.** ¼ yard 17″-wide brown huck. ¼ yard 36″-wide flannelette. 3 skeins light-pink six-strand floss. Light-pink standard-width bias tape. Light-pink mercerized sewing thread.

**Directions.** Cut a 6½″ square of huck. Work weaving on it, following diagram on following page. For border, first work back-and-forth pattern, then straight lines running through it.

Using this square as a pattern, cut one more square of huck and four squares of flannelette. To assemble, follow instructions for round pot holder, substituting bias tape for huck strips.

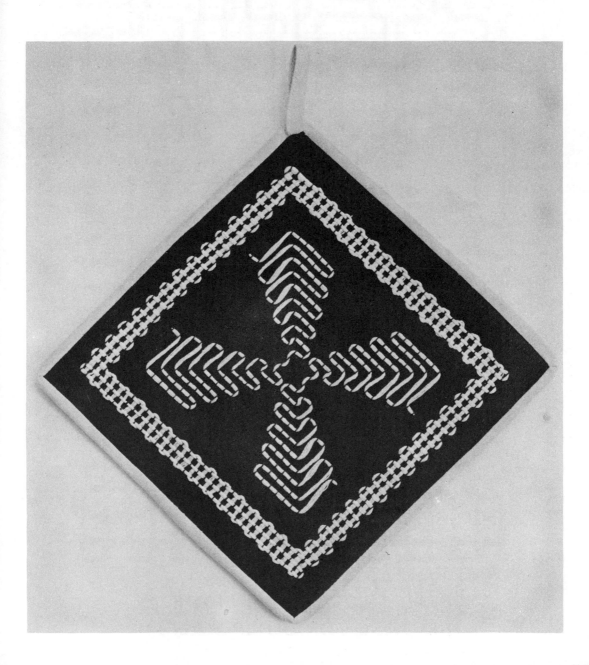

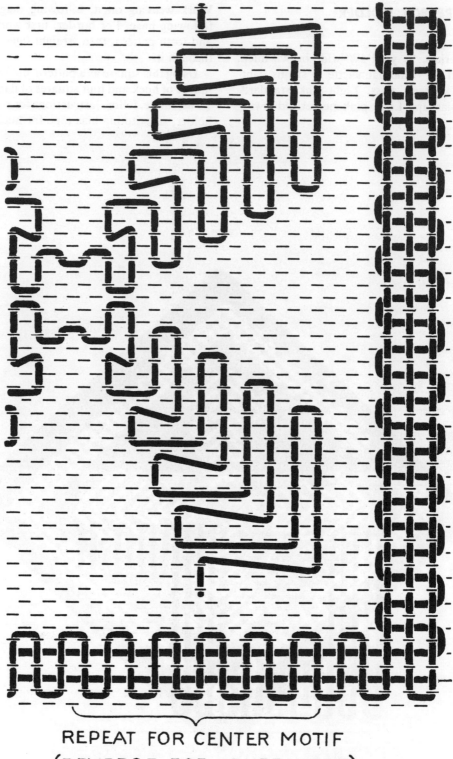

REPEAT FOR CENTER MOTIF
(REVERSE FOR OTHER HALF)

## PLACE MAT

**Materials.** ½ yard 36″-wide red huck. (*Note:* 1¼ yard cut lengthwise, will yield

four place mats. 3 skeins white six-strand floss. Red mercerized sewing thread.

**Directions.** Work border along both ends, allowing for ½″ hems. Make narrow, rolled hems along long edges, ½″ hems at ends, all by hand.

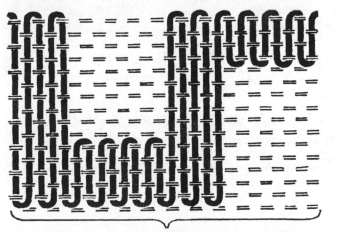

REPEAT ACROSS — REVERSE FOR OTHER END OF PLACEMAT

## GUEST TOWELS

**Materials for Each.** ½ yard 36″-wide huck. 4 skeins, for continuous border, and 2 skeins, for fish border, six-strand floss. Mercerized sewing thread to match huck.

**Directions.** Cut 14½″ by 25″ towel. Work border on one end, allowing for a 1″ hem. Make narrow hems along each side, 1″ hem at ends. Machine-stitch.

**Color Plate 4 — Four Designs for English Smocking**

Diagrams and instructions for making these four smocking patterns are given in Chapter 4, Smocking.

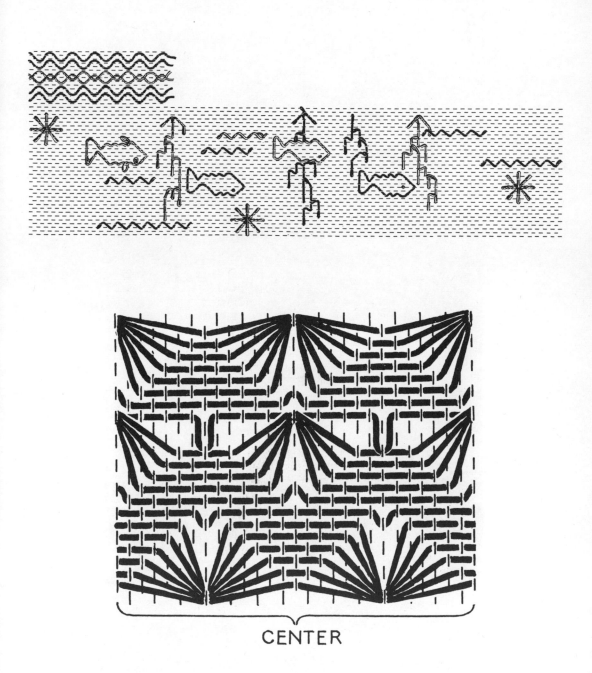

CENTER

## BORDER PATTERNS

Suitable for decorating aprons, towels, curtains, place mats, children's wear, etc. Follow general instructions when applying patterns in color combinations of your choice.

150

↑
CENTER

REPEAT

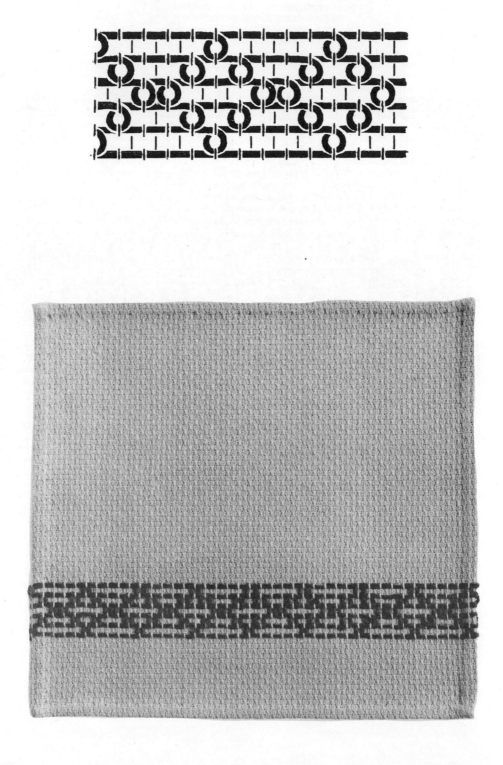

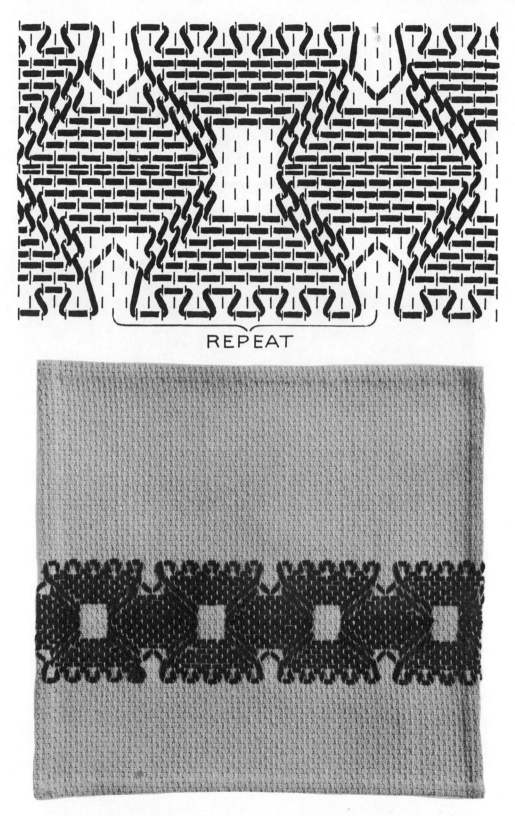

REPEAT

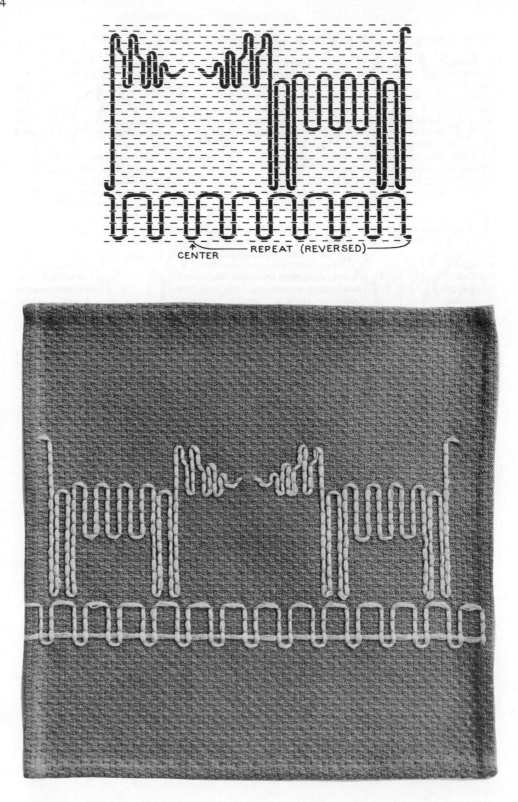

CENTER   —REPEAT (REVERSED)—

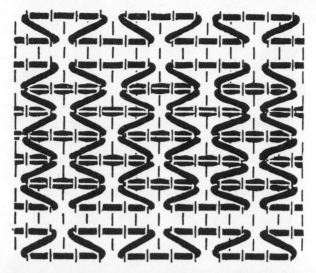

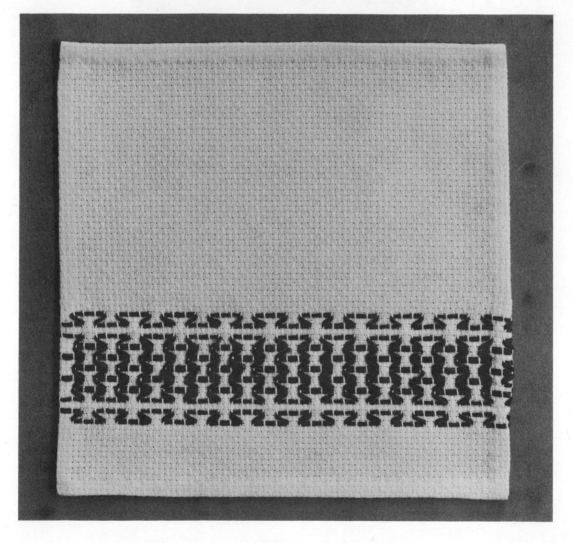

## Buttonhole Stitch

(For true buttonhole stitch see Chapter I, How to make hand made buttonholes.)

Work from left to right like blanket stitch but with the stitches placed close together. Buttonholing is used for scallops or edges of cut-work designs. The purling is always worked on the edge which is cut away. Scallops may be padded with running or outline stitch.

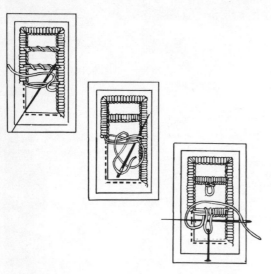

**Buttonhole Bars.** Work simple buttonhole stitch along one side of opening and along opposite side up to the place where bar is to be. Carry thread across to the finished row and bring needle up from below through one loop. Carry thread back and forth until there are 3 threads. Cover these threads with buttonhole stitches or simply wind them closely with thread to make a bar. Do not catch into fabric. A simple picot may be made in the center of the buttonholed bar by leaving the loop of the center stitch longer. Hold it with a pin. Then work next stitch around it.

## Eyelets

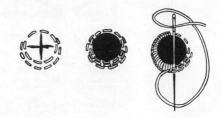

Mark a circle. Work running stitches on the line for padding. If circle is small, punch a hole with a stiletto. If large, cut a cross in the center. Overcast edges turning them under as work proceeds. Buttonhole stitch may

also be used. Leaves and petals may be worked in the same way. Slash fabric lengthwise. Round eyelets may be worked gradually widening edge as shown.

## COLOR PLATE 2

The colorful sampler "I Know My Stitches" is worked on checked gingham and is not at all difficult to do. You can make it or a similar one by following the checks on the gingham and the diagrams given showing the stitches used in the various borders. Substitute other stitches as desired.

Follow the color plate for placement of designs, borders, and colors used, or arrange them to suit yourself. The color photograph has been reduced. Checked gingham with eight squares to the inch (measuring crosswise of the fabric) was used. Have the selvage run lengthwise on the sampler.

You will need a piece of gingham about 14″ by 19″. This will leave a border of about 2″ around the embroidery. In order that the design be placed in the center as well as to

have it symmetrical, begin in the center and work outward.

Bright red, Kelly green, medium orange, and royal blue thread were used, but colors can be chosen which look well on the gingham you have selected.

Be sure to sign your sampler by working your name or initials as well as the date in one of the lower corners. Back-stitch is good for this purpose.

## COMBINING STITCHES

After learning a few of the stitches shown here, try combining some of them to make interesting borders. Some unusual and lovely effects can result. They will be very useful for decorating any number of articles, such as children's wear, place mats, pillows, table cloths, and skirts, and in any place where a flat decoration would look well.

158

Here are a few examples of combinations of stitches and where they might be used, from place mats and cushions to aprons and little girls' dresses.

Our great-grandmothers combined stitches when they set their "crazy quilts" together. Some of the results of their imaginations are delightful. Here are a few taken from an old silk "crazy quilt." These would be particularly suitable for trimming baby things and little girls' dresses.

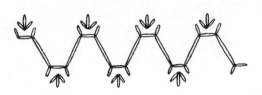

**Briar and Hen Tracks**

**Ball and Briar**

**Fagot and Turkey Track**

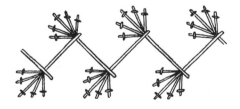

**Witch Hazel**

## Rickrack Plus Embroidery

Many color combinations are possible. The one shown was all white on gray linen. This motif is suitable for trimming place mats, guest towels, aprons, children's garments, etc.

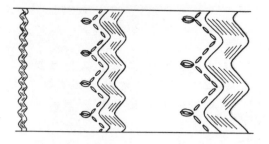

Arrange medium size rickrack into five-pointed star flowers (see photograph), and sew to fabric with invisible stitches. Using 2 strands of embroidery floss, work blanket stitch around petals. Work stem in outline stitch and leaves in lazy daisy stitch. Finish edge with narrow hem and rickrack on top.

A border of rickrack in graduated sizes plus simple embroidery stitches gives an elaborate effect without much work (see photograph). Running stitch and lazy daisy stitch were used. The model shown was bright red on white organdy, but many other color arrangements would be equally effec-

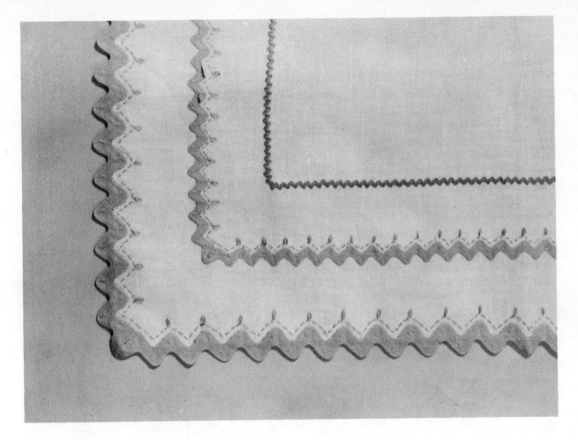

tive. Suitable for borders on place mats, aprons, or little girls' pinafores.

## Appliqué

See quilt chapter for appliqué with edges turned under.

Appliqué patches may also be held in place with blanket stitches. Cut the patch on the line (no turn-under allowance) and hold in place with blanket stitches.

## Cross Stitch Motif

This simple design in cross stitch can be done by counting threads on linen or other fabric with an even weave. It can be repeated any number of times to make runners, table cloths, pillows, etc.

The cross stitch is worked over 3 threads each way of the material. The dividing lines are worked in herringbone stitch over 6 threads in depth with 3 threads picked up on the needle.

Arrange the design as a border, corner pattern, or as an all-over design.

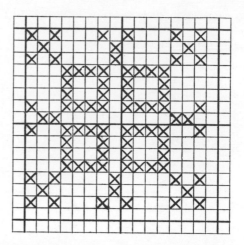

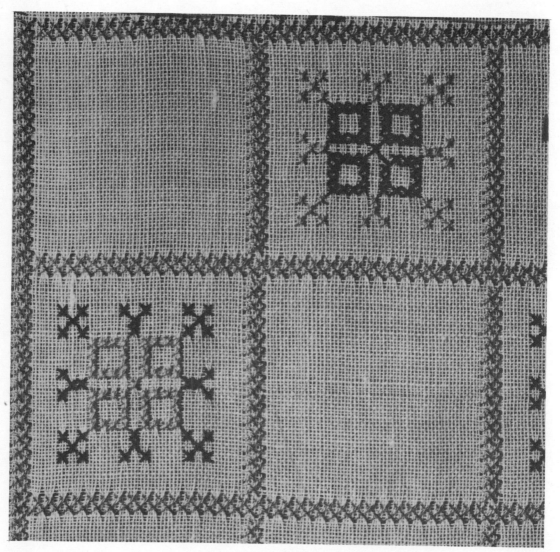

A suggestion for a color scheme: On cream linen, use deep beige or gray for the herringbone dividing lines and light red and black for the cross stitch motifs. Finish edge with a narrow hand hem.

Follow the photograph when working the design.

## EMBROIDERY STITCHES OF MORE INTRICACY

### Hemstitching

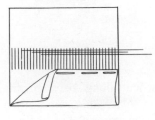

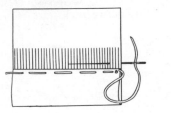

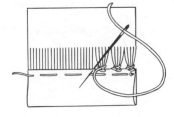

Simple hemstitching is not difficult, and it is given here as a prelude to the more elaborate types.

Figure the width of the hem. At the top of the hem draw out the number of threads necessary to make the desired width of hemstitching. Turn up and baste the hem.

*a*. Working from right to left, take up several threads; pull needle through with thread *under* the needle.

*b*. Take next stitch through very edge of hem and draw up tightly. Continue these two stitches (*a* and *b*) across row.

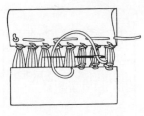

For double or ladder hemstitching with straight bars, work along other side of drawn threads picking up same group of threads.

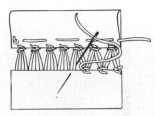

For diagonal hemstitching, be sure to pick up an even number of threads when working first row. When working second row, pick up half from each group, making a zigzag line.

### Italian Hemstitching

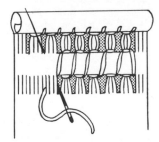

Draw out two rows of threads above hem leaving a narrow space of linen between. Make a row of regular hemstitching just above the hem. Starting at right and using same clusters above and below, pass needle under first group of threads of lower row.

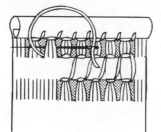

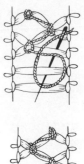

*Insert needle at right of this group and bring out at left of group above. Pass needle under top group and draw up. Bring needle out at left of lower group. Repeat from * across.

The thread is carried along between the stitches. In a wider space this same stitch may be used in zigzag fashion. Do not pull thread tightly between clusters.

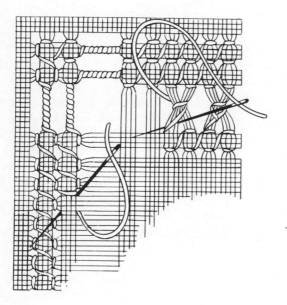

Corner showing Italian hemstitching and drawn work.

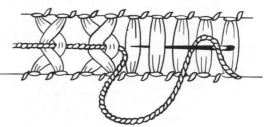

Another simple drawn-work stitch; bring needle from right to left under the second cluster of threads. Turn needle from left to right on top of and picking up the first cluster. This causes the clusters to cross each other. Do not pull thread too tight.

## Drawn Work

Draw threads in a somewhat wider space than for regular hemstitching (½ to ¾ inch wide). Work plain hemstitching on both edges in spoke or ladder effect. Work down the center with a chain stitch which holds together groups of three clusters (see diagram).

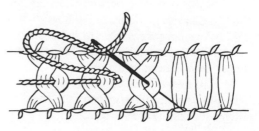

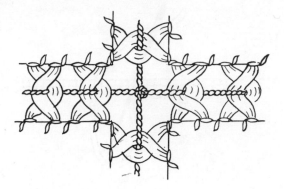

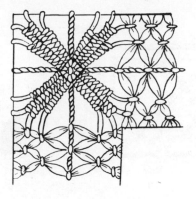

If working a corner, knot the second thread over the first.

In wider drawn work more long stitches may be added from corner to corner.

Weave as shown.

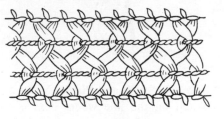

For a wider area, two rows or a double twist may be made.

### Italian Cutwork

This work is not for the beginner. It may be simple or elaborate, but must have the lines drawn or stamped on the linen as a guide for working.

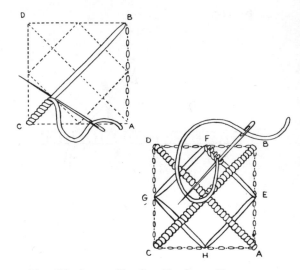

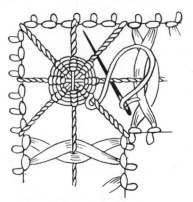

Finishing corners in open drawn work:

Cut and loosen threads on both sides of corner and conceal ends in hem.

Work hemstitching on edges or overcast. Add long stitches from corner to corner and weave center in spider-web fashion.

**To Work a Simple Design.** Draw a simple diagram, as given here, on the linen. Make small running stitches from A to B, then from B carry the thread diagonally to C. Overcast this thread without catching fabric. Make running stitches from B to D; then carry thread diagonally from D to A catching diagonals together at center. Overcast

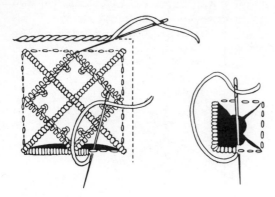

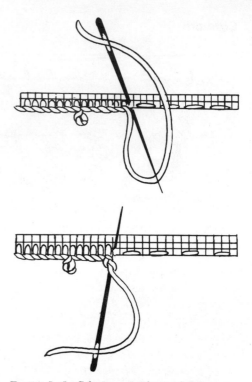

this diagonal, which brings you back to D. Work running stitches from D to C, from C to A, and from A to E (center of side). Run diagonal threads from E to F, from F to G, from G to H, and back to E, passing needle through diagonal bars and catching into fabric on the running stitches. Buttonhole over the diagonals, working picots in center if desired. Cut away linen close to running stitches and cover with overcasting or with buttonhole stitch.

## Picots

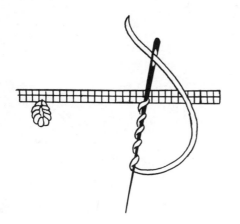

**Single Picot.** The thread is carried inside the hem to the point where picot is to be worked. Bring needle out; turn thread around needle 12 or 15 times. Draw thread through this spiral and insert needle in same place where it was drawn out. Slip needle through to next place.

**Buttonhole Stitch and Picots.** Make a running stitch on the line where hem is to be turned. Turn the hem and, with edge of linen toward you, make several buttonhole stitches. Insert needle in last buttonhole stitch (not the fabric) and pull it through. Take another buttonhole stitch in the same thread. This makes a picot. Insert needle under last buttonhole stitch and bring needle out in correct position to continue buttonhole stitches.

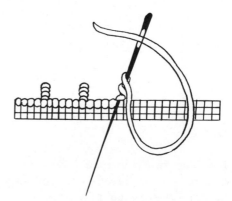

**Overcast Edge with Picot.** Hold edge away from you. Work overcast stitches and single picot as described above.

## Cutwork

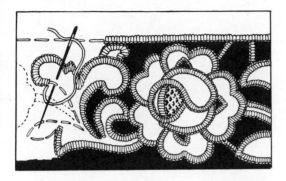

This type of work is sometimes called Richelieu embroidery and must be transferred to linen in some manner such as stamping or tracing so that there are clear-cut lines to follow. Very handsome designs can be purchased stamped on linen ready to work.

The entire design is done in narrow buttonhole stitch and the background is then cut away to leave the design in relief. The purl of the buttonhole stitch must come on the edge which is to be cut away. A running stitch may be worked between the narrow lines before buttonholing to serve as padding. This gives a more raised effect. Some designs have bars added to connect the more open places. These are worked like the Buttonhole Bars described previously, without catching into the fabric.

## Fagoting

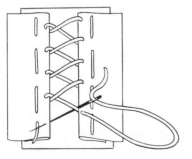

**Criss-Cross Fagoting.** Baste bias or straight folded edges on strips of paper an even distance apart. The stitch into the edge of the fabric is always taken from beneath. Bring

needle out at upper right hand; then take a stitch on opposite side ¼ inch down. *Pass needle behind last stitch and bring out on opposite side ¼ inch down. Repeat from *.

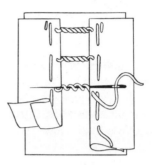

**Bar Fagoting.** Bring needle out at left side and insert directly opposite. Pull up stitch but leave enough to twist. Twist the stitch just made around the needle several times and being needle out at left again. Slip needle down inside fabric to the place for the next stitch.

**Blanket-Stitch Fagoting.** A blanket stitch is worked first on one side then on the other. Stitches should be the same length and evenly spaced.

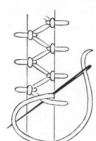

**Knotted Fagoting.** Work one stitch as for blanket-stitch fagoting. Then work another blanket stitch over loop of the stitch just made. This makes a firm knot. Repeat on opposite side a little lower down.

**Fagoted Medallion.** The design should be drawn or stamped on a foundation of heavy paper, stiff cambric, or scrim. Use double-fold bias binding and baste to the foundation following the design. Bias binding should be long enough to complete entire design if possible. If not, have as few "ends" as you can and always conceal them under another fold of the bias.

Use criss-cross fagoting to fill in the spaces, catching into the bias fold on each side.

**Whipped Blanket-Stitch Insertion.** Work a row of blanket stitches along both edges of fabric. Hold together by catching into the loops of the blanket stitches.

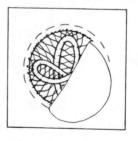

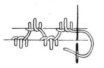

**Blanket-Stitch Insertion.** Work groups of blanket stitches (with center stitch longer) first on one side then on the other. Keep stitches evenly spaced and close together.

Remove the basting; this frees the medallion. Baste the medallion in place on the fabric. On the wrong side attach with fine running stitch, catching outside row of bias fold. Cut away fabric from beneath leaving a narrow edge. Roll and whip raw edge to medallion.

## Candlewicking or Tufting

This stitch was used on early American coverlets. A special heavy soft thread is used. It is composed of many strands with little or no twist. Candlewicking thread, a large needle, and muslin which has not been laundered are needed.

The design is indicated by dots. The stitch is a simple running stitch. Pick up about ⅛ inch on the needle and leave about ¾ inch between stitches. Several stitches may be taken on the needle at one time. Do not draw thread tightly enough to pucker fabric.

Cut each top stitch in half. When all tufts have been completed, dip in water to shrink fabric. This will hold tufts in place. Dry without ironing. Shake and brush tufts to fluff them into little balls. Use single thread for small tufts, double thread for large ones.

## Maltese or Tassel Stitch

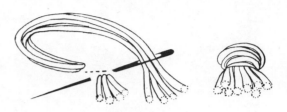

This stitch produces small tassels instead of tufts. It can also be used for tufting patterns. It was originally used for making rugs. Make a short stitch slanting slightly upward to the left and leaving an end (cluster of strands). Insert needle to right of center, in line with the point where it came out and bring it out at the center. Cut all strands the same length.

## Crewel Embroidery

This type of embroidery was very popular in England in the latter part of the seventeenth century. It was also known as Jacobean Embroidery. It should be done with a loosely twisted woolen yarn known as crewel wool and worked on linen. The designs were typical and inspired by printed cottons brought from the Far East. They were usually tree-like forms covering large areas with many unusual leaves and flowers and sometimes birds among the branches. A variety of stitches are used, sometimes filling the motifs. The colorings, soft rich blendings of blues, greens, muted reds, and tawny yellows, look particularly well on natural linen.

Crewel embroidery is used for the most part on upholstery and drapery fabrics, coverings for footstools, etc. The variety and combination of stitches is endless. Blanket stitch, outline stitch, cross stitch, chain stitch, coral stitch, herringbone, Kensington stitch, satin stitch, French knot, feather stitch, and so on, are some of the stitches employed in this work.

Some of the loveliest examples of crewel work can be seen in museums on early American pieces of bed draperies and spreads. It was probably the earliest form of embroidery done in this country by pioneer women. The photograph shows a sample of crewel work embroidered in India on hand-woven cotton. It is worked almost entirely in chain stitch.

### Armenian Needlepoint Lace

All loops or meshes are made with knotted buttonhole stitch.

Hold fabric piece with edge away from you and point the needle away from you. Fasten thread and insert needle. Thread coming from the cloth lies first over the needle, then under it. Thread coming from the eye lies under the needle, then over it (study

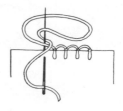

There are two principle stitches used in hardanger: satin or kloster stitch for the solid parts and a weaving stitch for the drawn work.

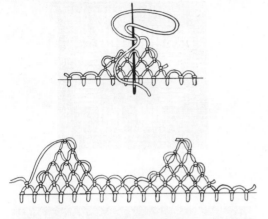

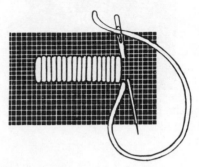

diagram). Pull needle through and tighten the knot close to edge. Take the next stitch ⅛ inch away. Succeeding rows of loops are made in the same manner, forming a knot in each loop.

The satin stitch is usually worked in groups of five over four threads of canvas. This is called a kloster block.

## Hardanger Embroidery

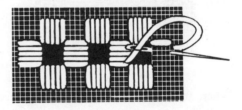

Hardanger work may be done on any fabric with an even weave. This means there are the same number of threads in a given space when counted either crosswise or lengthwise of the fabric. Fabric with 20 to 26 threads to the inch is best. This work can be done only by the accurate counting of threads as you work.

These groups are worked horizontally or vertically to form squares. The squares may be set together in rows on the straight or on the diagonal.

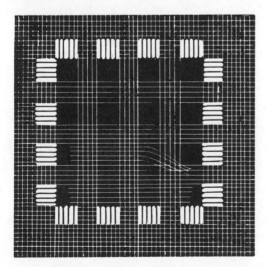

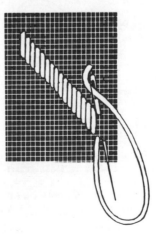

The satin stitch may be worked on the diagonal by raising (or lowering) each stitch

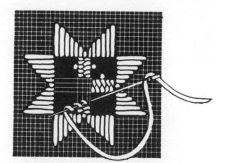

one mesh. Blocks with diagonal edges may also be made.

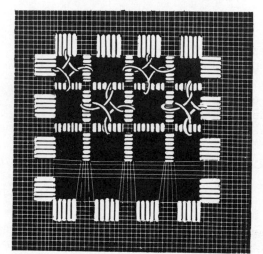

When blocks are completed the threads are cut. Care must be taken in cutting the threads for the openwork, being sure to leave attached those over which the weaving is to be done.

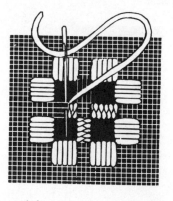

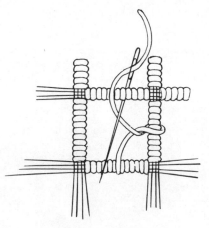

The remaining threads may be ornamented by weaving or by overcasting. Weave the the bars closely and evenly. Picots may be worked on the woven bars (see previous illustration).

On more elaborate pieces the open spaces may be ornamented with loop stitch or twisted bars to make lace work.

# USING YOUR STITCHES

## Embroidered Tablecloth

This square cloth, with a sheaf-of-wheat motif, is appropriate for a breakfast table or for a buffet serving table.

**Materials.** 1½ yards 54″-wide curry-color (or color of your choice) heavy linen. (For smaller cloth, use 48″ or 50″ square.) 1 yard 36″ cream-color linen for four 18″-square napkins. 1 tube or 6 skeins cream-color size-3 perle cotton. Tracing and carbon paper. 1 skein 6-strand embroidery floss to match linen. Embroidery needles.

**Making the pattern.** Pull threads and even the ends of linen to make a square. Lay folded tracing paper on center line of design shown on following page. Trace; turn paper; trace other half. Center and trace design on corners of cloth about 14″ from points.

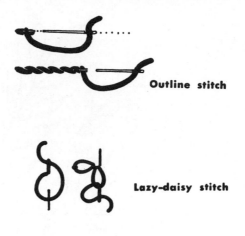

Outline stitch

Lazy-daisy stitch

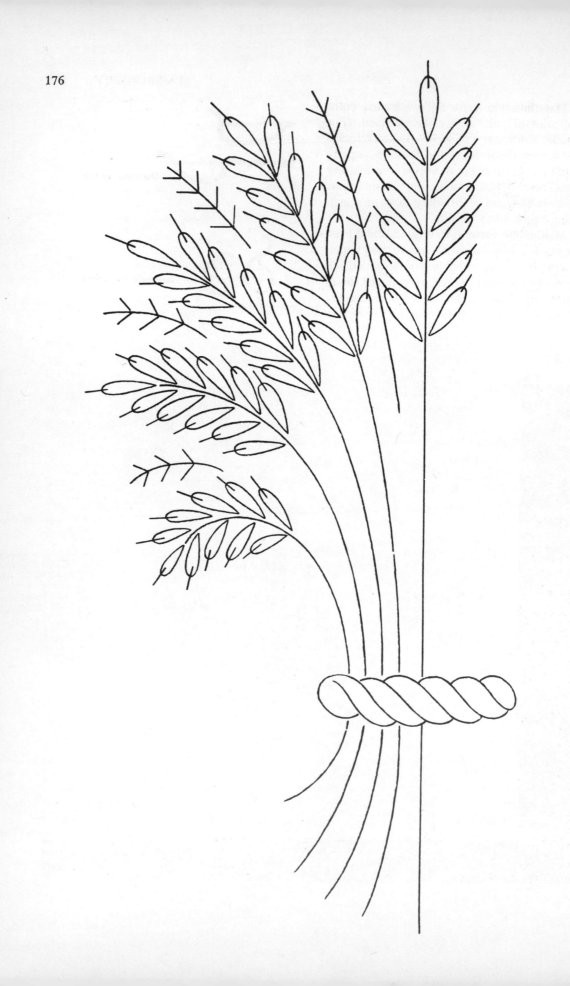

**Embroidering.** With single thread of perle cotton, work all stems and center scroll in outline stitch. Work flowers in lazy-daisy stitch. (See stitch diagrams.) Then, with double metallic thread, take a stitch at loop end of lazy-daisy stitches on top of stitch that holds down loop.

**Finishing Edge of Cloth.** With matching thread, machine zigzag all around edge of cloth. Turn edge ⅜″ to wrong side, and press. Topstitch ⅛″ from edge of cloth. Repeat twice, ⅛″ from previous row of stitching. Finish napkins same way.

**Couching and Tassels.** Use double thread of perle cotton 6″ to 10″ longer than one side of cloth. Fasten thread under hem near one corner; then bring out needle exactly at corner and ⅜″ from edge (top of hem). Insert needle in following corner at corresponding point. Thread another needle with three strands of colored embroidery floss and one gold thread. Follow diagram in section on

Couching

stitches for couching. Do not let perle threads twist. When corner is reached, fasten both threads on wrong side. Repeat on remaining three sides.

**Making Tassels** (make 12). Cut 1¼″- wide strip of cardboard. Wind 20 times with perle cotton. Tie at one edge, leaving 3″ end of thread; cut at other edge. Tie tassel near top with gold thread. With the long thread in needle, attach tassels to the tablecloth (one at corner and one each side).

CHAPTER 3 *Quilting*

The purpose of quilting is to hold together the various layers of materials and prevent the interlayer of cotton from slipping. In addition to this practical purpose, an infinite variety of decorative effects may be obtained. Quilting itself is an ancient art. It probably originated in a cold climate by the attempt to keep layers of cloth together for warmth. Examples of quilting have come down to us from many early sources. The knights of the Middle Ages wore quilted jackets under their armor for protection. And in ancient Egypt quilting was used in place of armor. It is still worn in northern China for warmth, and it is revived periodically by today's fashion designers for robes, jackets, etc.

But a "quilt" in our minds is a bed covering, and pieced quilts are truly American. They were the result of pioneer women making the best of things. The pieced quilt came before the appliquéd one and was born of necessity since women in those early days had to use and re-use every inch of cloth which came into their hands.

The first quilts were of the "crazy quilt" variety, made with shapeless scraps without attention to design. Simple patterns developed next, and finally the more intricate designs with interesting names such as Turkey Track, Indian Hatchet, Washington's Plumes, Churn Dash, Log Cabin, Delectable Mountains, and so on. A thorough study of old American quilts is a study of American history revealing the sturdy character, ingenuity, and sense of humor of our pioneer mothers.

Every pioneer bride aimed to have at least a dozen quilts in her dower chest. When a girl became engaged she started her "bride's quilt." These were especially beautiful and a great deal of work went into them.

Later the appliqué quilt appeared. Since two scraps pieced together go farther than one laid on top of the other, "laying on" a design was considered something of a luxury and was, therefore, indicative of better times. Appliqué, also, is very old as a technique, having been used by all people in all ages. But only in America was it associated with bed quilts.

**Color Plate 5 — Needlepoint Designs**

The fruit design is done in petit point. Instructions are given in Chapter 5, Needlepoint, for adapting this design and the scalloped all-over pattern for various uses.

The appliqué quilt offers more possibilities of variation in design than the pieced one. If at all possible, look at some examples of lovely old quilts in museums. They are a wonderful inspiration, and we can all take pride in this expression of the skill and imagination of our forebears.

For those whose enthusiasm for quilts is great enough for them to want to make one, we have tried to give here as many practical hints as possible. If you like to sew you will like to quilt; it takes only care and time.

## CHOOSE YOUR DESIGN

Whether you make a pieced quilt or one designed for appliqué is a matter of personal choice. Putting together small pieces by hand (certain patterns can be done on the machine), may seem monotonous and boring or it may appeal to you as being as much fun as solving an interesting puzzle. Certainly the finished effect is lovely and the geometric designs highly suitable to modern interiors.

Appliqué work is also fascinating and since this technique allows for curves, it is possible to use florals and other natural shapes. These are usually simplified but can be very charming indeed.

## FABRICS

The most important thing to keep in mind is to use the best materials you can afford. This is of course true of all handwork. Good quilt fabrics are not expensive, and it would be the height of foolishness to put all of the work into a quilt using cheap fabric which will not wear and may run or fade in washing. Choose a fabric with a firm weave but with a soft texture, such as fine percale or broadcloth. A thin interlining or batting is best since it allows for closer rows of quilting. A cotton bat is better than flannelette as it gives the much wanted puffy effect. Sheet wadding is too stiff for easy quilting.

For the lining or backing choose a soft unstarched fabric which is similar in texture to the top.

Thread for piecing should be a good 6 cord No. 50 or 60. If the piecing is done by machine, No. 70 is best. Also use No. 70 for appliqué work.

## PATCHWORK OR PIECED QUILTS

### Making Patterns

Your design will be made up of basic units. Trace or draw the shape of these unit pieces onto tracing or bond paper. Cut out each piece. To make a more durable pattern place each piece on top of a blotter or fine sand paper (either of which has the advantage of not sliding around on the fabric while you are cutting) and cut out exactly on the edge. Make more than one pattern of each piece so that when one becomes worn another is at hand. Sheet brass or tin, thin enough to cut with shears, may be used in place of blotting or sand paper and is still more durable.

### Cutting

Press fabric thoroughly. Use a damp cloth if necessary to remove wrinkles. Place the pattern on lengthwise grain. A square must be laid on true lengthwise and cross grain.

Diamonds should be placed so that two opposite sides are on lengthwise grain which gives two bias sides. Otherwise there will be four bias sides, which are difficult to piece without stretching.

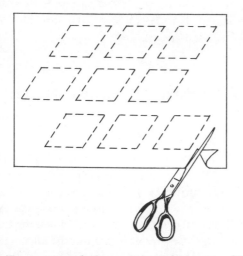

Trace around the pattern; then cut with a ¼″ (seam allowance) all around. All pieces must be cut exactly alike if the quilt is to fit together properly and be true to pattern.

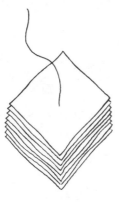

Each block must come out even at all corners and edges. If desired, after pieces are cut the pattern may be laid on the wrong side of each piece and the seam allowance pressed back over the edge. This slows down the work but insures uniform seams.

Group pieces of a kind together; our grandmothers ran a thread through each pile.

## Piecing

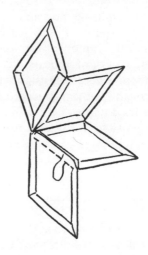

A poorly pieced quilt can never be made to look right. Unless each small piece in a patchwork block is true and even and unless all pieces are sewed to each other with the same width seam the block will be crooked and will not lie flat. The next step of sewing blocks together or to strips will be difficult and the whole result will be disappointing.

A rule of patchwork is to join the patches or units from the center out. Lay 2 pieces with right sides together and join on the seam line with fine running stitches. Use a short length of thread and be careful not to stretch any bias edges. Give special attention to corners where more than 2 pieces meet so that a perfect joining is made. Press seams open as you go; it makes for better-looking quilts. If this is not possible, press each block, taking care not to stretch bias seams.

## Setting the Quilt Together

Blocks are joined in strips and the strips are sewed together. The border is put on last. Pieced blocks are often alternated with plain, or set together with strips of plain between in one or both directions. There are many ways of varying the "set." It should be worked out on paper first. Make all seams match and press the whole top very carefully after setting together.

### Marking the Quilting Pattern

Marking or transferring the quilting pattern onto the quilt is usually done before putting the quilt into the frame (see paragraph on Quilting Frames). If you are using a hot iron transfer pattern it is best to do it at this point. Cut the pattern apart and lay it in the proper places. Be sure joinings match. If not using a hot iron transfer, run a colored basting up and down the center and cross-wise for a guide if needed.

If the marking is done in the frame it is done as the quilt is rolled marking all reach-able space on four sides. Quilt and roll.

In early days there were many methods of transferring quilting patterns onto the quilt top. Some of them are still practical. One was with models or templates. These could be wood, heavy paper, cardboard, even homely articles such as plates, cups, spools, or anything which could be used to make interesting scrolls, curves, etc. Some quilters scratched around the object, then worked quickly before the line disappeared. Others used pencil or chalk for marking.

A plain, all-over pattern such as diagonal lines or diamonds can be used and is very effective. One can change the direction of the lines for variation. If the quilt has plain and pieced blocks, it is more effective if the plain block is quilted more elaborately than the pieced one. Sometimes the design of the pieced or appliqué block is used for a quilt-ing pattern on the plain. Transfer patterns for more elaborate designs can be purchased.

## APPLIQUÉ QUILTS

This is an entirely different technique from piecing. To appliqué, one piece is laid upon another, edges turned under and secured with fine hemming stitches.

### How to Appliqué

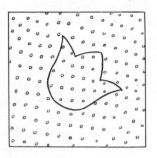

Trace each design part and make a cutting pattern of each piece using heavy paper or thin cardboard.

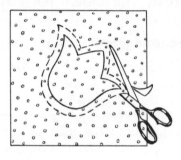

Lay the pattern on the fabric and trace around. Cut out allowing 3/16″ for turning under. The traced line is the turning line.

Unless the design is very simple, it should be traced or stamped onto the quilt top to show where the cut-out patches are to be placed.

Place the patch where it belongs, pin carefully, turn under on the line, and baste in place. Clip corners where necessary. Let flowers, buds, leaves, etc., overlap stems. All raw edges are turned under unless they end at the edge of a block and will be sewed in with the seam. Sew patches on with invisible hemming stitches, barely catching the edge of the patch and keeping its true shape.

It is possible to purchase this type of quilt ready-stamped; that is, the top of the quilt is stamped with both the appliqué design and the quilting pattern and the patches are stamped with both cutting and turning lines. See color plate for this type of quilt.

## PUTTING THE QUILT TOGETHER

### Preparing the Backing

The backing is made of widths of fabric stitched together. Usually a 36″ width is used in the center and a narrower strip on each side. Remove selvages before sewing strips together. The back of the quilt is usually cut a little larger than a pieced top because the latter has more "give" to it. If you wish to bring the edges of the backing over the top for a binding, as is often done, cut the back about 3 inches larger all around.

### Interlining

Cotton batting is most often used and most practical. One bat is sufficient for a single-size quilt.

### Placing Layers Together

Lay the quilt lining flat on the floor wrong side up, smoothing it out. Place cotton batting on top, arranging it in an even thickness over the lining and with no wrinkles or lumps. Place the quilt top, right side up, and baste all three thicknesses together.

## Basting

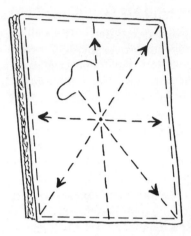

Start at the center of the quilt and baste out to the sides in four directions. Then starting at the center, baste to the four corners. Baste all outer edges together.

## QUILTING

### Frames and Hoops

Perfect results require the use of a quilting frame of some kind. The purpose of the quilting frame is to hold the work taut while it is being quilted. Quilting frames may be made of four strips of wood; two short bars (2″ wide by 24″ to 36″ long) and two long bars (2″ wide by about 92″ long, or a little longer than the quilt is wide), and a contrivance (a clamp) at corners for control. The corners must be held at right angles. A tape or strip of muslin is tacked the length of the long bars and the top and bottom edges of the quilt are sewed to these tapes. Roll one side until the width of the narrow bars is reached. The part exposed should be as much as can be reached comfortably from either side. Clamp the corners. To hold sides taut, sew over and over through the edge of the quilt and around end bars using heavy thread. Some frames are made with two strips of wood a little longer than the quilt and two of a length corresponding to the width of the quilt, but these take more space when set up. A curtain stretcher may also be used às a quilting frame. The frame may be set on saw horses or four straight-back chairs.

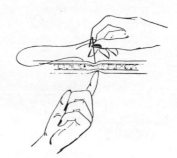

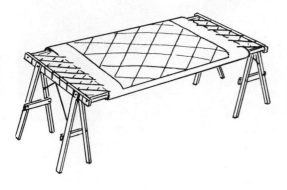

Place the forefinger of left hand over the spot where the needle should come through. Push needle through with right hand until it touches finger. Change hands and pull through with right hand. Forefinger of left hand should now be underneath. With right hand push needle down through the 3 layers to touch forefinger. Pull through with right hand.

Large hoops, 22″ or more in diameter, are available and can be used on quilts. Begin in the center and work outward.

**Quilting without a Frame.** It is possible to quilt without a frame. Two things are necessary. (1) The quilt must be basted closely all over. Start by basting as explained under "Basting" and then add many rows between so that layers are held firmly together. (2) There must be space (such as a ping-pong table or even the floor) where the quilt may remain until finished. Always work on this surface and from the center out as much as possible. Unless you are agile do not attempt quilting in this way.

Work alternately in this fashion. Fasten end of each thread securely by running between layers. This upward and downward movement through the layers is one correct way to quilt. Some experienced quilters prefer to take 2 or 3 stitches on the needle at one time. This can be done on a quilt with thin batting.

If working in a frame, when you have quilted all space within reach undo the threads at the sides, roll up and begin again.

After quilting is completed use art gum to erase pencil lines (if any), and bind the edges of the quilt.

## How to Quilt

Use a short needle especially made for quilting to speed the work. Also use quilting thread; it is strong and smooth and less likely to knot. Use a short length of thread and pull the knot through to the batting so it will not show.

## DOUBLE IRISH CHAIN QUILT

This is a variation of a favorite old pieced quilt. It may be made of plain or printed fabric combined with white.

The blocks are 11″ square (finished) and are made up of the following units (all given without seam allowance).

Unit no. 1 is a rectangle 1″ by 7″.

Unit no. 2 is a rectangle 1″ by 5″.

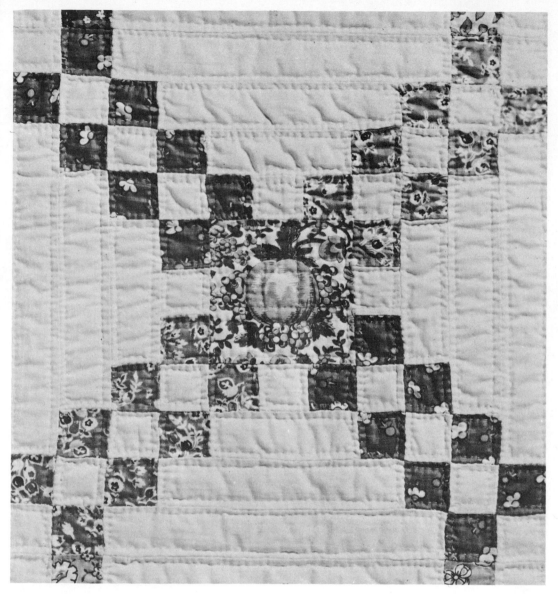

Unit no. 3 is a rectangle 1″ by 3″.
Unit no. 4 is a 1″ square.
Unit no. 5 is a 3″ square.
Make a pattern for each unit.
Number of each unit to cut for one block:
Unit no. 1: cut 4 white.
Unit no. 2: cut 4 white.
Unit no. 3: cut 4 white.
Unit no. 4: cut 20 white and 32
   print.
Unit no. 5: cut 1 print.

See General Directions for Making Pattern Pieces and Cutting (allow ¼″ seams all around units).

For a single quilt multiply the above numbers by 70.

For a double quilt multiply the above numbers by 90.

A single-size quilt takes 70 blocks set 7 by 10.

A double-size quilt takes 90 blocks set 9 by 10.

## How to Join to Form a Block

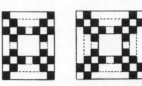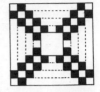

Start with a no. 5 unit in the center. Follow diagrams for setting together. Piece together each narrow row before setting it to the block; this avoids having to sew a block into a corner. Match seams carefully.

After all blocks are made set blocks together; see general directions for lining, interlining, and quilting. As shown in photograph this quilt looks well quilted each side of all seams, 1/8" away. Quilt the center block as though it were pieced of 9 (unit 4) 1" squares. Bind edges with print or plain.

## HORN-OF-PLENTY APPLIQUÉ QUILT

The quilt pictured on Color Plate 3 is available stamped ready to make up and appliqué (top only).

The Cherry Tree Quilt shown is an adaptation of a very old quilt which is in a museum

collection. It is of the appliqué type and can be purchased as a kit (top only). The cherry trees in tan, red and green, and the yellow birds are set off by the rich cream background color. Many hours of patient work are required to make the quilt, but the result is an heirloom piece.

## PIECE- AND QUILT-AS-YOU-GO QUILT

This is an unusual method of quilt making which holds much fascination because it has the advantage of being padded and "quilted" as you go. Each block is a square folded to make a triangle. Before folding, padding in the form of sheet wadding is laid on the square, edges of the square are turned and whipped together. These puffy triangular units are then whipped together. The quilt may be made of print or plain fabric combined with white and other arrangements of the blocks than the one given here are possible. It is especially delightful done in a delicate color with white for a child's quilt. This is also a good way to use up silk or fine wool scraps for a bed throw or lap robe.

## Child's Quilt or Carriage Cover

For a quilt 30 by 40 inches you will need:
  1½ yards white batiste, broadcloth, or other fine cotton.
  1½ yards colored cotton of fine quality.
  3 yards sheet wadding.
  Cotton batting.
Cut a piece of cardboard 3½″ square (this is guide for cutting wadding only).

### Cutting

Cut 96 squares of each color (on grain of fabric) 4½″ square. This gives a seam allowance of ½″ all around. The easiest way to do this is to use a yardstick and pencil to mark off the squares on the fabric and then cut.

Cut 96 squares of sheet wadding the size of the cardboard guide.

### Making

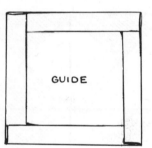

Center the cardboard guide on each fabric square, fold seam allowance over edges, and press.

Place a square of sheet wadding inside the square of fabric; trim corners of fabric. Fold square diagonally, edges even, and pin at point. Insert a small amount of cotton batting into triangle to make it puff slightly. Baste edges of triangle together. Prepare all triangles in this manner.

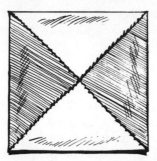

Pin the basted sides of two triangles together, matching white to a color. Whipstitch, taking in all thicknesses. Repeat; then assemble the two parts to form a block as shown.

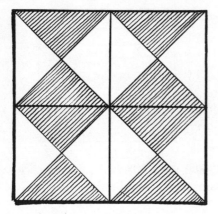

After making four blocks, whipstitch the folded edges together on the wrong side, white to white, color to color, as shown. Child's quilt is 6 blocks by 8 blocks. See photograph. For larger quilts and throws, make desired size.

## BISCUIT QUILT

This is a puff quilt reminiscent of the "biscuit" pillows our grandmothers made from left-over pieces of silk. This is made of print and plain cotton and stuffed with dacron. It is practical for an extra coverlet or can be used in place of a spread.

The quilt pictured is 64″ by 85″ in size. The squares are 2½″ finished and the quilt is 27 squares by 34 squares. Any size can be made.

Materials needed for this size:
   6½ yards cotton print.
   6½ yards plain color cotton.
   4¾ yards white cotton for backing.
   7 yards light weight unbleached muslin.
   9 yards 1″ bias binding to match plain cotton.
   Cotton, Orlon, or Dacron for stuffing (large package).

### Cutting

Cut one 3″ and one 4″ square from cardboard.

Use the cardboard patterns or mark off directly on the fabric with pencil and ruler. The plain and printed cotton is cut into 4″ squares. The unbleached muslin is cut into 3″ squares. The whole quilt may be cut at one time; or you may cut enough squares for one row across, which would be 14 squares print, 13 squares plain (alternate rows will be 14 squares plain and 13 squares print). Cut also 27 squares muslin.

### Making

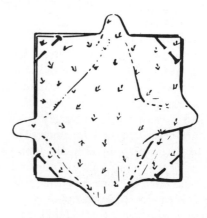

¼″ seams have been allowed. Pin the corners of a 4″ square to corners of a 3″ square (muslin).

Fold and pin excess fabric into a pleat at center of each side. Always fold in the same direction. Before pinning the fourth side insert a wad of cotton about the size of a walnut.

Baste square all around.

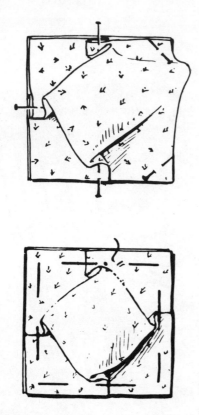

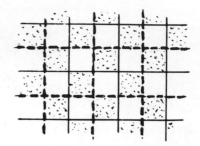

*Lining:* Cut white backing crosswise in two parts. Trim off selvages and sew the two pieces together lengthwise. Press seam open.

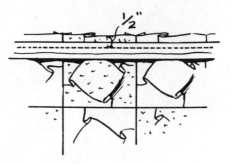

After preparing 27 squares in this manner, baste them together in a row, right sides together, taking ¼″ seams and alternating colors. Stitch and then press seams open. The row should begin and end with the same color.

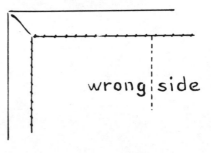

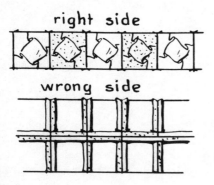

Make another row, beginning and ending with the second color. Rows are then sewed together in a crosswise seam.

*Quilting:* Quilt on the seam lines. This may be done on every row or every other row as desired, and it may be done by hand or by machine. Bind edge.

## OLD PIECED QUILT PATTERNS

Here are three old-time patterns for pieced blocks which can easily be enlarged and reproduced. They are made up for the most part of squares and triangles and are therefore easy to make.

### Maple Leaf

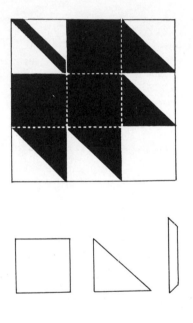

Draw a 9″ square and divide in thirds each way as shown. Mark off triangles and the line for stem. Only two patterns are needed: a 3″ square and a triangle which is one half of this square. Trace these off and make patterns. The stem is a piece of bias about ¾″ wide. Turn under the edges of the bias and appliqué it to a white square before piecing together. Allow ¼″ for seams on all blocks when cutting. Set together with alternate plain blocks and make sure that all the stems point in the same direction.

### Steps to the Altar

Draw a 12″ square and divide as shown. Allow ¼″ for seams on all pattern pieces. Follow the general rules for piecing. Set the blocks diagonally on the quilt with plain

blocks between. Finish sides and ends with half blocks and corners with quarter blocks.

### Whirlwind or Pin Wheel

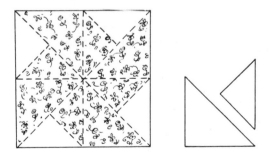

Draw a 8″ square and divide as shown. The pattern will consist of two triangles, one large and one small. Allow ¼″ seams when cutting. This is charming in a bright color for a child's quilt and can be set together with plain wide strips or with alternate plain blocks.

## TO MAKE A COMFORTER

Comforters are tufted rather than quilted. Where more warmth is wanted, the interlining is made of feathers, wool or Dacron batting, or two layers of cotton batting. An old woolen blanket can also be used.

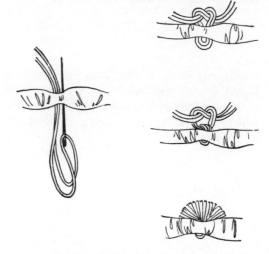

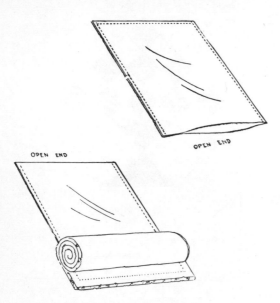

Sew the top and backing together to form a tube which is closed at one end. With tube wrong side out and on a flat surface, place the batting on smoothly and evenly. To give the comforter a nice rounded finish, allow the bat to extend beyond the edges about 1 inch all around. Baste the bat or interlining to all four sides of the top and turn right side out as you would a pillow slip. Sew up the open end and complete by tufting or by very wide quilting.

### Tufting

Tufting is the process of tying the layers of a comforter together at intervals closely enough to hold them in place (4 to 6 inches). Use 4-ply Germantown or knitting worsted wool yarn or nylon yarn and a heavy needle (one large enough to make a hole for the yarn to go through). Use double thread. Force the needle straight down through the layers and then straight up about ¼″ away from where it went in. Pull yarn through leaving ends to tie. Tie a firm double knot and cut leaving ½″ ends for tufts.

## TRAPUNTO OR ITALIAN QUILTING

This type of quilting does not cover the whole area but is done only on certain parts. A design with double lines is used. Trace or stamp design onto a soft open-weave muslin or any thin loosely-woven cotton fabric. Baste muslin to under side of the top (which is often of satin or taffeta) with design

showing. Work running stitch on all lines of the design sewing through the muslin and taffeta.

To raise the design, a heavy yarn is inserted between the double lines. Use a blunt needle and soft yarn such as Germantown. Use double or as many strands as necessary to fill the space. Insert the needle through muslin, and follow the design pushing the needle between the double lines of stitching. To turn around curves bring needle out through muslin and insert again in same hole. On sharp corners yarn may be left to form a small loop outside. Insert needle and proceed.

## STUFFED QUILTING

Other types of designs such as larger areas of flowers, animals, etc., may be padded by making small slits in the muslin and forcing cotton batting into the spaces. Sew up slits later.

This "stuffing" was done on many early all-white quilts to bring out parts of the elaborate designs. It is also sometimes used under appliqué patches to give a more raised effect.

## CARING FOR QUILTS

A beautiful quilt is deserving of the best of care, and a well made one should keep its puffy shape after many launderings.

Quilts should not be allowed to become too soiled. It is then possible to wash them in the automatic washer using the short washing cycle intended for fine fabrics. Use a mild soap or detergent.

*Never wring by hand or spin dry in the washer*. Instead arrange the wet quilt on the line matching corners and let it drip dry. Never touch it with an iron.

After washing look over carefully to see if any quilting stitches have broken and, if so, repair at once.

**CHAPTER 4** ## Smocking

Smocking is a beautiful old art which seems never to go out of style. In Anglo-Saxon times women wore a loose undergarment or "smock" with breeches and a woolen dress over them. It gradually became the fashion to decorate the upper part of the undergarment with fine stitching and to cut the neck of the overdress lower to display the hand work.

Later, as recently as 150 years ago, men wore loose smocks or dusters which were ornamented with a smocking design to denote their trade.

Today these lovely rows of stitches are used extensively on children's wear, such as dresses and coats, and to a lesser degree on women's blouses, lingerie, bed jackets, etc.

Real English smocking is done after very careful preparation of the foundation fabric. It is symmetrical and elastic, and a limitless number of designs exquisite in coloring and stitch arrangement can be achieved. It is not at all difficult if the rules are followed carefully.

## HOW TO DO ENGLISH SMOCKING

### Fabrics and Thread

Many fabrics are suitable for smocking but it probably is at its best on fine crisp cottons such as Pima cotton, fine gingham, chambray, dotted Swiss, fine lawn, muslin, and percale.

Use six-strand embroidery floss varying the number of strands according to the fineness of the fabric and smocking pattern. Four strands is a good average. Use crewel needles for the smocking and sharps or crewels for the gathering.

### Preparation of the Fabric

There are several points to keep in mind when preparing the fabric for English smocking.

**Amount or Width of Fabric.** For every inch of finished smocking allow about 3 inches of fabric. Measure the yoke space or wherever the smocking is to be used and multiply by three. This means adding width in cutting if the pattern was not designed to allow for smocking.

**Marking.** There are hot-iron transfers available for the rows of dots needed when gathering, or you can dot your own fabric (a tedious process). The *dots* should be ⅜" to ⅝" apart depending upon the fineness of the fabric. The *rows* are spaced ½" apart. The dots must be spaced uniformly and on the rows each dot must be exactly below the one above.

Instead of marking the dots it is entirely possible to follow the stripes on a striped fabric (rows will have to be marked), the checks on checked gingham, or the dots on dotted Swiss when doing the gathering or "gauging."

If using a transfer pattern, iron it onto the wrong side so that the larger pleat will come on the right side and the dots will not show on finished work. Also when placing transfer in position line up the dots with the thread or grain of the fabric leaving a seam allowance at the top.

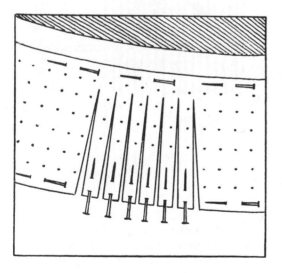

On a curved neckline clip the pattern at regular intervals to fit it to the curve.

## Gathering or Gauging

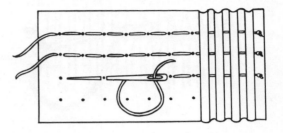

Each row of gathering must have a separate thread. Working on the wrong side, start with a knot and a double stitch at the right. Pick up a very short stitch (1/16") on each dot, then slip the needle to the next dot. This makes a uniform running stitch.

By setting the stitches exactly below each other in rows, a foundation of small "organ" pleats is formed upon which the smocking stitches are done. The rows of gathering serve as a guide for the rows of smocking as well as to hold the pleats in place. The gathering is removed after the smocking is completed.

Do not pull the gathers too tightly; pleats will form and they should be movable in order to insert the needle between them when smocking. Leave the threads in loose ends. Fasten them later by tying 2 together in a slip knot or winding each separately on a pin.

There is a small gathering machine available which does this part of the work for you in even and accurate rows. If you intend to do much smocking, it would be well to investigate it.

## Smocking Stitches

There are several basic stitches in smocking. The lovely designs which can be made are the result of combining and arranging them in different ways.

Do not pull the smocking stitches too tightly; the work should "give." Some calculation is necessary to make a design symmetrical if you wish the points or waves to come out even on each side.

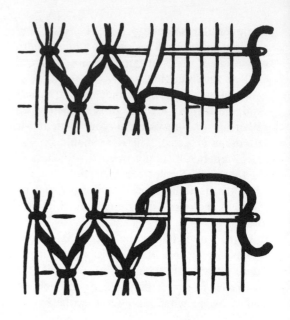

**Outline, Stem, or Rope Stitch.** This is worked from left to right. Keep the thread under the needle and pick up one pleat at a time.

be called Surface Honeycomb or Diamond Stitch. It may be varied by working several cable stitches instead of one before moving up or down (see diagram for dress).

**Cable Stitch.** Work this the same as outline stitch but throw the thread first above the needle and then below, alternately.

**Double Cable.** Two rows of single cable worked close together.

**Single Wave Stitch.** Work up and down from one row of gathers to another picking up stitches as shown. A cable stitch is made at the top and at the bottom. This is sometimes called Van Dyke Stitch, and when several rows are used close together it may

**Trellis Stitch.** Similar to Single Wave Stitch but with stitches closer together. It may be varied by taking 3, 4, or 5 stitches on each diagonal with the cable stitch at top and bottom. Keep stitches evenly spaced. This is sometimes called Chevron or Step Wave Stitch. Work from left to right.

**Honeycomb Smocking.** This is more elastic than other types of smocking. It is usually worked from right to left and is done on 2 rows of dots. Two dots are picked up for each stitch, alternating from one row to the other. Follow the steps as shown in the diagrams and work as follows:

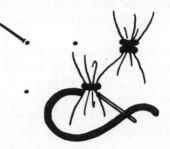

over it bringing needle out 2 dots to the left of stitch made on top row. Repeat the first stitch and continue back and forth in this

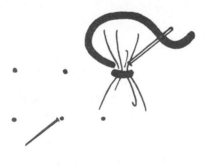

Bring the needle out at the second dot from the end at the right of the first row. Keep the thread above the needle and pick up the first dot of this row and also the second.

manner. The long stitch between dots is on the wrong side of the fabric leaving only dots on top forming a honeycomb effect.

Draw up. Take a second stitch over the first bringing needle out at third dot on the row below. Pick up the 2nd and the 3rd dot of that row and draw up. Take a second stitch

**Embellishments.** Sometimes smocking is embellished in the open spaces of the design with embroidery stitches such as lazy daisy stitch, rambler rose, bullion stitch, French knots, etc. (See Embroidery section.)

Also, embroidered dots and bars can be added by sewing over and over in satin stitch.

**Staying the Back.** This is a "trick" which can be used on certain types of smocking patterns.

The pleating or gauging of English smocking is so attractive in itself that it is not necessary to cover it entirely with smocking stitches. Large areas can be left open with borders at top and bottom plus a scattered design (see strawberry design on color plate). To do this, it is necessary to hold the pleats in place by working rows of smocking outline stitch at about 1" intervals on the *back* of the pleating. These stitches are elastic and will "give," holding the pleat in place since the gathering stitches are removed after the smocking is finished.

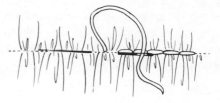

This is done by working embroidery stitches over rows of machine gathering. Put in the rows of gathering ½" to 1" apart; then work the embroidery stitches on top of the stitching. There is no elasticity to this type of "smocking." The stitches used here are Closed Feather stitch, Creton stitch and Back-stitch. Herringbone stitch, Chain stitch, or other decorative stitches may also be used.

## MOCK SMOCKING

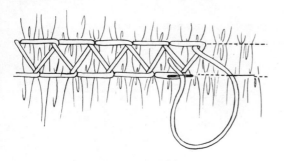

## "BOX PLEAT" SMOCKING

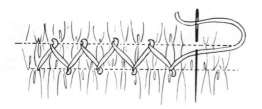

A novel way of getting a smocked effect. Make 1" tucks one inch apart and press them into small box pleats. Baste down the center of each pleat to hold it in place. Draw lines across the pleats lightly about 2" apart and baste on the lines. Work fine feather or other decorative stitching on these lines. Using embroidery floss, pick up the two edges of the pleat half-way between the rows of embroidery and sew together with double back-stitches. The effect is somewhat like honeycomb smocking. There is no elasticity to this work.

## No. 1 Pattern on Color Plate (on white fabric)

## COLOR PLATE 4

The color plate shows four designs for English smocking; two are fairly simple and two are rather elaborate. Diagrams are given here for all four so they can be copied if desired.

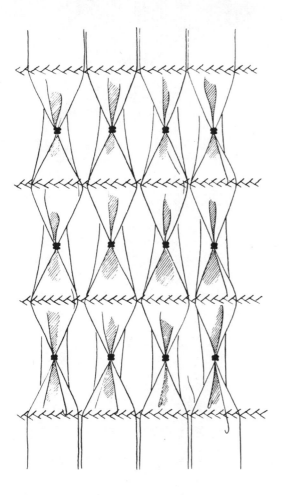

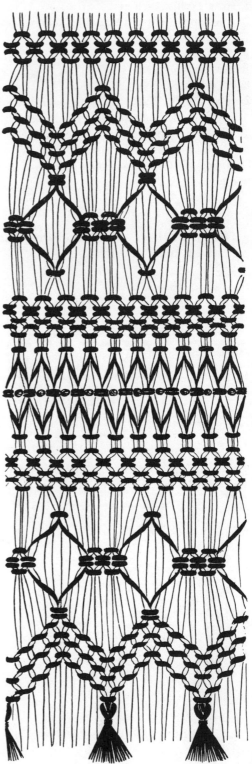

Description of rows beginning at top:

2 rows Cable stitch, Kelly green

3 rows Trellis stitch, red

2 rows Single Wave stitch, royal blue
   (3 Cables where rows meet)

1 row Cable, gold

1 row Cable, green

* 1 row Cable, gold

2 rows Single Wave, red with gold French
   knots worked on top where they meet

Repeat in reverse from * ending with 3
rows Trellis stitch. Make small (½″ to ¾″
long) red tassels and sew one to every other
point.

## No. 2 Pattern on Color Plate (on light blue fabric)

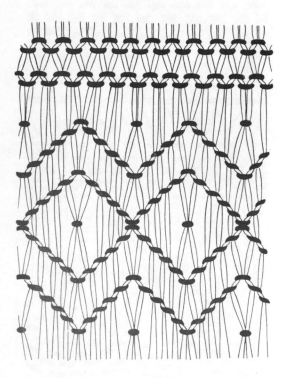

Beginning at top:

2 rows Cable, red about ⅜″ apart

1 row Trellis, white with red dots between
   points

2 rows Trellis, royal blue worked to form
   diamonds with red dot in center of each
   diamond

1 row Trellis, white with red dots

## No. 3 Pattern on Color Plate (Strawberry Design)

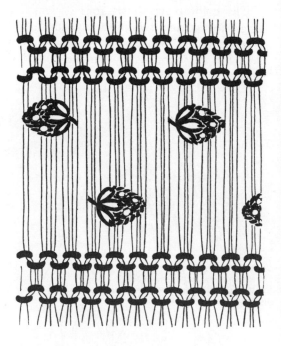

Beginning at top:

1 row Cable, royal blue

1 row Cable, red

Space (about 1¾″) for scattered strawberry
   design. Work 3 rows Outline stitch on
   back in this space to keep pleats in place.

Strawberries are outlined and filled in with
   red Outline stitch, leaves in green Lazy
   Daisy stitch, seeds in yellow Seed stitch.

## No. 4 Pattern on Color Plate (Dress)

Top half of pattern is given; repeat rows
in reverse after center rows of cable stitch
(the bottom row on the diagram) for lower
half.

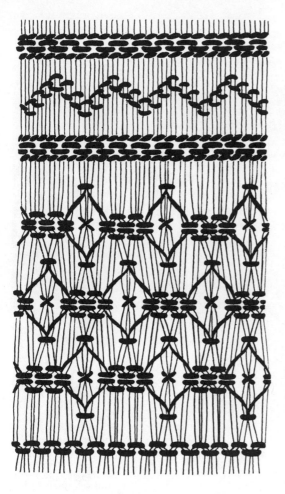

Repeat remainder of pattern in reverse ending with navy Outline stitch.

Any portion of the wide border patterns may be used.

Hot-iron transfers can be purchased for smocking designs. When using them it is not necessary to do the gathering or gauging. Follow the directions which come with the pattern for transferring the pattern and for doing the smocking. The appearance is somewhat different from English smocking but is attractive.

## ADDITIONAL SMOCKING DESIGNS

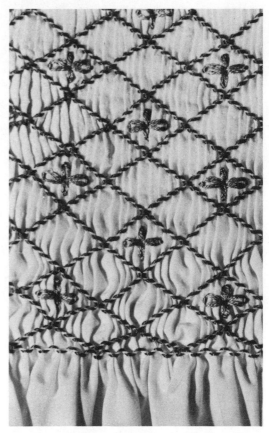

Beginning at top:
1 row Outline, navy
1 row Cable, bright blue } work close together
1 row Outline, navy
1 row Feather stitch, orange
1 row Outline, navy
1 row Cable, bright blue } work close together
1 row Outline, navy
* 2 rows Single Wave to form diamonds with 3 Cable stitches where they meet Small x stitch inside of diamond, navy
Repeat from * using light blue instead of orange.
Repeat again using gold instead of orange.
Navy x stitch in all diamonds.
1 row Cable, bright blue. This forms center of pattern. Do not repeat this row.

A dainty all-over pattern is shown above.

Row after row of Trellis stitch, making a diamond pattern and embellished with Lazy Daisies.

Pattern was worked in blue on white fabric.

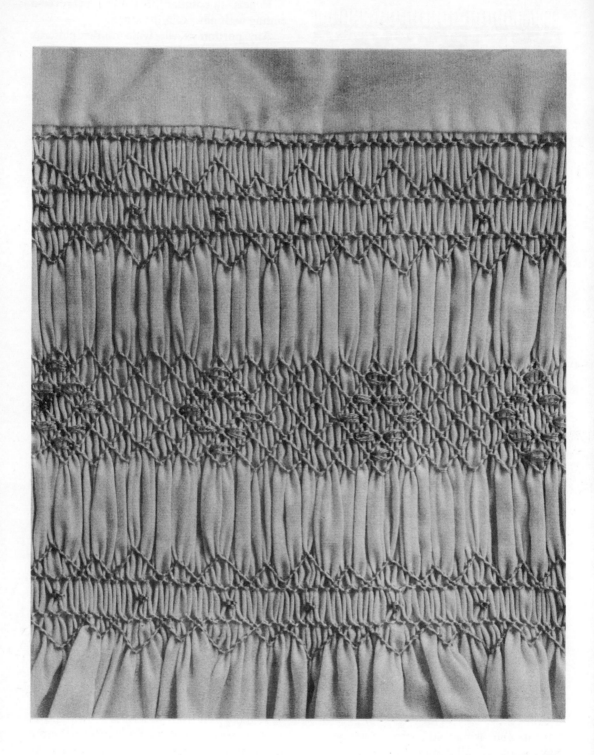

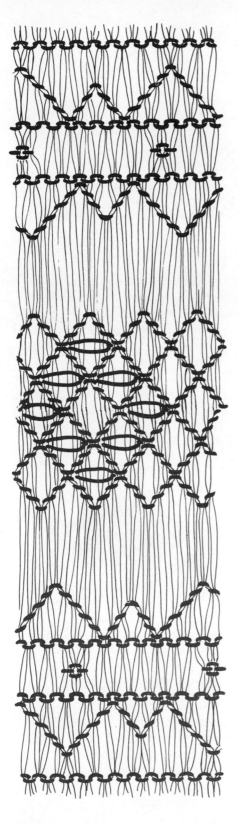

Beginning at top, as shown in diagram and photograph at left. Pattern was worked in all pink, with dots and Lazy Daisies in blue, on white fabric.

1 row Cable
1 row Trellis
1 row Cable
1 row "dots" made with Cable
1 row Cable
1 row Trellis
6 rows Trellis to make diamond pattern, embellished with horizontal Lazy-Daisy stitches
1 row Trellis
1 row Cable
1 row "dots" made with Cable
1 row Cable
1 row Trellis

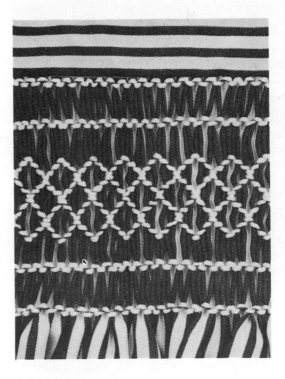

Beginning at top, as shown in photograph above. Pattern was worked in white on blue-and-white-striped fabric.

2 rows Cable
4 rows Trellis
2 rows Cable

CHAPTER 5  ## *Needlepoint*

Needlepoint is considered by some to be the highest art of the needle. Inspired by the old tapestries, it began in medieval times when queens and court ladies plied their needles making lovely hangings for their castles while their lords were away. It was an aristocratic art, and the pieces usually told a story or recorded history or the fashions of the periods.

However, it has now been for more than a hundred years a popular needlework art at which any woman may try her hand. Tinted or started needlepoint patterns are widely available, or you may design your own or have one designed for you. There is a particular kind of fascination in watching these tiny stitches grow under your fingers into something decorative and useful.

Needlepoint is durable; it will outlast most other decorative materials. Used as upholstery it almost never needs to be replaced. It is adaptable; the stitch is extremely simple, but almost any type of design can be developed with it. Also the uses to which this embroidery can be put are legion—from pictures to chair seats, from purses to pillows, and from screens to men's vests—all handsome and infinitely suitable.

Patterns may be geometric, naturalistic, or something in-between. Flowers, fruits, animals, houses, ecclesiastical designs, and many other motifs have been expressed in needlepoint. Original designs stemming from individual interests and hobbies or family activities have been the inspiration for rugs, pictures, hangings, and so on. After you have mastered the technique on a simple project you may wish to try your hand at an original creation.

If possible, visit museums and exhibits and look at fine tapestries and needlepoint pieces to appreciate this great hand art.

## WHAT IS NEEDLEPOINT?

Needlepoint is a type of embroidery worked on canvas and is a general term used for petit point and gros point, which are one and the same stitch differing only in size. The size of the mesh of the canvas determines the size of the stitch.

## DESIGNS

Needlepoint designs may be purchased with the motifs ready-worked and only the background to be filled in. One can also buy canvas with designs tinted or stamped on, in which case the whole piece must be worked.

Tramé patterns have the design and background indicated with threads "laid on." These are used as a guide and covered with needlepoint stitches.

One can also work from a chart. These can be purchased, or you may design your own. Use graph paper 10 squares to 1″ or a size corresponding to the mesh of the canvas you will use. Each square represents one mesh of canvas or one stitch. On your first design do not attempt much shading. Try simple motifs in all-over or border arrangements. All-over patterns can be very lovely; they often resemble old brocades. Indicate the design in pencil, crayon, or water color on the graph paper. Find the center of the design and the center of the canvas and work from the center out, unless you are willing to do a great deal of mesh counting to locate the different parts of the design.

## MATERIALS

As in other hand work do not be satisfied with anything less than the best in materials. The labor involved merits the best in canvas and a fine quality of yarn.

There are two types of needlepoint canvas, single-mesh and double-mesh. The former has single, evenly-spaced threads running in both directions (crosswise and lengthwise). Double-mesh canvas, as the name implies, is woven with double threads instead of single, leaving evenly-spaced square meshes for the needle to work through.

Any stitch method (see How to Work Needlepoint) may be used on double-thread canvas. Any stitch method *with the exception of Plain Half Cross Stitch* may be used on single-thread canvas.

Canvas is made in many qualities, sizes (number of meshes to the inch), and widths.

Choose a strong canvas with an even weave (square meshes). It should be somewhat stiff. Choose a yarn especially made for the purpose, with body enough to cover the meshes and in a good color selection.

Since needlepoint can be worked in the hand, it has the advantage that it can be carried about. Many people, however, prefer to use a frame which helps the piece to keep its shape better. An old picture frame or strips of wood with clamps will do as a frame. If working in a rigid frame you do not have to hold the work. This is more time-consuming, but even arthritic people can work in this way. Never use a hoop as it pulls the work out of shape.

Use a tapestry needle, which is a blunt needle with elongated eye large enough to let the thread slide easily. These needles are especially made for working needlepoint.

Purchase enough yarn of one dye lot to complete the piece.

## GENERAL RULES

After measuring the space to be covered, add 1″ all around for turning under (add more for slip seat furniture). Also make allowance for a slight shrinkage from working. On small items, such as handbags and glasses cases, work only a few meshes beyond the finished area.

The piece will look more uniform if you can develop a rhythm as you work. Pull the yarn evenly on each stitch. Work a little every day to avoid tension and to keep the rhythm. For a smoother finish work in one direction only; do not turn work and go back.

Practice each stitch method to find which one is best suited to you and to the piece on which you are working. If you are left-handed turn the stitch diagrams upside down.

For blocking purposes make a note of the size of the canvas before starting to embroider. Mark with crayon or basting stitch the outer edges of the background area to be covered.

The selvages of the canvas should be at the sides. If you are using a started piece the design will probably have a top and a bottom.

If you are not working in a frame, roll the canvas as you work—from bottom up and from top down. In this way the work can be grasped more easily.

If buying a started piece, be sure the canvas is large enough for the object for which you will use it. There should be at least 2″ of unworked canvas all around for attaching.

Also choose a design that harmonizes in style and is in proportion to the chair or other piece on which you will use it.

## HOW TO WORK NEEDLEPOINT

The tent or half cross stitch can be made in various ways. The appearance on the right side of the work is the same but the wrong side is different. Also the amounts of yarn used differs.

Continental and diagonal stitches both work up with more thickness on the back than on the front. This is especially desirable for upholstery and rugs because it serves as a pad and saves wear on the needlepoint. Plain half cross stitch leaves little yarn on the back and is the most economical as far as yarn is concerned.

Gros point means large point and petit point means small point. They both can be done in any of the various methods. The mesh size of the canvas determines the size of the stitch. *Plain half cross stitch cannot be done on a single-mesh canvas.*

Study the stitch diagrams and directions for making. One stitch method may be better than another for a certain article. For example, it would not be necessary to use continental stitch, which pads the back, on a picture.

To avoid fraying, use a strand of yarn in the needle not longer than 18″ to 20″. Use

a shorter length for petit point.

Use a tapestry needle size 18 or 19 for gros point and size 22 or 24 for petit point. To thread the needle, fold the yarn over the needle, then slip needle out. The resulting loop will easily thread through the eye. If you have to thread a short length, cover the end of the yarn with a small piece of folded paper or tape; then slip it through the eye.

For petit point, split the yarn or use stranded mercerized cotton, using as many strands as necessary to cover the mesh.

### Gros Point

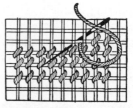

**Continental Stitch.** Work from right to left. The needle is brought out a mesh ahead and slanting. Study the diagram and top photograph below. Tent or half cross stitch is produced on the top but a long slanting stitch

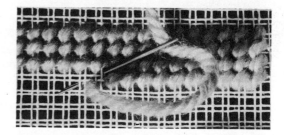

Right Side

Wrong Side

appears on the back, see photograph above. Very good for chair seats, foot stools, rugs, or any place where a padded back is desirable. This stitch uses about 1¼ yards of yarn to cover a square inch of canvas.

**Plain Half Cross Stitch.** This must be done on double-thread canvas. It may be done from right to left, from left to right, or from bottom to top working vertically. It forms a straight stitch on the back. Try all three methods and find the one which is easiest

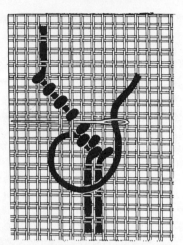

Right Side

Right Side

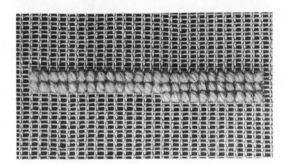

Wrong Side

for you. Follow the diagram. Plain Half Cross is adequate for small items which need no padding on the back. It uses about 1 yard of yarn for a square inch of canvas. This stitch has a tendency to pull the piece out of shape but this can be corrected in blocking.

**Diagonal Stitch.** Beginning at lower right hand corner, take a half cross stitch bringing needle out horizontally under 2 groups of threads to the left. Follow diagram closely. For second row, begin again at lower right corner taking stitches between those of the previous row. This stitch also leaves a thick pad on the back using about the same amount of yarn as continental stitch. This stitch does not pull the canvas out of shape.

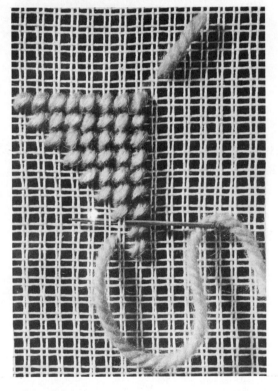

Right Side

**Basket Weave or Bias Tent Stitch.** This is started in the upper right hand corner, (see next page). Fasten thread in usual way or insert needle a few meshes down and a few meshes to the left, leaving knot on the surface. The piece of yarn on the back will be covered with stitches as you work. Clip off the knot

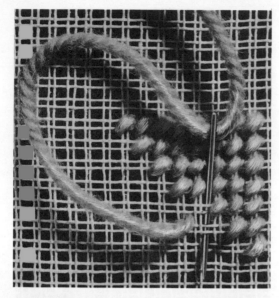

Right Side

## Petit Point

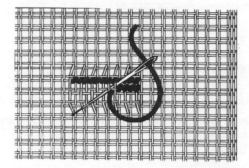

Petit point is usually worked over a single-thread canvas but can be done on double-thread. Very fine double-thread (Penelope) is quite suitable if available.

All the stitch methods given except plain half cross can be done on single-thread canvas. Continental stitch is most often used for petit point.

When a portion of the design on a gros point pattern is to be done in petit point, the stitch is done over a single thread. To facilitate this, dampen this portion of canvas and push the threads until the spaces are even.

Work the areas of petit point first. Silk or mercerized thread is sometimes used for petit point. Use as many strands as necessary to cover the mesh. Wool is also used but the yarn must be split. Petit point is especially suitable for designs with fine detail, such as faces, flowers, figures, etc., because subtle shading is possible.

If you are working a piece with a petit point center and background of gros point, work gros point up as far as there are 2 canvas threads to work over. Work also any open spaces within the petit point area. Then split the background yarn and fill in the small spaces, working over 1 thread of canvas, in petit point.

when you reach it. Bring needle out at upper right hand corner and take a stitch. Take an-

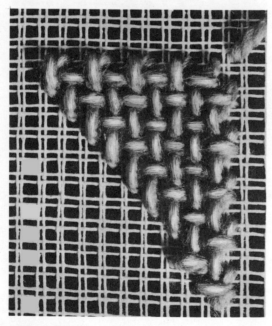

Wrong Side

other stitch to the left but bring needle out below first stitch. Follow diagrams. Rows are worked up and back diagonally leaving a thick basket weave on the under side. This uses about 1¾ yards of yarn per square inch.

## Tramé

This type of needlepoint has long threads "laid on" indicating the design and change of colors.

Tramé pieces can be purchased and usually come complete with yarn in the correct amounts and colors for completing the piece. Half cross stitch is worked over these long stitches which also serve as padding.

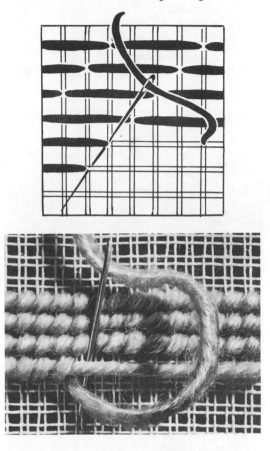

If you are working on tinted canvas, you may wish to prepare the piece in this manner yourself.

To lay on the stitches: Bring needle up through canvas from right-hand side between the double threads on one row. Carry it across the top of the double mesh and insert at point where color changes. Work half cross stitch back over the laid thread or you may do all of the tramé before covering with needlepoint stitches.

## Other Canvas Stitches

**Gobelin Stitch.** Like gros point, this stitch is used for backgrounds. It is worked over 2 or more meshes in height but only one in width, which makes it slightly slanted; or it may be worked over meshes directly above, which gives a vertical stitch. This should be worked on double mesh canvas unless the stitches are long (over more than 1 mesh).

**Long and Short Oblique Stitch.** Work in vertical rows. Long diagonal stitches are crossed at one end with a short stitch. The cross stitch may be done as you go or all

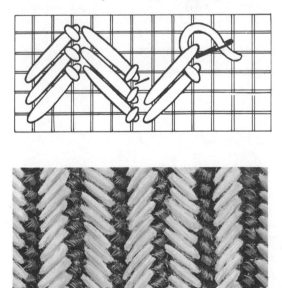

210

the long stitches done first and the short ones later, in which case two colors may be used.

**Long Oblique Stitch with Running Stitch.** Work rows of oblique stitches and fill space between with 2 rows of running stitch, backstitch, or chain stitch.

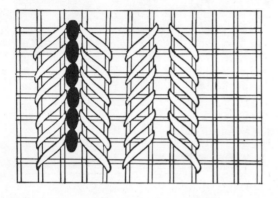

**Greek Herringbone Stitch.** This is a long-legged herringbone worked from left to right. Turn and work back.

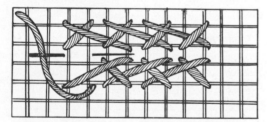

**Fern or Fishbone Stitch.** Work in vertical rows starting at upper left hand corner. Follow diagram.

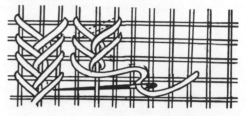

**Kelim Stitch.** Rows of oblique stitches slanted alternately. Two or more colors may be used. To save time use a needle for each color.

**Color Plate 6 — Hooked Rug**

An example of a hand-hooked rug. The rich coloring enhances the design, which is an interesting arrangement of simple forms. See Chapter 6, Rug Making, for instructions for this rug.

**Bargello or Florentine Stitch.** This is also called Flame embroidery and is a variation of long and short stitch. It is usually done on single-thread canvas following a chart and is worked from left to right (or right to left) over 2 or more meshes. After working one or two rows the counting is simple because all repeats are alike. The shading can be soft and gradual or more striking contrasts can be used. Several charts are given here for designs from a simple zigzag to the skyscraper effect.

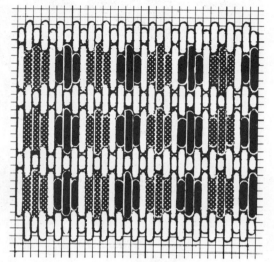

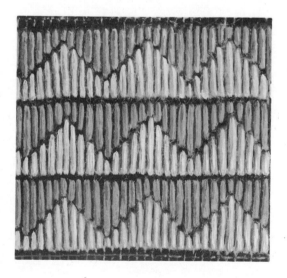

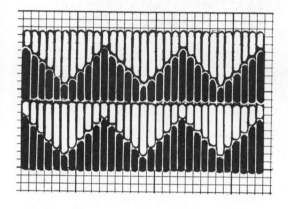

**Simple Long and Short Stitch.** In two shades of a color, this makes an attractive all-over pattern.

**Shadow Design.** Use three colors in soft shades for a subtle effect.

**Diamond Checkerboard.** Very striking if strong colors are used.

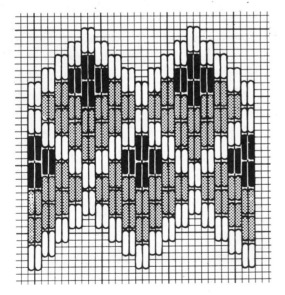

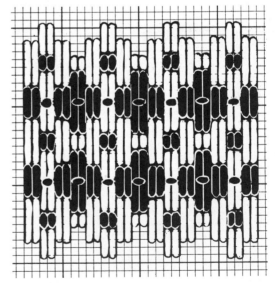

**Shaded Diamond.** Has many possibilities in color arrangements suitable for modern settings.

**Forget-me-not.** A floral-like pattern with lots of appeal.

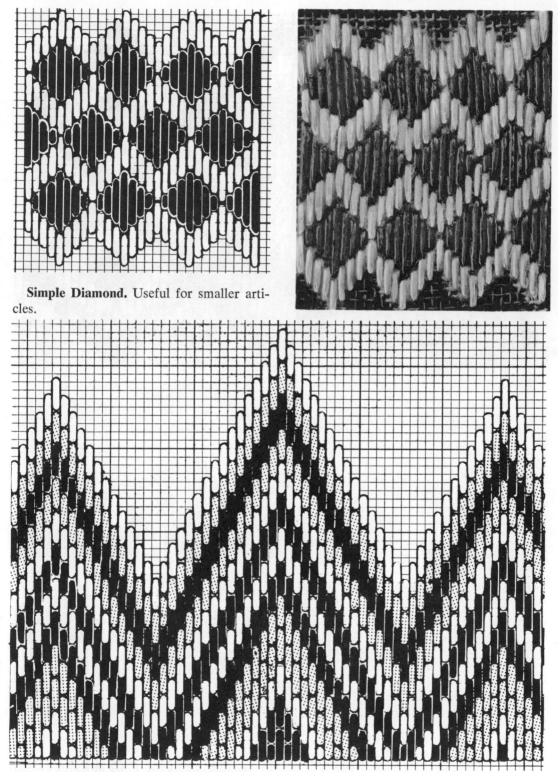

**Simple Diamond.** Useful for smaller articles.

**Sawtooth Design**

**Sawtooth Design.** A typical flame pattern with many possibilities for color shading.

**Skyscraper Design.** A typical Bargello or Florentine design which can be done in multicolor.

The size of the mesh of the canvas will determine the size of the design. An easy way to enlarge a design is to use a coarser canvas. A suitable yarn must be selected —one that covers the mesh well.

All of these patterns may be adapted for different articles. Worked on medium-coarse canvas (about 8 or 10 meshes to the inch) they are right for footstools, pillows, chair seats, and knitting bags. On finer canvas they might be used for handbags, glasses cases, or small bedroom pillows.

On coarse canvas very handsome rugs can be fashioned in this type of work.

## HOW TO PIECE NEEDLEPOINT

There are times when it is necessary to piece needlepoint canvas.

The canvas to be added must always be of exactly the same size mesh as the original. Be sure that selvages are running in the same direction on both pieces so the double threads will match.

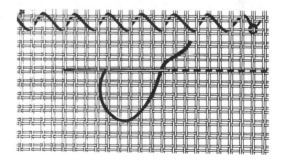

If these precautions are taken, canvas may be pieced either horizontally (crosswise) or vertically (lengthwise).

With right sides together and edges even, pin and baste canvas together taking a 5/8″ seam. Overcast the raw edges, matching 2 sets of double threads; back-stitch (by hand) through these double threads with strong linen thread or use a thread drawn from edge of canvas. Press seam open. The seam line on the right side is considered as a row of mesh when working over it.

Work up to and over this row *not catching* in the seam allowance. When working the seam line, instead of picking up the whole stitch from the right side, use an up and down movement, pushing needle to wrong side, catching with left hand, and pushing through to right side. Continue across row.

## BLOCKING

If the piece has become pulled out of shape in working this can be remedied by correct blocking.

Do not cut into canvas before blocking. Roll the piece in a very damp Turkish towel and leave overnight or until thoroughly damp.

Using the dimensions you made note of before starting work (see General Directions), lay piece face down on marked board. Stretch into shape and tack with rust-proof thumb tacks ¾″ apart around edges. Allow piece to dry thoroughly even if it takes several days. It should not be necessary to press but if desired you may do so. Remove from board, cover with damp cloth, and steam with a hot iron to fluff the yarn. Do not touch iron to needlepoint.

Mounting, especially of upholstery, should be done by an expert.

Pictures are framed like any painting. Pillows are made up in the usual ways. Handbags should be mounted by specialists. Rugs must be hemmed or faced with heavy tape and are sometimes lined.

### Fringing

If fringe is used on rugs and pillows be sure to use the same yarn as was used in the background. See directions for Making Fringe.

## COLOR PLATE 5

The fruit design on the color plate is worked in petit point. The threads of double-thread canvas were dampened and pushed apart until evenly spaced as shown on the diagram under Petit Point.

This design was drawn and tinted on graph paper and then worked on canvas following the tinted diagram as closely as possible.

A drawing of the design is given here actual size. It can be traced off using tissue or tracing paper and transferred to canvas or graph paper using carbon paper. The design can also be worked in gros point, but not as much detail will be possible since there will be fewer stitches to the inch. It would be advisable to enlarge the pattern first.

To enlarge the design: trace off the design; then using red pencil mark off ½″ squares all over the design (see diagram). To make it twice the original size: on a larger piece of paper mark off 1″ squares (or 2″ or 3″ for a still larger design). Now draw into the larger squares the same parts of the design as they appear in the smaller squares. Use the new drawing for a pattern. Trace it onto the canvas with carbon paper between.

The all-over design shown on the color plate is suitable for a footstool, chair seat, pillow, purse, or bag. A design of this kind necessitates some counting of meshes on the first row, but after one row is completed the

placing of the colors is almost automatic. See photograph for color arrangement. It shades from yellow through orange to deep red with the scallops separated by a row of green and black. Other color combinations would be equally effective.

For this pattern also a canvas of coarser mesh would enlarge the design.

## NEEDLEPOINT

The needlepoint sampler and chair shown are typical of the many lovely designs which can be purchased in needlework shops and departments. The design is ready worked and only the background is to be filled in.

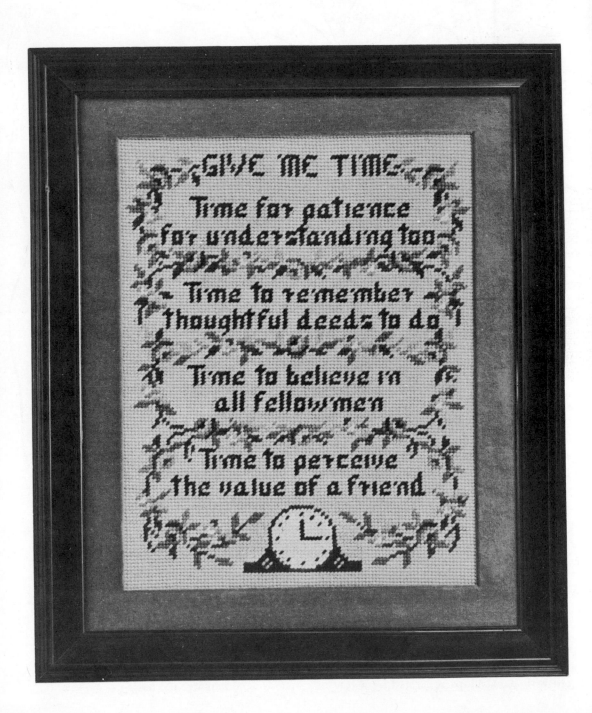

# CHAPTER 6 Rug Making

There are several ways of making hand-made rugs. None is very difficult nor does any of them, with the exception a hand-woven one, require much equipment.

Hooking is an old American craft, and there are many fine examples in museums and private collections of early hooked rugs which show much artistic feeling, not to mention patience and industry. Some are primitive, quaint, and simple and others are more intricate and even elaborate. For the most part they were made of left-overs and partly worn fabrics.

Modern hooked rugs are still made of fabric strips, but many are made of yarn. Jute is also being used. There is a growing interest in hooking using many types of materials such as fabric strips, yarn, jute, and even fur scraps in the same rug. Unusual texture effects are achieved in this way.

Braided rugs are also easy to make and lovely to look at when done with skill and taste. They are warm and cheerful and furnish a further use for scraps and pieces and partly worn clothing.

Needlepoint and cross stitch rugs are more elaborate in feeling and take longer to make. Designs with more detail can be executed in this technique and the effect is richer. It is fascinating and rewarding hand work.

The possibilities for achieving fine artistic effects for decorative use are very great in hand-woven rugs. They can be very handsome indeed. One must first master weaving in order to make them.

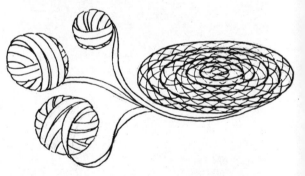

Crocheted rugs have a very definite place. Made in soft cotton or wool yarns they are extremely useful in bedroom and bath or children's rooms. Some very interesting textured rugs are being made of jute, which is suitable for more general use.

The knotted rug is another technique growing in favor. It is a revival of an old method and is done on coarse canvas or base cloth by knotting in loops of yarn. This method of working has great possibilities.

These are the important basic techniques of making hand-made rugs and the methods are given in the following pages. Designs can be simple and still be in wonderfully good taste. You can even plan them yourself. Plan

your rug for the place it is to be used taking into consideration size, color, and texture in relation to the room and its furnishings. Ready-prepared designs in several of the techniques can be purchased.

## COLOR PLATE 6

The rug shown **on** Color Plate 6 was hooked of strips of **fabric** much of which was specially dyed to produce the rich color arrangement. A diagram of the pattern is given on the preceding page and it can be enlarged.

The original rug was approximately 39″ by 69″ finished. To make your own pattern draw this size on light weight wrapping paper and mark it off in 3½″ squares. Trace off the design given using tissue or tracing paper. Mark it off in ½″ squares. Both large and small patterns should be 10 squares wide and 19 squares long. To transfer the pattern onto the wrapping paper draw into the squares the lines of the design which appear in the corresponding small squares.

Cut burlap or other foundation material 39″×69″ plus 3 or 4 inches around for hemming. Place heavy carbon paper face down between pattern and burlap. Center the design and trace with blunt end of crochet hook.

The motifs are simple and lend themselves to other arrangements. If you wish a rug of different size and shape the motifs can be arranged in various ways with good results.

The color arrangement can also be changed, and if you do not wish to use fabric strips, we suggest jute, which comes in beautiful tones.

## HOOKED RUGS

Hooked rugs are easy to create and, since they can be made of left-over materials, they are within the reach of everyone. Until you have tried your hand at this simple craft, you cannot know how much real pleasure can be derived from it.

### Foundation and Designs

For the foundation, heavy closely-woven burlap, warp cloth, monk's cloth, heavy linen, osnaburg, or any fairly coarse unbleached cotton may be used.

Designs can be simple. Several shades of a soft rich color can be arranged in blocks, rows, shells, diamonds, or scallops for a beautiful rug. Simple floral arrangements are not difficult to do if you have drawing ability. Many types of designs can be purchased ready-stamped or tinted on foundation fabric, but for many people half the fun of hooking a rug is creating the design. Remember that a border tends to make a rug look smaller. Draw the design on a light weight wrapping paper. If the paper is too heavy it is difficult to transfer. Trace the design onto the foundation fabric using heavy carbon paper and the blunt end of a crochet hook. If there are rows or straight lines in the design be sure they are in line with the weave of the foundation fabric when placing pattern. Leave a margin of 3 or 4 inches for fastening to the frame and later hemming the rug. The piece is put into the frame by lacing, or tacking.

## Materials

Many types of materials can go into a rug: fabric of various kinds cut into strips or yarns in different weights. Jute is again available and makes beautiful rugs. Yarn is almost always used in punch and automatic needles. Woolen fabric is better than cotton, although many of the lovely old rugs were cotton. As a general rule it is best to use the same fiber throughout in one rug. However if you enjoy experimenting with texture effects you may use a variety of materials. There is no standardization as to materials and this lends to the charm of hooked rugs.

## Preparing Strips

The strips should run lengthwise of the fabric. Strips may be cut in the hand using scissors (a rather slow process) or the fabric may be rolled (jelly roll fashion) and cut with a sharp knife or razor blade. Also a rug-cutting machine or stripper can be purchased. Never tear the strips, as this leaves threads which make the rug look fuzzy. Firmly woven fabrics can be cut ¼" wide or even less for the more detailed parts of the design. If a quickly-made and coarse type of rug is desired cut the strips wider.

## Ways of Hooking

The method you use is a matter of personal taste and preference. Experiment with all of them before you decide which to use.

**Hooking from the Right Side.** The fabric strip or yarn is held underneath with the left hand; the hook is pushed through from the top with the right hand. Catch the end of the strip and pull it through. Push the needle in again a thread or two away (depending upon the foundation fabric) and pull up a loop. Repeat, following the design. Keep loops about ¼" in length and uniform throughout. Skill develops with practice. Any length of strip can be used. Always pull ends through to the right side. Loops should be left uncut on rugs made of fabric strips. If not working in a frame, always start in the center of the rug. Do the design and then the background. Hooking may be done in straight rows or following the contour of the design.

**Hooking from the Wrong Side.** Strictly speaking this is not hooking but "punching," but the final result is much the same. It is done with either a punch or shuttle type needle. The punch type needle is a tube-like affair through which the yarn runs. It is made in different sizes for different weights of yarn and it always has some sort of adjustable stop to prevent the needle from being pushed farther than is wanted. This makes it possible to produce loops of different lengths. The shuttle type of punch hook is worked up and down with both hands and

**Hooking from the Right Side**

"walks" along, punching through at regular intervals. It is the quickest way of hooking, and is usually done with yarn.

Hooking from the back requires that the rug be stretched in a frame. The frame may be very simple (an old picture frame will do) with thumb tacks for holding the rug in place. Excellent frames which are made especially for the purpose are also available.

Both types of needles when raised leave a loop on the under side (the right side of the rug). Do not lift the needle above the surface but push it in again a short distance away. Some rug makers recommend doing the whole rug in rows changing colors as needed. Others prefer to work following the shape of the motifs (flowers, etc.), maintaining that a more natural result is achieved (see photograph). Certainly it is much easier to shade flowers by this last method. When using the punch needle hold the finished row back with the left hand so loops will not be caught with the needle. Leave an unhooked border 2″ to 3″ wide for hemming.

**Hooking from the Wrong Side**

## Clipping

Rugs made of yarn are often clipped and this is done while the rug is still in the frame. Use long, narrow, sharp scissors (some have bent handles for this purpose), and slide the points into the loops. Several loops can be cut at one time.

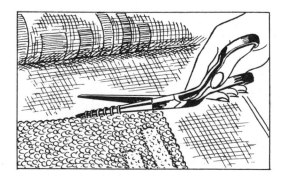

## Sculpturing or Beveling

## Sizing, Hemming, and Blocking

Some designs lend themselves to sculpturing or beveling. This means shaping parts of the design by clipping the pile. Exaggerated sculpturing is not practical because it is difficult to walk on, but there are times when a limited amount will bring out the design.

There is a special rug sizing which can be used on the back of burlap rugs. It is used only on unclipped rugs and its purpose is to prevent the loops from slipping out of the burlap. Many prefer not to size rugs maintaining that it cheapens them and also causes

them to slip easily. Remove the rug from the frame, trim, and make a 1½" hem all around. The edge of the hem may be taped instead of being turned under, which makes a flatter finish (see photograph). The rug may be steamed and pressed lightly over a soft surface, or it may be placed face down on the floor with paper underneath and walked on for a while to set the stitches.

## BRAIDED RUGS

This is one of the easiest ways of making rugs and almost any size can be made—from 2 by 4 feet to 9 by 12 or larger. Also oval, oblong, round, and many variations of these are possible.

### Materials

Wool, cotton, and silk can all be used but should not be combined in the same rug. Cotton soils easily and therefore is more suitable for small rugs which can be laundered. Silk can be braided into small mats and rugs for use where they will get little wear. Wool is best because of its body and wearing quality. Collect pieces left from sewing and save partly worn clothing. Mill ends may also be used and these can be purchased by the pound.

### Color

Decide upon a color scheme and dye colors if necessary. If the rug is to have bands of shaded colors, it is well to start

with a dark center, or to have a dark band near the center. This gives the appearance of weight and solidity.

## Size and Shape, Amounts and Preparation

Decide upon the size and shape you will make. If the rug is to be oval, subtract the width from the length to find out how long the first braid should be. The size of the rug helps to decide the size of the braid. A very large rug should be made of heavy braids; for smaller rugs use smaller braid.

Depending upon the thickness of braid desired, it takes about ¾ pound of wool per square foot of rug. It is well to know in figuring amounts that about ⅓ of the length of the strip is taken up in braiding.

Fabric should be carefully washed before using. Wash and rinse each color separately until water is clear if you want a color-fast rug.

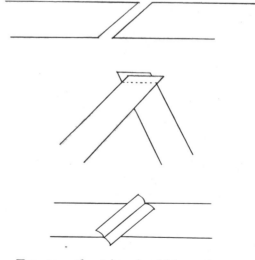

For strength, strips should be cut or torn lengthwise of the fabric. Before cutting, experiment a little to get the size of braid you want. Braids that are too narrow are tedious to sew together; if too large the rug will be coarse and heavy and be hard to clean. A good medium size is a 1″ wide finished braid.

For this, cut strips about 2″ wide. If fabric is light weight, it will need to be cut wider. Strips are joined by sewing together on the bias. Fold in the raw edges and then fold the strip down the center. Experienced rug makers fold as they braid. There are

"braiders" available at needlework counters which fold automatically. Prepare colors separately and roll into balls.

## Braiding

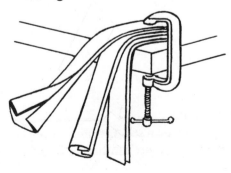

The simplest type of braiding is with 3 strips but it is possible to use 4 or more. The

rug may be made by sewing the braids together or by interbraiding as you work.

If you are sewing braids together, begin by anchoring the ends firmly by tacking or

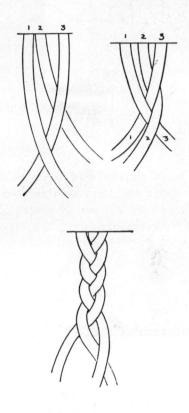

clamping to a solid surface. Braid tightly, keeping tension firm and steady. Stretch strips slightly as you work. Whenever you let go of the braids, pin ends together. To avoid bumps, space pieced seams so no two come together.

## Sewing Rug Together

After braiding several yards, start sewing them together. If the rug is oval start with a straight length down the center. Double the braid back on itself and continue down the side, around the end, up the other side, and on around. Allow "fulness" on curves so rug will lie flat.

## Multiple Braiding

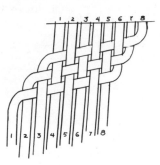

Use heavy carpet thread, lacing back and forth through the loops so thread will be invisible and the rug will be reversible. To end the last braid cut each strand to a tapered point; whip edges and braid together.

The principle is the same whether you braid with three strands or more. Begin with the last strip to the right and weave it over and under from right to left. Repeat, beginning again at the right.

## Interbraiding

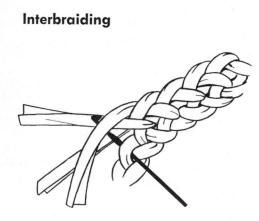

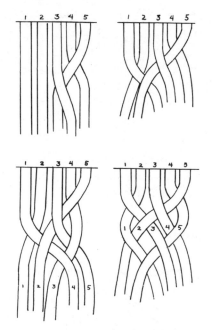

This method joins the braids as they are made using a heavy crochet hook. When ready to join, as each strand comes to the inside it is pulled through the finished loop of the previous row with the hook. On curves it is necessary to bring two successive strips through the same loop. This method of braiding makes a very neat and finished-looking rug. Work on a flat surface when joining the rug so it will lie flat.

**Fancy Five-strand Braiding.** Number the strips from left to right. Bring last strip (No. 5) over No. 4 and under No. 3. Bring No. 1 over No. 2 and under No. 5. Re-number strips and repeat these two steps.

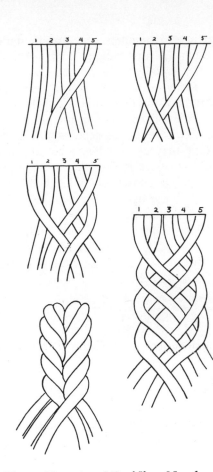

**Heavy Five-strand Braiding.** Number strips from left to right. Bring last strip, No. 5 over Nos. 4 and 3; bring No. 1 over Nos. 2 and 5. Re-number strips and repeat these two steps.

**Fancy Eight-strand Braiding.** Number strips from left to right. Bring No. 4 over No. 5, under Nos. 6, 7, and 8. Bring No. 5 over Nos. 3, 2, and 1. Grasp Nos. 6, 7, and 8 as one unit and bring under Nos. 1, 2, and

3 as one unit. Bring No. 4 over Nos. 1, 2, and 3 and bring No. 5 under Nos. 6, 7, and 8. Bring No. 5 over No. 4 at center. Repeat these last two steps, continuing to braid first the three-strand units and then the single-strand units.

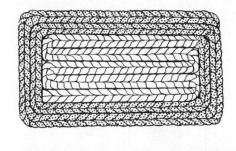

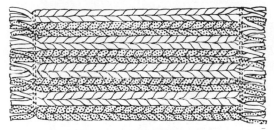

Since the wider the braid, the more difficult it is to turn curves and corners, it is better to use the wide braids in oblong rugs where strips run lengthwise only. Ends may be unravelled to form a fringe.

## RUGS WORKED ON CANVAS— KNOTTED RUGS

### Turkey Work, Smyrna Rug Stitch, or Pile Stitch

These are different names for the same stitch. It is done with needle and thread on canvas. A tapestry needle is used and it can be done on heavy single-thread linen canvas, rug, or base cloth in which case it is called Turkey Work. Persian rug wool, which is a loosely twisted 3-ply yarn, is used; or regular rug yarn can be used if the canvas or base cloth is coarse enough. Have several needles at hand to avoid changing colors as much as possible.

When done on double-thread canvas using the same stitch it is sometimes called Smyrna Rug stitch or Pile stitch. Diagrams show working the stitch on canvas. It is not necessary to put the canvas in a frame as it can be worked in the hand or on a table top. It can be rolled up when not in use.

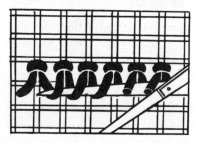

If working on a table hold canvas down with a weight. Have the first row at edge of table. Start at the lower left hand corner

leaving several squares for turning under. The stitch is very simple. First pass the needle horizontally to the left under a vertical thread. Draw up tight. Work the next stitch to the right of the first holding the thread in a loop against the canvas, or use a ½″ wide gauge made of a tongue depressor. It is very important that all the loops be the same length. The design is done first and then the background, but each row is finished before going on to the next. After working a half dozen loops or so they are cut.

**Finishing Edge.** Fold edges under one square on coarse canvas or about ½″ on single thread canvas. Work over edge with close blanket stitch.

## Needlepoint and Cross Stitch Rugs

These rugs are made on regular needlepoint canvas for a fine textured rug or on coarser canvas which gives a bolder effect and works up more quickly.

Cross stitch on double-thread canvas is shown here. See Needlepoint section for how to do needlepoint and other canvas stitches for which finer canvas may be used.

Any cross stitch pattern can be followed. Simple borders can be repeated to make rows; or motifs can be arranged in block effect. On the whole soft color combinations are more pleasing and easier to live with.

Cross stitch designs stamped on burlap squares can be purchased for add-a-block rugs.

There are many stitches other than needlepoint and cross stitch which can be worked on canvas to make handsome rugs. See Embroidery section and Needlepoint section for stitches. Learn to experiment with various threads and yarns on different sizes of canvas for unusual and interesting texture. More than one stitch may be combined in the same rug. Also, cross stitch or other canvas stitches may be combined with knotting or pile stitch for very interesting effects.

## Knotted with Latch Hook

This type of knotting is similar to but not exactly like knotting with needle and thread. It is done on coarse double-thread canvas with a special latch hook.

Rug yarn is used and it is cut in short lengths before knotting into the canvas. Cut yarn in lengths of about 3 inches and keep each color separate.

Place the canvas on the table and mark off a border of about 2″ all around. This is for turning under after rug is completed. Work with the rug on the table or in the lap; the selvage edges should be at the sides.

Start at the lower right-hand corner on the first row just inside of the margin. If you are working on tinted canvas, follow the colors of the tinting, selecting yarn to match.

Fold the piece of yarn in half over the shank of the hook just below the latch.

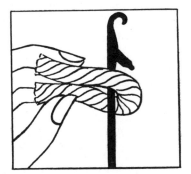

Match the two loose ends and hold with thumb and forefinger of left hand. Hold the hook in the right hand and keep the latch down with the forefinger.

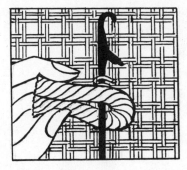

With yarn still folded over the hook, push the hook through the first hole under the first row of horizontal threads and up through the hole directly above. Push far enough so the latch is above the threads.

Now pull the hook toward you until the latch is almost vertical but not closed. Slip the ends (which are held in the left hand) between the latch and the hook.

Draw hook back until latch is closed; let go of the ends and pull loose ends through the loop. The hook slips out.

Tighten the loop by pulling the loose ends. This is one stitch. Continue across making a loop in each square. Work rows from right to left, keeping finished part toward you.

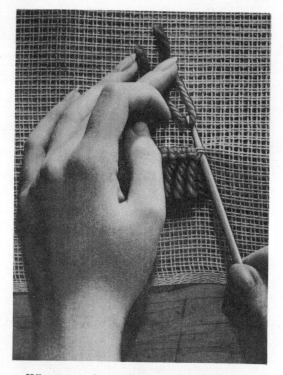

When complete, trim any uneven ends and shake rug well.

Turn under the margin and sew on rug binding. Apply binding flat, covering the raw edges. Hem down both edges using a curved needle and strong thread. Apply binding loosely and miter the corners.

It is possible to do the stitch with an ordinary crochet hook also.

## CROCHETED RUGS

Crocheted rugs can also be made of various kinds of yarn or thread or of fabric strips. Use all of one kind of fabric (wool or cotton preferably) in one rug. The strips are cut wider than for hooking but not as wide as for braiding (½″ to ¾″ depending on the thickness of fabric used). It is wise to make a swatch. Some prefer to cut the fabric on the bias for crocheting. Knitted fabrics work up well.

If you have many odds and ends of yarn they can be worked up into a "hit or miss" round or oval rug in single crochet (picking up both top stitches) with a very pleasing result. All weights of yarn can be used by doubling the finer ones. Increase just enough to keep the rug flat and not enough to make it ripple. Increase equal amounts on each side.

There are many other stitches which make attractive crocheted rugs such as loop stitch, popcorn, etc.

The rug and pillow shown here are crocheted of two tones of jute. The rug is worked in squares which are set together. This makes it possible to make any size rug desired by adding blocks.

### Directions for Crocheted Jute Rug

(*See Crochet chapter for abbreviations*)

JUTE-TONE: 7 tubes Dk. Green and 15 tubes each Willow Green and Spun Gold, or colors of your own choice.

No. K Crochet Hook.

Work tightly for best results.

Rug measures 34″ × 51″.

NO. 1—BLOCK (17″ square): Using 2 cords Gold, ch 2.

RND 1: 8 sc in 2d ch from hook, join with sl st in 1st sc.

RND 2: Ch 1, turn, 2 sc down in same st where sl st was made, (sc in next sc, 3 sc in next sc) 3 times, sc in next sc, * sc in same place with 1st 2 sc, join with sl st in 1st sc. *

RND 3: Ch 1, turn, 2 sc down in same st where sl st was made. Start all rnds in this way. (Sc in next 3 sc, 3 sc in next sc) 3 times, sc in next 3 sc, end as in last rnd from * to *. Mark the right side of this rnd as right side of Block.

RND 4: Ch 1, turn and start as in last rnd, (sc in next 5 sc, 3 sc in next sc) 3 times, sc in next 5 sc, end as in Rnd 2 from * to *.

RND 5: Ch 1, turn, start as in previous rnds, * sc in each sc across (2 more than last rnd and always an uneven no. of sc), 3 sc in next (corner) sc; repeat from * around; end as in Rnd 2 from * to *. Repeat Rnd 5 twice for Rnds 6 and 7.

RND 8: Ch 1, turn, start as before, * (ch 1, sk 1 sc, long sc under base of next sc) 6 times, ch 1, sk 1 sc, ** 3 sc in next (corner) sc; repeat from * twice and from * to ** again; end as in Rnd 2 from * to *.

RND 9: Ch 1, turn, start as before, * (ch 1, sk 1 sc, long sc in sc under next ch-1 sp)

7 times, ch 1, sk 1 sc, ** 3 sc in next (corner) sc; repeat from * twice and from * to ** again; end as in Rnd 2 from * to *.

RND 10: Ch 1, turn, start as before, * (ch 1, sk 1 sc, long sc in sc under next ch-1 sp) repeat across (1 more long sc than previous rnd), ch 1, sk 1 sc, ** 3 sc in next (corner) sc; repeat from * twice and from * to ** again; end as before. Repeat Rnd 10 five times (thru Rnd 15).

RND 16: Ch 1, turn, 3 sc in same st with sl st, * (sc in next sc, long sc in sc under next ch-1 sp) 14 times, sc in next sc, ** 5 sc in next (corner) sc; repeat from * twice and from * to ** again, 2 sc in same place with 1st 3 sc, join.

RND 17: Ch 3, turn, 1 dc and 1 hdc in same st with sl st, * sc in next 3 sc, hdc in next 2 sc, holding back the last lp of each dc make 2 dc in next sc, yo and draw thru all 3 lps on hook at same time for a Cluster, 1 dc in next sc, a 2-dc Cluster in next sc, hdc in next 2 sc; repeat from * twice; sc in next 3 sc, ** (1 hdc, 3 dc, 1 hdc) in next (corner) sc; repeat from * twice and from * to ** again; 1 hdc and 1 dc at base of ch-3, join to top of ch-3.

RND 18: Ch 2 and without turning, 2 hdc in same st, * sc in next 3 sts, (sk 1 st, sc in next 4 sts, 3 sc in next dc, sc in next 4 sts) 3 times, sk 1 st, sc in next 3 sts, ** 5 hdc in next (corner) dc; repeat from * twice and from * to ** again; 2 hdc at base of ch-2, join to top of ch-2. Fasten off.

RND 19: Turn, attach 2 cords Willow Green with 2 sc in center hdc at 1 corner, ch 3, 2 sc in same st, ** sc in next 5 sts, sk 1 sc, sc in next 4 sc, (sc, ch 2, sc) in next sc, sc in next 4 sc, * sk 2 sc, sc in next 4 sc, (sc, ch 2, sc) in next sc, sc in next 4 sc; repeat from * once; sk 1 sc, sc in next 5 sts, (2 sc, ch 3, 2 sc) in next (corner) hdc; repeat from ** around, join and fasten off.

RND 20: Turn, attach 2 cords Dk. Green with 2 sc in back lp of 1st sc on left side of 1 corner p and working in back lps, sc in next 2 sc, * hdc in next 2 sc, dc in next sc, (dc in next 2 sc) made into a Cluster-dec, dc in next sc, hdc in next 2 sc, sc in next sc, ** sk p, sc behind p in next sc on left side of p; repeat from * twice and from * to ** again; sc in next sc, 2 sc in next (end) sc, sk corner p, 2 sc in next sc on left side of p, sc in next 2 sc; repeat from * around; sk p, join to 1st sc. Fasten off. Make 3 Blocks.

NO. 2—BLOCK: With 2 cords Willow Green, repeat thru Rnd 18; make Rnd 19 in Gold; repeat Rnd 20. Make 3 Blocks.

JOINING: Using 1 cord Dk. Green, sew 1 Willow Green Block, 1 Gold Block and 1 Willow Green Block tog into a strip, going thru both lps of sts and sewing adjoining ps tog.

2d STRIP: Sew 1 Gold Block, 1 Green Block and 1 Gold Block tog. Sew 2 Strips tog exactly matching corners and ps.

EDGE: RND 1: With 2 cords Dk. Green, make a rnd of sc, putting 3 sc thru top lp of p at each corner. Fasten all other ps down with sc thru top lp into sc directly behind p.

RND 2: Make sl st in each sc around, join and fasten off. Stretch and pin Rug right-side-down in true shape on a padded table or on floor. Steam and press dry through a cloth.

## TV Cushion

JUTE-TONE: 4 tubes Dk. Green, 2 tubes Willow Green, and 7 tubes Spun Gold.

No. K Crochet Hook.

Foam rubber cushion, 18″×18″, 3″ or 4″ deep. Cloth or plastic material for bottom of cushion.

TOP: Make a No. 1—Block as for Rug.

EDGE: Repeat Rnd 1 of edge around Rug. If Block still does not measure 18″ when stretched, make a 2d rnd of sc, with 5 sc in each corner; join and fasten off.

SIDES: With 2 Cords Dk. Green, ch 7, sk 1 ch, sc in next 6 ch. (Ch 1, turn, sc in 6 sc) repeat for 18″. Join Willow Green through final sc, fasten off Dk. Green, (ch 1, turn, sc in 6 sc ) repeat for 18″. Join Dk. Green, fasten off Willow Green and make 18″. Join Gold, fasten off Dk. Green and make 18″.

EDGE: Ch 1, sc in same end sc, sc in each row across Gold section, join Dk. Green and work across next section, join Willow Green and work across 3d section, join Dk. Green and work across 4th section, fastening off each color in turn. Repeat on other side of Band.

Stretch and pin Block and Band right-side-down in true size. Steam and press dry through a cloth. Sew ends of Band tog, then sew Band to Block, using 1 cord of Dk. Green and going through 1 lp of each sc. Cut cloth or plastic to fit bottom of cushion. Sew to free edge of Band around 3 sides, insert cushion and complete closing.

# CHAPTER 7 *Knitting*

Knitting was at one time considered to be a manly accomplishment. Although women now regard the craft as almost exclusively their own, they are relative newcomers to it. During the Middle Ages in England in the years of the "Crafts and Guilds" a man worked six years to become a master-knitter. He served an apprenticeship under a qualified master, went abroad to learn foreign techniques, and returned to "sit" for an extremely difficult examination.

The machine age and the Industrial Revolution changed all of that and knitting was left to the women. In early America, women knit to provide warm clothing for the family and Knitting became a necessary occupation. Every stocking had to be knit at home by hand and even the children were obliged to help out. They often knew how to knit before they could read and carried their work to school and knit during recess periods.

Knitting is a simple technique, done for the most part on two needles, but it can fashion things of delicate beauty or of sturdy warmth and practicality for children and adults. Every girl should learn to knit because at some time in her life she is almost sure to find this skill to be useful either from a practical point of view or as an outlet for her creative energy.

## YARNS

There are many types of yarns and threads suitable for knitting although they vary as to size, twist, and texture. They also differ in fiber content and may be made of silk, wool, cotton, linen, or man-made fibers such as nylon, Orlon, Dacron, and others. A yarn may also be a combination of two or more fibers. The kind and size of yarn determines its use, and this must be taken into consideration when choosing a suitable yarn for the article to be made.

The size or ply of yarn to be used is usually given with the knitting instructions (novelty yarns excepted) and should be followed as closely as possible if the result is to be satisfactory. Only an expert knitter dares to make changes in size or type of yarn. Some yarns are interchangeable, but this must be carefully determined by knitting a swatch to check the gauge. Also be sure to buy all of the yarn needed for a garment at one time because dye lots differ.

## KNITTING NEEDLES

Knitting "pins" or needles vary in size and length and the proper ones are specified in the instructions. It is not advisable to change sizes unless necessary in order to obtain the proper gauge. (See "Gauge.")

### Straight Needles

These come in pairs. When using them the work is done in rows back and forth. Sizes are numbered—the larger the number, the coarser the needle.

### Circular Needles

These come in different sizes and in several lengths. The longest will hold enough stitches for a skirt width. They can also be used for smaller articles and in places where it is desirable to avoid a seam. They are usually used for knitting round and round instead of back and forth.

### Double-Pointed Needles

These come in sets of 4 or 5 and, as the name implies, are pointed at each end. They also are used to knit in rounds, especially for socks.

## GAUGE

Do not overlook the "Stitch Gauge" given at the beginning of each instruction. It is very important to the size and fit of your garment. It is always well to make a swatch at least 2 inches square with the yarn and needles specified. Block it, then measure. (See diagram.) The number of stitches to the inch and the number of rows to the inch should be the same as those given in the

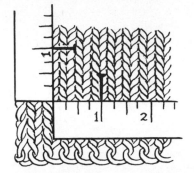

gauge of the instructions you are following. If this is not so, then it means that you are either a very loose or a very tight knitter and it may be necessary to change the size of the needles. The size of the needle does not matter as long as the stitch gauge is correct.

## ABBREVIATIONS

| | |
|---|---|
| k | knit |
| p | purl |
| inc | increase |
| dec | decrease |
| rnd | round |
| sl | slip |
| st(s) | stitch(es) |
| yo | yarn over |
| psso | pass slip stitch over knit stitch |
| tog | together |
| beg | beginning |
| dp | double pointed |
| pat | pattern |

\* This symbol (asterisk) means that the instructions immediately following it are to be repeated the given number of times.

A row is once across the needle. "Work even" means to work without increasing, keeping the pattern as is.

Abbreviations for crochet may be found in chapter on crochet.

# HOW TO KNIT

## Casting On (putting the first stitches onto the needle)

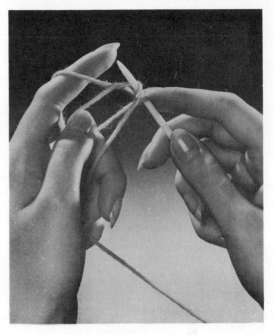

**Method 1 (With One Needle).** Make a slip knot, leaving a long end (allow 1 inch or a little less for each stitch), and slip needle into the loop.

*Slip the needle under the outside strand on the thumb, draw through the yarn attached to the ball slipping the thumb out of the loop.

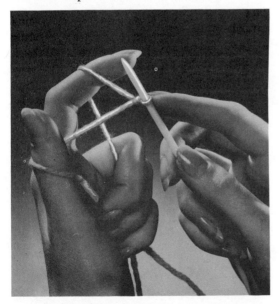

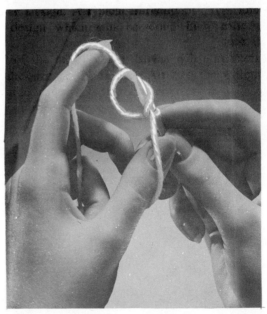

With the loose end make a loop over left thumb and with the strand attached to the ball make a loop over the left forefinger.

Immediately slip the thumb under yarn coming from front of needle and make another loop on the thumb while drawing up the stitch on the needle. Repeat from * for desired number of stitches.

**Method 2 (With Two Needles).** Make a slip knot on left needle. * Insert right needle into the loop from the front. Pass yarn around point of right needle and draw yarn through.

Slip this loop onto left needle, inserting the needle from right to left. Repeat from * for desired number of stitches keeping loops as even as possible.

## Plain Knitting or Garter Stitch

**What to Do with the Left Hand.** In the left hand, hold the needle with the stitches which you have just cast on. Hold the first stitch lightly with the index finger near the tip of the needle.

**What to Do with the Right Hand.** Hold the right needle between the thumb and the index finger as if you were holding a pencil. Place the yarn over the first finger, under the second, over the third, and under fourth above the middle joint. As you practice, you will learn to adjust the yarn to get the best results.

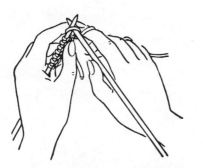

**First row.** 1. Bring your hands close together. Adjust the yarn and insert needle into the front of first stitch from the left side.

2. Steady the right needle against the forefinger of the left hand. Keep yarn to the back of your work.

3. With the right hand bring the yarn over the point of the right needle.

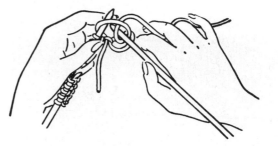

4. Draw the yarn through the stitch.

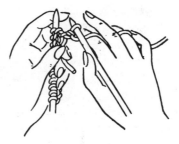

5. Slip the old stitch off the left needle, thus completing the first stitch. This starts a new row on the right needle. Always keep pushing your work up on the left needle so that the stitch on which you are working is near the tip.

Repeat steps 1 to 5 until all the stitches have been knitted off the left needle. Now you have knitted one row.

**Second and Succeeding Rows.** Change the needle with the stitches into the left hand.

With empty needle in right hand, slip yarn over fingers as before. When using a long needle many knitters tuck one end of the right needle under the right arm to relieve strain and speed up work.

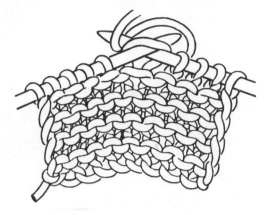

Insert right needle into front of first stitch on the left needle from the right side and slip the first stitch off and onto the right needle without knitting. Do this with the first stitch of each succeeding row and you will have a smooth edge known as chain edge.

**How to Bind Off.** Knit 2 stitches. * Slip the first stitch over the second (on right needle). Knit another stitch and repeat from * until desired number of stitches are bound off. If you are at the end of the row, break yarn and draw through last loop. Do not bind off too tightly.

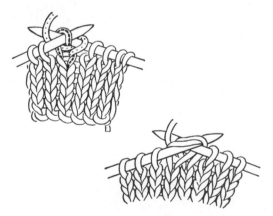

*Note:* This chain edge is not used in all cases; it makes a smooth edge on straight knitting. However, the closed edge produced by knitting every stitch is used when shaping various parts of a garment.

Bring yarn to the back of the work and proceed as before. Knit in this manner for a number of rows and you have garter stitch.

**To Increase.** Knit first into the front of the stitch, then into the back before slipping stitch from needle. This makes two stitches on right needle instead of one. To increase in purling, purl into the front, then into back of stitch.

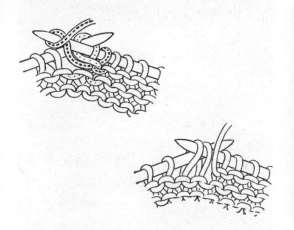

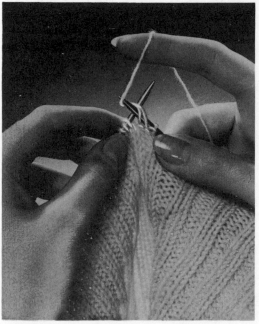

**To Decrease.** On a knit row, knit two stitches together. On a purl row, purl two stitches together. Another method used is to slip one stitch, knit one stitch, then pass the slipped stitch over the knit stitch on right needle as in binding off.

You should now be able to make the baby's surplice shown in baby section.

in plain knitting). **Pass** yarn around back of right needle from right to left and draw through loop backward, allowing stitch to slip off needle. Continue, keeping yarn in front of work.

**To Purl.** The needles are held in the same way as for plain knitting but the yarn is held in front of the work. Insert the right needle in the front of stitch on the left needle from *right* to *left* (instead of from the left side as

**Stockinette Stitch.** Knit across and purl back. Repeat these two rows. On circular or sock needles knit continuously to produce stockinette.

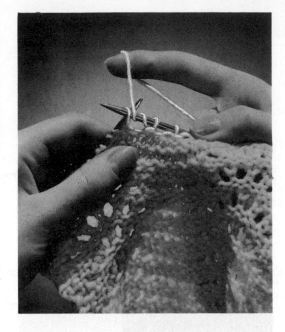

244

**Ribbing.** For a k 2 p 2 ribbing, cast on a multiple of 4 sts, then * k 2 sts, bring yarn forward and p 2 sts. Repeat from * across row and end with p 2. Turn work and repeat this row. In ribbing, when smooth side of stitch is toward you, the stitch is to be knitted; and when the rough side is toward you, the stitch is to be purled. There are other types of ribbing; the pattern depends upon changes in the number of k and p stitches.

**To Slip a Stitch.** Slip the stitch from the left to the right needle as for purling without knitting it.

Before a purl stitch, wrap yarn completely around right needle and purl the next stitch in the usual way. These "yarn overs" form holes and are used for open work patterns.

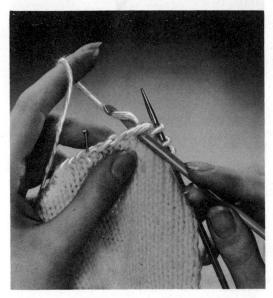

**Yarn Over.** Before a knit stitch, bring yarn in front of right needle and then knit the next stitch. This makes an extra stitch because a loop is formed on the right needle.

**To Pick up Stitches.** Stitches are most frequently picked up around neck and armholes. Divide and mark the space into quarters. Be sure to pick up ¼ of the total number of stitches in each space so work will look smooth. On an irregular edge insert needle into every row to avoid holes. With right side toward you, work from right to left. Hold free end of ball of yarn against back of garment with left hand until you get started. Insert crochet hook into first row in from edge and draw yarn through. Place stitch on knitting needle. Continue around. Stitches may also be picked up directly onto the knitting needle.

You should now be able to make any knitted article worked on 2 needles in stockinette stitch, garter stitch, and ribbing. Pattern stitches, unless very simple take a little more practice.

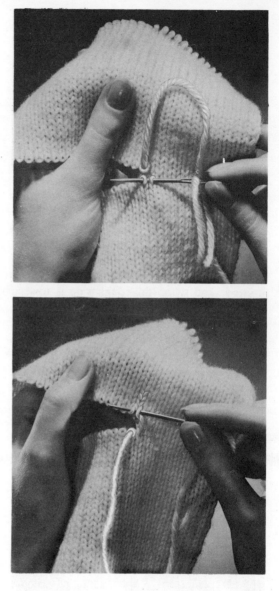

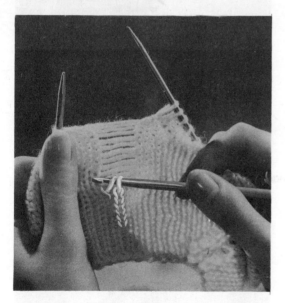

**Dropped Stitches.** In stockinette or ribbing, always pick up stitches with the knit side toward you. Insert a crochet hook in loop of dropped stitch; draw yarn of the row above through the loop. Continue until you reach the row on which you are working. Slip last loop onto needle. Do not twist stitches.

**To Weave Stockinette.** Use a wool needle (or any needle with blunt point) and the same yarn as the garment. Bring pieces to be joined close together. Fasten yarn on the under side at the right. Draw yarn from wrong side through first stitch on upper piece. Insert needle in first stitch on lower piece and bring through next stitch on lower piece from wrong side. Draw up yarn. * Insert needle in same stitch as before on upper piece and bring through next stitch on upper piece from wrong side. Draw up yarn. Insert needle from right side in same stitch as before on lower piece and draw through next stitch on lower piece from wrong side. Repeat from * until stitches are joined. Fasten yarn on wrong side.

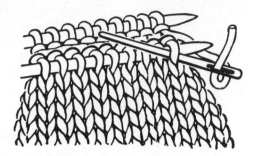

**Weaving Toes of Socks.** There must be an equal number of stitches on each of two needles. Break the yarn off from ball leaving a long length. Thread this into a wool needle. The knitting needles with the stitches are held even and parallel having the end of yarn coming from right at back of needle.

1. Insert the wool needle as if to purl in first stitch of front needle. Draw yarn through leaving stitch on needle.

2. Insert wool needle as if to knit into first stitch of back needle. Draw yarn through leaving stitch on needle.

3. Insert wool needle as if to knit in first stitch of front needle (same stitch as before) and slip the stitch off the needle. Insert needle in next stitch of front needle as if to purl; draw yarn through but leave stitch on needle.

4. Insert wool needle as if to purl in first stitch of back needle and slip this stitch off. Insert wool needle in next stitch of back needle as if to knit. Draw yarn through but leave stitch on needle.

5. Repeat steps 3 and 4 until all stitches are worked off.

Arrange the three needles in a triangle with free end of yarn on right-hand needle. Make certain that the stitches haven't become twisted. With fourth needle start working on the first needle. This is called joining.

**How to Knit with Four Needles.** This is round knitting and is usually used on socks. It is always worked in one direction. (See Casting On.) Using method number one, cast on one needle ⅓ the number of stitches required. Place another needle alongside of and a little forward of the first and cast on the second ⅓ of stitches. Repeat on third needle.

**How to Knit with Circular Needle.** Cast on the desired number of stitches using one or both points of the needle. Lay the needle on a flat surface and make sure the cast-on edge is not twisted. Insert point of right needle (yarn from ball is attached at left needle) into first stitch of left side and begin to knit. In working on a circular needle, continue in one direction. This forms stockinette stitch.

**Knots.** Whenever possible have knots come at the end of a row. If not possible, leave 3- or 4-inch ends on both pieces but do not make a knot. After several rows of knitting these ends can be tied firmly.

**Raveling Stitches.** Rip the last row stitch by stitch and place each stitch on a fine needle. Knit these onto the needle you are using.

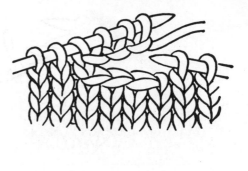

**Markers.** Instructions sometimes say to slip a marker on the needle. A small safety pin or a loop of yarn made with a slip knot and of contrasting color may be used. Slip onto right needle and on next row slip from one needle to the other.

There are many small knitting aids available such as stitch holders, counters, bobbins for holding the various shades of yarn in multicolor knitting. These are usually made of plastic and are sold in needlework departments and yarn shops.

## Buttonholes

Bind off the given number of stitches (to fit size of button desired). Cast on the same number of stitches on next row directly over the bound-off stitches. Work around holes with buttonhole stitch.

Girls' and women's cardigans can be faced with grosgrain ribbon down each side of front. Mark for buttonholes and machine-stitch around markings. Cut through for buttonholes and work buttonhole stitch around opening. Sew buttons on left side. Or make machine-made buttonholes through the grosgrain. These are usually done vertically.

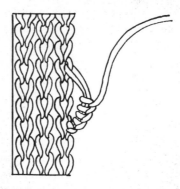

**Loop Buttonholes.** Mark spaces at edge of opening for placing buttonholes. Thread needle with yarn and make a loop of 2 strands of yarn long enough to admit button. Work buttonhole st over the loop.

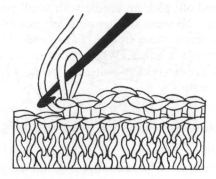

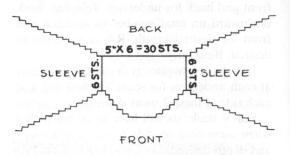

**Crocheted Buttonholes.** Sometimes used on edges which are finished with single crochet. Mark spaces. Work in sc to marking. Chain st for number of sts required for the button. Skip this space on the edge and work sc to the next mark. Buttonholes may also be made in the center of a wide crocheted band in the same way, by working rows of sc before and after making buttonholes.

## Knit-in Raglan Sleeve on Slip-on Sweater

For this type of sweater you begin at the neck and work down. The following method tells you how to arrive at the number of stitches to be cast on.

Measure the width at the back of the neck (we will assume it is 5 inches), and allow 1 inch for each sleeve top. This makes 7 inches; multiply this by the number of stitches per inch of your gauge (we will assume it is 6). This makes 42 sts. Now add 4 seam sts, 8 sts for raglan increasing, and 1 st for each side of front. This makes 56 sts in all. This total will vary with the width at the back of neck and the gauge.

Cast stitches on circular needle. Mark the seam sts. Work back and forth, increasing on each side of the seam sts at the beginning and end of every alternate row (every knit row). At the same time shape neck as follows: For a round neck increase 1 st at beg and end of every second k row 7 times (or as desired). Then cast on the number of sts required to complete neck (straight across front, see diagram). The number of sts for front must equal or exceed number of sts in back section. For example: if there are 58 sts in back and 20 sts in each front section, cast on 18 sts. Join and work round and round as in plain knitting. At the same time continue to inc before and after each of four seam sts every other round until raglan seam is the required length (to reach to underarm plus "ease") and the front and back are wide enough.

Now place front, back, and one sleeve on stitch holders and work on one sleeve only.

To sleeve sts add ½ inch each side for underarm and work downward decreasing as necessary for width and length of sleeve desired. Work second sleeve in same manner.

To body sts add ½ inch on each side of front and back for underarm. Join and work downward on total number of sts back and front for desired length. Rib at waistline as desired. Bind off.

If a shaped sweater is desired, select 2 sts at each underarm for seam line and dec 1 st each side of these 2 sts as desired.

For V neck, sts will have to be calculated when increasing on side fronts to get shape and depth desired.

For cardigan, divide measurements of front in half and add 1 inch to each side of center front for lap. Cardigans may have round or V neck.

## Set-in Pocket

Knit the body of the sweater to proper placement of pocket. Bind off number of stitches desired for width of pocket. Knit to end of row. Drop this piece temporarily. On separate needles, cast on same number of stitches as were bound off for pocket and knit for desired depth of pocket. Be sure to end piece on the same row as stitches of body of sweater were bound off. Drop this piece of work. Pick up body of sweater. Knit across row as far as space made by stitches

bound off; pick up needle with small pocket piece, slip these stitches onto left needle and knit across these stitches and to end of row. Continue knitting. When garment is completed, sew pocket lining to wrong side of garment.

## How to Turn the Heel on a Sock

When it is time to make the heel, the stitches must be rearranged on the needles. The directions tell how many stitches to place on each needle.

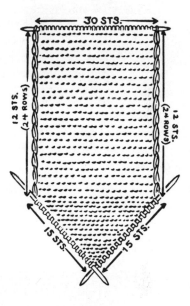

For example: if you are working with 60 sts, place 30 sts on the heel needle and 15 sts on the other two needles. These two needles are left idle while a heel flap is made on the 30 sts. Work straight for 24 rows. (For longer wear nylon yarn may be substituted for the heel part or a thread of matching nylon sewing thread may be knitted in with the yarn.) For extra strength the heel is knitted in alternate rows as follows:

Row 1: P across. Row 2: * Sl 1, k 1, repeat from * across. Work for the number of rows (or inches) indicated in the directions—depending upon size of socks. Now this heel portion must be brought into position to make it possible to knit on three needles

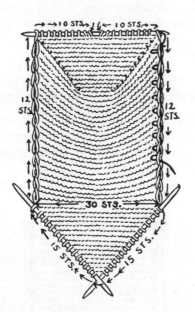

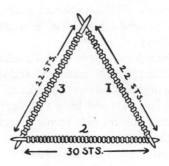

again. This shaping is achieved by a series of decreases on each side of work. This is called "turning the heel."

When shaping is completed, there are 20 sts on the needle (or as many as size indicates). Now pick up side sts according to directions and resume work on 3 needles. Pick up the inside loop of stitches at side of heel.

## PATTERN STITCHES

### Moss, Seed, or Rice Stitch

To make an even slant in opposite directions two kinds of decreases must be used. When working on the wrong side, dec by purling 2 tog. When working on the right side, decrease with sl 1, k 1, psso.

Cast on an uneven number of sts. Row 1: * K 1 st, p 1 st, repeat from * across row ending with k 1. Repeat this row. Always be sure to k above the p sts and p above the k sts of the preceding row.

## Simple Rib Stitch

Cast on a multiple of 7 sts plus 2. Row 1: * P 2, k 5, repeat from * across row and end with p 2. Row 2: * K 2, p 5, repeat from * across row and end k 2. Repeat these 2 rows.

## Oblique Rib Stitch

Cast on a multiple of 7 sts plus 2. Row 1: * P 2, k 5, repeat from * across row and end with p 2. Row 2: K 3, p 4, repeat from * across row and end with k 2. Row 3: * P 2, k 3, p 1, k 1, repeat from * across row and end with p 2. Row 4: * K 2, p 2, k 1, p 2, repeat from * across row and end with k 2.

Row 5: * P 2, k 1, p 1, k 3, repeat from * across row and end with p 2. Row 6: K 2, * p 4, k 3, repeat from * across row and end k 3. Repeat these 6 rows.

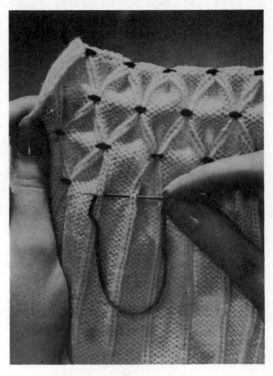

## Smocked Ribbing

This is done on a simple rib pattern of k 5, p 1. The p 5, k 1 side is the right side of the garment. Thread a blunt-end needle with contrasting yarn. * Working from left to right and following the same row of knitting across, * bring needle from wrong side to the left of the first k st; insert needle from right to left under k st of next rib and under the first k st. Draw up. Work another stitch in the same place. Bring needle to wrong side at right of stitches just made. Bring needle out at left of k st on next rib. Do not draw up. Repeat from * across. Skip about 8 rows of knitting. On the next row, pick up alternate ribs and work across to form diamonds or "honeycomb" smocking. This may be worked on other types of ribbing and spacing can be varied.

252

## Block Stitch

Cast on a multiple of 10 sts. Row 1: * K 5, p 5, repeat from * across row and end with p 5. Repeat row 1 for 6 rows. Row 7: * P 5, k 5, repeat from * across row and end k 5. Repeat row 7 for 6 rows. Repeat these 12 rows to make pattern.

## Diagonal Rib Stitch

Cast on a multiple of 8 sts. Row 1: * K 4, p 4, repeat from * across row and end p 4. Row 2: P 1, * k 4, p 4, repeat from * across row and end p 3. Row 3: K 2, * p 4, k 4, repeat from * across row and end k 2. Row 4: P 3, * k 4, p 4, repeat from * and end p 1. Row 5: * P 4, k 4, repeat from * across row and end k 4. Row 6: K 1, * p 4, k 4, repeat from * across row and end k 3. Row 7: P 2, * k 4, p 4, repeat from * across row and end p 2. Row 8: K 3 * p 4, k 4, repeat from * across row and end k 1. Repeat these 8 rows for the pattern. *Note:* In forming a diagonal rib pattern any number of k and p sts can be used and the bias effect attained by moving the k and p st one st to the right on one side and one st to the left on reverse side.

## Diamond Stitch

Cast on a multiple of 8 sts plus one. Row 1: K 4, * p 1, k 7, repeat from * across row p 1, k 4. Row 2: P 3, * k 1, p 1, k 1, p 5, repeat from * across row and end p 3. Row 3: K 2, * p 1, k 3, repeat from * across row and end k 2. Row 4: * P 1, k 1, p 5, k 1, repeat from * across row and end p 1. Row 5: * P 1, k 7, repeat from * and end row p 1. Row 6: Same as row 4. Row 7: Same as row 3. Row 8: Same as row 2. Repeat these 8 rows for pattern.

## Chevron Stitch

Cast on a multiple of 4 sts plus 2. Row 1: (right side) * K 2, yarn forward sl 2 sts, yarn back. Repeat from * across row and end k 2. Row 2: P 1, * yarn back (when sts are slipped on wrong side, the yarn must always be on k side), sl 2 sts, yard forward, p 2. Repeat from * across row and end p 3. Row 3: * Yarn forward, sl 2 sts, yarn back, k 2. Repeat from * across row and end yarn forward, sl 2 sts. Row 4: P 3, * yarn back, sl 2 sts, yarn forward, p 2. Repeat from * across row and end p 1. Repeat these 4 rows twice (12 rows in all); then shift pattern to produce slant effect in opposite direction as follows: Change to contrasting color. Row 1: * With yarn forward, slip 2 sts, yarn back, k 2. Repeat from * across row and end with sl 2 sts. Row 2: P 1, * yarn back, sl 2 sts, yarn forward, p 2. Repeat from * across row and end p 3. Row 3: K 2, * yarn forward,

sl 2 sts, yarn back, k 2. Repeat from * across row and end k 2. Row 4: P 3, * yarn back, sl 2 sts, yarn forward, p 2. Repeat from * across row and end p 1. Repeat these last 4 rows twice (12 rows in all). Repeat these 24 rows for pattern.

## Mock Cable

Cast on a multiple of 6 sts plus 3. Row 1: * P 3 and k 3. Repeat from * across row and end p 3. Row 2: * K 3 and p 3. Repeat from * across row and end k 3. Row 3: * P 3, k into third st on needle and leave on needle, k into first st on needle then k into second st on needle, drop 3 sts off left needle. Repeat from * across row and end p 3. Row 4: Same as row 2. Repeat these 4 rows for pattern.

## Simple Cable

Cast on a multiple of 14 sts. Rows 1, 4, 5, 7, and 9: K 2, * p 10, k 4, repeat from *

across row and end with k 2. Rows 2, 4, 6, and 8: P 2, * k 10, p 4, repeat from * across row and end p 2. Row 10: P 2, * slip next 5 sts onto double-pointed needle and place in back of work, k next 5 sts, then k 5 sts from double-pointed needle, p 4, repeat from * across row and end p 2. Repeat these 10 rows for pattern.

### Plaited Cable

Cast on a multiple of 14 sts plus 1. Rows 1 and 3: * P 1, k 2, p 9, k 2, repeat from * across row and end k 2, p 1. Row 2: * K 1, p 2, k 9, p 2, repeat from * across row and end p 2, k 1. Row 4: * K 1, p 2, slip next 3 sts onto double-pointed needle and place in front of work, k next 3 sts, then k 3 sts from double-pointed needle, k 3, p 2, repeat from * across row and end k 3, p 2, k 1. Rows 5 and 7: Same as row 1. Row 6 same as row 2. Row 8: * K 1, p 2, k 3, slip next 3 sts onto double-pointed needle and place in back of work, k next 3 sts, then k 3 sts from double-pointed needle, p 2, repeat from * across row and end p 2, k 1. Repeat these 8 rows for pattern st.

## Lattice Cable

Cast on a multiple of 4 sts plus 2. Rows 1, 3, 5, and 7: * K 2, p 2, repeat from * across row and end k 2. Rows 2, 4, and 6: * P 2, k 2, repeat from * across row and end p 2. Row 8: * P 2, slip next 4 sts onto double-pointed needle and place in back of work, K 2 from left needle, slip 2 p sts from double-pointed needle, repeat from * across row and end p 2. Rows 9, 11, 13, and 15: Same as row 1. Rows 10, 12, and 14: Same as row 2. Row 16: P 2, k 2, * p 2, slip 4 sts onto double-pointed needle and place in front of work, k 2 from left needle, slip 2 p sts from double-pointed needle to left needle and p these 2 sts, k 2 from double-pointed needle, repeat from * across row and end p 2. Repeat these 16 rows for pattern.

## Lace Stitch with Pointed Border

Cast on a multiple of 13 sts, plus 1. Row 1: P across. Row 2: * K 1, yo, k 4, k 2 tog twice, k 4, yo. Repeat from * across row, end with k 1. Repeat these two rows for pattern.

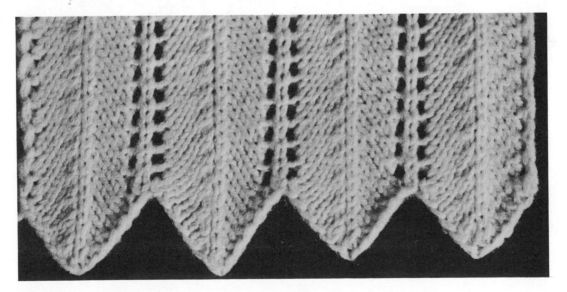

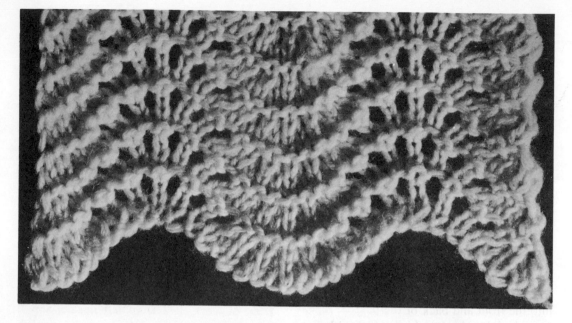

## Lace Stitch with Scalloped Border

## Medallion Lace Stitch

Cast on a multiple of 18 sts. Row 1: K across. Row 2: P across. Row 3: K 2 tog 3 times, * (yo and k 1 for 6 times), k 2 tog 6 times, repeat from * across row and end k 2 tog 3 times. Row 4: K across. Repeat these 4 rows for pattern.

Cast on a multiple of 8 sts plus 2. Row 1: K 1, p 3, * k 2, p 6, repeat from * across row and end k 2, p 3, k 1. Row 2: K 4, p 2, * k 6, p 2, repeat from * across row and end k 4. Row 3: Same as row 1. Row 4: Same as row 2. Row 5: K 1, p 2, * k 2 tog, yo,

slip 1, k 1, psso, p 4, repeat from * across row and end k 2 tog, yo, slip 1, k 1, psso, p 3. Row 6: K 3, * p 1, k into back of next st, then k into the front of the same st, p 1, k 4, repeat from * across row and end k 3. Row 7: K 1, p 1, * k 2 tog, yo, k 2, yo, slip 1, k 1, psso, p 2, repeat from * across row and end p 2. Row 8: K 2, * p 6, k 2, repeat from * across row and end k 2. Row 9: K 1, * k 2 tog, yo, k 2 tog, yo, slip 1, k 1, psso, yo, slip 1, k 1, psso, repeat from * across row and end k 1. Row 10: K 1, p 3, * k into the front and back on the next st, p 6, repeat from * to last 5 sts, then k into the front and back of the next st, p 4. Row 11: K 1, * yo, slip 1, k 1, psso, yo, slip 1, k 1, psso, k 2 tog, yo, k 2 tog, repeat from * and end yo, k 1. Row 12: K 1, k into back of next st, * p 6, k into the front and back of the next st, repeat from * and end k into back of next st, k 1. Row 13: K 1, p 1, * yo, slip 1, k 2 tog, psso, yo, k 3 tog, wrap yarn all the way around needle, p 2. Row 14: K 2, * k into back of next st, p 1, k into the front and back of the next st, p 1, k into back of next st, k 2, repeat from * across row and end k 2. Row 15: K 1, p 2, * yo, slip 1, k 1, psso, k 2 tog, wrap yarn around needle, p 4, repeat from * across row and end p 2, k 1. Row 16: K 3, * k into back of next st, p 2, k into back of next st, k 4, repeat from * and end k 3. Repeat the last 14 rows (rows 3 to 16 inclusive) for pattern.

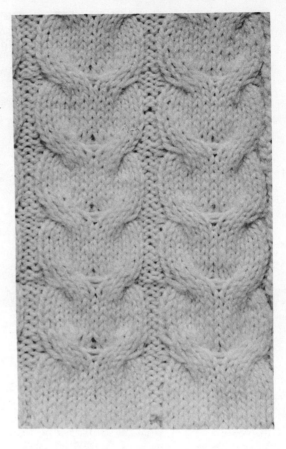

dp needle; sl next 3 sts on dp needle and hold in front of work, k next 3 sts, k sts from dp needle, p 3, repeat from * across. Repeat these 12 rows for pattern.

## Chain Cable

Cast on a multiple of 15 sts plus 3 sts. Row 1 (wrong side): K 3, * p 12, k 3, repeat from * across. Row 2: P 3, * k 12, p 3, repeat from * across. Rows 3 through 11: Repeat Rows 1 and 2. Row 12 (right side): P 3, * sl next 3 sts on dp needle and hold in back of work, k next 3 sts, k sts from

## Woven Stitch

Cast on an uneven number of sts. Row 1 (right side): Sl 1, k 1, * put right needle behind left needle and k the 2nd st on left needle as usual, but do not slip it off the needle; bring needle to front and k first st on left needle, slipping the 2 sts off left needle (4 sts on right needle), repeat from * across,

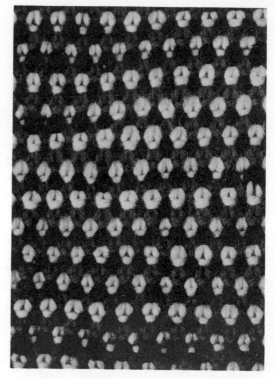

k last st. Row 2: Sl 1, p 1, * put right needle in front of next st, p 2nd st, leaving it on the left needle, p the first st on left needle, sl the 2 sts off left needle, repeat from * to within last st, p 1. Repeat these 2 rows for pattern.

**Popcorn Stitch**

### Tri-Color Stitch

Cast on an even number of sts. Use 3 colors—indicated by A, B, and C. Row 1: With B, * k 1, bring yarn to front of work and sl 1, repeat from * to end of row. Row 2: With C, * p 1, hold yarn in back of work and sl 1, repeat from * to end of row. Repeat these 2 rows for pat, working 1 row each of A, B, and C alternately.

Cast on a multiple of 4 sts. Row 1 (right side): Purl. Row 2: * K, p and k in next st (3 sts made in 1 st), sl 1, k 2 tog, psso, repeat from * to end of row. Row 3: Purl. Row 4: * Sl 1, k 2 tog, psso; k, p and k in next st (3 sts made in 1 st), repeat from * to end of row. Repeat these 4 rows for pattern.

### Knitting Patterns in Colors

Known as Scandinavian or Fair Isle Knitting. Certain patterns are typical of certain countries.

There are two methods of carrying the yarn across the wrong side of the work.

Method 1: When the spaces between where the color occurs in the design are not more than 4 sts wide, the yarn not in use is carried loosely across the back. Try to keep it the same tension as the knitting, never taut. Method 2: When the spaces are more than 4 sts, the colors should be caught in by twisting around the yarn being used. Hold the thread you are carrying in the left hand. K 1 st in the usual manner but before catching

thread to k, be sure yarn is over the yarn you are carrying. Break the yarn only when you are finished with that color. Leave an end 4 or 5 inches long on the back to be fastened in later with a sewing needle. In this type of knitting it is possible to work designs from cross stitch patterns. You can design your own on graph paper using symbols to represent different colors. It is well to have the colors in quite strong contrast.

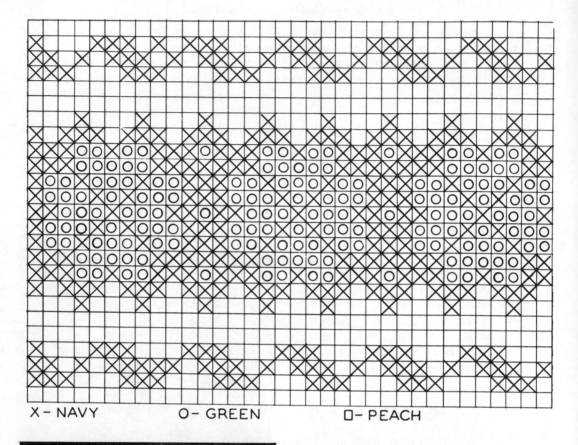

X – NAVY      O – GREEN      □ – PEACH

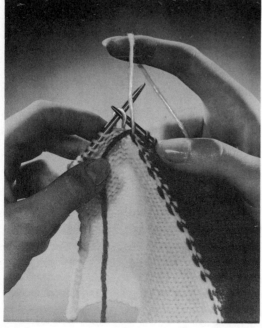

## Changing Colors in Knitting

When working with 2 or more colors for wide spaces, always be sure to twist the colors to prevent holes.

# BODY MEASUREMENT CHARTS

## Infants and Children (boys and girls)

| Size | 6 mo | 1 | 2 | 3 | 4 | 5 | 6 | 7 | 8 | 10 | 12 | 14 |
|------|------|---|---|---|---|---|---|---|---|----|----|----|
| Chest | 19 | 20 | 21 | 22 | 23 | 23½ | 24 | 25 | 26 | 28 | 30 | 32 |
| Waist | 19 | 19½ | 20 | 20½ | 21 | 21½ | 22 | 22½ | 23 | 24 | 25 | 26 |
| Hip | | | | | | 25 | 26 | 27 | 28 | 30 | 32½ | 35 |
| Back Waist Length | | | | | | | | 11 | 11½ | 12½ | 13 | 13¾ |
| Sleeve Length | 6 | 7 | 8 | 8¾ | 9½ | 10¾ | 11 | 11½ | 12 | 13½ | 14½ | 16 |

## Misses and Women

| Size | 10 | 12 | 14 | 16 | 18 | 20 | 40 | 42 |
|------|----|----|----|----|----|----|----|----|
| Bust | 31 | 32 | 34 | 36 | 38 | 40 | 42 | 44 |
| Waist | 24 | 25 | 26 | 28 | 30 | 32 | 34 | 36 |
| Hip | 33 | 34 | 36 | 38 | 40 | 42 | 44 | 46 |
| Back Waist Length | 15¾ | 16 | 16¼ | 16½ | 16¾ | 17 | 17⅛ | 17¼ |
| Sleeve Length | 16¼ | 16½ | 17 | 17½ | 18 | 18 | 18 | 18 |

## Men

| Chest | 32 | 34 | 36 | 38 | 40 | 42 | 44 |
|-------|----|----|----|----|----|----|----|
| Waist | 28 | 30 | 32 | 34 | 36 | 38 | 40 |

## Women's Half Sizes

| Size | 12½ | 14½ | 16½ | 18½ | 20½ | 22½ |
|------|-----|-----|-----|-----|-----|-----|
| Bust | 33 | 35 | 37 | 39 | 41 | 43 |
| Waist | 27 | 29 | 31 | 33 | 35 | 37 |
| Hip | 37 | 39 | 41 | 43 | 45 | 47 |
| Back Waist Length | 15¼ | 15½ | 15¾ | 16 | 16¼ | 16½ |

## To Change Instructions for Individual Measurements

Take the measurements of the individual accurately. See measurement chart to find which measurements to take and to decide which size to follow in the directions. Knitted garments, like other wearing apparel, are made with a certain amount of "ease"; that is, somewhat larger than actual body measurements. This varies with personal taste and also with the type of garment. For example, an evening top should fit more snugly than a ski sweater.

Instructions in this book are given with "ease" allowed for each size. When changing instructions for sizes not given here, compare the measurements you have taken with those given in the instructions and add or deduct the number of stitches equal to the difference in measurements. If the instructions are for a pattern stitch, be sure the number of stitches you are going to use is a multiple of this pattern stitch.

# FINISHING HAND-KNITS

## Blocking

Blocking must be done properly and before the seams are sewed up in order to achieve a professional-looking job. Block each piece separately using rust-proof pins. Place the pieces on a flat padded surface or pressing board wrong side up. Pin all edges, stretching to the blocking measurements given with the instructions. Use plenty of pins, placing them close together to avoid scalloped edges.

Place a damp cloth over the piece and press *lightly* with a moderately hot iron, allowing the steam to go through garment. Leave until thoroughly dry. A skirt knit on the round may be blocked double or on a skirt blocker. Do not stretch or press ribbing but steam lightly.

## Sewing Seams

Place right sides of pieces together and pin matching the pattern, if any. Beginning at bottom, sew ¼ inch from edge with back stitches. Do not draw stitches too tight. Press seams open.

If the garment has shoulder seams, reinforce them with seam binding to prevent stretching. Pin tape flat along seam on wrong side and sew to garment with invisible hemming stitches using matching mercerized thread.

When sewing in sleeve, pin sleeve seam at underarm and center top of sleeve at shoulder seam. Ease in fulness.

## Laundering

Use mild soap and lukewarm water. Squeeze suds through until garment is thoroughly clean. Handle carefully; do not stretch. Rinse thoroughly in several warm waters. Squeeze, do not wring. Place on a clean bath towel; roll tightly to absorb moisture. Do not hang garment but leave flat on towel to dry. Block to measurements. Special soaps are available for washing woolens.

## Casing for Top of Skirt

This is best done with crochet. With right side toward you, work several rows of sc around top of skirt. With wrong side toward you, work 1 sc in first st of first round of sc, * ch 5, skip 5 sts on last round and work 1 sc in the sixth st. Ch 5, skip 5 sts on first round and work 1 sc in sixth st. Repeat from * around. End with sl st in first sc. Skip more or less sts to produce an even beading.

## Duplicate Stitch

# KNITTING FOR THE HOME AND FAMILY

## Baby's Surplice for Beginners

Follow the chart for placing sts according to design. Thread a tapestry needle with yarn and fasten on the wrong side of work. * Insert the needle from the back and bring thread through to right side of work in the center of a stitch. Slip the needle under the 2 strands of the st above as shown and draw thread through. Now insert needle in center where it came out and draw through to wrong side. Repeat from *.

## HOME KNITTING MACHINES

Many different makes of home knitting machines are now available. They vary somewhat in the number of needles (width of knitting space), automatic devices for the different knitting processes, size, and ease in handling. Before purchasing, it is well to investigate several to find the one that suits your needs best.

Most of the machines will accommodate a number of kinds and weights of yarn and do a variety of stitches (but not all that can be done by hand). After developing skill in using a knitting machine, it is possible to make many types of garments and other articles such as afghans, stoles, scarves, etc.

**Materials.** Jumbo Pompadour 3 ozs. Knitting Needles No. 7. Plastic Crochet Hook, Size 3.

**Gauge.** 5 sts—1".

*Directions.* Cast on 45 sts for lower edge of back. Work even in garter st until 6" from beg or desired length to underarm. Cast on 30 sts at beg of each of next 2 rows for sleeves—105 sts. Work even until sleeve edge measures 3". Next row, k 44 sts, slip these sts on a holder; bind off 17 sts for back of neck; k 44 sts. Work even on 44 sts for 1", ending at neck edge. Inc 1 st at neck edge on next row, repeat inc every 2nd row 6 times, then every row until sleeve measures 7" from beg, ending at sleeve edge. Bind off 30 sts beg next row, inc 1 st at end. Continue increasing at neck edge every row until there are 45 sts on needle. Work even until front measures same as back. Bind off. Beg at neck edge, work other side to correspond, reversing shaping.

**Finishing.** Sew underarm and side seams. From right side, work 1 row sc around front and neck edge. Work 1 row sc around sleeve edges. Block. Ribbon Ties: Sew ribbon at top and bottom of even edge of each front and at corresponding places at underarm seams.

**Kitten Bonnet and Bootees**

**Materials.** Baby Wool (1 oz. Skeins): 1 skein of White and small amount of Baby Pink. Knitting Needles: 1 pair each No. 0 and No. 2. Steel Crochet Hook No. 2.

**Gauge.** 8 sts—1". 11 rows—1".

**Bonnet.** Starting at front edge with baby pink and No. 0 needles, cast on 88 sts. Work in stockinette st (k 1 row, p 1 row) for 6 rows. Change to white and No. 2 needles and continue in stockinette st until piece measures 4½ inches in all, ending with a p row.

TO SHAPE BACK: Row 1: * K 2 tog, k 9. Repeat from * across. Row 2: P. Row 3: * K 2 tog, k 8. Repeat from * across. Row 4: P. Row 5: * K 2 tog, k 7. Repeat from * across. Continue to dec 8 sts evenly on each k row in this manner, having 1 st less before decs on each dec row, until 16 sts remain. P next row, then k 2 tog across. Leaving 12-inch end, break yarn. Draw end through remaining sts, fasten tightly, then sew back seam to within 3¾ inches of front edge. With white and right side facing, work 1 row single crochet around neck opening. Press through a damp cloth, allowing first 4 rows to roll back against front of bonnet. Ears: With white and No. 2 needles, cast on 18 sts. Row 1: K. Row 2: P. Row 3: K 1, k 2 tog, k to last 3 sts, k 2 tog, k 1. Repeat Rows 2 and 3 until 6 sts remain. P next row; turn, k 1, k 2 tog twice, k 1, turn; p 2 tog twice, turn; k 2 tog. Break yarn and fasten off.

EAR LININGS: Using pink, make same as ears. Sew lining to ears, purl sides together. Sew ears to bonnet, 3½ inches apart and 2 inches from front edge, cupping them forward.

TIES: Cut 3 strands of pink, each 24 inches long, knot together at one end and twist tightly in one direction until they buckle, then fold in half and twist in opposite direction and tie end. Make a small loop at tied end and sew to corner of bonnet. Make 2.

**Bootees.** Starting at top with pink, cast on 48 sts. Work in stockinette st for 6 rows. Change to white and continue in stockinette st for 1¾ inches, ending with a p row.

BEADING ROW: K 3, * yo, k 2 tog. Repeat from * to last 3 sts, yo, k 2 tog. k 1, p 1 row.

TO SHAPE INSTEP: K 32, turn, p 16, turn. Work back and forth on center 16 sts for 1½ inches, ending with a p row. Break yarn. With right side facing you, slip first 16 sts on left-hand needle. Attach pink and k first 16 sts, pick up and k 12 sts along side of instep, k instep sts, pick up and k 12 sts along other side of instep, k last 16 sts, k next row on wrong side (72 sts). Work in stockinette st for ¾ inch, ending with a p row.

TO SHAPE SOLE: Row 1: * K 1, k 2 tog, k 30, sl 1, k 1, psso, k 1; slip a marker on needle. Repeat from * once more. Row 2: P. Row 3: * K 1, k 2 tog, k to within 3 sts of marker, sl 1, k 1, psso, k 1. Repeat from * once more. Repeat Rows 2 and 3 twice. Bind off remaining sts. Sew sole and back seams. Block, allowing top to roll over.

CORDS: Cut 3 strands pink each 40 inches long. Make same as bonnet ties and run cords through beading. Make two.

## Four-Piece Knitted Baby Set

Directions are for size 6 months to 1 year.

**Materials.** Orlon or Fingering Yarn 3 ply—5 ozs., Baby Pink. Knitting Needles Nos. 1 and 2. 2 Stitch Holders. 1 Double-Pointed Needle No. 2. Steel Crochet Hook No. 3. 4 Buttons; 1½ yds. ¾" Ribbon; 2 yds. narrow Ribbon.

**Gauge.** 8 sts—1".

**Sacque.** RIGHT FRONT: With No. 2 needles cast on 55 sts and work in garter st for 7 rows. Next row p to within 4 sts from end. K 4 for border. Work these 4 sts in garter st for front border. Work in stockinette st until piece measures 5½" ending with a p row.

Start pattern: Row 1: K 4 sts for border, then k 5, * with yarn in front of work slip next 5 sts to right-hand needle (slip as if to p), k 3, repeat from * across ending with k 1.

Row 2 and all even rows: Purl, working 4 sts of border in garter st. Rows 3 and 5: Repeat Row 1. Row 7: K 4 sts for border, k 7, * insert right-hand needle under 3 loops of the 3 slipped rows, k into next st on left-hand needle knitting the loops and st tog, k 7, repeat from * across ending k 3. Row 9: K 4 sts for border, k 1, * with yarn in front of work, slip 5 sts, yarn in back of work, k 3, repeat from * across ending k 5. Rows 11 and 13: Same as Row 9. Row 15: K 4 sts for border, k 3, * insert needle under 3 loops of the 3 slipped rows, k into next st. knitting loops and st tog, k 7, repeat from * to end of row.

SHAPE ARMHOLE: At arm edge bind off 5 sts. Dec 1 st at arm edge every row 2 times. Work even in pat until armhole measures 2½" from last dec of underarm ending with last row of pat. Shape Neck: At front edge bind off 16 sts. Work 8 rows even. Dec 1 st at neck edge every other row 4 times. Work even on 28 sts for 7 rows. Sl sts on holder.

LEFT FRONT: Work to correspond to right front for 5½", reversing the 4 border sts ending with a p row. Next row: Start pat: K 1, * sl 5, k 3, repeat from * across ending k 9. Last 4 sts are for border. Complete to correspond to right front.

BACK: Cast on 25 sts for back of neck, cut

yarn. Join to right front by picking up sts from holder to same needle, join yarn and p across row (81) sts. Keeping pat uniform, work in pat until 4 pat have been worked from the 25 cast on sts of neck ending with last row of pat. Inc 1 st each end every other row 4 times. Cast on 5 sts beg of next 2 rows. Work 13 more rows in pat, then work in stockinette st until same length as fronts ending with border same as fronts. Bind off.

SLEEVES: Cast on 49 sts and work in garter st (K each row) for 7 rows. Row 8: K 1, * sl 5, k 3, repeat from * across row. Continue in pattern same as Sacque for 15 more rows. Work in stockinette st until sleeve measures 6″ from start. Shape Cap; Bind off 5 sts at beg of next 2 rows. Work 1 row even. Next row: Dec 1 st each end of row. Repeat last 2 rows until 19 sts remain. Bind off.

FINISHING: Block. Sew seams and set in sleeves. Neckband: With right side toward you and using No. 1 needles, pick up 70 sts around neck edge, k 6 rows. Bind off. Crocheted Edge Trim: With right side of work toward you, join yarn at left side of neck edge, * ch 3 and working down left front, 1 sl st in each of the next 3 ridges, repeat from * down front, * ch 3, and working across lower edge, 1 sl st in each of the next 3 sts, repeat from * across lower edge, work up right front same as left front and work around neck edge same as lower edge, join, cut yarn. Work edge trim on sleeves in same manner. Sew buttons in place.

**Cap.** With No. 2 needles, cast on 17 sts. Work in stockinette st for 7 rows. On the next row inc 1 st each end and repeat this inc every 7th row until there are 29 sts. Work even until piece measures 4″. Cast on 30 sts at beg of next 2 rows—89 sts. Pattern: Row 1: K 2, * sl 5, k 3, repeat from * ending k 2. Continue in pat until cap measures 9¾″ from start, ending with a p row. Work in garter st for 8 rows. Bind off.

FINISHING: Block. With wrong side facing you, work edge trim on bound off sts. Sew sides. Turn back garter st border. With No.

1 needles, pick up 40 sts along side of cap, 16 sts across back and 40 sts along other side. K the next row dec at even intervals to 83 sts. Work in garter st for 5 rows. Bind off. Crochet edge trim around neck edge. Sew ribbons in place as shown.

**Bootees.** With No. 2 needles, cast on 41 sts. Work in garter st for 7 rows. Pattern: K 2, * sl 5, k 3, repeat from * ending k 2. Continue in pat for 15 rows. Work in stockinette st until piece measures 2½″ from start, ending with a p row. Beading: K 1, * yo, k 2 tog, repeat from * across. Work in stockinette st for 3 rows. Divide for Foot: K 14 sts and slip them on a holder; k 13 sts for instep; slip remaining 14 sts on another holder. Work in stockinette st on instep sts for 2″, ending with a p row. Slip these sts on a dp needle. Slip 14 sts from first holder onto needle, pick up 11 sts along side of instep, k 13 sts of instep, pick up 11 sts along other side of instep, k 14 sts from other holder. Work in garter st on 63 sts for 10 rows. K the next row dec 4 sts at even intervals. K 3 rows. Dec 1 st in center of next row. Work 1 row even. Bind off.

FINISHING: Sew sole and back seams. Work edge trim around upper edge. Lace ribbon through beading.

**Mittens.** With No. 2 needles, cast on 41 sts. K 2 rows. Pattern: K 2, * sl 5, k 3, repeat from * across ending k 2. Continue pat for 15 more rows ending with a p row. K 1 row. P 1 row. Beading: K 1, * yo, k 2 tog, repeat from * across. Work in garter st for 3 rows. Next row: * K 8, k 2 tog, repeat from * 3 times, k 1 (37 sts). P 1 row. Work in stockinette st until piece measures 3½″, ending with a p row. Next row: * K 5, k 2 tog, repeat from * 4 times, k 2 (32 sts). P 1 row. Work in stockinette st for 12 rows ending with a p row. Next row: K 2 tog across row. Cut yarn leaving an end long enough to draw through remaining sts. Thread into blunt needle, draw through stitches and sew side of mitten. Join yarn at edge of mitten and crochet edge trim. Lace ribbon through beading.

## Knitted Carriage Cover

**27 × 34 inches**

**Materials.** Baby Wool or Orlon—9 ozs. Knitting Needles No. 2.

**Gauge.** 7 garter sts—1″.

Cast on 195 sts and work in garter st for 20 rows.

**Pattern.** Row 1: K 12 sts for border; k 5, * with yarn in front of work sl next 5 sts to right-hand needle, yarn to back of work, k 3, repeat from * across ending k 13. Row 2 and all even rows: P each row always keep-ing 12 sts each end in garter st for border. Rows 3 and 5: Repeat Row 1. Row 7: K 12 for border, k 7, * insert right-hand needle under 3 loops of the 3 slipped rows, k into next st on left-hand needle knitting the loops and st tog, k 7, repeat from * across ending k 15. Row 9: K 12 for border, k 1, * with yarn in front of work sl 5 sts, yarn in back of work, k 3, repeat from * across ending k 17. Rows 11 and 13: Same as Row 9. Row 15: K 12 for border, k 3, * insert needle under 3 loops of the 3 slipped rows, k into next st knitting loops and st tog, k 7, repeat from * across, k last 12 sts. Row 16: Same as Row 2. Repeat these 16 rows until piece measures 32″ or 2″ less than desired length. K 20 rows for border. Bind off. Block.

## Ruffled Baby Afghan
## Approximately 32 × 38 inches

**Materials.** Super Fingering (1 oz. Skeins): 12 skeins of White and 5 skeins of Lt. Pink. Knitting Needles: 1 pair No. 7.

**Gauge.** 6 sts—1″. 11 rows—1″ (2 rows make 1 ridge).

**Center Section.** (Make 1 white and 1 pink.) Starting at narrow end, cast on 120 sts. Work in garter st (k every row) for 26 inches. Bind off. Make other piece exactly the same number of rows.

**Border.** With white and spare needle, pick up and K 1 st in each st across narrow end of pink section. With white, insert needle through first st on narrow end of white section and first st on needle and k 1; k tog 1 st from white section and 1 st from needle, across. Work these sts in garter st, inc 1 st at both ends of every other row 6 times. Bind off loosely. With spare needle, and white, pick up and k 1 st in each ridge along side edge of pink section. Complete this border same as first border, then work border along other 2 sides in same way.

**Ruffle.** With white, cast on 30 sts. Row 1: K. Row 2: P. Row 3: K. Repeat these 3 rows until piece measures 132 inches unstretched. Bind off. Sew ends of ruffle together. Sew ruffle evenly around afghan, gathering at corners.

## Baby Cardigan

Directions are for infants Size 2. Changes for Size 3 are in parentheses.

**Materials.** Baby Wool—3 (4) ozs. Knitting Needles No. 3. Contrasting scraps of yarn for trim. 4 Buttons.

**Gauge.** 7 sts—1″. 9 rows—1″.

**Border Pattern.** Rows 1 and 2: * K 2, p 2, repeat from * across. Row 3: K 3, * p 2, k 2, repeat from * ending p 1. Row 4: K 1, * p 2, k 2, repeat from * ending p 2, k 1. Repeat these 4 rows for pattern.

**Back.** Cast on 72 (80) sts. Work in pat for 1½″. Now work in stockinette st until back measures 6½ (7)″ from start. SHAPE RAGLAN ARMHOLES: Dec 1 st each end every other row until 36 (40) sts remain. Bind off.

**Left Front.** Cast on 44 sts. Work in pat for 1½″. Keeping 10 sts in pat for front border, work remaining sts in stockinette st until piece measures same as back to underarm. SHAPE ARMHOLE AND NECK: Dec 1 st inside front border and 1 st at arm edge every other row until 14 sts remain. Keeping front edge even, continue to dec at armhole edge until 10 sts of front border remain. Continue in pat on these 10 sts for 1½″. Bind off.

**Right Front.** Work to correspond with left front, reversing shaping and working first buttonhole when piece measures ½ (1)″. BUTTONHOLE: Starting at front edge work 3 sts, bind off 2 sts, complete row. On the next row cast on 2 sts over 2 sts bound off previous row. Make 3 more buttonholes, evenly spaced, the last one to be made at start of neck shaping.

**Sleeves.** Cast on 44 (48) sts. Work in pat for 1″. K the next row inc 10 sts at even intervals. Continue in stockinette st until sleeve measures 7 (7½)″, or desired length to underarm. SHAPE CAP: Dec 1 st each end every other row until 28 sts remain, then dec 1 st each end every row until 8 sts remain. Bind off.

**Finishing.** Block pieces. Sew seams. Set in sleeves. Sew ends of front borders tog and sew in place to back of neck. Sew buttons in place. Embroider flowers as shown or as desired.

## Baby Jacket

Note the change in style in arrangement of instructions. This is done deliberately to familiarize you with the chart method of giving changes in instructions for the various sizes which is used in many knitting booklets.

| | | **Sizes** | | | |
|---|---|---|---|---|---|
| | | 1 | 2 | 3 | 4 |
| **Materials.** Nylo Germantown (2 oz skeins) . . . . . | | 2 | 2 | 3 | 3 |
| 1 pair No. 4 Knitting Needles | | | | | |
| 1 lightweight separating zipper . . . . . . . . .Inches | | 10 | 10 | 12 | 12 |
| *Gauge.* 6 sts=1″; 8 rows=1″. | | | | | |

### Directions

| | | 1 | 2 | 3 | 4 |
|---|---|---|---|---|---|
| **Back.** Cast on . . . . . . . . . . . . . . | Sts | 59 | 65 | 67 | 69 |
| K 1 row. Then work in pattern st as follows: Row 1: P . | Sts | 3 | 1 | 2 | 3 |
| * K 3, P 2, repeat from *, ending K 3, P . . . . . . | Sts | 3 | 1 | 2 | 3 |
| Row 2: K . . . . . . . . . . . . . . . | Sts | 3 | 1 | 2 | 3 |
| * P 3, K 2, repeat from *, ending P 3, K . . . . . . | Sts | 3 | 1 | 2 | 3 |
| Repeat last 2 rows once more. Row 5: P . . . . . . | Sts | 3 | 1 | 2 | 3 |
| * skip next 2 sts, K the 3rd st, then K the skipped 2 sts, P 2 *, repeat between *'s, ending P . . . . . . . . | Sts | 3 | 1 | 2 | 3 |
| Repeat Rows 2 through 5 twice more. Then work as follows: | | | | | |
| Row 1 (wrong side): P . . . . . . . . . . . . | Sts | 21 | 24 | 25 | 26 |
| * K 2, P 3, repeat from * twice more, K 2, P . . . . | Sts | 21 | 24 | 25 | 26 |
| Row 2: K . . . . . . . . . . . . . . . . . | Sts | 21 | 24 | 25 | 26 |
| * P 2, K 3, repeat from * twice more, P 2, K . . . . . | Sts | 21 | 24 | 25 | 26 |
| Repeat last 2 rows until piece measures . . . . . .Inches | | 7 | 7½ | 8 | 9 |

ending with a wrong side row.

TO SHAPE ARMHOLE: At the beg of each of the next 2 rows bind off 2 sts. Dec 1 st each end of needle every other

| | | 1 | 2 | 3 | 4 |
|---|---|---|---|---|---|
| row . . . . . . . . . . . . . . . . . . .Times | | 8 | 9 | 10 | 10 |

ending with a right side row. K the next row to form a ridge. Continuing in pattern as established, on next row dec 1 st

| | | 1 | 2 | 3 | 4 |
|---|---|---|---|---|---|
| each end of needle and repeat this dec every other row . .Times | | 8 | 9 | 9 | 9 |
| more. Bind off remaining . . . . . . . . . . . | Sts | 21 | 23 | 23 | 25 |
| **Left Front.** Cast on . . . . . . . . . . . . | Sts | 31 | 33 | 34 | 35 |
| K 1 row. Then work in pattern st as follows: Row 1: P . . | Sts | 2 | 4 | 0 | 1 |
| * K 3, P 2, repeat from * to last 4 sts, K 4 (front band). | | | | | |
| Row 2: K 6, * P 3, K 2, repeat from *, ending P 3, K . . | Sts | 2 | 4 | 0 | 1 |
| Repeat last 2 rows once more. Row 5: P . . . . . . | Sts | 2 | 4 | 0 | 1 |

Repeat between *'s of Row 5 of back to last 4 sts, K 4. Repeat Rows 2 through 5 twice more. Then work as follows: Row 1: K 6, P 3, K 2, P to end of row. Row 2: K to last 11 sts, P 2, K 3, P 2, K 4. Repeat last 2 rows until piece meas-

| | | 1 | 2 | 3 | 4 |
|---|---|---|---|---|---|
| ures . . . . . . . . . . . . . . . . . . .Inches | | 7 | 7½ | 8 | 9 |

ending with a wrong side row.

TO SHAPE ARMHOLE: At arm edge bind off 2 sts. Dec 1 st

| | | 1 | 2 | 3 | 4 |
|---|---|---|---|---|---|
| at same edge every other row . . . . . . . . .Times | | 8 | 9 | 10 | 10 |

ending with a right side row. K the next row to form a ridge. On next row dec 1 st at arm edge and repeat this dec every

| | | 1 | 2 | 3 | 4 |
|---|---|---|---|---|---|
| other row . . . . . . . . . . . . . . . .Times | | 5 | 6 | 6 | 6 |

more, ending at front edge.

| | | 1 | 2 | 3 | 4 |
|---|---|---|---|---|---|
| TO SHAPE NECK: At front edge bind off . . . . . . | Sts | 9 | 9 | 9 | 10 |

Continuing to dec 1 st at arm edge every other row 3 times more, at neck edge dec 1 st every row 3 times. Fasten off.

**Right Front.** Work to correspond to left front reversing pattern and all shaping.

| | | Sizes | | | |
|---|---|---|---|---|---|
| | | 1 | 2 | 3 | 4 |
| **Sleeves.** Cast on . . . . . . . . . . . . . | Sts | 35 | 39 | 41 | 45 |
| K 1 row. Then work in pattern st as follows: Row 1: P . | Sts | 1 | 3 | 4 | 1 |
| * K 3, P 2, repeat from *, ending K 3, P 1 . . . . . . | Sts | 1 | 3 | 4 | 1 |
| Row 2: K . . . . . . . . . . . . . . . . | Sts | 1 | 3 | 4 | 1 |
| * P 3, K 2, repeat from *, ending P 3, K . . . . . . | Sts | 1 | 3 | 4 | 1 |
| Repeat these 2 rows once more. Row 5: P . . . . . . | Sts | 1 | 3 | 4 | 1 |
| repeat between *'s of Row 5 of back, ending P . . . . | Sts | 1 | 3 | 4 | 1 |
| Repeat Rows 2 through 5 once more. Then work as follows: | | | | | |
| Row 1 (wrong side): P . . . . . . . . . . . . | Sts | 14 | 16 | 17 | 19 |
| K 2, P 3, K 2, P . . . . . . . . . . . . . . | Sts | 14 | 16 | 17 | 19 |
| Row 2: K . . . . . . . . . . . . . . . . | Sts | 14 | 16 | 17 | 19 |
| P 2, K 3, P 2, K . . . . . . . . . . . . . . | Sts | 14 | 16 | 17 | 19 |
| Continue in pattern as established, inc 1 st each end of needle every 1 inch 5 times. Work even on . . . . . . | Sts | 45 | 49 | 51 | 55 |
| until piece measures . . . . . . . . . . . . .Inches | | 7½ | 8½ | 9½ | 10½ |
| ending with a wrong side row. | | | | | |
| TO SHAPE CAP: At the beg of each of the next 2 rows bind off 2 sts. Work decreases and ridge in same manner as on back. Bind off remaining . . . . . . . . . . . | Sts | 7 | 7 | 7 | 11 |
| **Finishing.** Sew sleeves to front and back armholes. Sew underarm and sleeve seams. NECKBAND: With right side facing you, pick up . . . . . . . . . . . . . | Sts | 56 | 58 | 58 | 62 |
| around neck. K 8 rows (4 ridges) in garter st, dec 1 st each end of needle every other row 4 times. Bind off remaining . | Sts | 48 | 50 | 50 | 54 |
| Block. Sew in zipper. | | | | | |

## Cabled Slipon
## Toddler Size 3

**Materials.** Baby Wool—3 ozs. Knitting Needles Nos. 1 and 4. Double-pointed Needle. 2 small Pearl Buttons.

**Gauge.** 8 sts—1". 10 rows—1".

**Pattern.** Row 1 (wrong side): * P 4, k 1, repeat from * ending p 4. Row 2: * K 4, p 1, repeat from * ending k 4. Row 3: Same as Row 1. Row 4: K 4, p 1, k 4, * p 1, sl next 2 sts on dp needle and hold in back of work, k next 2 sts, k 2 sts from dp needle (cable twist), p 1, k 4, repeat from * until 7 cable twists have been made, p 1, k 4 twice. Repeat these 4 rows for pattern.

**Back.** With No. 1 needles, cast on 68 sts. K 1, p 1 in ribbing for 1¼". Change to No. 4 needles. K the next row, inc at even intervals to 84 sts. Work in pat until back measures 8". ARMHOLES: Work 6 sts and slip them onto a holder, work across to last 6 sts and slip these onto another holder. Continue in pat on remaining 72 sts for 3½". SHAPE NECK: Row 1: Work in pat across 19 sts, * k 4 sts, k 2 tog, k 2, k 2 tog, repeat from * 2 more times, k 4, continue in pat to end of row. Row 2: Work in pat across 19 sts, k 28 sts, work in pat to end of row. Repeat Row 2 four more times. Bind off loosely in pat.

**Front.** Work in same manner as back until 2" above armholes. Now work neck in same manner as back (do not bind off). SHAPE NECK: Work in pat across 19 sts, k 4, join another ball of yarn and bind off center 20

sts, complete row. Working on both sides at the same time, work 4 sts in garter st at each neck edge and remaining sts in pat until arm edge measures same as back. Bind off in pat.

**Sleeves.** Starting at arm edge, sew shoulder seam for 1½″. With right side toward you and No. 4 needles, sl 6 sts from one holder onto needle, pick up 52 sts around arm edge, then k across 6 sts of other holder. Work in pat as on front for 3 rows. Row 4: (K 4, p 1) 3 times; (cable twist, p 1, k 4, p 1) 4 times; k 4, p 1, k 4. Work in pat as set up for 2″. Continue in pat, dec 1 st each end every 1″ 7 times. Work on 50 sts until sleeve measures 9″, or 1½″ less than desired length. Change to No. 1 needles and k 1, p 1 in ribbing for 1½″. Bind off loosely in ribbing.

**Finishing.** Block. Crochet 1 row sc around each shoulder opening, making a ch-3 loop on each front edge. Sew seams. Sew buttons in place.

## Dolls

**Materials.** Nylon or Fingering Yarn, 3 ply—1 oz. each of White, Gray, and Green; small amounts of Pink, Dark Brown, Red, and Walnut. Knitting Needles No. 1. 1 Steel Crochet Hook No. 5. 2 Steel Beads. Stuffing.

**Gauge.** 17 sts—2″.

**Note.** Head and body are knitted upside down in two pieces for *Girl*.

**Girl.** HEAD: Using Pink and starting at top of head, cast on 10 sts. Work in stockinette st, casting on 2 sts at end of *every row* 6 times. Work even on 22 sts until piece measures 2″. Break off Pink.

BODY: Join White and work even until body measures 4″, ending with a p row. Break off and put sts on a holder. Make another piece in same manner.

LEGS: Starting at center, put last 11 sts of one piece and first 11 sts of the other piece on one needle, thus closing side seams and having leg seams at inside of leg. Work even in stockinette st until leg measures 2½″. Break off White. *Shoe:* Join Dark Brown and work even for 1″. On the next row

work 2 sts tog 11 times. Break off, leaving a 6″ end. Draw end tightly through all sts on needle and seam edges of foot. Work other leg in same manner.

ARMS: Make 2. Using White, cast on 14 sts. Work even in stockinette st for 1½″. Break off White. GLOVES: Join Dark Brown and continue in stockinette st until piece measures 2″. On the next row work 2 sts tog 7 times. Break off, leaving a 6″ end. Draw end through all sts on needle and fasten off tightly.

FINISHING: Sew back and front pieces together, leaving ample opening for stuffing. Sew arm seams. Stuff with cotton. Sew on arms. Wind yarn tightly, 2″ from top of head to form neck and 3¾″ from neck to form waist.

SKIRT: Using Green, cast on 80 sts. K 4 rows (2 ridges) in garter st. Break off Green. Join Gray and k 10, p 10 in ribbing until piece measures 3″. Bind off. Using Green, crochet 1 row sc on bound-off edge, holding in to size of waistline. Seam skirt. BIB TOP: Keeping first k panel for center back and third k panel for center front, using Gray, crochet 7 sc across front panel, ch 1, turn. Work 6 rows more of sc, ch 20, turn. Work 1 sc in 2nd ch from hook and in each st to end of ch for strap, 1 sc in each of next sc, ch 20, 1 sc in 2nd ch from hook and in each st to end of chain for 2nd strap, join with sl st to next sc. Fasten off.

FINISHING: Block. Sew skirt to body, crossing straps at back and sewing to skirt.

HAT: Crochet as follows: Using Green, ch 2. Rnd 1: 6 sc in 2nd st from hook. Rnd 2: 2 sc in each sc—12 sc. Rnd 3: * 2 sc in next sc, 1 sc in next sc, repeat from * to end of rnd—18 sc. Rnd 4: Ch 3, 1 dc in each of next 2 sc, * 2 dc in next sc, 1 dc in next sc, repeat from * to end of rnd—27 dc. Break off Green. Join Gray. Rnd 5: 2 sc in top of next ch 3, 1 sc in each of next 2 dc, * 2 sc in next dc, 1 sc in each of next 2 dc, repeat from * to end of rnd—36 sc. Rnd 6: Ch 3, 1 dc in each of next 4 sc, * 2 dc in next sc, 1 dc, in each of next 3 sc, repeat from * to end of rnd—45 dc. Break off Gray.

**Color Plate 7 — Modern Scandinavian Pullover**

A colorful sweater for sportswear done in pattern knitting. Instructions are given in Chapter 7, Knitting.

Join Green. Rnd 7: 1 sc in each dc. SHAPE RIM: Row 1: Ch 1, turn, 1 sc in first dc, 1 hdc in next dc, 1 dc in next dc, * 1 dc in each of next 2 dc, 2 dc in next dc, repeat from * 8 times more, 1 dc in next dc, 1 hdc in next dc, 1 sc in next dc, ch 1, turn, leaving last 12 sc. free for back of neck. Row 2: 1 sc in each of the 42 sts of last row, ch 1, turn. Row 3: Sl st over first 10 sts, 1 sc in each of next 22 sts, sl st over last 10 sts. Fasten off.

FINISHING: Sew hat to back of head. Using Gray, ch 30. Fasten off. Tie into small bow to trim crown.

BRAIDS: Cut 12 6″ strands of Walnut. Make 2 braids and sew around face as shown in photograph. Tie with bows of Green.

EMBROIDERY: Embroider face, using Dark Brown for eyes and eyebrows and Red for mouth and nose. Embroider 2 White daisies with Green stems on each p panel of skirt as shown in photograph.

**Boy.** HEAD: Work in same manner as head of girl doll. Break off Pink.

BODY: Join Green. K 38 rows (19 ridges) in garter st. Break off Green. Join Gray. K 28 rows (14 ridges) in garter st. Break off and put sts on a holder. Make another piece in same manner.

LEGS: Work in garter st in same manner as for legs of girl doll for 38 rows (19 ridges). On next row k 2 tog 11 times. Break off, leaving a 6″ end. Run end through sts on needle and draw up tightly. Fasten off.

ARMS: Make 2. Using Green, cast on 14 sts. Work even in garter st for 2″. On the next row k 2 tog 7 times. Break off yarn, leaving a 6″ end. Run end through sts on needle and draw up tightly.

FINISHING: Sew seams. Sew back and front together, leaving an ample opening for stuffing. Stuff with cotton. Stuff arms and sew to body. Wind pink yarn tightly 2″ from top of head to form neck. Using Gray, make a 12″ ch and tie around waist with a bow in back. Using Green, make 2 chains of 10″ each. Starting at end of side seams, lace chain through 7 ridges of Gray and tie bow at start of Green.

HAT: Crochet as follows: Using Green, ch 2, Rnd 1: 6 sc in 2nd st from hook. Rnd 2: 2 sc in each sc—6 sts inc. Rnd 3: * 1 sc in next sc, 2 sc in next sc, repeat from * to end of rnd—6 sts inc. Rnd 4: * 1 sc in each of next 2 sc, 2 sc in next sc, repeat from * to end of rnd—6 sts inc. Continue in this manner to inc 6 sts in *every rnd* 5 times more —54 sc. Rnd 10: 1 dc in each sc. Rnd 11: 1 sc in each dc. Fasten off. Using Gray, make a chain 11″ long. Sew around crown and tie in a bow. Sew hat to back of head. HAIR: Using Walnut, ch small loops and sew around face as shown in photograph. Embroider face.

## Child's Cardigan

Directions are for Size 4. Changes for Sizes 6 and 8 are in parentheses. Directions are for girl's cardigan; for boy's cardigan make buttonholes on *left side*.

**Materials.** Fingering Yarn—4 (5–6) 1 oz. Balls. Knitting Needles: 1 pair each No. 1 and No. 3. 6 Buttons.

**Gauge.** 7 sts—1″.

**Back.** With No. 1 needles, cast on 80 (88–94) sts and work in k 2, p 2 ribbing for 2½ (2½–3)″. Change to No. 3 needles and work even in stockinette st until piece measures 10 (11–11½)″ from start. SHAPE ARMHOLES: At the beg of each of the next 2 rows, bind off 4 sts. Dec 1 st each end of needle every other row 4 times. Work even on 64 (72–78) sts until armholes measure 4½ (5–5½)″. SHAPE SHOULDERS: Work next 8 rows, keeping center 22 (24–26) sts in stockinette st and 21 (24–26) sts on each end in garter st. Bind off 22 (24–26) sts at beg of each of the next 2 rows and slip center sts on a holder.

**Left Front.** With No. 1 needles cast on 44 (48–52) sts. Row 1: K 2, p 2 in ribbing to last 8 sts, k 8. Row 2: K 10, p 2, k 2 in ribbing to end of row. Repeat these 2 rows for 2½ (2½–3)″. Change to No. 3 needles and work as follows: Starting at side edge, K 31, p 1, k 12. Row 2: K 8, p 32. Repeat these 2 rows until piece measures same as back to underarm. SHAPE ARMHOLE: At arm edge bind off 4 sts. Dec 1 st at same edge every other row 4 times. Work on 36 (40–44) sts until armhole measures 3 (3½–4)″. SHAPE NECK: Slip the 8 garter sts at front edge to a holder. At front edge, bind off 2 sts and then dec 1 st at same edge every other row 5 times. *At the same time,* when starting the second dec at neck edge, continue the shoulder part of front in garter st to correspond to back shoulders.

**Right Front.** Work to correspond to left front, reversing all shaping, but make 6 buttonholes, evenly spaced, starting the first one 1″ from bottom. To make buttonhole, k 2 from front edge, bind off 3 sts and finish row. On next row, cast on 3 sts over those bound off. Top buttonhole is made after the front border sts at neck are taken from holder and worked till they match height of neckband.

**Sleeves.** With No. 1 needles, cast on 52

(56–64) sts and work in k 2, p 2 ribbing for 2 (2½–2½)″. Change to No. 3 needles and work in stockinette st, inc 1 st at each end every ¾″ 14 times, 66 (70–78) sts on needle. Work even until sleeve measures 10½ (11½–12½)″ from start. SHAPE CAP: Bind off 4 sts at beg of next 2 rows. Dec 1 st each end every other row for 3 (3¼ – 3½)″. Bind off 3 sts at beg of next 4 rows. Bind off remaining sts.

**Finishing.** Sew shoulder seams. With right side facing you, pick up 92 (96–100) sts around neck edge, with No. 1 needles, and work in k 2, p 2 ribbing for 1½″. Bind off loosely in ribbing. Slip 8 sts from holders at top of front border and continue in garter st for 1½″. Bind off. Sew neatly to edge of neckband. Sew seams and set in sleeves. Work 1 row of single crochet along front edges. Finish buttonholes. Sew buttons in place.

## Boy's Suit

Directions are for Size 2. Changes for Sizes 3 and 4 are in parentheses.

**Materials.** Sock and Sport Yarn—5 ozs. Knitting Needles Nos. 1 and 3. Steel Crochet Hook Size 1.

**Gauge.** 8 sts—1″. 21 rows—2″.

**Measurements.** Vest—Chest: 22½ (24½ – 25½)″. Width across back at underarm: 11 (11½–12)″. Pants: Width below waistband: 21 (22–23)″.

**Vest.** BACK: With No. 3 needles, cast on 80 (84–88) sts. Work in stockinette st, inc 1 st each end every ¾″ 4 times. Work on 88 (92–96) sts until back measures 4 (4½–5)″, or desired length to underarm. SHAPE ARMHOLES: Bind off 6 sts at beg of next 2 rows. Dec 1 st each end every other row 6 times. Work on 64 (68–72) sts until armholes measure 4½ (4¾–5)″. SHAPE SHOULDERS:

Bind off 7 sts at beg of next 4 rows; then 6 (7–8) sts at beg of next 2 rows. Bind off remaining 24 (26–28) sts.

RIGHT FRONT: With No. 3 needles, cast on 40 (44–48) sts. Work in stockinette st, inc 1 st at side edge every ¾″ 4 times. Work on 44 (48–52) sts until front measures same as back to underarm. SHAPE ARMHOLE AND NECK: Bind off 6 sts at arm edge. Dec 1 st at arm edge every other row 6 times and *At The Same Time,* dec 1 st at front edge every other row until 20 (21–22) sts remain. Work even until armhole measures same as back. SHAPE SHOULDER: At arm edge bind off 7 sts every other row 2 times, then bind off remaining 6 (7–8) sts.

LEFT FRONT: Work to correspond to right front, reversing all shaping.

FINISHING: Block pieces. Sew seams. Crochet 2 rows sc across lower edge. Work 1 row sc along each front and neck edge, working 3 sc in each corner st of V-neck shaping to keep work flat. Mark position of 4 buttons evenly spaced on right front, having first marker 2 sts above lower edge and last marker at beg of neck shaping. Row 2: Ch 1, turn, work 1 sc in each st, working 3 sc in corners and ch 2, skip 2 opposite each marker for buttonhole. On the next row work 1 sc in each st, 3 sc in each corner and 1 sc in each ch over buttonholes. Fasten off. Work 2 rows sc around armhole edges.

**Pants.** FRONT: With No. 3 needles, cast on 52 sts loosely for lower edge of right leg. K 1, p 1 in ribbing for 10 rows. P 1 row. Short Rows—Row 1: Inc 1 st in first st, k 46, turn. Row 2 and all even rows: Sl 1, p to end of row. Row 3: K 40, turn. Row 5: Inc 1 st in first st. k 31, turn. Row 7: k 25, turn. Row 9: Inc 1 st in first st, k 16, turn. Row 11: K 10, turn. Row 12: Sl 1, p to end of row. Inc 1 st in first st, k 8, with right-hand needle take up st directly below slipped st and slip to left needle, k this st tog with sl st to prevent a hole, k to end of row working all slipped sts in this manner. Continue in stockinette st, inc 1 st at beg of every k row 2 (4–6) times more—58 (60–62) sts. P 1

row. Break yarn. Sl sts onto a holder. With No. 3 needles, cast on 52 sts for left leg. Work in ribbing for 10 rows. K 1 row.

SHORT ROWS: Row 1: P 47, turn. Row 2: Sl 1, k to within 2 sts of end, inc 1 st in next st, k last st. Row 3: P 40, turn. Row 4: Sl 1, k to end of row. Row 5: P 32, turn. Row 6: Same as Row 2. Row 7: P 25, turn. Row 8: Sl 1, k to end of row. Row 9: P 17, turn. Row 10: Same as Row 2. Row 11: P 10, turn. Row 12: Sl 1, k to end of row. On the next row p all sts, working each sl st tog with st directly below. Continue in stockinette st, inc 1 st at end of every k row 3 (5–7) times—58 (60–62) sts. P 1 row. Join as follows: K across sts of left leg, k sts of right leg onto same needle—116 (120–124) sts. P 1 row, placing a marker on needle between 2 center sts. Center Dec Row: K to within 3 sts of marker, sl, k and pass, k 2, k 2 tog, k to end of row. Repeat this dec row every other row 7 times; then every 4th row 8 times. Work on 84 (88–92) sts until piece measures 8 (8½–9)″ from beg, or desired length (measured at side edges). Waistband: Change to No. 1 needles and k 1, p 1 in ribbing for 1½″. Bind off in ribbing.

BACK: Work in same manner as front to waistband, ending with a p row. Short Rows: K to within 8 sts of end, turn. * Sl 1 st, p to within 8 sts of end, turn. Sl 1 st, k to within 16 sts of end, turn. Sl 1, p to within 16 sts of end, turn. Sl 1, k to within 24 sts of end, turn. Sl 1, p to within 24 sts of end, turn. Break yarn, slip all sts onto one needle. Join yarn and work across being careful to avoid holes. Change to No. 1 needles and k 1, p 1 in ribbing for 1½″. Bind off in ribbing.

STRAPS: Make 2. With No. 1 needles, cast on 12 sts. K 1, p 1 in ribbing for 1″. Buttonhole: Work 4 sts, bind off 4 sts, work to end of row. On the next row cast on 4 sts over 4 sts bound off previous row. Continue in ribbing until 10 (11–12)″ from buttonhole, allowing 3″ for stretching. Make another buttonhole. Bind off.

FINISHING: Block pieces. Sew seams. Sew buttons in place.

## Girl's Slipon

Directions are for size 4. Changes for sizes 6 and 8 are in parentheses.

**Materials.** Nylon or Fingering 3 ply (1 oz. pull skeins) 4 (5–5). Knitting Needles Nos. 1 and 2. 1 Steel Crochet Hook No. 2. 3 small Buttons.

**Gauge.** 8 sts—1″. 12 rows—1″.

**Back.** With No. 1 needles, cast on 92 (96–104) sts. K 1, p 1, in ribbing for 1¾″. Change to No. 2 needles and work in stockinette st until piece measures 9 (10–11)″. SHAPE ARMHOLES: Bind off 4 (4–6) sts at the beg of each of the next 2 rows. Dec 1 st each end every other row 3 times. Work even on 78 (82–86) sts until armholes measure 2 (2½–3)″, ending with a k row. BACK OPENING: P 36 (38–40) sts. Cast on 6 sts for underlap, sl remaining 42 (44–46) sts onto a holder. Work on 42 (44–46) sts of left back until armhole measures 4½ (5–5½)″. SHAPE SHOULDER: At arm edge bind off 6 sts 3 times and 5 (6–8) sts once. Sl remaining 19 (20–20) sts onto a holder. RIGHT BACK: Starting at center back, work to correspond to left back reversing shaping and forming first buttonhole when back opening measures ½″. Buttonhole: Starting at center back, p 2, bind off the next 2 sts, p to end of row. On the next row cast on 2 sts over those bound off previous row. Make 2 more buttonholes, evenly spaced—the last one to be made in neckband.

**Pattern Stitch for Front.** Multiple of 4 sts plus 1. Row 1: P 2, * k 1, yo, k 1, pass the 3rd st from end of right-hand needle over the last 2 sts, p 2, repeat from * across row. Row 2: K 2, * p 2, k 2, repeat from * across row. Repeat these 2 rows for pattern stitch.

**Front.** With No. 1 needles, cast on 92 (96–104) sts. K 1, p 1 in ribbing for 1¾″. Change to No. 2 needles and work as follows: P 15 (15–17), put a marker on needle, p 62 (66–70), put a marker on needle, p 15 (15–17). Row 1: K 15 (15–17), work Row 1 of pat st on next 62 (66–70) sts, k to end of row. Row 2: P to first marker, work Row 2 of pat st on next 62 (66–70) sts, p to end of row. Keeping the 62 (66–70) sts between markers in pat st and remaining sts in stockinette st, work even until piece measures 9 (10–11)″. SHAPE ARMHOLES: Bind off 4 (4–6) sts at the beg of each of the next 2 rows. Dec 1 st each end every other row 3 times. Work on 78 (82–86) sts until armholes measure 3½ (4–4½)″, ending with a right side row. SHAPE NECK: Work 29 (30–32) sts, sl center 20 (22–22) sts onto a holder, join another ball of yarn and work last 29 (30–32) sts. Working on both sides at once, at each neck edge dec 1 st *every row* 6 times. Work on 23 (24–26) sts of each side until armholes measure 4½ (5–5½)″. SHAPE SHOULDERS: At each arm edge bind off 6 sts 3 times and 5 (6–8) sts once.

**Sleeves.** With No. 1 needles, cast on 44 (46–48) sts. K 1, p 1 in ribbing for 2″. Change to No. 2 needles and p next row, inc at even intervals to 58 (60–62) sts. Work in stockinette st, inc 1 st each end every 1″ 7 (8–9) times. Work even on 72 (76–80) sts until piece measures 10½ (11½–12½)″. SHAPE CAP: At the beg of the next 2 rows bind off 4 (4–6) sts. Dec 1 st each end every other row for 2¾ (3–3¼)″. At the beg of each of the next 6 rows bind off 3 sts. Bind off remaining sts.

**Finishing.** Block pieces. Sew seams. Set in sleeves. NECKBAND: With No. 1 needles and right side facing you pick up 93 (93–95) sts around neck, including sts from holders. K 1 p 1 in ribbing for 3 rows. On the next row work another buttonhole in same manner as before on right back. Continue in ribbing until neckband measures ½″. Bind off in ribbing. With right side facing you, crochet 1 row sc on each edge of back opening. Sew underlap of back opening in place. Press seams. Sew buttons in place.

## Boys' or Girls' Blazer

Note the change in style in arrangement of instructions. This is done deliberately to familiarize you with the chart method of giving changes in instructions for the various sizes which is used in many knitting booklets.

### Girls' Blazer

| Materials. | Sizes | | | |
|---|---|---|---|---|
| | 6 | 8 | 10 | 12 |
| Nylo Germantown (2-oz skeins) | | | | |
| MC (main color). . | 4 | 5 | 5 | 6 |
| CC (contrasting color) . . . | 1 | 1 | 1 | 1 |
| One pair No. 8 knitting needles | | | | |
| Five buttons | | | | |
| **Gauge.** | | | | |
| 5 sts=1"; | | | | |
| 7 rows=1". | | | | |

| Blocking Measurements. | Sizes | | | |
|---|---|---|---|---|
| | 6 | 8 | 10 | 12 |
| Chest . . Inches | 24 | 26 | 28 | 30 |
| Shoulder . . . | 3 | 3¼ | 3½ | 3¾ |
| Armhole depth. . | 5 | 5½ | 6 | 6½ |
| Bottom to underarm . . . | 10 | 11 | 11½ | 12 |
| Underarm sleeve length . . . . | 11½ | 12½ | 13½ | 15 |
| Sleeve width at underarm . . . | 9½ | 10 | 11 | 11½ |
| Waist . . . . | 22 | 23 | 24 | 25 |
| Hips . . . . | 26 | 28 | 30 | 32½ |

### Directions

| | | Sizes | | | |
|---|---|---|---|---|---|
| | | 6 | 8 | 10 | 12 |
| **Back.** Using MC, cast on . . . . . . . . . . . | Sts | 64 | 68 | 74 | 78 |

Work even in stockinette st for 1 inch, ending with a k row. K the next row to form hemline. Continue in stockinette st

| | | | | | |
|---|---|---|---|---|---|
| until piece measures . . . . . . . . . . .Inches | | 10¼ | 11¼ | 11¾ | 12¼ |

above hemline.

TO SHAPE ARMHOLES: At the beg of each of the next 2

| | | | | | |
|---|---|---|---|---|---|
| rows, bind off . . . . . . . . . . . . . | Sts | 3 | 4 | 5 | 5 |
| Dec 1 st each end of needle every other row . . . . .Times | | 3 | 3 | 4 | 4 |
| Work even on . . . . . . . . . . . . . . | Sts | 52 | 54 | 56 | 60 |
| until armholes measure . . . . . . . . . .Inches | | 5¼ | 5¾ | 6¼ | 6¾ |

TO SHAPE SHOULDERS: At the beg of each of the next 4

| | | | | | |
|---|---|---|---|---|---|
| rows, bind off . . . . . . . . . . . . . | Sts | 5 | 5 | 5 | 6 |
| At the beg of the next two rows, bind off . . . . . . | Sts | 5 | 6 | 6 | 6 |
| Bind off remaining . . . . . . . . . . . . | Sts | 22 | 22 | 24 | 24 |

*Note:* When changing colors, always twist yarns on wrong side of work to avoid making holes.

| | | | | | |
|---|---|---|---|---|---|
| **Left Front.** Using MC, cast on . . . . . . . . . | Sts | 30 | 32 | 35 | 37 |

Work even in stockinette st for 1 inch, ending with a k row. K the next row to form hemline. K the next row, join CC at front edge, and cast on 13 sts for front band and facing. You

| | | | | | |
|---|---|---|---|---|---|
| now have . . . . . . . . . . . . . . . | Sts | 43 | 45 | 48 | 50 |
| Row 1: p 13 CC, p . . . . . . . . . . . . | Sts | 30 | 32 | 35 | 37 |

MC.

| | | | | | |
|---|---|---|---|---|---|
| Row 2: k . . . . . . . . . . . . . . . | Sts | 30 | 32 | 35 | 37 |

MC, k 6 CC, sl 1, k 6 CC. Repeat these 2 rows until piece

| | | | | | |
|---|---|---|---|---|---|
| measures . . . . . . . . . . . . . . .Inches | | 10¼ | 11¼ | 11¾ | 12¼ |
| TO SHAPE ARMHOLE: At arm edge, bind off . . . . | Sts | 3 | 4 | 5 | 5 |
| Dec 1 st at same edge every other row . . . . . .Times | | 3 | 3 | 4 | 4 |
| ending with a p row. You now have . . . . . . | Sts | 37 | 38 | 39 | 41 |

|  | | **Sizes** | | |
|---|---|---|---|---|
|  |  | 6 | 8 | 10 | 12 |

TO SHAPE NECK: On next row, k to 2 st before front band; k 2 tog (dec); work front band. Continue in this manner to

| | | 6 | 8 | 10 | 12 |
|---|---|---|---|---|---|
| dec 1 st inside of front band every other row . . . . . | Times | 8 | 8 | 9 | 9 |
| more. Work even on . . . . . . . . . . . . | Sts | 28 | 29 | 29 | 31 |
| until armhole measures . . . . . . . . . . | Inches | 5¼ | 5¾ | 6¼ | 6¾ |

TO SHAPE SHOULDER: At arm edge, bind off . . . .

| | | 6 | 8 | 10 | 12 |
|---|---|---|---|---|---|
| TO SHAPE SHOULDER: At arm edge, bind off . . . . | Sts | 5 | 5 | 5 | 6 |
| twice and . . . . . . . . . . . . . . . . | Sts | 5 | 6 | 6 | 6 |

once. Using CC only, continue in pattern established on 13 sts of front band for . . . . . . . . . . . Inches 2¼ 2¼ 2½ 2½
more. Bind off.

**Right Front.** Using MC, cast on . . . . . . . . . Sts 30 32 35 37
Work even in stockinette st for 1 inch, ending with a k row. K the next row to form hemline. On next row, join CC at front edge, and cast on 13 sts. Work to correspond to left front, but reverse all shaping and form first double buttonhole when piece measures 1 inch above hemline.

TO FORM DOUBLE BUTTONHOLE: Starting at front edge, work 2 sts; bind off next 2 sts; work until there are 5 sts after bound-off sts; bind off the next 2 sts; work to end of row. Work the next row, casting on 2 sts over the bound-off sts. Make 4 more double buttonholes, evenly spaced, the last one to be made ½ inch below start of neck shaping.

**Sleeves.** Using CC, cast on . . . . . . . . . . Sts 36 36 38 38
Work even in stockinette st for 1 inch, ending with a k row. K the next row to form hemline. Continue in stockinette st until piece measures 1 inch above hemline. Break off CC. Join MC, and work in stockinette st, inc 1 st each end of

| | | 6 | 8 | 10 | 12 |
|---|---|---|---|---|---|
| needle every 1 inch . . . . . . . . . . . . | Times | 7 | 8 | 10 | 11 |
| Work even on . . . . . . . . . . . . . . | Sts | 50 | 52 | 58 | 60 |
| until piece measures . . . . . . . . . . . | Inches | 11½ | 12½ | 13½ | 15 |

above hemline.

TO SHAPE CAP: At the beg of each of the next two rows,

| | | 6 | 8 | 10 | 12 |
|---|---|---|---|---|---|
| bind off . . . . . . . . . . . . . . . . | Sts | 3 | 4 | 5 | 5 |
| Dec. 1 st each end of needle every other row for . . . | Inches | 3¼ | 3½ | 3¾ | 4 |

At the beg of each of the next 6 rows, bind off 2 sts. Bind off remaining stitches.

| | | 6 | 8 | 10 | 12 |
|---|---|---|---|---|---|
| **Pocket (Make 2).** Using MC, cast on . . . . . . . | Sts | 17 | 18 | 19 | 20 |
| Work even in stockinette st for . . . . . . . . . | Inches | 3 | 3¼ | 3½ | 3¾ |

Break off MC, and join CC. Work even in stockinette st for 1 inch, ending with a k row. K 1 row to form hemline. Continue in stockinette st until piece measures 1 inch above hemline. Bind off.

**Finishing.** Sew underarm, shoulder, and sleeve seams. Set in sleeves. Turn under and hem lower edge of sweater, sleeves, front and pocket facings. Sew in neckband, and seam at center back. Sew pockets in place 1¼ inches from front band. Finish buttonholes. Block. Sew on buttons.

| | Sizes | | |
|---|---|---|---|
| 6 | 8 | 10 | 12 |

### Boys' Blazer

**Materials.** Nylo Germantown (2-oz skeins)

| | 6 | 8 | 10 | 12 |
|---|---|---|---|---|
| MC . . . . . . . . . . . . . . . . . . . . . . . . . | 4 | 5 | 5 | 6 |
| CC . . . . . . . . . . . . . . . . . . . . . . . | 1 | 1 | 1 | 1 |

One pair No. 8 knitting needles
Five buttons
Gauge: 5 sts=1"; 7 rows=1".

### Directions

**Back.** Work in same manner as back of girls' blazer.

**Right Front.** Work in same manner as right front of girls' blazer, but omit buttonholes.

**Left Front.** Work in same manner as left front of girls' blazer, and form first double buttonhole when piece measures 1 inch above hemline. Make 4 more double buttonholes, evenly spaced, the last one to be ½ inch below start of neck shaping.

**Sleeves, Pockets, and Finishing.** Work in same manner as for girls' blazer.

## CHILDREN'S CAPS

### Fair Isle Cap, 3 to 5 years

Instructions are for cap with Fair Isle pattern. For plain cap, disregard pattern and follow instructions, using one color throughout.

**Materials (for Fair Isle Cap).** We have specified exact amounts required: One oz each dark-brown (color A) and white (color B); ½ oz light-brown (color C); 10 yds yellow (color D). Nylon 'n Wool Germantown.

(For Plain Cap). 2 ozs Nylon 'n Wool Germantown. One pair size-7 plastic knitting needles. One size-3 plastic crochet hook.

**Gauge.**  5 sts=1 inch
7 rows=1 inch

**Directions.** LEFT EARLAP: With A, cast on 5 sts. Work stockinette st (p 1 row, k 1 row) for 3 rows. Continuing stockinette st, inc 1 st each side of every row 11 times; end with k row (27 sts). Break yarn. Place sts on holder.

RIGHT EARLAP: With A, cast on 5 sts. Work same as for left earlap, casting on 4 sts at end of last row for back edge; and with k row (31 sts).

JOINING ROW: P 31 sts of right earlap; cast on 19 sts; pick up the 27 sts of left earlap on the free needle, and p onto same needle with sts of right earlap, casting on 3 sts at end of last row for back edge (80 sts). *Note:* Carry color not being used loosely along on wrong side of work to keep work flat.

PATTERN: Row 1 – (on right side), * k 4 A, 1 B, 3 A; repeat from * to end. Row 2 – * p 2 A, 3 B, 3 A; repeat from * to end. Beg with row 3 on chart; continue pat, following chart until 22 rows of pat are completed. Break off A, C, and D.

FIRST DEC ROW: With B, * k 6, k 2 tog; repeat from * to end (70 sts). P 1 row.

SECOND DEC ROW: * K 5, k 2 tog; repeat

from * to end (60 sts). P 1 row. Continue in this manner to dec 10 sts every second row, having 1 st less before decs in each successive dec row until 20 sts remain; end with p row.

FINAL DEC ROW: K 2 tog 10 times in succession (10 sts). Break off, leaving an end. Draw end through 10 sts twice; draw tog, and fasten end securely.

FINISHING: Sew back seam, matching pat rows.

CROCHET EDGE: With A, beg at center back, from right side, work 1 row sc around entire edge of cap, keeping work flat; join with sl st in first sc. Row 2: Ch 1; working from same side as last row, work 1 sc in each sc to center of first earlap; ch 49, work 1 sl st in horizontal loop of each st of ch for tie string; continue sc around to center of second earlap, and work tie string as before; work sc to end of rnd; join with sl st in first sc. Fasten off. With B and C, make small pompon, and sew to top of cap, as illustrated. Block.

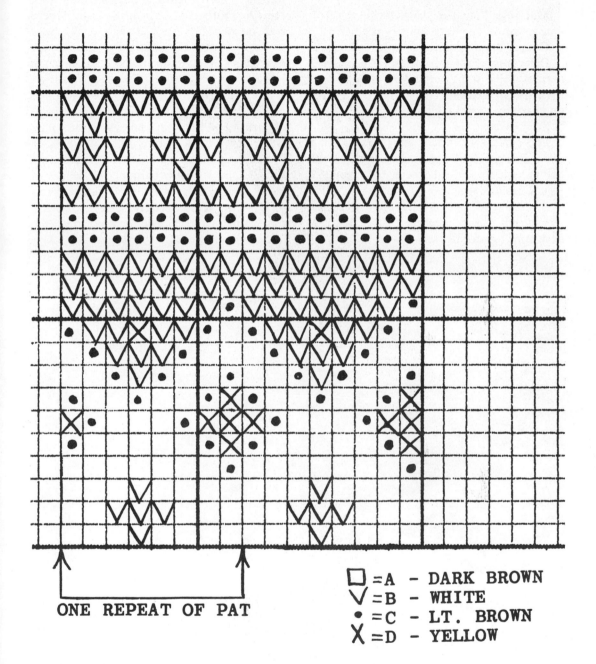

ONE REPEAT OF PAT

□ =A - DARK BROWN
V =B - WHITE
• =C - LT. BROWN
X =D - YELLOW

## Skating Cap, 6 to 10 years

**Materials.** Four 1-oz skeins Nylon 'n Wool. One set size-3 dp plastic knitting needles.

**Gauge.** 8 sts=1 inch; 21 rnds=2 inches

**Directions.** Cast on 44 sts on each of 3 needles (132 sts); join, taking care not to twist sts on needles. Mark end of rnds; carry up marker; k around until 12 inches from beg.

FIRST DEC RND: * K 1, slip, k and pass, k 60, k 2 tog, k 1 * ; place a second marker before next st; repeat between *'s once (128 sts). K 3 rnds even.

SECOND DEC RND: * K 1, slip, k and pass, k to within 3 sts of marker, k 2 tog, k 1; repeat from * once (124 sts).

Repeat last dec rnd every fourth rnd 9 times (88 sts), then every round until 8 sts remain. Fasten off, leaving an end. Thread end on tapestry needle, and draw twice through all sts. Fasten tightly. Turn under 3½ inches of lower edge, and hem on wrong side for border. Steam.

TASSEL: Wind 1 strand of yarn 440 times over 4-inch cardboard. With a double piece of yarn, tie securely at one end; cut at other end; trim. Cut 4 strands of yarn about 15 inches long; twist tog to make a cord; fold in half, and let retwist; loop over center of tassel; pull tightly; sew other end neatly to top of cap. Wind separate piece of yarn 5 times around tassel, 1 inch below tied end; fasten off. Trim ends.

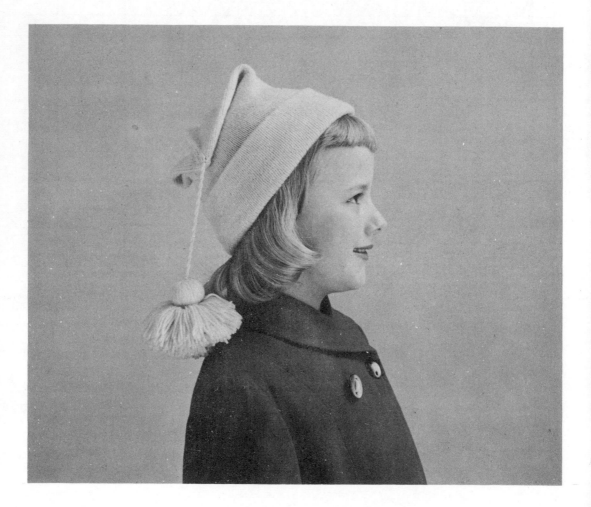

## Pixy Cap, 6 to 10 years

**Materials.** Two 1-oz skeins Nylon 'n Wool. One set size-3 dp plastic knitting needles.

**Gauge.** 21 rnds=2 inches.

**Directions.** Cast on 48 sts on each of 3 needles (144 sts); join, taking care not to twist sts on needles.

RND 1: * K 1, p 2; repeat from * to end of rnd; place a marker for end of rnd. Carry up marker. Repeat rnd 1 until 4½ inches from beg.

FIRST DEC RND: * K 1, p 2, slip 1 as if to k, k 1, psso, work next 63 sts, k 2 tog, p 2 * ; place second marker before next st; repeat between *'s once (140 sts). Carry up markers. Work 3 rnds even, matching sts.

SECOND DEC RND: * K 1, p 2, slip, k and pass as before, work to within 4 sts of marker, k 2 tog, p 2; repeat from * once (136 sts).

Repeat last dec rnd every fourth rnd 9 times (100 sts), with care to keep pat; then repeat dec rnd every second rnd 20 times (20 sts). Bind off. Working from wrong side, fold cap on dec ribs, and sew top tog, neatly matching sts. Steam lightly.

## Pony-tail Cap, 6 to 12 years

**Materials.** Two 1-oz skeins Sport and Sweater Yarn. Two cards of handi-wool, in contrasting color, for edging. One pair size-4 plastic knitting needles. One size-3 steel crochet hook.

**Gauge.** 17 rows=2 inches.

**Directions.** Cast on 99 sts for lower edge of cap. Row 1: On wrong side, p 3; * k 3, p 3; repeat from * to end. Row 2: K 3; * p 3, k 3; repeat from * to end. Repeat last 2 rows until 4 inches from beg; end on wrong side.

FIRST DEC ROW: K 1, k 2 tog, * p 1, p 2 tog, k 1, k 2 tog; repeat from * to end (66 sts). Work ribbing of p 2, k 2 until 6½ inches from beg; end on wrong side.

SECOND DEC ROW: K 2 tog; * p 2 tog, k 2 tog; repeat from * to end (33 sts). Work ribbing of p 1, k 1 for 5 rows; end on wrong side. Bind off tightly in rubbing. Do not break yarn. Working from right side, work 1 row of sc around entire cap; keeping edge even, join with a sl st in first sc. Fasten off.

EDGING: With contrasting color and working from same side as last row, work 1 sc in first sc, † ch 4; * yo, insert hook in fourth ch from hook and draw up a loop; repeat from * 3 times; yo and draw through all 9 loops on hook, ch 1, sl st into same ch st in which pat was worked, skip 1 sc, 1 sc in next st; repeat from † around entire cap; join with a sl st in first sc. Fasten off. Steam lightly. Fold cap in half, and tack tog along side edges of last 4 rows of ribbing.

CORD: Using main color: Cut 4 strands of yarn, each about 54 inches long; twist tightly together; fold in half; let cord retwist. Tie knot at cut ends. Make two. At knotted ends, make a small double bow, and tack firmly at lower front edge of cap, leaving about 16 inches of cord for tying.

## Cable Mittens

Directions are for Size 4. Changes for Sizes 5, 6, 7, 8, 9, 10, 11, 12, 13, and 14 are in parentheses.

**Materials.** Knitting Worsted, 4 ply—Sizes 4–12; 2 ozs. Sizes 13 and 14; 4 ozs. Double-Pointed Sock Needles, 1 set each No. 3 and No. 5.

**Gauge.** 5 sts—1″. 7 rnds—1″.

**Right Mitten.** Starting at cuff with No. 5 needles, cast on 26 (26–28–28–30–30–32–32–34–34–36) sts. Divide sts among 3 needles and join, being careful not to twist sts. Change to No. 3 needles and work in k 1, p 1 ribbing for 1¾ (2–2–2–2¼–2¼–2¼–2½–2½–2½–2½)″; inc 1 st on last rnd on Sizes 5, 7, 9, 11, and 13. Change to No. 5 needles and work as follows: Rnd 1: K 15 (16–16–17–17–18–18–19–19–20–20) sts, p 2, k 4 for cable rib, p 2, k 3 (3–4–4–5–5–6–6–7–7–8) sts. Repeat rnd 1 1 (1–1–2–2–2–3–3–3–3–3) more time. Now work thumb gore as follows: Rnd 1: Place a marker on needle, p and k in first st, k in front and in back of next st, place a marker on needle, knit 13 (14–14–15–15–16–16–17–17–18–18) sts, p 2, k 4, p 2, k 3 (3–4–4–5–5–6–6–7–7–8) sts. Inc 1 st following the first marker and 1 st preceding the 2nd marker on every 3rd rnd, slipping the markers on every rnd until there are 8 (8–8–10–10–10–10–10–12–12–12) sts in thumb gore, *at the same time* making a cable over the cable rib on the 6th rnd and every 6th rnd thereafter (to make a cable, sl 2 sts onto a spare dp needle and hold in front of work, k next 2 sts on left-hand

needle, k the 2 sts from the spare dp needle). When thumb gore is completed, work even for 2 (2–2–3–3–3–3–4–4–4–4) rnds. Next rnd: Slip the sts of the thumb gore onto a safety pin or stitch holder to be worked later, cast on 2 sts for inner side of thumb, join and work in pat over these 26 (27–28–29–30–31–32–33–34–35–36) sts until mitten, when tried on, reaches tip of little finger, or measures from last rnd of

cuff 4½ (4½–4¾–5–5–5¼–5¼–5½–5¾–5¾–6)″. SHAPE TIP: Rnd 1: Sl 1, k 1, psso, k 9 (10–10–11–11–12–12–13–13–14–14) sts, k 2 tog, place a marker on needle, sl 1, k 1, psso, work in pat to within last 2 sts, k 2 tog. Rnd 2: Work in pat around without decreasing, sl the marker. Rnd 3: Sl 1, k 1, psso, k to within 2 sts preceding the marker, k 2 tog, sl marker, sl 1, k 1, psso, work in pat to within last 2 sts, k 2 tog. Repeat rnds 2 and 3 alternately until 14 (15–16–17–18–19–20–21–22–23–24) sts remain. Next rnd: On Sizes 5, 7, 9, 11, and 13, work in pat around dec 1 st at center back of hand. Next rnd: Repeat rnd 3. On all sizes, place the sts of the palm on one needle and the sts of the back of hand on another needle and weave sts tog.

**Thumb.** Slip the sts for the thumb onto 3 needles, pick up 2 sts over the 2 cast-on sts. K around until thumb reaches ¼″ from tip, or measures 2 (2–2–2¼–2¼–2¼–2¼–2¼–2½–2½–2½)″. SHAPE TIP: Rnd 1: * K 1, k 2 tog. Repeat from * around. Next Rnd: K around. Next Rnd: * K 2 tog. Repeat from * around. Break off, leaving an 8″ length of yarn. Thread this length into a needle and draw through remaining sts. Pull up tightly and fasten securely on wrong side.

**Left Mitten.** Work as for Right Mitten until cuff has been completed. Change to No. 5 needles and work as follows: Rnd 1: K 3 (3–4–4–5–5–6–6–7–7–8) sts, p 2, k 4 (cable rib), p 2, k 15 (16–16–17–17–18–18–19–19–20–20) sts. Work as for Right Mitten to within first rnd of thumb gore. Work Thumb Gore as follows: Rnd 1: Work in pat to within last 2 sts, place a marker on needle, p and k in next st, k in front and in back of next st, place a marker on needle— position of Thumb Gore has now been established. Complete as for Right Mitten.

**Finishing.** Press Mittens through a damp cloth.

## Boy's and Man's Ribbed Cardigan

Directions are for Size 4. Changes for Sizes 6, 8, 10, 12, 36, 38, 40 and 42 are in parentheses.

**Materials.** Fingering Yarn 3 ply—8 (9–10–10–11–12–12–13–14) ozs. Knitting Needles Nos. 1 and 3. 7 Buttons.

**Gauge.** 7 sts—1″; 9 rows—1″.

**Pattern.** Row 1: P 1 (p 2–p 2–k 1, p 2–k 1, p 2–p 1–p 2–p 2–k 1, p 2), * k 4, p 2, repeat from * ending p 1 (p 2–p 2–p 2–k 1–p 2–k 1–p 1–p 2–p 2–p 2–k 1). Row 2: K 1 (k 2–k 2–p 1 k 2–p 1 k 2–k 1–k 2–k 2–p 1 k 2), * p 4, k 2, repeat from * ending k 1 (k 2–k 2–k 2 p 1–k 2 p 1–k 1–p 2–p 2–p 2 k 1). Repeat these 2 rows for pattern.

**Back.** With No. 1 needles, cast on 84 (92–98–106–112–126–134–140–148) sts. Work in pat for 1 (1–1½–1½–2–2–2–2½–2½)″. Change to No. 3 needles and continue in pat until back measures 10 (10¾–11½–12¼–13–14–14½–14½–15)″. SHAPE ARMHOLES: Bind off 3 (4–4–5–5–5–6–6–7) sts at beg of next 2 rows. Dec 1 st each end every other row 3 (3–4–4–5–6–6–7–8) times. Work on 72 (78–82–88–92–104–110–114–118) sts until armholes measure 5½ (6–6½–7–7½–8½–8¾–9–9¼)″. SHAPE SHOULDERS: Bind off 23 (25–26–29–30–34–36–37–38) sts at beg of next 2 rows. Bind off remaining sts.

**Right Front.** With No. 1 needles, cast on 60 (63–67–70–74–80–85–91–98) sts. Starting at front edge, k 8 (9–8–9–8–9–8–8–8) sts, sl 1, k 8 (9–8–9–8–9–8–8–8) sts, * p 2, k 4, repeat from * ending same as first row of pat. Row 2: Work same as Row 2 of pat to within last 17 (19–17–19–17–19–17–17–17) sts, p to end of row. Repeat these 2 rows for 1 (1–1½–1½–2–2–2–2½–2½)″. Change to No. 3 needles and continue in pat until front measures same as back to underarm. SHAPE ARMHOLE AND NECK: At arm edge bind off 3 (4–4–5–5–5–6–6–7) sts. Dec 1 st at arm edge every other row 3 (3–4–4–5–6–6–7–7) times and, *at the same time,* dec 1 st inside front border every third row until 40 (44–44–47–48–53–53–54–55) sts remain. Work even until armhole measures same as back. SHAPE SHOULDER: At arm edge bind off 23 (25–27–29–30–34–36–37–38) sts once. Work on remaining border sts for 1¾ (2–2–2–2¼–2½–2½–2¾–2¾)″. Bind off.

**Left Front.** Work to correspond with right front, reversing shaping and pat and working double buttonholes when piece measures ¾″ above lower edge. DOUBLE BUTTON-HOLE: Starting at front edge p 2 (3–2–3–2–3–2–2–2) sts, bind off next 4 sts, p 5 (7–5–

7–5–7–5–5–5) sts, bind off next 4 sts, complete row. On the next row cast on 4 sts over each 4 sts bound off previous row. Make 6 more double buttonholes, evenly spaced, the last one to be made at start of neck shaping.

**Sleeves.** With No. 1 needles, cast on 50 (56–56–62–62–68–68–74–74) sts. Work in pat for 2 (2–2½–2½–3–3–3–3½–3½)″. Change to No. 3 needles and continue in pat, inc 1 st each end every 1½ (1½–1½–1½–1¼–¾–¾–1–1)″ until there are 60 (64–70–76–84–102–104–106–108) sts. Work even until sleeve measures 10½ (12–13½–15–16½–19–19½–20–20½)″. SHAPE CAP: Bind off 3 (4–4–5–5–5–6–6–7) sts at beg of next 2 rows. Dec 1 st each end every other row until 30 (30–30–30–34–42–42–44–44) sts remain; then dec 1 st each end every row until 20 sts remain on all sizes. Bind off.

**Pockets.** Make 2. With No. 3 needles, cast on 26 (26–26–32–32–32–32–32–32) sts. Work in pat for 3 (3½–3½–4–4–4½–4½–4½–4½)″. Bind off.

**Finishing.** Block pieces. Sew seams and set in sleeves. Sew pockets in place, matching ribs. Sew neckband ends tog and sew to back of neck. Turn under front facing and sew in place. Finish double buttonholes. Sew buttons in place.

### Boy's and Man's Slipon Sweater with Sleeves

Directions are for Size 4. Changes for Sizes 6, 8, 10, 12, 36, 38, 40, 42, and 44 are in parentheses.

**Materials.** Orlon Fingering Yarn 3 ply—4 (5–6–7–8–9–10–11–12–13) ozs. Knitting Needles Nos. 1 and 2.

**Gauge.** 7 sts—1″. 12 rows—1″.

**Back.** With No. 1 needles, cast on 92 (98–104–110–116–134–140–146–152–158) sts. K 2, p 2 in ribbing for 2½ (2½–2½–3–3–3½–3½–3½–3½–3½)″. Change to No. 2 needles. Row 1 (right side): K * 3 (2–*3–2–*3–2–*3–2–*3–2) sts, p 1 st, k 0 (*3–0–*3–0–*3–0–*3–0–*3) sts, p 0 (1–0–1–0–1–0–1–0–1), repeat from * 22 (22–25–25–28–31–34–34–37–37) times, ending with k 0 (3–0–3–0–3–0–3–0–3). Row 2: K 2 (1–2–1–2–1–2–1–2–1) sts, p * 1, k 3, repeat from * 21 (23–24–26–27–32–33–35–36–38) times, ending with p 1, k 1 (0–1–0–1–0–1–0–1–0). Repeat these 2 rows until piece measures 11 (11–11–12–12–13–14–14–14½–14½)″, or desired length. SHAPE ARMHOLES: Bind off 3 (3–4–4–5–8–8–9–9–10) sts at beg of next 2 rows. Dec 1 st each end every other row 2 (3–3–4–4–4–5–5–6–6) times. Work even on 82 (86–90–94–98–110–114–118–122–126) sts until armhole measures 5 (5½–6–6½–7–8–8½–8½–9–9)″. SHAPE SHOULDERS: Bind off 9 (10–10–11–11–13–14–14–14–15) sts at beg of next 4 rows, then bind off 9 (8–9–9–10–11–10–11–12–12) sts at beg of the next 2 rows. Bind off remaining 28 (30–32–32–34–36–38–40–42–42) sts for back of neck.

**Front.** Work same as back until armholes measure 3 (3–3½–3½–4–4½–5–5–5½–5½)″. SHAPE NECK: Work across 32 (34–35–37–39–44–45–46–48–49) sts; join another ball of yarn and bind off center 18 (18–20–20–20–22–24–26–26–28) sts, complete row. Working on both sides at the same time dec 1 st each neck edge every 4th row until 27 (28–29–31–32–37–38–39–40–42) sts remain on each side. Work until armholes measure same as back. Shape same as on back.

**Sleeves.** With No. 1 needles cast on 48 (48–52–52–56–60–64–64–68–68) sts. K 2, p 2 in ribbing for 2½ (2½–2½–2½–3–3–3½–3½–3½–3½)″. Change to No. 2 needles; Row 1: K * 3, p 1, repeat from * 11 (11–12–12–13–14–15–15–16–16) times. Row 2: K 2, p * 1, k 3, repeat from * 10 (10–11–11–12–13–14–14–15–15) times, ending with p 1, k 1. Repeat last 2 rows inc 1 st each end of every 6th row until there are 88 (88–94–94–100–106–112–112–118–118) sts. Work even until sleeve measures 14 (15–15½–16–17–18–18–18½–18½–

19)″ or desired length to underarm. SHAPE CAP: Bind off 7 (7–7–9–9–10–10–10–11–11) sts at beg of next 2 rows. Dec 1 st each end every other row until 32 (32–36–36–40–40–44–44–50–50) st remain. Bind off 2 sts at beg of next 4 rows. Bind off remaining sts.

**Finishing.** Block pieces.

**Back Neck Band.** With No. 1 needles pick up and k 24 (24–28–28–32–32–36–36–40–40) sts across neck edge. K 2, p 2 in ribbing ¾ (¾–¾–1–1–1–1–1¼–1¼–1¼)″. Bind off in ribbing.

**Front Neck Band.** With No. 1 needles pick up and k 80 (84–84–84–88–88–88–92–92–92) sts evenly spaced around neck edge. Work in ribbing for ¾ (¾–¾–1–1–1–1–1¼–1¼–1¼)″. Bind off. Sew seams and sew sleeves in position.

## Boy's and Man's Sleeveless Cable Sweater

Directions are given for Size 4. Changes for Sizes 6, 8, 10, 12, 36, 38, 40, 42, and 44 are in parentheses.

**Materials.** Fingering Yarn: 4 (4–4–5–5–6–7–8–8–9) ozs. White. Knitting Needles Nos. 1 and 2; Double-Pointed Needle No. 2.

**Gauge.** STOCKINETTE ST: 7 sts—1″. 11 rows—1″. CABLE PAT: 9 sts—1″.

**Back.** With No. 1 needles, cast on 92 (98–104–110–116–134–140–146–152–158) sts and work in k 2, p 2 ribbing for 2½ (2½–2½–3–3–3–3½–3½–3½–3½)″. Change to No. 2 needles and work even in stockinette st until piece measures 7 (8–9–10½–12–13–14–14–14–14½)″ or desired length. SHAPE ARMHOLE: Bind off 8 (9–9–10–11–10–11–12–12–13) sts beg next 2 rows, then bind off 2 (2–2–2–2–2–2–2–2–2) sts beg next 6 rows. Dec 1 st beg and end of every other row 8 (8–9–9–9–10–10–10–11–11) times. Work even on 48 (52–56–60–64–82–86–90–94–98) sts until armhole measures 5½ (6–6–6½–7½–8½–8½–9–9½–10)″. SHAPE SHOULDERS: Bind off 3 (3–3–4–5–7–8–8–9–9) sts beg next 4 rows. Bind off 4 (6–6–6–6–9–9–9–9–9) sts beg next 2 rows.

Change to No. 1 needles and work in k 2, p 2 ribbing on 28 (28–32–32–36–36–40–40–44) sts for ¾″. Bind off in ribbing.

**Front.** With No. 1 needles, cast on 92 (98–104–110–116–134–140–146–152–158) sts and work in k 2, p 2 ribbing for 2½ (2½–2½–3–3–3–3½–3½–3½–3½)″ and inc 26 (28–30–32–34–34–36–38–40–42) sts evenly spaced on last row of ribbing. Row 1: With No. 2 needles and working on 118 (126–134–142–150–168–176–184–192–200) sts, k 0 (2–0–0–0–0–0–0–0–3) sts, p 0 (2–0–0–0–0–0–0–1–2) sts, k 10 (10–0–4–8–0–3–7–10–10), p 2 (2–2–2–2–1–2–2–2–2), k * 4 (*4–*4–*4–*4–*4–*4–*4–*4–*4), p 2 (2–2–2–2–2–2–2–2–2), k 10 (10–10–10–10–10–10–10–10–10), p 2 (2–2–2–2–2–2–2–2–2).

Repeat from * 4 (4–6–6–6–8–8–8–8–8) times, end with k 4 (4–4–4–4–4–4–4–4–4), p 2 (2–2–2–2–1–2–2–2–2), k 10 (10–0–4–8–0–3–7–10–10), p 0 (2–0–0–0–0–0–0–1–2), k 0 (2–0–0–0–0–0–0–0–3). Row 2: P 0 (2–0–0–0–0–0–0–0–3), k 0 (2–0–0–0–0–0–0–1–2), p 10 (10–0–4–8–0–3–7–10–10), k 2 (2–2–2–2–1–2–2–2–2), p * 4 (*4–*4–*4–*4–*4–*4–*4–*4–*4), k 2 (2–2–2–2–2–2–2–2–2), p 10 (10–10–10–10–10–10–10–10–10), k 2 (2–2–2–2–2–2–2–2–2), repeat from * 4 (4–6–6–6–8–8–8–8–8) times, end with p 4 (4–4–4–4–4–4–4–4–4), k 2 (2–2–2–2–1–2–2–2–2), p 10 (10–0–4–8–0–3–7–10–10), k 0 (2–0–0–0–0–0–0–1–2), p 0 (2–0–0–0–0–0–0–0–3). Rows 3 and 4: Repeat Rows 1 and 2. Row 5: K 10 (2–0–4–8–0–3–7–0–3), p 2 (2–0–2–2–0–2–2–1–2), work cable twist over next 0 (10–0–0–0–0–0–0–10–10) sts as follows: sl next 5 sts on dp needle and hold in back of work, k 5 sts, then k the 5 sts from dp needle, p 0 (2–2–0–0–1–0–0–2–2), k * 4 (*4–*4–*4–*4–*4–*4–*4–*4–*4), p 2 (2–2–2–2–2–2–2–2–2), cable twist over next 10 (10–10–10–10–10–10–10–10–10) sts, p 2 (2–2–2–2–2–2–2–2–2), repeat from * across row end with k 4 (4–4–4–4–4–4–4–4–4), p 2 (2–2–2–2–1–2–2–2–2), cable twist over next 0 (10–0–0–0–0–0–0–10–10) sts, p 0 (2–0–0–0–0–0–0–1–2), k 10 (2–

0–4–8–0–3–7–0–3). Rows 6, 8, 10, 12, 14, 16, and 18: Same as Row 2. Rows 7, 9, 11, 13, 15, 17: Same as Row 1. Row 19: Same as Row 5. Repeat from Rows 6 through 19 for pat.

Work even in pat until front measures same as back to underarm. Next row: Bind off 6 (7–8–10–10–10–10–12–12–13) sts beg next 2 rows. Bind off 2 (2–2–2–2–2–2–2–2–3) sts beg the next 6 rows. Next row: Dec 1 st at armhole edge, work in pat across next 45 (48–51–53–57–66–70–72–76–76) sts, tie in another skein of yarn and work in pat across remaining sts, dec 1 st at end of row and work both sides at same time. Next row: Keeping pat uniform, dec 1 st on each side of neck edge. Dec 1 st at armhole edges every other row 3 (4–5–7–11–8–10–12–16–16) times and at the same time dec 1 st on each side of neck edge every 3rd row 0 (3–3–3–3–5–5–5–4–4) times, then dec 1 st on each side of neck edge every other row 28 (23–21–21–21–25–23–23–24–24) times. Work even on 14 (18–22–22–22–28–32–32–32–32) sts until armhole measures same as back armholes.

SHAPE SHOULDERS: At armhole edge bind off 5 (6–7–7–7–9–11–11–11–11) sts beg next 4 rows. Bind off 4 (6–8–8–8–10–10–10–10–10) sts beg next 2 rows.

LEFT FRONT BAND: With right side of work toward you, starting at shoulder and with No. 1 needles, pick up 56 (56–60–64–68–76–76–80–80–80) sts, work in ribbing of k 2, p 2 for ¾″, dec 1 st at center front every row. Bind off in ribbing.

RIGHT FRONT BAND: Starting at center front, pick up same amount of sts as left front band and work same way.

ARMHOLE RIBBING: With No. 1 needles, pick up 124 (132–140–148–156–172–172–180–180–180) sts around armhole and work in ribbing of k 2, p 2 for ¾″. Bind off in ribbing. Finish other armhole in same manner.

**Finishing.** Block and sew shoulder seams. Sew ribbing at center front neck band. Sew side seams.

## Man's Vest

Sizes: small (36 to 38), medium (40 to 42), and large (44 to 46)

| Sizes. | Sm. | Med. | Lge. |
|---|---|---|---|

**Materials.** Sweater and sock yarn . . .     ozs  9     9     10
1 pair each No. 1 and No. 2 knitting needles. No. 7 steel crochet hook. 6 buttons. ½ yard 1″ grosgrain ribbon.

**Gauge.** 8 sts=1 inch
       16 rows=1 inch

**Blocking Measurements.** Width across

| | | Sm. | Med. | Lge. |
|---|---|---|---|---|
| Width across back at underarm . . . . . . . . . . . . . | inches | 18¾ | 19¾ | 20¾ |
| Width across each front at underarm . . . | inches | 8½ | 9 | 9½ |
| Underarm seams . . . . . . . . . . . . . | inches | 11 | 11½ | 12 |
| **Back.** With No. 1 needles, cast on . . . | sts | 118 | 126 | 134 |

and work in ribbing of k 1, p 1 for 2¼ inches. Change to No. 2 needles, and work in garter st (k every row) throughout garment, inc 1 st

Sizes. Sm.  Med. Lge.

at beg and end of row every ½ inch until there
are . . . . . . . . . . . . . . . . . . . . . . . . sts 150 158 166
Work even until back measures . . . . . . . inches 11    11½  12
from beg.

TO SHAPE ARMHOLES: Bind off 3 sts at
beg of next 4 rows; bind off 2 sts at beg of
next 8 rows; dec 1 st at beg of next . . . rows 10   12    14
Work even for 3 rows; dec 1 st at beg and
end of next row; then dec 1 st at beg and
end of every 4th row . . . . . . . . . . . times 10   11    11
more. Work even until armholes measure . inches 7½   8     8½
Inc 1 st at beg and end of next row; then inc
1 st at beg and end of row every ½ inch 4
times more. You now have . . . . . . . . sts 100  104   110
Work even for ½ inch.

TO SHAPE SHOULDERS: Bind off 4 sts at
beg of next 12 rows; bind off . . . . . . . sts 3    4     5
at beg of next 4 rows. Bind off remaining . sts 40   40    42
for back of neck.

**Right front.** With No. 1 needles, cast on . sts 104 108 112
and work in ribbing of k 1, p 1 for 2¼ inches.
Change to No. 2 needles, and work even until
front measures . . . . . . . . . . . . . . inches 6    6     6½
from beg.

TO SHAPE FRONT EDGE: Bind off 2 sts at
front edge every other row 6 times; then bind
off 2 sts at same edge every 4th row 6 times;
then dec 1 st at same edge every ½ inch until
front measures . . . . . . . . . . . . . : . . inches 11½ 12  12½
(½ inch more than length of back to under-
arm).

TO SHAPE ARMHOLE: Work armhole same
as for back (since you are working on *one*
front divide decreases in half). Continue
shaping at front edge every ½ inch until
there are 25 decs at the ½ inch intervals.

TO SHAPE SHOULDER: Bind off 3 sts at
armhole edge every other row 8 times; then
bind off . . . . . . . . . . . . . . . . . . . sts 3    4     5
every other row twice. Place 3 markers for
buttons along straight edge, with first marker
½ inch from lower edge and each of the next
2 markers about 2½ inches apart. Place
markers for second set of buttons about 5
inches from first set (see picture) and in corresponding position.

**Left front.** Work same as for right front.
reversing the shaping and working buttonholes to correspond to markers.

Buttonholes: Starting at front edge, k 4, bind off 4 sts, k 38, bind off 4 sts, k to end of row. In next row, cast on 4 sts over the bound-off sts.

Block each section. Sew shoulder seams; sew underarm seams to within 2 inches from lower edge.

ARMHOLE BINDING (make 2): With No. 1 needles, cast on 13 sts. Row 1: K 2 tog; k to end of row, increasing 1 st in last st. Row 2: P across row. Repeat these 2 rows until binding is long enough for armhole; bind off.

BINDING FOR STRAIGHT EDGE OF LEFT FRONT: With No. 1 needles, cast on 2 sts. Row 1: Inc 1 st in each st (4 sts). Row 2: P across row increasing 1 st at beg and end of row. Row 3: K across row, increasing 1 st at beg and end of row (8 sts). Row 4: P across row. Row 5: K 2 tog; k to end of row, increasing 1 st in last st. Repeat last 2 rows until binding measures . . . . . . . . . . . . . inches   6      6      6½
Bind off.

**Front Binding.** With No. 1 needles, cast on 15 sts, and work same as for armhole binding until binding is long enough to reach from shaped edge of left front, up left front, across back of neck, down right front, along straight edge to ¾ inch from lower edge, ending with a p row. Next row: K 2 tog; k across row to within 2 sts; k 2 tog. Next row: P 2 tog; p to end of row. Repeat last 2 rows until all sts are worked off.

**Finishing.** With right sides facing and starting at underarm seam, place armhole binding along edge of armhole. Seam edges close along outer edge. Seam short edges tog. Turn binding to wrong side of work, and tack in position; leave about ⅛ inch showing on right side for piping. Sew bindings for straight edge of left front and front in position in same manner, seaming the 2 pieces together. Face both sets of buttonholes with grosgrain ribbon, working buttonholes in ribbon; then face inside set of buttons of right front with grosgrain ribbon. Work a row of sc around slit at each side.

## Man's Muffler

**Materials.** 4 skeins (1-oz skeins) Fingering Yarn. 1 pair size-4 10-inch knitting needles. 1 size-3 steel crochet hook.

**Gauge.** 7 sts=1 inch

**Directions.** Cast on 67 sts. Work in pattern as follows: Row 1: * K 1; yarn forward, slip 1 as if to p; yarn in back, repeat from * across row, ending k 1. Row 2: P across row. Row 3: * Yarn forward, slip 1; yarn in back, k 1; repeat from * across row, ending slip 1. Row 4: P across row. Repeat these 4 rows for pattern until work measures 46 inches from start. Bind off. Work 1 row of sc along sides.

FRINGE: To make 4″ length strands wind yarn over a 2-inch cardboard. Cut loops at one edge. Fold 3 strands in half and with crochet hook, pull through and knot in every other st across each end of scarf.

## Man's Argyles

Directions are given for Medium Length. Changes for Bermuda Length are in parentheses.

**Materials.** Nylon Sweater and Sock Yarn—Main Color (M)—2(3) ozs.; 1 oz. each of the following colors: Diamond (X), Diamond (Z), Crossline (o), and Crossline (O); Knitting Needles No. 3; Double-Pointed Needles No. 2.

**Gauge.** 9 sts—1″ (No. 2 Needles). 8 sts—1″ (No. 3 Needles).

To prevent stitches from slipping off, place rubber band at one end of each of 2 No. 2 Needles and with M cast on 68 sts loosely. Work in k 2, p 2 ribbing for 3(1½)″. Change to stockinette st (for Bermuda Length, change to No. 3 Needles and work 1″ with M), then work pat from Chart twisting strands when changing color (by picking up the next color from underneath the color being dropped). Repeat the 33 rows of Chart

once more (4 times more) to heel, reversing colors, *at the same time,* when 3 Diamond Patterns have been completed, change to No. 2 Needles for remainder of Sock. Place 17 sts from each end onto st holders for heel. On center 34 sts, work 1 more Diamond, reversing colors. Sl these sts onto st holder.

**Heel.** Slip sts from holders onto one needle. Working on the 34 sts of heel only, work as follows:

Row 1: (Right side of work) * sl 1, k 1, repeat from * across row. Row 2: Sl 1, then p across row. Repeat these 2 rows 17 times more (36 rows).

TO TURN HEEL: Row 1: K 22, sl 1, k 1, psso, turn. Row 2: Sl 1, p 10, p 2 tog, turn. Row 3: Sl 1, k 10, sl 1, k 1, psso, turn. Repeat rows 2 and 3 until all sts are worked off each side (12 sts remaining on needle).

(Working on 2 needles). On wrong side of work pick up and p 18 sts at side of heel, turn. Row 1: K across the 30 sts on needle, pick up and k 18 sts at other side of heel (48 sts). Row 2: P across row. Row 3: K 2 tog, work across row, ending k 2 tog. Repeat rows 2 and 3 until 34 sts remain.

Work even on the 34 heel sts until work

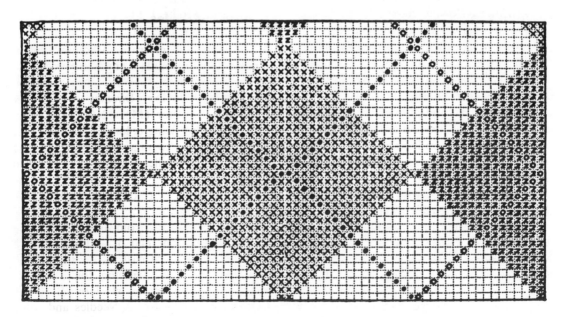

☐—M— Main Color   Z—Diamond   X—Diamond   ○—Crossline   ●—Crossline

measures same length as instep. K 17 to center of needle, then join sole to instep and work around as follows: 1st needle: k 17; 2nd needle: k across instep sts; 3rd needle: k 17. Work around (68 sts) until foot measures 9½" from back of heel (or desired length)—allowing 2" to finish toe.

**To Shape Toe.** Row 1—1st needle: K to last 3 sts on needle, k 2 tog, k 1; 2nd needle: k 1, slip 1, k 1, psso, k to last 3 sts, k 2 tog, k 1; 3rd needle: k 1, slip 1, k 1, psso, k to end of needle. Row 2–K. Repeat last 2 rows until 24 sts remain. With 3rd needle k across 6 sts of lst needle (12 sts on each of 2 needles). Weave sts tog. (See Weaving Toes of Socks.) Sew seams.

## Woman's Argyles

Directions are given for Medium Length. Changes for Bermuda Length are in parentheses.

**Materials.** Nylon Sweater and Sock Yarn—Main Color (M)—2(3) ozs. 1 oz. each of the following colors: Diamond (X), Diamond (Z), Crossline (o), and Crossline (O) Knitting Needles No. 2: Double-Pointed Needles No. 1.

**Gauge.** 9 sts—1" (No. 2 Needles); 10 sts—1" (No. 1 Needles).

Place rubber band at one end of each of 2 No. 1 (2) Needles and with M cast on 68 sts loosely. K 2, p 2 in ribbing for 2½ (1½)". Change to stockinette st (for Bermuda Length, work 1" with M), then work 1 pat from Chart (see Men's Argyles), twisting strands when changing color by picking up the next color from underneath the color being dropped. (Repeat the 33 rows of Chart 4 times more to heel, reversing colors. *At the same time,* when work measures 11½" from start, change to No. 1 Needles for remainder of Sock.) Place 17 sts from each end onto st holders for heel. On center 34

sts work 1 more Diamond, reversing colors. Slip these sts onto st holder.

**Heel.** Slip sts from holders onto one needle. Working on the 34 sts of heel only, work as follows: Row 1: (Right side of work) * Sl 1, k 1, repeat from * across row. Row 2: Sl 1, then p across row. Repeat these 2 rows 17 times more (36 rows).

TO TURN HEEL: Row 1: K 22, sl 1, k 1, psso, turn. Row 2: Sl 1, p 10, p 2 tog, turn. Row 3: Sl 1, k 10, sl 1, k 1, psso, turn. Repeat rows 2 and 3 until all sts are worked off each side (12 sts remaining on needle).

(Working on 2 needles.) On wrong side of work pick up and p 18 sts at side of heel, turn. Row 1: K across the 30 sts on needle, pick up and k 18 sts at other side of heel (48 sts). Row 2: P cross row. Row 3: K 2 tog, work across row, ending k 2 tog. Repeat rows 2 and 3 until 34 sts remain.

Work even on the 34 heel sts until work measures same length as instep. K 17 to center of needle, then join sole to instep and work around as follows: 1st Needle: K 17; 2nd Needle: K across instep sts; 3rd Needle: K 17. Work around (68 sts) until foot measures 8 inches from back of heel (or desired length—allowing 1½ inches to finish toe).

TO SHAPE TOE: Row 1—1st Needle: K to last 3 sts on needle, k 2 tog, k 1; 2nd Needle: K 1, slip 1, k 1, psso, k to last 3 sts, k 2 tog, k 1: 3rd Needle: K 1, slip 1, k 1, psso, k to end of needle. Row 2: K. Repeat last 2 rows until 24 sts remain. With 3rd Needle k across 6 sts of 1st Needle (12 sts on each of 2 needles). Weave sts tog. (See Weaving Toes of Socks.) Sew seams.

## Woman's Fireside Boots

Size: small (8 to 9), medium (9½ to 10½) and large (11 to 12)

**Materials.** Knitting Worsted

| | Sizes. | Sm. | Med. | Lge. |
|---|---|---|---|---|
| (1-oz. skeins) . . . . . . . . . . . . . . . . skeins | | 2 | 3 | 3 |

of navy, and 2 skeins of geranium. 1 set No. 2 dp needles

**Gauge.** Stockinette st 6 sts=1 inch

8 rows=1 inch

Sole pattern    8 st=1 inch

11 rows=1 inch

**Directions.** SOLE: Starting at heel with geranium and 2 needles, cast on 9 sts. Row 1: K 1; * leaving yarn in back of work, sl 1 as if to purl; k 1. Repeat from * across. Row 2: K and p in first st; purl to last st; p and k in last st (1 st inc at each edge). Row 3: Sl 1, * k 1, sl 1. Repeat from * across. Row 4: Repeat row 2. Rows 5 and 6: Repeat rows 1 and 2. Keeping sl sts directly over one another, continue to inc 1 st at both ends of every purl row . . . . . . . . . . . . . . times 0 1 2
more. Work even on . . . . . . . . . . . sts 15 17 19
until piece measures 4 inches.

TO SHAPE TOE: Inc 1 st at both ends of each of the next 3 purl rows; then inc 1 st at both ends of every 4th row until there are . sts 25 29 33
Work even until piece measures . . . . . . inches 7½ 8 8½
in all, or . . . . . . . . . . . . . . . . . . inches 1½ 2 2½
less than desired foot length. Dec 1 st at both ends of the next purl row and again every 4th row . . . . . . . . . . . . . . . . . . . . times 2 3 4
more, then every other row . . . . . . . . times 2 3 4
Dec 1 st at both ends of every row 3 times. Bind off remaining 9 sts.

TOP: Starting at ankle with geranium, cast on . . . . . . . . . . . . . . . . . . . sts. 48 52 56
Divide sts on 3 needles, and join, taking care not to twist sts. Work in ribbing of k 2, p 2 for 5 rnds. Change to navy, and k . . . . . . . rnds. 5 9 13

TO SHAPE HEEL: With first needle (heel needle), k . . . . . . . . . . . . . . . . . . . sts 12 13 14
sl . . . . . . . . . . . . . . . . . . . . . . . sts 12 13 14
on other end of same needle. Turn. Divide remaining . . . . . . . . . . . . . . . . . . sts 24 26 28
on 2 needles for instep, to be worked later. Row 1: P across. Row 2: K across. Repeat these 2 rows until heel measures . . . . . . inches 2 2¼ 2½
ending with a p row. On the next row, bind off, retaining last st on heel needle.

| Sizes. | Sm. | Med. | Lge. |
|---|---|---|---|

TO SHAPE GUSSETS: With same needle (first needle), pick up and k . . . . . . . . sts 10 12 14 along side of heel; with free needle (second needle), k across all . . . . . . . . . . . . sts 24 26 28 of the instep; with third needle, pick up and k . . . . . . . . . . . . . . . . . . . sts 10 12 14 along other side of heel. You now have . sts 45 51 57 on needles. Turn. Row 1: P across. Row 2: On first needle, k to last 3 sts, k 2 tog, k 1; k across second needle; on third needle, k 1, sl 1, k 1, psso, k to end of row. Repeat these 2 rows until . . . . . . . . . . . . . . . 8 9 10 dec rows have been worked in all and . . . sts 29 33 37 remain on needles. Slip all sts on one needle, and continue without decreasing until piece, when folded in half, measures . . . . . . . inches 7½ 8 8½ from center back of heel, or . . . . . . . . inches 1½ 2 2½ less than desired foot length.

TO SHAPE TOE: Dec 1 st at both ends of the next row, again every fourth row twice, then every other row . . . . . . . . . . . . times 2 3 4 You now have . . . . . . . . . . . . . . . sts 19 21 23 Dec 1 st at both ends of every row until 9 sts remain. Bind off. Press through a damp cloth. Sew top to sole, matching center of heel and toe.

POMPONS: Wrap geranium 25 times around 4 fingers. Tie securely at center of strands. Clip ends until pompon is about the size of a nickel. Sew pompons in place.

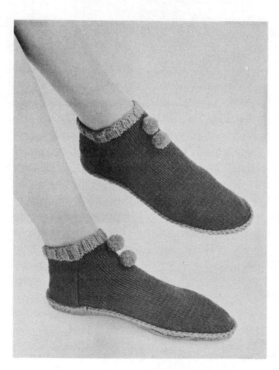

## COLOR PLATE 7

### Modern Scandinavian Ski Sweater

Directions are for Women's Small Size (32). Changes are in parentheses for: Women's Medium Size or Men's Small Size (34–36), Women's Large Size or Men's Medium Size (38–40), and Men's Large Size (42–44).

**Materials.** Knitting Worsted—4 ply (1 oz. skeins)—Black (MC), 22 (24–26–28) skeins; Salmon (X), 2 (2–3–3) skeins;

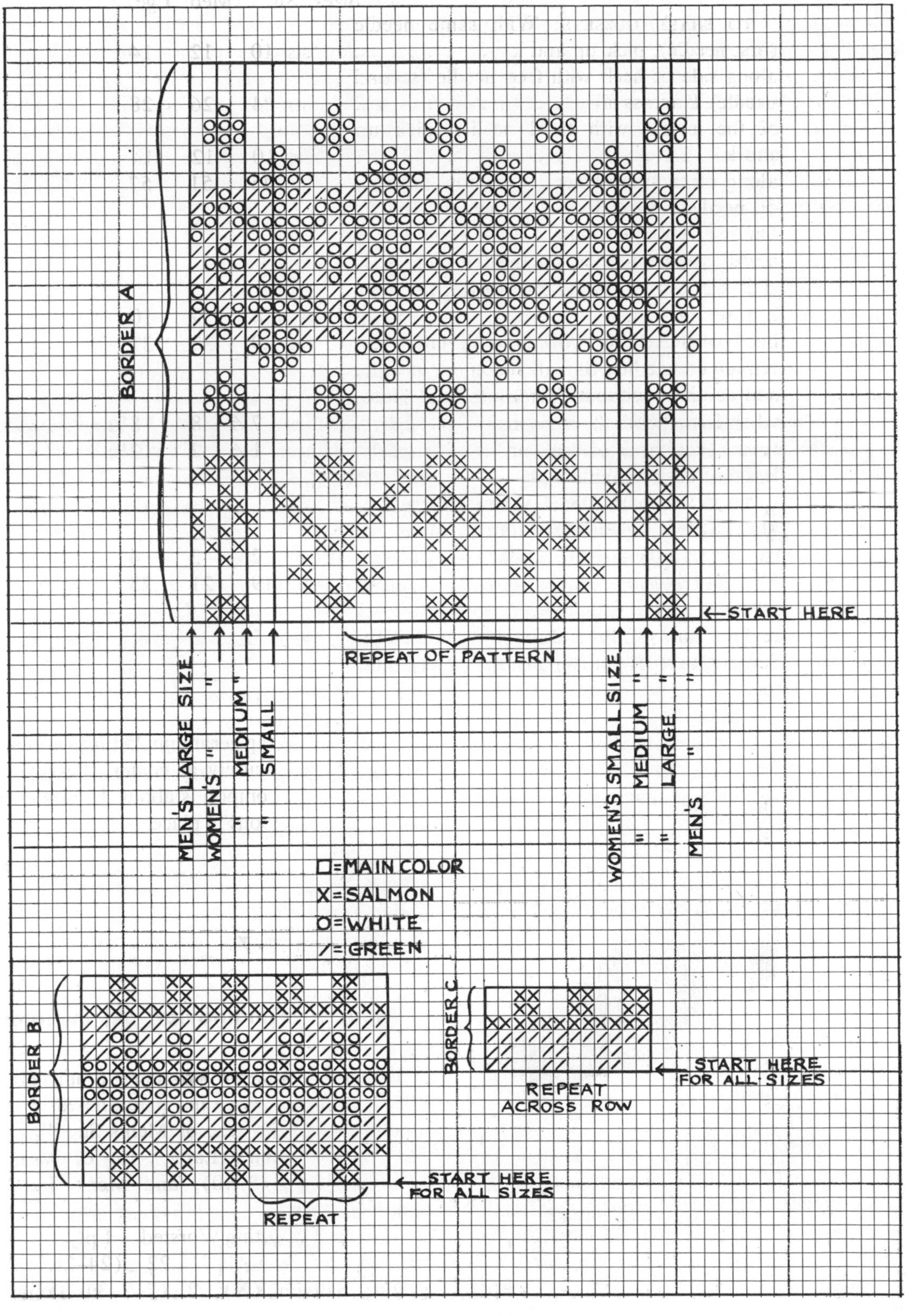

BORDER A

←START HERE

REPEAT OF PATTERN

MEN'S LARGE SIZE
WOMEN'S "
MEDIUM "
SMALL
" "
" "

WOMEN'S SMALL SIZE
MEDIUM "
LARGE "
MEN'S "

□=MAIN COLOR
X=SALMON
O=WHITE
∕=GREEN

BORDER B

BORDER C

START HERE
FOR ALL SIZES

REPEAT
ACROSS ROW

START HERE
FOR ALL SIZES

REPEAT

White (o), 1 (1–2–2) skeins; Woodland Green (/), 1 (1–2–2) skeins. Knitting Needles: Nos. 6 and 10.

**Gauge.** 9 sts—2″. 6 rows—1″.

**Measurements.** Width across back or front at underarm: 20 (20¾–21½–22½)″. Depth of armhole: 8 (8¼–8¾–9¼)″. Width of sleeve at upper arm: 17 (17¾–18¾–19¾)″. Length of sleeve seam: 18 (19–20–21)″.

**Front.** With MC and No. 6 needles, cast on for Women's Sizes 80 (84–88) sts and for Men's Sizes 92 (96–100) sts. K 2 p 2 in ribbing for 3″. Change to No. 10 needles and work in stockinette st, inc for Women's sizes only, 1 st at each end every 1½″ 4 times. When front measures 8 (8–9–10)″ above ribbing, inc 1 st in last row, not at edge; 89 (93–97–101) sts. With right side of work toward you, start pat with Border A, following the diagram. SHAPE ARMHOLES: Place a marker for start of armhole at each end of Row 11 of Border A (about 2″ above start of pat). *Note:* Inc 1 st in last plain row of Border A. Starting on a knit row work Border B on the 90 (94–98–102) sts. P 1 row with MC. Change to No. 6 needles and k 2, p 2 in ribbing for 4 (6–8–10) rows. SHAPE SHOULDERS: Bind off 8 sts at beg of next 4 rows, then bind off 7 (7–9–9) sts at beg of next 2 rows. Sl remaining 44 (48–48–52) sts on a holder.

**Back.** Work same as front omitting Border A and place border B in corresponding place to Border B on front. Block pieces. Sew one shoulder seam. Neck: With MC and No. 6 needles, pick up sts from holder, k 2, p 2 in ribbing on 88 (96–96–104) sts of neck for 2 (2–2½–2½)″. Change to Color X and k 1 row with right side toward you, then continue in ribbing for 2½ (2½–3–3)″ more. Bind off tightly. Sew other shoulder seam and ribbing tog.

**Sleeves.** With MC and right side of work toward you, using No. 10 needles pick up and k 76 (80–84–88) sts, starting and ending at armhole markers. Work in stockinette st, dec 1 st each end every 4th row 6 (6–8–8) times, then every 6th row 10 times. Work

even if necessary on the 44 (48–48–52) sts until sleeve measures 14 (15–16–17)″, dec 4 sts evenly spaced across last purl row. Work Border C on 40 (44–44–48) sts. Work 1 row with MC. Change to No. 6 needles and p 2, k 2 in ribbing for 3″. Bind off.

**Finishing.** Block sleeves and neck ribbing. Sew seams. Press seams lightly.

## Aran Cardigan

This is for experienced Knitters only.

Directions are for Size 12. Changes for Sizes 14, 16, and 18 are in parentheses.

**Materials.** Knitting Worsted, 4 ply, 14 (14–15–15) 2 oz. skeins. Knitting Needles Nos. 4 and 6. 1 Double-Pointed Needle. 7 Buttons.

**Gauge.** STOCKINETTE ST: 5 sts—1″; 7 rows—1″. PATTERN ST: 7½ sts—1″.

**Blocking Measurements.** Bust (cardigan buttoned): 35½ (37½–39½–41½)″. Width across back at underarm: 17½ (18½–19½–20½)″. Width across each front at underarm: 9½ (10–10½–11)″. Length from lower edge to underarm: 14 (14–14½–14½)″. Length of sleeve seam: 13 (13–13½–13½)″. Width across sleeve at upper arm: 13 (13½–14–14½)″.

**Back.** With No. 4 needles, cast on 88 (93–98–103) sts. Work in stockinette st for 9 rows. K 1 row on purl side of work to form hemline. Change to No. 6 needles and continue in stockinette st until back measures 14 (14–14½–14½)″ above hemline. SHAPE ARMHOLES: Bind off 5 sts at beg of the next 2 rows. Dec 1 st each end every other row 5 (6–7–8) times. Work on 68 (71–74–77) sts until armholes measure 8 (8¼–8½–8¾)″. SHAPE SHOULDERS: Bind off 6 sts·at beg of next 6 rows; then bind off 4 (5–6–7) sts at beg of next 2 rows. Bind off remaining 24 (25–26–27) sts for back of neck.

**Left Front.** With No. 4 needles, cast on 63 (68–73–78) sts. Work in stockinette st

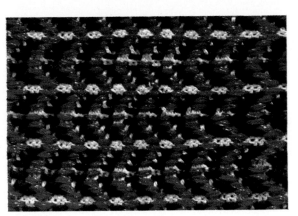

**Pattern 1**

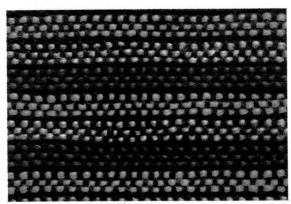

**Pattern 2**

**Pattern 3**

**Pattern 4**

## Color Plate 8 — Crocheted Fabrics

A new departure in crochet is the making of fabrics in interesting and unusual textures. These are suitable for cushions, chair seats, footstools, etc. Instructions for making the designs on the color plate are given in Chapter 8, Crochet.

for 9 rows. K 1 row on purl side to form hemline. Continue in stockinette st for 8 rows. Change to No. 6 needles and work in pat as follows: Row 1: K 1 (2–3–4) sts; skip next st, k in st below skipped st, k skipped st and pass first st over second st (raised k st); p 2, k 6, p 2 (for cable); work a raised k st; p 8 (k 4, p 8 for lozenge pat; work a raised k st; p 2, k 6, p 2; work a raised k st; p 12 (16–20–24) sts for popcorn pat; work a raised k st, k 5 (front border). Row 2: K 5; skip next st, p in st below skipped st. p skipped st and pass first st over second st (raised p st), * k, p and k in next st, sl l, k 2 tog, psso, repeat from * 2 (3–4–5) times more for popcorn pat, raised p st, k 2, p 6, k 2, raised p st, k 8, p 4, k 8, raised p st, k 2, p 6, k 2, raised p st, p 1 (2–3–4) sts. Row 3: K 1 (2–3–4) sts; raised k st, p 2, k 6, p 2, raised k st; p 7; sl next st on dp needle and hold in back of work, k next 2 sts, p st from dp needle (k–2 rib moved to right); sl next 2 sts on dp needle and hold in front of work, p next st, k sts from dp needle (k–2 rib moved to left), p 7, complete same as Row 1. Row 4: K 5, raised p st, * sl l, k 2 tog, psso; k, p and k in next st, repeat from * 2 (3–4–5) times more for popcorn pat (these 4 rows constitute popcorn pat), raised p st, k 2, p 6, k 2, raised p st, k 7, p 2, k 2, p 2, k 7, raised p·st, k 2, p 6, k 2, raised p st, p 1 (2–3–4) sts. Row 5: K 1, (2–3–4) sts, raised k st, p 2; sl next 3 sts on dp needle and hold in back of work, k next 3 sts, k sts from dp needle (cable twist); p 2, raised k st, p 6, move k–2 rib to right, p 2, move k–2 rib to left, p 6; raised k st. p 2, twist cable, p 2, complete row. Row 6: Same as Row 2 through 3rd raised p st, k 6, p 2, k 4, p 2, k 6, complete same as Row 2. Row 7: Same as Row 1 to lozenge pat, p 5, move k–2 rib to right, p 4, move k–2 rib to left, p 5, complete same as Row 1. Row 8: Same as Row 4 through 3rd raised p st, k 5, p 2, k 6, p 2, k 5, complete row. Row 9: Work to lozenze pat, p 4, move k–2 rib to right, p 6, move k–2 rib to left, p 4, complete row. Row 10: Same as Row 2 through 3rd raised p st, k 4, p 2, k 8,

p 2, k 4, complete row. Row 11: Work to lozenge pat, p 3, move k–2 rib to right, p 8, move k–2 rib to left, p 3, complete row. Row 12: Same as Row 4 to 3rd raised p st, k 3, p 2, k 10, p 2, k 3, complete row. Row 13: Working a cable twist as on Row 5, work to lozenge pat, p 2, move k–2 rib to right, p 10, move k–2 rib to left, p 2, complete row. Row 14: Same as Row 2 through 3rd raised p st, k 2, p 2, k 12, p 2, k 2, complete row. Row 15: Work to lozenge pat, p 1, move k–2 rib to right, p 12, move k–2 rib to left, p 1, complete row. Row 16: Same as Row 4 through 3rd raised p st, k 1, p 2, k 14, p 2, k 1, complete row. Row 17: Work to lozenge pat, p 1, move k–2 rib to *left,* p 12, move k–2 rib to *right,* p 1, complete row. Row 18: Repeat Row 14. Row 19: Work to lozenge pat, p 2, move k–2 rib to left, p 10, move k–2 rib to right, p 2, complete row. Row 20: Repeat Row 12. Row 21: Working cable twists as on Row 5, work to lozenge pat, p 3, move k–2 rib to left, p 8, move k–2 rib to right, p 3, complete row. Row 22: Repeat Row 10. Row 23: Work to lozenge pat, p 4, move k–2 rib to left, p 6, move k–2 rib to right, p 4, complete row. Row 24: Repeat Row 8. Row 25: Work to lozenge pat, p 5, move k–2 rib to left, p 4, move k–2 rib to right, p 5, complete row. Row 26: Repeat Row 6. Row 27: Work to lozenge pat, p 6, move k–2 rib to left, p 2, move k–2 rib to right, p 6, complete row. Row 28: Repeat Row 4. Row 29: Working cable twists as on Row 5, work to lozenge pat, p 7, move k–2 rib to left, move next k–2 rib to right, p 7, complete row. Row 30: Repeat Row 2. Row 31: Work to lozenge pat, p 8, sl next 4 sts on dp needle and wrap yarn tightly around them twice, k these 4 sts, p 8, complete row. Row 32: Same as Row 4 to 3rd raised p st, k 8, p 4, k 8, complete row. Repeat these 32 rows for pattern. Work in pat until front measures same as back to underarm. SHAPE ARMHOLE: At arm edge bind off 5 sts. Dec 1 st at same edge every other row 5 (6–7–8) times. Work on 53 (57–61–65) sts until armhole measures 6 (6¼–6½–6¾)". SHAPE NECK: At front edge work 14 (16–18–20) sts and slip these sts on a holder. (Work any broken popcorn pats in stockinette st.) Dec 1 st at neck edge every row 4 (5–6–7) times. Work on 35 (36–37–38) sts until armhole measures same as back. SHAPE SHOULDERS: At arm edge bind off 6 sts every other row 5 times, then bind off remaining 5 (6–7–8) sts.

**Right Front.** Work same as left front for 4 rows. Buttonhole: Starting at front edge work 2 sts, bind off next 2 sts, complete row. On the next row cast on 2 sts over 2 sts bound off previous row. Complete hem as on left front working a buttonhole on the 5th row above hemline. Change to No. 6 needles. Set up pat as follows: K 5 (front border), raised k st, p 12 (16–20–24) sts for popcorn pat; raised k st; p 2, k 6, p 2 for cable pat; raised k st; p 8, k 4, p 8 for lozenge pat; raised k st, p 2, k 6, p 2, for cable; raised k st, k 1 (2–3–4). Work to correspond to left front, reversing all shaping. Work 6 more buttonholes, evenly spaced, the last one to be made in neckband.

**Sleeves.** With No. 4 needles, cast on 42 (44–46–48) sts. Work in stockinette st for 7 rows, k next row on purl side to form hemline, continue in stockinette st for 7 rows. P the next row, inc at even intervals to 50 (52–54–56) sts. Change to No. 6 needles and set up pat as follows: Row 1: K 7 (8–9–10) sts, raised k st; p 2, k 6, p 2 for cable pat; raised k st; p 12 for popcorn pat; raised k st; p 2, k 6, p 2 for cable; raised k st, k 7 (8–9–10) sts. Working raised sts, cables, and popcorn pat as set up and remaining sts in stockinette st, inc 1 st each end every 6th row 11 (11–12–12) times. Work on 72 (74–78–80) sts until sleeve measures 13 (13–13½–13½)" above hemline. SHAPE CAP: Bind off 5 sts at beg of next 2 rows. Dec 1 st each end every other row until 36 sts remain, then dec 1 st each end every row until 16 sts remain. Bind off.

**Pockets.** With No. 6 needles, cast on 25 sts. Work in stockinette st for 5". Bind off. Make one more.

**Finishing.** Block pieces to measurements. Block without destroying raised effect of pattern sts. Fronts have more sts than backs. "Full" in front to back on shoulders. Sew shoulder seams. NECKBAND: With No. 4 needles, and right side facing you, pick up 80 (84–88–92) sts around neck, including sts from holders. P 1 row, k 1 row, p 1 row. Work a buttonhole on right front of next 2 rows. K 1 row, p 1 row, k 2 rows (hemline). Row 1: K 5, p 2, * k 2, p 2, repeat from * to last 5 sts, k 5. Row 2: P 5, k 2, * p 2, k 2, repeat from * to last 5 sts, p 5. Repeating these 2 rows, work a buttonhole on the next 2 rows, work 3 more rows. Bind off. Leaving a 5" opening on each side 2½" above hemline for pockets, sew side seams. Sew shoulder and sleeve seams. Set in sleeves. Sew pockets to back edge of opening, tack to front on wrong side. Turn under hems and sew in place. Finish buttonholes. Press seams. Sew buttons in place.

## Woman's Cardigan

Directions are for Size 36. Changes for Sizes 38, 40, and 42 are in parentheses.

**Materials.** Sock and Sport Yarn—10 (11–12–12) ozs. Knitting Needles Nos. 1 and 2. 7 Buttons.

**Gauge.** 17 sts—2".

**Measurements.** Bustline (buttoned): 41 (43–45–47)". Width of back at underarm: 19 (20–21–22)". Sleeve width at underarm: 13½ (14–14½–15)".

**Back.** With No. 1 needles, cast on 152 (160–168–176) sts. K 1, p 1, in ribbing for 4". Change to No. 2 needles and work in stockinette st, inc 1 st each end every 1½" 5 times. Work on 162 (170–178–186) sts until back measures 14". SHAPE ARMHOLES: Bind off 5 (6–7–8) sts at beg of next 4 rows. Dec 1 st each end every other row 11 times. Work on 120 (124–128–132) sts until armholes measure 7¾ (8–8¼–8½)". SHAPE SHOULDERS: Bind off 7 (8–9–9) sts at beg of next 8 rows; then 10 (8–6–8) sts at beg of next 2 rows. Bind off remaining 44 sts.

**Front Border Pattern.** Worked on 11 sts.

Row 1: P 1, k 2, k 2 tog, yo, k 1, yo, slip, k and pass, k 2, p 1. Row 2 and all even rows: K 1, p 9, k 1. Row 3: P 1, k 1, k 2 tog, yo, k 3, yo, slip, k and pass, k 1, p 1. Row 5: P 1, k 2 tog, yo, k 5, yo, slip, k and pass, p 1. Row 6: Same as Row 2. Repeat these 6 rows for pat.

**Left Front.** With No. 1 needles, cast on 91 (95–99–103) sts. Row 1 (right side): K 1, p 1 in ribbing to last 15 sts, k 7, sl 1, k 7 (front border). Row 2: P 15, k 1, p 1 in ribbing to end of row. Repeat these 2 rows for 4″, ending with a right side row. On the next row, p 15, k 1, p 1 in ribbing on next 16 sts, inc 1 st in next st and in every 6th st 9 times more, complete row—101 (105–109–113) sts. Change to No. 2 needles. K to within last 26 sts, put a marker on needle, work Row 1 of pat on next 11 sts, put a marker on needle, complete front band. Work pat on 11 sts between markers, front border as before and remaining sts in stockinette st, inc 1 st at side edge every 1½″ 5 times. Work on 106 (110–114–118) sts until front measures ½″ longer than back to underarm.

SHAPE ARMHOLE AND NECK: At arm edge bind off 5 (6–7–8) sts, k to within 2 sts of first marker, k 2 tog, complete row. Dec 1 st at arm edge every other row, and k 2 sts tog just before marker every 4th row until armhole measures 4¾ (5–5¼–5½)″, ending with a p row.

DART: K 20 (21–22–23) sts, slip, k and pass, put a marker on needle, k 2 tog, complete row. Continue to dec at front edge until 24 decreases have been worked, dec 1 st each side of dart marker in same manner as before every 1″ 3 times more—53 (55–57–59) sts.

SHAPE SHOULDER: At arm edge bind off 7 (8–9–9) sts every other row 4 times; then 10 (8–6–8) sts once. Continue on the 15 border sts for 2½ (2½–2¾–2¾)″. Leaving an 8″ end for weaving, break yarn and slip sts on a holder.

**Right Front.** Work to correspond with left front, reversing all shaping and working first buttonhole when piece measures ¾″. Double Buttonhole: K 2, bind off next 3 sts, work 5 sts, bind off 3 sts, complete row. On the next row cast on 3 sts over each 3 sts bound off previous row. Make 6 more double buttonholes, evenly spaced, the last one to be made at start of neck shaping.

**Sleeves.** With No. 1 needles, cast on 68 (68–72–72) sts. K 1, p 1 in ribbing for 3″. P the next row inc at even intervals to 78 (82–86–90) sts. Change to No. 2 needles and work in stockinette st, inc 1 st each end every ¾″ 18 times. Work on 114 (118–122–126) sts until sleeve measures 18″, or desired length to underarm. SHAPE CAP: Bind off 5 (6–7–8) sts at beg of next 2 rows; then 5 sts at beg of next 2 rows. Dec 1 st each end every other row 29 (30–31–32) times; then every row 4 times. Bind off remaining sts.

**Finishing.** Block pieces. Sew seams, holding in extra ½″ length of front at bust. Set in sleeves. Weave neckband edges tog and sew neckband to back of neck. Fold under facings and hem in place. Finish buttonholes, working through both thicknesses. Press seams. Sew buttons in place.

## Lace Yoke Blouse for Half Sizes

Directions are for Sizes 14½. Changes for 16½, 18½, 20½ and 22½ are in parentheses.

**Materials.** Boucle or other Dress Yarn—10 (11–12–13–15) 1 oz. skeins. Knitting Needles Nos. 2 and 3. 14 Buttons.

**Gauge.** 7 sts—1″; 11 rows—1″.

**Measurements.** Width across back at underarm: 18½ (19½–20½–21½–22½)″. Width across each front at underarm (excluding facings): 11½ (12–12½–13¼–13½)″. Width across back above armhole shaping: 15¼ (15¾–16¼–16¾–17½)″. Length from back of neck to lower edge: 19½ (20–20½–21–21½)″. Sleeve width at underarm: 13 (13½–14–14½–15)″.

312

**Pattern Stitch.** Multiple of 4 sts plus 2. Row 1: * Yo, k 2 tog, k 2, repeat from * ending yo, k 2 tog. Row 2: Purl. Repeat these 2 rows for pattern st.

**Back.** With No. 2 needles, cast on 104 (110–118–126–132) sts. K 1, p 1, in ribbing for 4". Change to No. 3 needles and p the next row inc at even intervals to 114 (120–128–136–142) sts. Work in stockinette st, inc 1 st each end every 6th row 8 times. Work on 130 (136–144–152–158) sts, until back measures 11 (11½–11½–12–12)", or desired length to underarm. SHAPE ARM-HOLES: Bind off 6 (7–8–9–10) sts at beg of next 2 rows. Dec 1 st each end every other row 6 (6–7–8–8) times. Work on 106 (110–114–118–122) sts until armholes measure 7½ (7½–8–8–8½)". SHAPE SHOULDERS: Bind off 7 sts at beg of next 8 (10–8–4–2) rows; then bind off 6 (0–8–8–8) sts at beg of each of the next 2 (0–2–6–8) rows. Bind off remaining sts.

**Left Front.** With No. 2 needles, cast on 79 (83–87–91–95) sts. Row 1 (right side): K 1, p 1 in ribbing to last 25 sts, k 12, sl 1, k 12 (front border). Row 2: P 25, work in ribbing to end of row. Repeat these 2 rows for 4", ending with a right side row. Change to No. 3 needles and p the next row inc at even intervals to 84 (88–92–96–100) sts. Work in stockinette st, slipping 13th st from front edge on right side of work and inc 1 st at side edge every 6th row 8 times. Work on 92 (96–100–104–108) sts until front measures 8½ (9–9–9½–9½)". SHAPE DART: Bind off 7 sts at side edge every other row 4 times, then cast on 7 sts at same edge every other row 4 times. YOKE: With right side toward you, k to last 35 sts, * yo, k 2 tog, k 2, repeat from * once more, yo, k 2 tog, complete row. P the next row. Repeat these 2 rows once more. Next row work to last 39 sts, work in pat across next 14 sts, complete row. Continue to work 4 sts more in pat toward side edge every 4th row once more, then every 8th row 2 times, then every 12th row until there are 10 fagotting stripes on yoke and *at the same time,* when front

measures 12½ (13–13–13½–13½)" (1½" longer than back, allowing for dart), SHAPE ARMHOLE: Bind off 6 (7–8–9–10) sts at arm edge. Dec 1 st at same edge every other row 8 (8–9–10–10) times. Work on 78 (81–83–85–88) sts until armhole measures 5½ (5½–6–6–6½)". SHAPE NECK: At front edge bind off 26 (28–29–29–31) sts once, then bind off 3 sts at same edge every other row 4 times. Dec 1 st at same edge every other row 6 times. Work on 34 (35–36–38–39) sts until armhole measures same as back. SHAPE SHOULDER: At arm edge bind off 7 sts every other row 4 (5–4–2–1) times; then bind off 6 (0–8–8–8) sts every other row 1 (0–1–3–4) time.

**Right Front.** Work to correspond to left front, reversing shaping and pat and working first double buttonhole when piece measures ½" above lower edge. Double Buttonhole: Starting at front edge, k 4 sts, bind off 4 sts, k 4 sts, sl 1, k 4, bind off 4 sts, complete row. On the next row cast on 4 sts over each 4 sts bound off previous row. Make 13 more double buttonholes, evenly spaced, the last one to be made 1" below neck shaping.

**Sleeves.** With No. 2 needles, cast on 76 (78–82–86–90) sts. K 1, p 1 in ribbing for 1". Change to No. 3 needles and p the next row inc at even intervals to 82 (84–88–92–96) sts. Work in stockinette st, inc 1 st each end every 4th row 5 times. Work on 92 (94–98–102–106) sts until sleeve measures 5 (5–5–5½–5½)", or desired length. SHAPE CAP: Bind off 6 (7–8–9–10) sts at beg of next 2 rows. Dec 1 st each end every other row until 32 sts remain. Bind off 2 sts at beg of next 6 rows. Bind off remaining sts.

**Collar.** With No. 3 needles, cast on 92 (96–100–100–104) sts. Keeping 3 sts each end in garter st, work remaining sts in pat for 2". Work all sts in garter st for 5 rows. Bind off loosely.

**Finishing.** Block pieces. Sew darts. Sew seams and set in sleeves. Turn under front facing and sew in place. Finish double buttonholes. Sew cast-on edge of collar around neck to within ¾" of each front edge. Sew buttons in place.

## Twin Sweater Set

Directions are for Size 12. Changes for Sizes 14 and 16 are in parentheses.

**Materials.** Cashmere-type Yarn. (½ oz. pull skeins) 9 (10–10) skeins for Slipon; 13 (14–14) skeins for Cardigan. Knitting Needles: 16" Circular Needle No. 2; 24" Circular Needle No. 2; Knitting Needles No. 0; 1 set Dp Needles No. 0. 9 Buttons; 1½ yds 1" Grosgrain Ribbon.

**Gauge.** 8 sts—1"; 12 rows—1".

**Slipon.** FRONT: Starting at neck and using 16" needle, cast on 82 (86–90) sts. P 1 row. Work back and forth as follows: Row 1: K 1, yo, p 1, k 6, p 1, yo, k 4, yo, p 1, k 6, p 1, yo, k 40 (44–48), yo, p 1, k 6, p 1, yo, k 4, yo, p 1, k 6, p 1, yo, k 1. Rows 2, 4, 6, and 8: Purl. Row 3: Inc 1 st in first st, k 1, yo, p 1, k 6, p 1, yo, k 6, yo, p 1, k 6, p 1, yo, k 42 (46–50), yo, p 1, k 6, p 1, yo, k 6, yo, p 1, k 6, p 1, yo, k 1, inc 1 st in last st. Row 5: Inc 1 st in first st, k 3, yo, p 1, sl next 3 sts on dp needle and hold in back of work, k next 3 sts, k 3 sts from dp needle (cable twist), p 1, yo, k 8, yo, p 1, cable twist on next 6 sts, p 1, yo, k 44 (48–52), yo, p 1, cable twist on next 6 sts, p 1, yo, k 8, yo, p 1, cable twist on next 6 sts, p 1, yo, k 3, inc 1 st in last st. Row 7: Inc 1 st in first st, k 5, yo, p 1, k 6, p 1, yo, k 10, yo, p 1, k 6, p 1, yo, k 46 (50–54), yo, p 1, k 6, p 1, yo, k 10, yo, p 1, k 6, p 1, yo, k 5, inc 1 st in last st. Rows 9 and 11: Inc 1 st in first st, k to first p 1, * yo, p 1, k 6, p 1, yo, k to next p 1, repeat from * ending inc 1 st in last st. Rows 10 and 12: Purl. Row 13: Repeat Row 9, making a cable twist on each group of k 6 between yo's. Row 14: Purl. At beg of the next row cast on 26 (30–34) sts; k to first p 1, * yo, p 1, k 6, p 1, yo, k to next p 1, repeat from * to end of row. Join and work as follows: Rnd 1: Knit. Rnd 2: K to next p 1, * yo, p 1, k 6, p 1, yo, k to next p 1, repeat from * to end of rnd. Repeat these 2 rnds being sure to work a cable twist every 8th rnd until there are 44 (46–48)

holes on each raglan—472 (496–520) sts on needle. *Note:* When there are too many sts on 16" needle, change to 24" needle. DIVIDE WORK: Starting at the beg of a rnd, k to center of second cable and sl the last 100 (104–108) sts just worked onto a holder for left sleeve; k to center of next cable and sl these 136 (144–152) sts on a holder for back; k to center of next cable and sl these 100 (104–108) sts on a holder for right sleeve. On remaining 136 (144–152) sts, WORK FRONT: Work back and forth in stockinette st for ½". On the next row dec 1 st each end and repeat this dec every ¾" 9 times more. Work even on 116 (124–132) sts until piece measures 8½ (8½–9)" from underarm. Change to No. 0 straight needles and k 1, p 1, in ribbing for 3". Bind off in ribbing.

BACK: Work to correspond to front.

SLEEVES: Sl 100 (104–108) sts from holder onto No. 2 Needle. Work back and forth in stockinette st for ½". On the next row dec 1 st each end and repeat this dec every ½" 4 times more. Work on 90 (94–98) sts until piece measures 3 (3–3½)". Change to No. 0 straight needles and k 1, p 1 in ribbing for 1". Bind off in ribbing.

FINISHING: Sew seams. Neckband: With right side facing you and dp needles, pick up 130 (130–134) sts around neck. K 1, p 1 in ribbing for 1". Bind off loosely in ribbing. Block.

**Cardigan.** Work in same manner as slipon for 14 rows. At the beg of each of the next 2 rows cast on 20 (22–24) sts. Rows 1 and 3: With right side facing you, p 1, k 1 in ribbing for 11 sts (front border), * k to next p 1, yo, p 1, k 6, p 1, yo, repeat from * to last 11 sts, p 1, k 1 in ribbing to end of row. Rows 2 and 4: K 1, p 1 in ribbing for 11 sts, p to last 11 sts, k 1, p 1 in ribbing to end of row. Row 5: Work in ribbing for 11 sts, * k to next p 1, yo, p 1, cable twist on next 6 sts, p 1, yo, repeat from * to last 11 sts, work in ribbing to end of row. Rows 6 and 8: Repeat Row 2. Row 7: Repeat Row 1. Repeat these 8 rows, being sure to work a cable twist every 8th row and forming first

buttonhole on right front border when work measures 2″ above cast on sts. BUTTONHOLE: Starting at right front edge, work 3 sts, bind off next 5 sts, work to end of row. On the next row cast on 5 sts over those bound off previous row. Make 7 more buttonholes, spaced 2¼ (2¼–2½)″ apart. Continue to work in this manner until there are 46 (48–

50) holes in each raglan seam—502 (526–550) sts, ending with a k row. *Note:* When there are too many sts on the 16″ needle, change to 24″ needle. DIVIDE WORK: P 77 (81–85) sts and put these sts on a holder for right front; p next 104 (108–112) sts and put these sts on a holder for right sleeve; p next 140 (148–156) sts and put these sts on a holder for back; p next 104 (108–112) sts and put these sts on a holder for left sleeve; on remaining 77 (81–85) sts work as follows: LEFT FRONT: Keeping 11 sts at front edge in ribbing as established, work back and forth in stockinette st for 1″. On the next row at arm edge dec 1 st and repeat this dec every ¾″ 9 times more. Work on 67 (71–75) sts until piece measures 9½ (9½–10)″ from underarm. Change to No. 0 straight needles and k 1, p 1 in ribbing for 3″. Bind off in ribbing. RIGHT FRONT: Sl 77 (81–85) sts of right front onto No. 2 needles and work to correspond to left front, forming buttonholes in same manner as before. BACK: Sl 140 (148–156) sts from holder onto No. 2 needle and work back and forth in stockinette st for 1″. On the next row dec 1 st each end and repeat this dec every ¾″ 9 times more. Work on 120 (128–136) sts until piece measures 9½ (9½–10)″ from underarm. Change to No. 0 needles and k 1, p 1 in ribbing for 3″. Bind off in ribbing. SLEEVES: Sl 104 (108–112) sts of sleeve onto No. 2 needle and work back and forth in stockinette st for 3″. On the next row, dec 1 st each end and repeat this dec every ½″ 21 (22–23) times more. Work on 60 (62–64) sts until piece measures 15 (15–15½)″. Change to No. 0 straight needles and k 1, p 1 in ribbing for 3″. Bind off.

FINISHING: Sew seams. Neckband: With No. 0 straight needles and right side facing you pick up 137 (137–141) sts around neck. K 1, p 1 in ribbing for 3 rows. On the next row on right front form a buttonhole in same manner as before. Continue in ribbing until band measures 1″. Bind off in ribbing. Block to size. Face fronts with ribbon. Finish buttonholes. Sew buttons in place.

## Plain Skirt (not shown)

Directions are for Size 12. Changes for Sizes 14, 16, 18 and 20 are in parentheses.

**Materials.** Boucle or other Dress Yarn—12 (12–14–14–16) ozs. Circular Needle No. 2. Steel Crochet Hook Size 2.

**Gauge.** 8 st—1″.

**Note.** To make skirt longer or shorter, work more or less inches before first dec rnd.

Cast on 410 (420–430–440–450) sts. Join, being careful not to twist sts. K around for 8 (9½–11–11–12½)″. Next rnd dec 10 sts at evenly spaced intervals. Continue to dec 10 sts (having 1 st less between dec on each dec rnd) every 1½″ 10 (9–8–8–7) times more—300 (320–340–350–370) sts on needle: (Hipline—23″ from start). Work even 1″, dec 10 sts as before, then every 1″ 2 (1–1–1–1) times, then every ½″ 6 (8–8–8–8) times—210 (220–240–250–270) sts on needle. When skirt measures 30″ (or desired length) from start, bind off.

**Finishing.** Work 1 rnd sc around lower edge of skirt. CASING: Join yarn to inside waistband. With wrong side toward you, * ch 5, skip 2 sts, sl st in st ½″ below next st, ch 5, skip 2 sts, sl st in next st ½″ above next st, repeat from * around. Fasten off. Run elastic, which has been cut to waist measurement, through beading and sew ends tog.

## Narrow Rib Skirt

Directions are for Size 12. Changes for Sizes 14, 16, 18, and 20 are in parentheses.

Materials. Boucle or other Dress Yarn—12 (13–14–15–16) ozs. Circular Knitting Needle No. 2. Steel Crochet Hook Size 2.

**Gauge.** 8 sts—1″.

**Note.** To make skirt longer or shorter, work more or less inches before first dec rnd.

Cast on 363 (374–385–396–407) sts.

Join, being careful not to twist sts. Rnd 1: * K 5, p 6, repeat from * to end of rnd. Repeat this rnd until piece measures 17″. First Dec Rnd: * K 5, p 2, p 2 tog, p 2, repeat from * to end of rnd—33 (34–35–36–37) sts dec. Now k 5, p 5 in ribbing for 6″. On the next rnd, dec 1 st in center of each p rib. You now have 297 (306–315–324–333) sts. Work in k 5, p 4, ribbing for 2½″. On the next rnd, dec 1 st in center of each p rib and repeat this dec every 2½″ once more—231 (238–245–252–259) sts. Work in k 5, p 2 ribbing until skirt measures 30″, or desired length. WAISTBAND: K the next rnd dec 31 (26–21–12–3) sts at even intervals. K 1, p 1 in ribbing for 1¼″. Bind off in ribbing.

## Wide Graduated Rib Panel Skirt

Directions are given for Size 12. Changes for Sizes 14, 16, 18, and 20 are in parentheses.

**Materials.** Boucle or other Dress Yarn—1 oz. balls—13 (14–16–17–19); 29″ Circular Knitting Needle No. 2. Steel Crochet Hook Size 2.

**Gauge.** 8 sts—1″.

Cast on 360 (360–396–396–432) sts, join, being careful not to twist sts. Rnd 1: * K 18, p 18, repeat from * around. Repeat Rnd 1 for 17″ (for 30″ Skirt—for shorter or longer skirt adjust accordingly). Next row dec 1 st at center of each panel and work even for 2 (3–2–3–2)″. Dec as before, then

**Finishing.** Crochet 1 rnd sc around lower edge of skirt. CASING: Join yarn to inside waistband. With wrong side toward you, * ch 5, skip 2 sts, sl st in st ½″ below next st, ch 5, skip 2 sts, sl st in next st ½″ above next st, repeat from * around. Fasten off. Run elastic, cut to waist measurement, through beading and sew ends tog.

every 2″ 2 times (3″ 1 time, 2″ 2 times, 3″ 1 time, 2″ 2 times) more. There are now 280 (300–308–330–336) sts on needle and skirt is at hipline, 23″ from start. When skirt measures 24½ (24½–25–25–25)″ dec 1 st in each panel as before, then every 1½″ 3 times (1½″ 3 times, 2″ 2 times, 1½″ 3 times, 2″ 2 times) more. There are now 200

(220–242–242–264) sts on needle. Work even until skirt measures 30″ or desired length from start.

**Waistband.** Work in ribbing of k 1, p 1, dec 8 sts for Size 14, 18 sts for Size 16, and 8 sts for Size 20, across row. Work even for 1½″, bind off loosely in ribbing. Crochet casing for elastic inside of Waistband. Crochet 1 row of sc around lower edge.

## Shoulderette
## Length, 50 inches

**Materials.** Fingering Yarn 3 ply—6 ozs. Knitting Needles Nos. 3 and 10. Steel Crochet Hook Size 2.

**Gauge.** 5 sts—1″.

**Jiffy Garter Pattern.** Row 1: With No. 10 needles, knit across. Row 2: With No. 3 needles, knit across. Repeat these 2 rows for pattern continuing to change needles.

Starting at cuff, with No. 3 needles, cast on 50 sts. K 1, p 1 for 5″. On the next row knit, inc 1 st in each st. Now work in pat until piece measures 45″ from start, or 5″ less than desired length. K 2 sts tog across the next row. With No. 3 needles, k 1, p 1 in ribbing for 5″. Bind off in ribbing.

**Finishing.** Sew cuffs and sleeves for 12″ from each end. Edging: Join yarn at one end of opening. Crochet 1 row sc around opening. Row 2: * Ch 3, sc into first ch, skip 1 st, sc in next st, repeat from * around. Fasten off.

## Slippers

Directions are for small size (4½–6). Changes for medium size (6½–8) and large size (8½–10) are in parentheses.

**Materials.** Fingering 3 ply (1 oz. pull skeins)—1 (2–2). Knitting Needles No. 4. 1 Aluminum Crochet Hook No. 3/D. 3 doz. Multicolor Shells or other trimming.

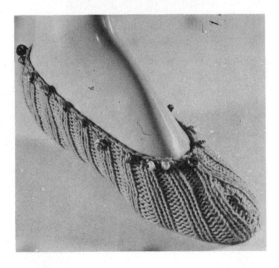

**Gauge.** 11 sts—2″; 7 rows—1″.

**Note.** Yarn is used double throughout.

Using a double strand of yarn, cast on 34 (38–42) sts. Row 1 (right side): K 2, * p 2, k 2, repeat from * across row. Row 2: P 2, * k 2, p 2, repeat from * across row. Repeat these 2 rows twice more. ** On the next row inc 1 st each end of needle and repeat this inc every 4th row twice more, forming new patterns as sts are increased. Work even on 40 (44–48) sts for 5 rows, ending with Row 2. On the next row dec 1 st each end of needle and repeat this dec every 4th row twice more. Work even on 34 (38–42) sts for 5 rows, ending with Row 2. Repeat from ** once more. Bind off in ribbing.

**Finishing.** Fold in half lengthwise and sew seams. Using yarn double, work 1 row sc around slipper, working 1 sc in each rib. Using a fine sewing needle, sew trimming around top, spacing at even intervals.

### Socks for the Family

Directions are for Children's Size 7½. Changes for Women's Size 9½ and Men's Size 11½ are in parentheses.

**Materials.** Nylon and Wool, 3 ply—1 oz. for Children and Women, 2 ozs. for Men. Double-Pointed Sock Needles No. 2.

**Gauge.** 9 sts—1″. 12 rows—1″.

Cast on 52 (64–68) sts, 18 (22–24) sts on each of 2 needles and 16 (20–20) sts on third needle. Join, being careful not to twist sts. K 2, p 2 in ribbing for 1¾ (2¼–3½)″. On Children's socks only, dec 2 sts on last rnd. Now k round and round until work measures 4½ (5–11)″ from start, working to within last 12 (17–17) sts of third needle. Slip last 12 (17–17) sts of third needle and first 12 (17–17) sts of first needle onto one needle for heel and remaining 26 (30–34) sts onto 2 needles for instep.

**Heel.** Row 1 (right side): * Sl 1, k 1, repeat from * across row. Row 2: Sl 1, p to end of row. Repeat these 2 rows 11 (15–15) times more—24 (32–32) rows. TURN HEEL: K 14 (19–19), k 2 tog, k 1, turn. Row 2: Sl 1, p 5, p 2 tog, p 1, turn. Row 3: Sl 1, k 6, k 2 tog, k 1, turn. Row 4: Sl 1, p 7, p 2 tog, p 1, turn. Continue in this manner (k or p 1 st more every row) until 16 (20–20) sts remain on Row—8 (14–14). CHILDREN'S SOCKS ONLY: Row 9: Sl 1, k 12, k 2 tog, turn. Row 10: Sl 1, p 12, p 2 tog—14 sts on needle. ON ALL SIZES: K 7 (10–10) sts to center of heel. Divide sts on 3 needles as follows: 1st Needle: K remaining 7 (10–10) sts of heel, pick up and k 12 (16–16)

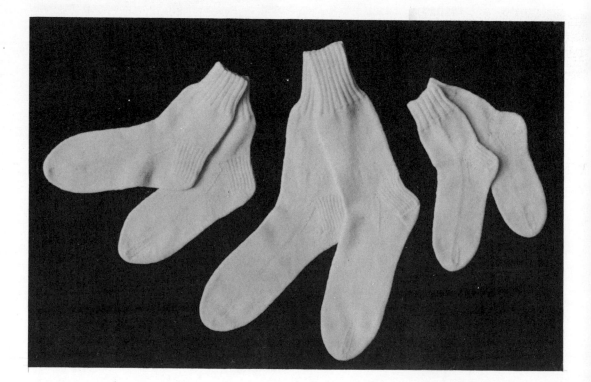

sts at side of heel—19 (26–26) sts; 2nd Needle: Work across instep sts; 3rd Needle: Pick up and k 12 (16–16) sts at other side of heel, k 7 (10–10) sts to center of heel. Work around as follows: Row 1: K to last 3 sts on 1st needle, k 2 tog, k 1; work across sts on 2nd needle; 3rd Needle; K 1, sl 1, k 1, psso, k to end of row. Row 2: Knit. Repeat these last 2 rows 6 (8–8) times more. ON CHILDREN'S SOCKS ONLY: dec 2 sts on instep needle. On Women's and Men's Sizes Only, sl 1 st from 1st and 3rd needles onto 2nd needle (32 sts on 2nd needle and 16 sts on 1st and 3rd needles). ON ALL SIZES: k round and round until foot measures 6¼ (7½– 9½)", or desired length, allowing 1¼ (2– 2)" to finish toe. SHAPE TOE: Row 1: 1st Needle: K to last 3 sts on needle, k 2 tog, k 1; 2nd Needle: K 1, sl 1, k 1, psso, k to last 3 sts, k 2 tog, k 1; 3rd Needle; K 1, sl 1, k 1, psso, k to end of needle. Row 2: Knit. Repeat these last 2 rows until 20 (24–24) sts remain. With 3rd Needle, k 5 (6–6) sts from 1st Needle—10 (12–12) sts on each of 2 needles. Weave or sew sts tog.

## Gloves for the Family

Directions are for Size 4. Changes for Sizes 5, 6, 7, 8, and 9 are in parentheses.

**Materials.** Nylon and Wool, 3 ply—1 oz. for Sizes 4 through 6; 2 ozs. for Sizes 7 through 9. Double-Pointed Needles No. 2.

**Gauge.** 9 sts—1"; 12 rows—1".

**Right Glove.** Cast on 46 (50–54–60–64–68) sts. Divide sts onto 3 needles and join, being careful not to twist sts. K 1, p 1 in ribbing for 2 (2–2½–2½–3–3)". K around for 6 rnds, then start thumb increases as follows: Rnd 1: Inc 1 st in each of first 2 sts (4 sts in thumb), k to end of rnd. Rnds 2 and 3: Knit. Rnd 4: Inc 1 st in first st, k 2, inc 1 st in next st, k to end of rnd. Rnds 5 and 6: Knit. Rnd 7: Inc 1 st in first st, k 4, inc 1 st in next st, k to end of rnd. Continue to inc 2 sts in this manner (having 2 sts more between increases) every 3rd rnd until there are 16 (18–18–20–20–22) sts in thumb. Slip these sts onto a holder and cast on 2 sts over these sts. K around on 46 (50–54–60–64–68) sts until piece measures 5 (5½–6½–

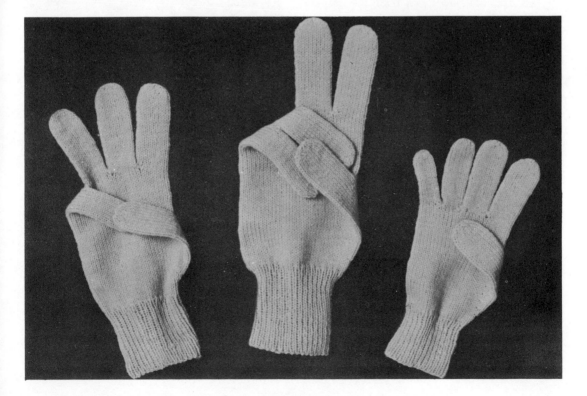

6¾–7½–7¾ )″ from start, or desired length to base of fingers. FIRST FINGER: K first 7 (7–8–8–9–9) sts of 1st Needle (palm), cast on 2 sts, then k last 7 (8–8–9–9–10) sts of 3rd Needle (back of hand) and place remaining sts on a holder. Divide sts on 3 needles. Join and k around on these 16 (17–18–18–19–20–21) sts for 2 (2¼–2¾–2¾–3–3)″. Next Rnd: * K 2 tog, k 1, repeat from * ending k 2 tog (k 2–0–k 2 tog–k 2–0). K 1 rnd even. Next Rnd: * K 2 tog, repeat from * to end of rnd. Cut yarn, draw through remaining sts and fasten. SECOND FINGER: Join yarn and k 6 (6–7–7–8–8) sts from palm of hand, cast on 2 sts, k next 6 (7–7–8–8–9) sts from back of hand, pick up 2 sts over the 2 sts cast on first finger. Join and k around for 2¼ (2½–3–3–3¼–3¼)″. Dec and finish as for first finger. THIRD FINGER: Join yarn and k next 5 (5–6–7–7–8) sts from palm of hand, cast on 2 sts, k next 5 (6–6–7–8–8) sts from back of hand, pick up 2 sts over cast on sts for second finger. Join and k around. Finish as for first finger. FOURTH FINGER: Pick up remaining sts and pick up 2 sts over the cast-on sts of third finger. Join and k around for 1¾ (1¾–2–2–2½–2½)″. Finish as for other fingers. THUMB: Pick up sts from st holder and 2 sts over cast on sts of hand. Join and k around on 18 (20–20–22–22–24) sts for 1¾ (2–2¼–2¼–2½–2½)″. Dec and finish as for other fingers.

**Left Glove.** Work to correspond to right glove, reversing all shaping.

## Cable Socks

Sizes 7½–12½

**Materials.** Nylon and Wool, 3 ply, Sizes 7½–9½, 3 ozs. Sizes 10–12½, 4 ozs. Double-Pointed Sock Needles, No. 1.

**Gauge.** 9 sts—1″; 12 rnds—1″.

Starting at cuff, cast on 68 sts loosely. Divide sts among 3 needles. Join, being careful not to twist sts. Work in k 1, p 1 ribbing for 2″, inc evenly to 72 sts on last rnd. Work in pat as follows: Rnd 1: * P 2, k 2, p 2, k 6. Repeat from * around. Rnd 2: * P 2,

k 2, p 2, make a cable over next 6 sts (to make a cable, slip the first 3 sts onto a spare needle and place in back of work, k the next 3 sts, then k the 3 sts from spare needle). Repeat from * around. Rnds 3 to 7: Repeat rnd 1. Rnds 2 to 7 constitute the pattern. Work in pat until piece measure 11″ in all, or desired length. Divide sts for heel as follows: With fourth needle, k across first 16 sts; sl 22 sts from third needle onto other end of fourth needle (38 sts on heel needle). Divide remaining 34 sts on 2 needles for instep. Work back and forth over the heel sts **only** as follows:

**Heel.** Row 1: Sl 1, p across, dec 4 sts evenly. Row 2: * Sl 1, k 1, repeat from * across. Row 3: Sl 1, p across. Repeat last 2 rows alternately until piece measures 2¼″, ending with a p row. TURN HEEL: Row 1: K 21, k 2 tog, k 1, turn. Row 2: Sl 1, p 9, p 2 tog, p 1, turn. Row 3: Sl 1, k 10, k 2 tog, k 1, turn. Row 4: Sl 1, p 11, p 2 tog, p 1, turn.

Row 5: Sl 1, k 12, k 2 tog, k 1, turn. Row 6: Sl 1, p 13, p 2 tog, p 1, turn, Row 7: Sl 1, k 14, k 2 tog, k 1, turn. Row 8: Sl 1, p 15, p 2 tog, p 1, turn. Row 9: Sl 1, k 16, k 2 tog , k 1, turn. Row 10: Sl 1, p 17, p 2 tog, p 1, turn. Row 11: Sl 1, k 18, k 2 tog, k 1, turn. Row 12: Sl 1, p 19, p 2 tog, p 1, turn. Row 13: K across (22 sts on heel needle).

**Instep.** With heel needle, first needle, pick up and k 16 sts along side of heel; with second needle, work in pat across instep sts; with third needle, pick up and k 16 sts along other side of heel; k 11 sts from heel needle. There are 27 sts on first and third needles; 34 sts on second needle. SHAPE INSTEP: Rnd 1: K to last 3 sts on first needle, k 2 tog, k 1; work in pat across second needle; on third needle k 1, sl 1, k 1, psso, k to end of rnd. Rnd 2: K across first needle, work in pat across second needle; k across third needle. Repeat the last 2 rnds until 34 sts remain on first and third needles. Work even until piece measures 2½″ less than required foot size.

**Shape Toe.** Rnd 1: On first needle, k to last 3 sts, k 2 tog, k 1; on second needle, k 1, sl 1, k 1, psso, k across to last 3 sts, k 2 tog, k 1; on third needle k 1, sl 1, k 1, psso, k to end of rnd. Rnd 2: K around. Repeat the last 2 rnds until 20 sts remain. With third needle, k across sts of first needle (10 sts on each of 2 needles). Weave sts tog.

## Knitted Afghan

**Materials.** 28 2-oz skeins jumbo size yarn; one pair No. 13 knitting needles; one dp needle; one No. 5 crochet hook.

**Gauge.** 5 sts=2 inches; 5 rows=1 inch.

**Center Panel.** Cast on 46 sts. K 10 rows (5 ridges). Now work in pattern as follows:

ROW 1: P 2, k 8, p 2 for wishbone cable; put a marker on needle; k 6, * yo twice, k 2 tog. Repeat from * 4 times more, yo twice, k 6 for fan pattern; put a marker on needle; p 2, k 8, p 2 for other cable (29 sts on fan pattern).

ROW 2: K 2, p 8, k 2; slip marker; k 7, * p 1, k 2. Repeat from * 4 times more; p 1, k 6; slip marker; k 2, p 8, k 2.

ROW 3: P 2, slip next 2 sts on dp needle, and hold in front of work; k next 2 sts; k sts from dp needle; slip next 2 sts on dp needle, and hold in back of work; k next 2 sts; k sts from dp needle (cable twist made), p 2; slip marker (always slip markers on every row); k to next marker, p 2, make cable twist, p 2.

ROW 4: K 2, p 8, k 2; k to last marker; k 2, p 8, k 2.

ROW 5: P 2, k 8, p 2; k 6, yo twice, k 2 tog, k 13, k 2 tog, yo twice, k 6; p 2, k 8, p 2 (31 sts on fan pattern).

ROW 6: K 2, p 8, k 2; k 7, p 1, k 16, p 1, k 6; k 2, p 8, k 2.

ROWS 7 AND 8: Repeat rows 3 and 4.

ROW 9: P 2, k 8, p 2; k 6, yo twice, k 2 tog, yo twice, k 2 tog, k 11, k 2 tog, yo twice, k 2 tog, yo twice, k 6 p 2, k 8, p 2.

ROW 10: K 2, p 8, k 2; k 7, p 1, k 2, p 1, k 14, p 1, k 2, p 1, k 6; k 2, p 8, k 2 (35 sts on fan pattern).

ROW 11: Repeat row 3.

ROW 12: K 2, p 8, k 2; k 11, * yo twice, k 1. Repeat from * 13 times more, yo twice, k 10; k 2, p 8, k 2.

ROW 13: P 2, k 8, p 2; k 6, yo twice, k 2 tog, yo twice, k 2 tog; yo twice; dropping the 15 double yarn overs, slip the next 14 sts on right-hand needle; slip them back on left-hand needle, and p 15 tog; yo twice, k 2 tog, yo twice, k 2 tog, yo twice, k 6; p 2, k 8, p 2 (29 sts on fan pattern).

ROW 14: Repeat row 2. Repeat rows 3 to 14 incl until piece measures about 52 inches, ending with row 14.

NEXT ROW: Discarding markers, k 16, * k 2 tog, k 1. Repeat from * to last 16 sts, k 16 (46 sts). K 9 rows. Bind off.

**Right Side Panel.** Cast on 38 sts. K 10 rows.

ROW 1: K 4 for side edge; slip marker on needle; p 2, k 8, p 2 for cable; slip marker on needle; k 6, * yo twice, k 2 tog. Repeat from

* 4 times more, yo twice, k 6 for fan pattern. Knitting the 4 sts at side edge on every row, work fan pattern and cable same as for center panel until piece measures same as center panel, ending with 14th row.

NEXT ROW: K across; dec 7 sts evenly over center of fan pattern. Discard markers. K 9 rows. Bind off.

**Left Side Panel.** Cast on 38 sts. K 10 rows.

ROW 1: K 6, * yo twice, k 2 tog. Repeat from * 4 times more; yo twice, k 6; slip marker on needle; p 2, k 8, p 2; slip marker on needle; k 4. Complete to correspond to right side panel. Sew panels tog. Block.

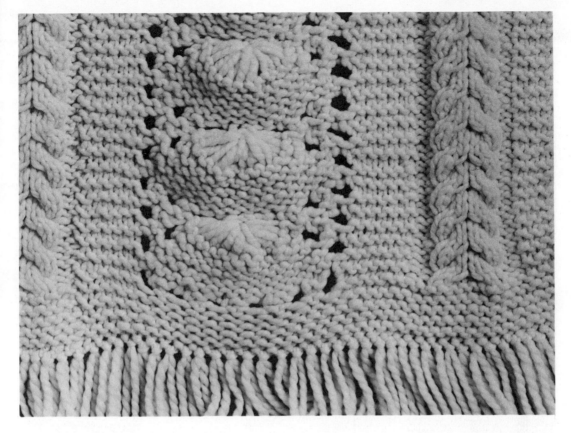

**Fringe.** Cut yarn 10½″ long. Fold in half. With crochet hook, pull loop to wrong side through first stitch of afghan; slip ends through loop, and pull up. Continue in every stitch across ends of afghan.

## Bedspread

**Materials.** Mercerized Bedspread Cotton: Single Size Spread—72×106″ (including fringe)—24 balls of White, Ecru, or Cream; Double Size Spread—92×106″ (including fringe)—30 balls of White, Ecru, or Cream. American Standard Steel Double-Pointed Knitting Needles No. 0.

**Gauge.** Block measures 10″ square.

**Block.** Starting at the center, cast on 8 sts on 4 needles. Rnd 1: * Yo, k 1, repeat from * around (16 sts). Rnd 2: K around. Rnd 3: * Yo, k 1, repeat from * around (32 sts). Rnd 4: K around. Rnd 5: * Yo, p 2, (k 1, yo) twice; k 1, p 2, yo, k 1, repeat from * around. Rnd 6: * P 3, k 5, p 3, k 1, repeat from * around (48 sts). Rnd 7: * Yo, p 3, k 2, yo, k 1, yo, k 2, p 3, yo, k 1, repeat from * around. Rnd 8: * P 4, k 7, p 4, k 1, repeat from * around (64 sts). Rnd 9: * Yo, p 4, k 3, yo, k 1, yo, k 3, p 4, yo, k 1, repeat from * around. Rnd 10: * P 5, k 9, p 5, k 1, repeat from * around (80 sts). Rnd 11: * Yo, p 5, k 4, yo, k 1, yo, k 4, p 5, yo, k 1, repeat from * around. Rnd 12: * P 6, k 11, p 6, k 1, repeat from * around

(66 sts). Rnd 15: * Yo, p 6, place thread along. Rnd 70: * k 2, yo, k 1 * rep 11 times. K 2, hook off work * ( 8 k 1 pws, k 4 k 2 nag 6 )...repeat from * around. Row. Rnd 37: * Yo, k 1 * repeat from * around. Rnd 14: ... 1, k 1... yo k 2 repeat from * around. Rnd 5...repeat from * around. (160)

(96 sts). Rnd 13: * Yo, p 6, place thread at back of work, sl 1, k 1, psso, k 7, k 2 tog, p 6, yo, k 1, repeat from * around. Rnd 14: * P 7, k 9, p 7, k 1, repeat from * around. Rnd 15: * Yo, p 3, yo, k 1, yo, p 3; sl 1, k 1, psso, k 5, k 2 tog, p 3, yo, k 1, yo, p 3, yo, k 1, repeat from * around. Rnd 16: * P 4, k 3, p 3, k 7, p 3, k 3, p 4, k 1, repeat from * around (112 sts). Rnd 17: * Yo, p 4, (k 1, yo) twice; k 1, p 3; sl 1, k 1, psso, k 3, k 2 tog, p 3, (k 1, yo) twice; k 1, p 4, yo, k 1, repeat from * around. Rnd 18: * P 5, k 5, (p 3, k 5) twice; p 5, k 1, repeat from * around (128 sts). Rnd 19: * Yo, p 5; k 2, yo, k 1, yo, k 2; p 3, sl 1, k 1, psso, k 1, k 2 tog, p 3; k 2, yo, k 1, yo, k 2; p 5, yo, k 1, repeat from * around. Rnd 20: * P 6, k 7, p 3, k 3, p 3, k 7, p 6, k 1, repeat from * around (144 sts). Rnd 21: * Yo, p 6, k 3, yo, k 1, yo, k 3, p 3, sl 1, k 2 tog, psso, p 3, k 3, yo, k 1, yo, k 3, p 6, yo, k 1, repeat from * around. Rnd 22: * (P 7, k 9) twice; p 7, k 1, repeat from * around (160 sts). Rnd 23: * Yo, (p 7, k 4, yo, k 1, yo, k 4) twice; p 7, yo, k 1, repeat from * around. Rnd 24: * P 8, k 11, p 7, k 11, p 8, k 1, repeat from * around (184 sts). Rnd 25: * Yo, p 8, sl 1, k 1, psso, k 7, k 2 tog, p 7, sl 1, k 1, psso, k 7, k 2 tog, p 8, yo, k 1, repeat from * around. Rnd 26: * P 9, k 9, p 7, k 9, p 9, k 1, repeat from * around (176 sts). Rnd 27: * Yo, p 9, sl 1, k 1, psso, k 5, k 2 tog, p 7, sl 1, k 1, psso, k 5, k 2 tog, p 9, yo, k 1, repeat from * around. Rnd 28: * P 10, k 7, p 7, k 7, p 10, k 1, repeat from * around (168 sts). Rnd 29: * Yo, p 10, sl 1, k 1, psso, k 3, k 2 tog, p 7, sl 1, k 1, psso, k 3, k 2 tog, p 10, yo, k 1, repeat from * around. Rnd 30: * P 11, k 5, p 7, k 5, p 11, k 1, repeat from * around (160 sts). Rnd 31: * Yo, p 11, sl 1, k 1, psso, k 1, k 2 tog, p 7, sl 1, k 1, psso, k 1, k 2 tog, p 11, yo, k 1, repeat from * around. Rnd 32: * P 12, k 3, p 7, k 3, p 12, k 1, repeat from * around (152 sts). Rnd 33: * Yo, p 12, sl 1, k 2 tog, psso, p 7, sl 1, k 2 tog, psso, p 12, yo, k 1, repeat from * around. Rnd 34: * P 35, k 1, repeat from * around (144 sts). Rnd 35: * Yo, k 35, yo, k 1, repeat from * around.

Rnd 36: * K 2, (yo, k 2 tog) 17 times; k 2, repeat from * around. Turn. Rnd 37: * Yo, p 37, yo, k 1, repeat from * around (160 sts). Now work back and forth across 1 needle only as follows: Row 1: Bind off 1 st, k across (39 sts), turn. Row 2 (right side): K 1, k 2 tog, * yo, k 2 tog, repeat from * across. Row 3: K 2 tog, * yo, k 2 tog, repeat from * across. Row 4: K 2 tog, * yo, k 2 tog, repeat from * across, ending k 1. Row 5: K 1, k 2 tog, * yo, k 2 tog, repeat from * across, ending k 1. Repeat the last 4 rows (2nd to 5th rows incl) until 4 sts remain. Next row: K 1, k 2 tog, k 1. Bind off.

With wrong side facing, join thread at next needle and, starting with Row 1, work across the next group of sts. Complete remaining two sides to correspond. For Single-Size Spread make 6 rows of 10 Blocks. Double-Size Spread make 8 rows of 10 Blocks. Sew Blocks neatly together on wrong side. Finish edges with Plain or Knotted Fringe or Tassels.

**Plain Fringe.** Cut 10 strands of thread, each 12″ long. Double these strands to form a loop. Insert hook in space on edge of bedspread and draw loop through. Draw loose ends through loop and pull up tightly to form a knot. Make a fringe in every other space (or every ½″) around spread. When fringe is completed, trim ends evenly.

**Knotted Fringe.** Cut 8 strands of thread, each 16″ long, and make a Plain Fringe around edges of spread. Pick up 8 strands of the first fringe and 8 strands of the second fringe and make a knot 1″ down and in the center between 2 previous knots. Pick up remaining strands of second fringe and first 8 strands of next fringe and knot as before. Continue in this manner around. Trim ends evenly.

**Tassel.** Cut a cardboard 4 × 5″. Lay two 8″ strands across width of cardboard. Wind thread around length of cardboard 60 times. Pick up the two 8″ lengths and tie securely. Remove from cardboard and cut loops at opposite end. Wind a strand of thread several times around top 1″ down from where tassel was tied. Trim ends evenly.

# CHAPTER 8 *Crochet*

Because it is so fascinating and versatile, crochet has become a well-loved hand art. Hook and thread plus agile fingers can produce an endless variety of designs in good taste, both modern in feeling and traditional, each with its special charm.

New threads, new stitches, or rather, variations of old ones, constantly appear and open up further possibilities to challenge the imagination of the crochet enthusiast.

The word crochet is derived from the French word "croche" meaning hook. Originally one of a number of lace-making tools, the hook came to be used alone to fashion a multitude of designs.

For many years crochet was carried on almost entirely in convents. The terrible Irish famine of 1846 gave crochet a great impetus due to the fact that pupils of the nuns' made and sold crocheted articles and the proceeds were used to alleviate the suffering. Rare patterns of old lace were skillfully copied by the Irish girls. One of the loveliest types of crochet work is known as "Irish Crochet," which is famous as far back as 1743 when the Royal Dublin Society awarded prizes for outstanding examples of the art. Crochet gradually became one of the graceful accomplishments of the well-born ladies of the time.

## ABBREVIATIONS

| | |
|---|---|
| ch | chain |
| sc | single crochet |
| hdc or half dc | half double crochet |
| dc | double crochet |
| tr | treble |
| d tr | double treble |
| sl st | slip stitch |
| st(s) | stitch(es) |
| tog | together |
| dec | decrease |
| inc(s) | increasing, increased, increase(s) |
| incl | inclusive |
| rnd | round |
| sp | space |
| bl(s) | block, blocks |
| pat | pattern |
| beg | beginning |
| pc | picot |

* This symbol (asterisk) means that the instructions immediately following it are to be repeated the given number of times.

Repeat instructions in parentheses as many times as specified. For example: "(ch 5, sc in next sc) 5 times," means to make all that is in parentheses 5 times in all.

## GAUGE

Gauge in crochet as in knitting is extremely important. It means the number of stitches and the number of rows equivalent to one inch and is given with each instruction when necessary. Make a swatch or practice piece at least 2 inches square using the hook and thread specified in the instructions. Block it; then measure. If it does not correspond with the gauge given, it will be necessary to use a smaller or larger hook. If you have more stitches to the inch you will need a smaller hook; if you have fewer, you need a larger hook. Practice until it is correct.

## THREADS

Many types of threads and yarns may be used for crochet and will produce a variety of effects. With very fine thread and a fine hook, laces can be fashioned which rival those made in almost any other way. Heavy threads and yarn give the bold effects often wanted in modern furnishings. Choose a tightly twisted thread for hard surface effects and long-wearing quality. Select a soft thread or yarn for softer textures. Crochet may be done with cotton, linen, silk, wool, man-made fibers, or combinations of any of these. The texture desired and the purpose of the article being made should determine the choice of thread.

Because sizes and dye lots vary and often cannot be matched, it is advisable to purchase enough thread or yarn to complete an item before beginning to work.

## HOW TO CROCHET

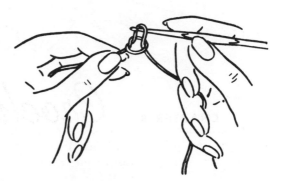

Begin by making a loop. Make a slip knot near the end of the yarn. Hold loop between thumb and forefinger, insert hook in loop and pull up close around end of hook but not too tight.

About 4 inches down from the loop slip thread between third and little fingers of left hand.

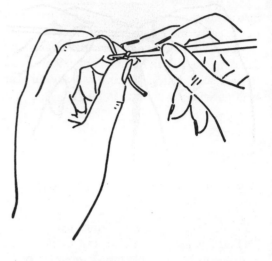

Bring thread to back of hand and over the little and the third finger; then under the middle finger and over the forefinger.

The middle finger of left hand regulates the tension. The motion of hook and thread should be easy and smooth.

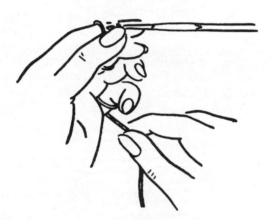

## Chain Stitch

Grasp needle and loop between thumb and forefinger of left hand. Pull ball thread so it lies around fingers firmly but not tightly.

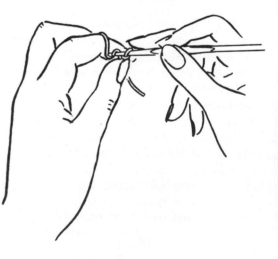

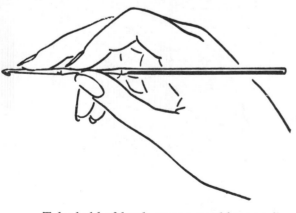

Take hold of hook as you would a pencil. Rest middle finger near tip of hook.

Slip hook under thread catching it and pulling it through loop on hook. This makes one chain. Do not pull tight.

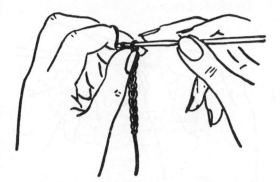

Repeat until you have as many chains as needed. One loop always remains on the hook. Keep thumb and forefinger of left hand near stitch on which you are working.

## Single Crochet

Make a foundation chain for a practice piece. Insert hook from the front under 2 top threads of second chain from hook.

Catch thread with hook ("thread over") and draw through stitch. There are now 2 loops on hook.

Thread over again and draw through these 2 loops. One loop remains on hook. This completes one single crochet.

Now insert hook under two top threads of next stitch and proceed as before.

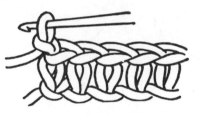

Repeat until you have made a sc in every chain; then ch 1 for turning.

Turn work, insert hook from front under 2 top threads of second st from hook and work as on first row.

*Note*: In all crochet it is customary to pick up the two top threads of every stitch unless otherwise specified. When only the back stitch is picked up a different effect is produced known as rib stitch.

## Turning Work

At the end of a row, a certain number of chain stitches is usually added to bring work into position for the next row. The piece is then turned and the work proceeds. The number of turning chains depends upon the stitch with which the next row begins. This is given in the directions. The turning chain always counts as the first stitch except in single crochet when ch 1 only raises the work to position.

## Joining to Form a Ring

Many instructions start with a row of ch sts which must be joined to form a ring. This is done by making a sl st into the first chain st.

## Double Crochet

First row: Make a chain foundation. Thread over and insert hook from front under two top threads of 4th ch from hook.

Thread over and draw through the stitch. There are now 3 loops on the hook.

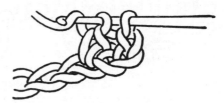

Thread over and draw through 2 loops. Two loops remain on the hook.

Thread over and draw through 2 loops. One loop remains. This completes 1 double crochet.

For next double crochet, thread over, insert hook from front under two top threads of next stitch and proceed as before.

Repeat across row. At end of row ch 3 and turn. The ch 3 counts as first dc in next row.

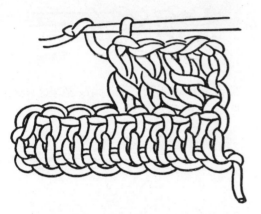

Second and following rows: Thread over, insert hook from front under two top threads of second st on previous row.

## Half Double Crochet

This stitch is made by repeating the first 2 steps of Double Crochet (to the point where there are 3 loops on the hook). Then thread over and draw through all three hoops at once. Ch 2 to turn.

## Slip Stitch

This stitch is used only in joining or where an invisible stitch is required. Insert hook from front through two top threads of stitch. Thread over and with one motion draw thread through st and loop on hook.

## Increasing and Decreasing

Instructions tell you where to increase. Make two sts in one st. Each time you do this you make an extra stitch on the row.

Instructions tell you where to decrease.

*How to Decrease Single Crochet:*

1. Work a single crochet to the point where two loops remain on the hook.

2. Insert hook from front under two top threads of next stitch.

3. Thread over and draw through one loop. There are now 3 loops on hook.

4. Thread over and draw through the 3 loops at once. One loop left on hook. You have worked 2 sc together and there is one less st on the row.

*How to Decrease Double Crochet:*

1. Work a double crochet to the point where there are two loops on the hook.

2. Thread over and insert hook from front under the two top threads of next stitch.

3. Thread over and draw through one loop. There are now 4 loops on hook.

4. Thread over and draw through two loops. There are now 3 loops on hook.

5. Thread over and draw through 3 loops. One loop on hook. You have worked 2 dc together and there is one st less on the row.

You are now ready to make the Baby Surplice or any simple crocheted article.

## Treble Crochet

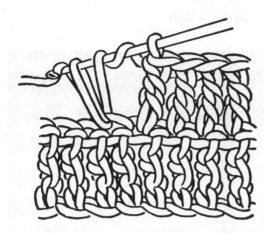

Make a foundation chain.

1. Thread over twice and insert from front under 2 top threads of 5th ch from hook.

2. Thread over and draw through ch. There are now 4 loops on hook.

3. Thread over and draw through 2 loops. Three loops remain.

4. Thread over and draw through 2 loops. Two loops remain.

5. Thread over and draw through 2 loops. One loop remains.

6. For next treble, thread over twice and proceed again with step No. 1, inserting hook under 2 top threads of next stitch.

7. At end of row ch 4 and turn.

## Double Treble

Thread over 3 times, insert hook in stitch and draw loop through. Now 5 loops are on hook. Thread over and draw thread through 2 loops at a time 4 times. This completes a double treble.

## Triple Treble

Thread over hook 4 times, insert hook in st and draw loop through. Now 6 loops are on hook. Thread over and draw thread through 2 loops at a time 5 times. This completes a triple treble.

All crochet is based upon these fundamental stitches. By combining them in various ways, many interesting effects may be produced. Some of the more popular fancy stitches are given here.

## Picot

There are two ways of making picots.

*Method 1:* Work a sc in edge of foundation, ch 3 or 4 or length desired, sl st in top of sc.

*Method 2:* Work a sc, ch 3 or 4 for picot and sc again in same space. Work as many sc's between picots as desired.

## Changing Colors in Crochet

Commence the sc or dc as usual and at the second step of the last sc or dc (inserting hook from front under two top threads of stitch) pick up the second color and pull it through loop or loops on hook. Drop first color, leaving thread to hang until it is picked up in the next row. Work across. If the first color is to

be discontinued, lay it along top of row and work over it for 3 or 4 stitches, then cut thread. The thread at the back must be loose enough to allow work to lie flat.

## FINISHING AND CARE

### Blocking

For woolen articles, follow the instructions for blocking knitted articles (Chapter 7). Cotton articles usually have to be stretched and pinned carefully to a flat padded surface to retain their design and shape.

### Sewing Together

With right sides together sew corresponding pieces together with whipping stitches. Do not pull too tight.

### Laundering

For woolen articles follow instructions given under knitting. Depending upon the article, cotton crocheted pieces usually are washed in mild suds and handled carefully to prevent stretching, then blocked.

## PATTERN STITCHES

### Open Mesh

Make a foundation chain and 5 extra ch sts to turn. Row 1: 1 dc in 6th ch from hook, * ch 2, skip 2 ch, 1 dc in next ch. Repeat from * across row and end with 1 dc in last ch. Ch 5 to turn. Row 2: * 1 dc in dc of previous row, ch 2, skip 2 ch of previous row. Repeat from * across row and end with 1 dc in 3rd ch of 5 ch of previous row. Repeat Row 2.

### Block or Solid Mesh

A block is formed of 4 dc; or 3 dc are required for each additional block when pattern calls for several blocks adjoining. For example: 2 adjoining blocks are formed of 7 dc and 3 adjoining blocks are formed of 10 dc. Spaces and blocks or "open and solid mesh" are used to make filet crochet, arranged to produce an interesting design. Filet designs are worked from a chart of squares. The dark squares represent solid mesh or blocks and the light squares represent open mesh.

## Star Stitch

## Lace Stitch

Make a foundation ch plus 8 extra chains. 1 sc in 9th st from hook, * ch 3, skip 2 ch, 1 dc in next st, ch 3, skip 2 ch, 1 sc in next ch. Repeat from * across row and end with 1 dc in last ch. Row 2: Ch 8, 1 dc in 2nd dc * ch 5, 1 dc in next dc, repeat from * across row and end 1 dc in 6th ch of original group. Row 3: Ch 5, * 1 sc in 3rd ch, ch 3, skip 2 ch, 1 dc in next dc, ch 3, repeat from * across row and end with 1 dc in 6th ch of original group of 8 ch. Repeat Rows 2 and 3 throughout.

Make a foundation chain. Row 1: Skip 1 ch and draw up a loop in each of next 5 sts, thread over and draw through 6 loops on hook. Ch 1, * draw a loop through the eye formed by ch just made, draw a loop through back of last loop of star just made, draw a loop through same chain where last loop of previous star was made, draw a loop through each of next 2 ch sts, thread over and draw through the 6 loops on hook, ch 1. Repeat from * across row and end ch 1. Row 2: Ch 4 and turn. Skip first ch, draw up a loop in each of the next 3 chains, draw a loop through side of first star, draw a loop through eye of next star, thread over and draw through 6 loops on hook. * Ch 1, draw a loop through eye formed by ch just made, draw a loop through back of last loop of star just made, draw a loop through same ch where last loop of previous star was made, draw a loop through side of star of previous row, draw a loop through eye of next star, thread over and draw through 6 loops on hook, ch 1. Repeat from * across row and end ch 1. Repeat Row 2 throughout.

## Shell Stitch

Make a foundation chain and 3 extra ch sts to turn. Row 1: 4 dc in 4th ch from hook, * skip 2 ch, 1 sc in next ch, skip 2 ch, 5 dc in next ch. Repeat from * and end with 1 sc. Row 2: Ch 3, turn, 4 dc in first sc, * 1 sc in 3rd dc of previous row, 5 dc in next sc of previous row. Repeat from * across row and

1 sc in last ch 3 of previous row. Repeat Row 2 throughout.

end with 1 sc in 3rd dc of last group. Repeat Row 2 throughout, working 5 dc in each sc of the previous row and 1 sc in the center dc of the group of 5 dc of the previous row. Shells may be made with as many dc in a group as desired.

## Shawl Stitch

## Brick or Crazy Shell

Make a foundation chain and 3 extra ch sts to turn. Row 1: 3 dc in 4th ch from hook, * skip 3 ch, 1 sc in next ch, ch 3, 3 dc in same ch. Repeat from * across row, and end with 1 sc. Row 2: Ch 3 and turn, 3 dc in sc of previous row, * 1 sc in the space made by ch 3 of previous row, ch 3 and 3 dc in same place. Repeat from * across row and end with

Make a foundation chain and 3 extra ch sts to turn. Row 1: 1 dc in the 4th ch, ch 2, 2 dc in same ch. * Skip 3 ch, 2 dc in next ch, ch 2 and 2 dc in same ch. Repeat from * across row. Row 2: Ch 3 and turn, 1 dc into space made by ch 2 of previous row, ch 2, 2 dc in same space, * 2 dc in next space made by ch 2 of previous row, ch 2 and 2 dc in same space. Repeat from * across row. Repeat Row 2 throughout.

most conceals the 4 dc just completed), * 1 sc between the 4th and 5th dc of next group of 8 dc, 4 dc in the next sc, then work 4 dc in the last dc of the previous group of 8 dc of row below (this almost conceals the 4 dc just completed). Repeat from * across row and end with 1 sc between the 4th and 5th dc of last group of 8 dc and 4 dc in the last dc of this group. Repeat Row 2 for pattern.

## Fancy Puff Stitch

Make a foundation chain plus 3 extra ch sts to turn. Row 1: Work 8 dc in 4th ch from hook. * Skip 4 ch and work 1 sc into next ch. Skip 4 ch and work 8 dc in next ch. Repeat from * across row and end with 4 dc. Row 2: Turn without making a chain, 4 dc in first sc, then work 4 dc in the last dc of the group of 4 dc of row below (this al-

## Knot Stitch

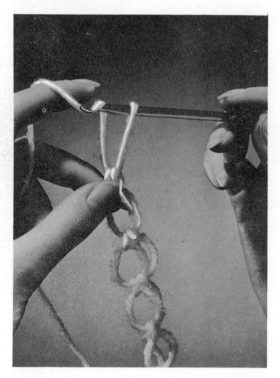

Make a foundation chain the desired length. * Draw up a loop ½ inch long, thread over and draw through chain, 1 sc in back strand of loop (this is a single knot); repeat from * to make a double knot. Skip 2 chains, 1 sc in each of next 2 chs. Repeat from first * across. End with one sc in last ch. Ch 3 to turn. Row 2: Make a single knot, * 1 sc

## Color Plate 9 — Summer Evening Scarf

A triangle of double organdy with wide tatted edging of wool. Instructions for making are given in Chapter 9, Tatting.

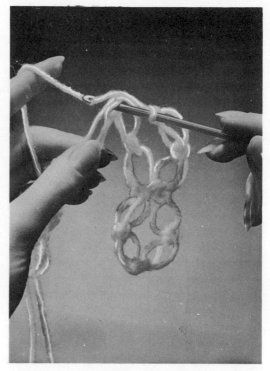

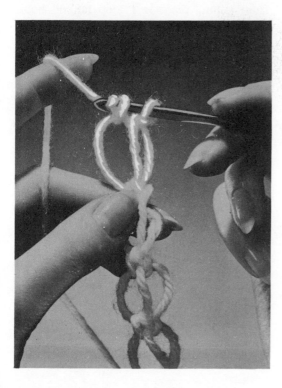

in center of double knot of previous row, make a double knot; repeat from * across row. Ch 3 to turn. Repeat Row 2 for pattern.

## Afghan Stitch

Make a foundation chain plus 1 to turn. Row 1: Beginning in 2nd ch from hook draw up a loop through each ch and keep all loops on hook. Row 2: Yo and draw through 1 loop, * yo and draw through 2 loops. Repeat from * until there is 1 loop left on hook. Row 3: Draw a loop through second upright stitch and through each one across row keeping all loops on hook. Repeat Rows 2 and 3 for pattern.

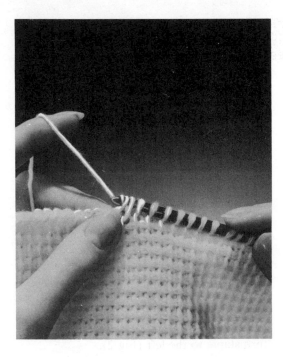

## Loop Stitch

Use a piece of cardboard ¼, ½, or ¾ inch wide or a tongue-depressor for a gauge. Make a chain desired length. Row 1: Work sc in each st across row. Row 2: * Hold cardboard in back of work, insert hook in next sc, wind yarn around cardboard from back to front, yarn over hook and draw loop through st, yarn over and draw through first

## Hairpin Lace

This is made on a hairpin fork or staple which comes in several sizes ½, 2, and 3 inches wide. This work probably originated by using fine thread and crocheting over an ordinary straight hairpin.

Hairpin lace is very simple to make and goes quickly. After learning the basic steps, you can make many attractive variations.

**Uses of Hairpin Lace.** With wool yarn and a large fork, a soft fluffy lace results which can be used for afghans, baby wear, carriage covers, stoles, etc.

With fine cotton thread, lace edgings and insertions of great delicacy can be made for various uses.

With coarse cotton, linen, or jute threads, bold lace for curtains, mats, pillows, or trimmings can be made.

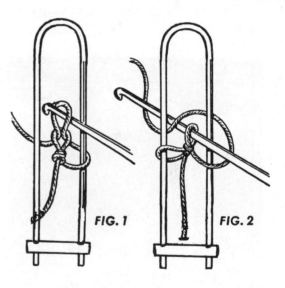

FIG. 1          FIG. 2

**How to Make Hairpin Lace.** BASIC STEPS: Hold staple with curve at the top. Bar at lower end is to keep stitches from slipping off.

1. Make a loop near the end of the ball of thread. Insert hook in loop and wind ball thread around right prong of staple. Thread over hook and draw through loop, keeping loop at center (Fig 1).

2. Raise hook to a vertical position and turn staple to the left (Fig 2).

loop, yo and draw through 2 loops on hook. Repeat from * to form each loop. Work 1 loop in each st. Repeat Rows 1 and 2 for pattern. This stitch can also be done by looping the thread over forefinger of left hand instead of using a gauge.

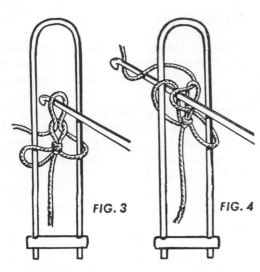

FIG. 3     FIG. 4

3. Thread over hook and draw through on hook (Fig 3).

4. Insert hook in loop of left prong (Fig 4). Thread over hook and draw loop through (2 loops on hook), thread over and draw through 2 loops.

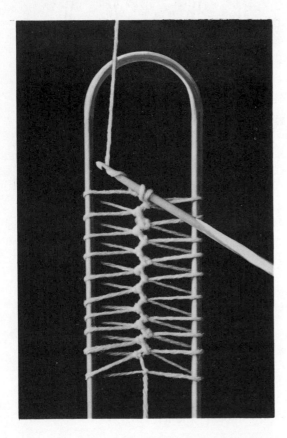

Repeat steps 2, 3, and 4 until staple is filled. Remove bar, slip off all but last few loops, replace bar, and proceed as before for length desired.

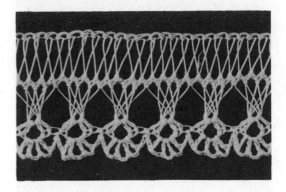

**Pattern No. 1.** Work hairpin lace for length desired keeping the twist in the loops. Across one side work a sc in each loop.

Scallop, Row 1: Working on opposite side, attach thread through first 4 loops, ch 3, 1 dc in same space, ch 3, 2 dc in same space, * 2 dc through next 4 loops, ch 3, 2 dc in same space (shell), repeat from * across row, turn. Row 2: * Ch 2, 4 dc with ch 2 between each dc in next shell, ch 2, sc between shells, repeat from * across row.

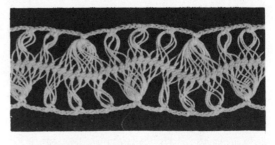

**Pattern No. 2.** Work hairpin lace for length desired. Join thread in three end loops and work 1 sc in same space, * ch 5, 1 sc over next 3 loops, repeat from * once, ** ch 5, 1 sc through next 9 loops, * ch 5, 1 sc over next 3 loops, repeat from * twice, repeat from ** across length. Join thread in first 9 loops of opposite side and work in same manner as first side reversing the clusters.

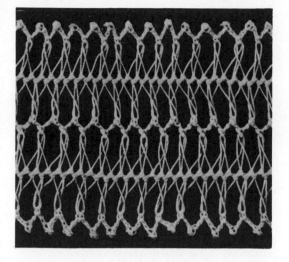

buds, stems, etc. The picot is used generously on both background and motif.

Given here is a typical background pattern and the rose motif which is also typical. Here also is a round medallion which can be repeated and used in many ways. On page 358 you will find instructions for an exquisite round mat using an elaborate border of Irish crochet on linen. It could be an extra special mat for dining or be used in the bedroom.

**Pattern No. 3.** Work 2 lengths of hairpin lace the desired length. Join thread in 2 end loops of first length and work 1 sc in same space, * ch 2, 1 sc over 2 corresponding loops of second length, ch 2, 1 sc over next 2 loops of first length, repeat from * across length.

Row 2: Edge. Join thread in 2 end loops of lace, 1 sc in same space, * ch 5, slip st in 3rd st from hook for picot, ch 2, 1 sc over next 2 loops, repeat from * across length. Work other side to correspond.

## Background Pattern

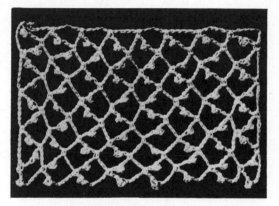

## IRISH CROCHET

This distinctive type of crocheted lace never goes out of style. It has a kind of timeless beauty of which one does not tire. It is suitable for many things from linens to wearing apparel and baby articles.

Irish crochet is worked not in rows like ordinary crochet but with a mesh background. The motifs are worked separately. The mesh can be worked in around the motifs or the motifs can be applied to the finished background. The latter is a more simplified method.

The most beautiful examples of Irish crochet are done with very fine thread. The motifs are varied: flowers, tendrils, leaves,

Ch ½″ to 1″ longer than actual measurement calls for, sc in 3rd st from hook (this forms the picot), ch 2, sc in 9th ch from picot, * ch 5, sl st in 3rd st from hook for picot, ch 2, skip 4 chs, sc in next ch (a single picot loop). Repeat from *. Ch 9, turn.

*2nd Row*—Sl st in 3rd st from hook for picot, ch 2, sc in next loop, * work a single picot loop, sc in next loop, repeat from * and repeat 2nd row.

### Irish Crochet Motif

Ch 5, join to form a ring, ch 6, dc in ring, * ch 3, dc in ring, repeat from * twice, ch 3, join in 3rd st of ch.

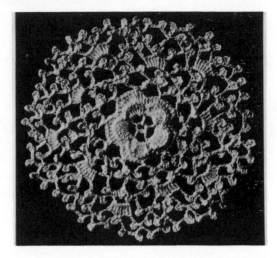

double picot loop, sc in 4th dc, ch 5, sc in same space, double picot loop, sc between picots of next loop, double picot loop, 7 dc in next ch 9 loop, double picot loop, sc between picots of next loop, repeat from * 4 times ending with sl st in same space as beginning.

*10th Round:* Sl st between next 2 picots, * double picot loop, sc between picots of next loop, double picot loop, sc between picots of next loop, double picot loop, sc in 4th dc, ch 5, sc in same space, double picot loop, sc between picots of next loop, double picot loop, sc between picots of next loop, repeat from * around, join, cut thread.

*2nd Round:* Ch 1, * 1 dc ,7 tr c, 1 dc in next ch 3 loop, sc in next dc, repeat from * all around.

*3rd Round:* * Ch 6, sc in next sc in back of petal, repeat from * all around.

*4th Round:* * 1 dc, 8 tr c, 1 dc in next loop, sc in next sc, repeat from * all around.

*5th Round:* Sl st to 2nd tr c, * ch 7, sl st in 5th st from hook for picot, ch 7, sl st in 5th st from hook for picot, ch 2 (double picot loop), skip 4 tr c, sc in next tr c, make another double picot loop, sc in 2nd tr c of next petal, repeat from * all around.

*6th Round:* Sl st to center of loop between picots, * double picot loop, sc between picots of next loop, repeat from * all around.

*7th Round:* Ch 10, * sl st in 5th st from hook for picot, ch 7, sl st in 5th st from hook for picot, ch 2, sc between picots of next loop, ch 9, sc between picots of next loop, double picot loop, dc in next sc, ch 7, repeat from * 3 times, sl st in 5th st from hook for picot, ch 7, sl st in 5th st from hook for picot, ch 2, sc between picots of next loop, ch 9, sc between picots of next loop, double picot loop, join in 3rd st of ch 10.

*8th Round:* Sl st between next 2 picots, * double picot loop, 7 dc in next ch 9 loop, double picot loop, sc between picots of next loop, ch 9, sc between picots of next loop, repeat from * 4 times ending with sl st in same space as beginning.

*9th Round:* Sl st between next 2 picots, *

## Irish Crochet Rose

Ch 7, join to form a ring, ch 5, dc in ring, * ch 2, dc in ring, repeat from * 5 times, ch 2, join in 3rd st of ch.

*2nd Round:* Ch 1 and over each mesh work 1 sc, 4 dc, 1 sc, join.

*3rd Round:* * Ch 5, sl st in back of work between next 2 petals, repeat from * 7 times.

*4th Round:* Ch 1 and over each loop work 1 sc, 6 dc, 1 sc, join.

*5th Round:* * Ch 6, sl st in back of work between next 2 petals, repeat from * 7 times.

*6th Round:* Ch 1, and over each loop work 1sc, 1 hdc, 7 dc, 1 hdc, 1 sc, join, cut thread.

## CROCHETING FOR CHILDREN

### Infant's Surplice for Beginners

**Materials.** Jumbo Pompadour, 3 ozs.; Plastic Crochet Hook, Size 6.

**Gauge.** 9 sts—2".

**Back.** Ch 47 for lower edge; 1 dc in 4th ch from hook and in each st to end (45 dc). Ch 3, turn (ch 3 counts as first dc), 1 dc in 2nd dc and in each st across. Repeat last row until 5½" from beginning or desired length to underarm. Ch 29 at end of last row for sleeve, turn. Work 1 dc in 4th ch from hook and in each ch across, work 1 dc in each dc to end of row; with another strand of yarn, ch 27 sts for 2nd sleeve, join this ch to end of row below; continue last row, working 1 dc in each st to end of ch (99 dc). Work dc on all sts until sleeve edge measures 3¼". Work across 42 sts for front. Work on these 42 sts only for 1" (end at sleeve edge). Shape opposite edge for neck as follows: Row 1: Ch 3, turn, work across row working 3 dc in last st (44 dc). Row 2: Ch 3, turn, 1 dc in 3rd ch from hook, 2 dc in next dc, work to end of row (47 dc). Repeat these two rows until sleeve edge measures 6½" (end at neck edge). Next Row: Continue incs. at neck

edge, work to within 27 sts of sleeve edge. Leave these 27 sts free for sleeve. Continue shaping neck edge as before until there are 45 dc. Work even until same length as back. Fasten off. Skip center 15 sts for back of neck. Join yarn in next st and work other side to correspond reversing shaping.

**Finishing.** Sew side and sleeve seams. Work 1 row sc around sleeve edges and around entire surplice keeping an even edge. Steam lightly. Sew ribbon at top and bottom of even edge of each front and at corresponding places at underarm seam.

### Crocheted Baby Set

**Materials.** Fingering Yarn, 5 ozs. Baby Pink; 1 oz. White for trim; Plastic Crochet Hook, Size E; 3½ yards narrow Ribbon; 1½ yards ⅝" Ribbon.

**Gauge.** 4 rows of pat—1"; 5 single knot sts—2".

**Sacque.** With Pink starting at neck, ch 61 to measure about 12½", sc in 2nd st from hook, 1 sc in each remaining st of ch, ch 1, turn. Row 2: 1 sc in each of the next 12 sc (front), 3 sc in next sc, 1 sc in each of the next 4 sc (shoulder), 3 sc in next sc, 1 sc in each of the next 24 sc (back), 3 sc in next sc, 1 sc in each of the next 4 sc (shoulder), 3 sc in next sc, 1 sc in each of the next 12 sc (front), ch 1, turn. Row 3: 1 sc in each sc, ch 1, turn. Row 4: 1 sc in each of the next 13 sc, 3 sc in next sc, 1 sc in each of the next 6 sc, 3 sc in next sc, 1 sc in each of the next 26 sc, 3 sc in next sc, 1 sc in each of the next 6 sc, 3 sc in next sc, 1 sc in each of the next 13 sc, ch 1, turn. Row 5: 1 sc in each sc, ch 1, turn. Row 6: 1 sc in each sc and 3 sc in center st at each of the 4 inc points, ch 1, turn. Row 7: 1 sc in each sc; ch 1, turn. Rows 8, 9, 10, 11: Repeat Rows 6 and 7, twice. Row 12: Draw up a ⅜" loop on hook, yo and pull through loop forming a ch st, sc over single loop of st (single knot st), sc in next sc, repeat from beg across row, turn. Row 13: * Work a single knot st, sc over the 2 loops of next single knot st (pat), repeat from * across row, turn. Repeat the last row 3 times (16th row is right side of work). Row 17: * Single knot st, sc over the 2 loops of next single knot st, repeat from * 16 times, ch 3, skip 15 single knot sts for sleeve, sc in next single knot st, work 34 pat across back, ch 3, skip 15 single knot sts for other sleeve, sc in next single knot st, work 17 pat across other front, turn. Row 18: * Single knot st, sc in next single knot st, repeat from * 16 times, single knot st, skip 1 st of ch, sc in next st of ch, * single knot st, sc in next single knot st, repeat from * 33 times, single knot st, skip 1 st of ch, sc in next st of ch, * single knot st, sc in next single knot st, repeat from * 16 times, turn. Work even in pat until Sacque measures 8" from neck edge, fasten off.

**Sleeve.** Working on wrong side of armhole, attach yarn at underarm and work 18 pat around armhole, join in 1st single knot st, turn. Next Row: * Single knot st, sc in next single knot st, repeat from * all around dec 1 pat at underarm (17 pat), join, turn. Next Row: * Single knot st, sc in next single knot st, repeat from * all around, join, turn. Repeat last row until sleeve measures 4" from underarm. Next Row: Working on right side of sleeve, * work 1 sc in each of the next 2 single knot sts, sc in next sc, repeat from * all around ending with sc in last single knot st, join. Next Row: Ch 1, 1 sc in each sc, join. Repeat the last row once, fasten off. Next Row: Edge: Attach White and * work a single knot st, skip 1 sc, sl st in next sc, repeat from * all around, join, fasten off. Work other sleeve in same manner. Beading: With right side toward you, attach Pink in 1st st at neck edge, ch 3, skip 1 sc, hdc in next sc, * ch 1, skip 1 sc, hdc in next sc, repeat from * across neck edge, fasten off. Attach White at opposite side of neck edge, * work a single knot st, sc in next hdc, repeat from * across neck edge, then work in pat down front skipping about ⅜" space between knot sts, work a single knot st in each single knot st across lower edge and work up opposite front to correspond to 1st front, join,

fasten off. Lace ribbon through beading.

**Cap.** With Pink ch 4, join to form a ring, ch 1 and work 8 sc in ring; do not join this or following rnds. Place a marker at beg of each rnd. Rnd 2: 2 sc in each sc. Rnd 3: * Sc in next sc, 2 sc in next sc, repeat from * all around. Rnd 4: Work 1 rnd sc. Rnd 5: Same as rnd 3. Rnd 6: Inc in every 3rd sc. Rnds 7 and 8: Work 2 rnds even in sc. Rnd 9: Inc in every 4th sc, sl st in next sc to even rnd. Rnd 10: Draw up a ⅜" loop on hook, yo and pull through loop forming a ch st, sc over single loop of st (single knot st), skip 1 sc, sc in next sc, * single knot st, skip 1 sc, sc in next sc, repeat from * around then sl st in 1st single knot st (30 single knot sts), turn. Rnd 11: * Work a single knot st, sc over the 2 loops of next single knot st, repeat from * 28 times, single knot st, sc in same sp as beg, then sl st in 1st single knot st, turn. Rnd 12: * Single knot st, sc over the 2 loops of next single knot st (pat), repeat from * 26 times (3 pat left free for back of cap), turn. Rnd 13: * Single knot st, sc over the 2 loops of next single knot st, repeat from * 26 times, turn. Repeat Rnd 13 until pat section measures 6" from Rnd 9, fasten off. Leaving last 6 rows or 1½" free for Turn Back and working on right side, attach Pink in next st, working across lower edge of cap, work 38 sc across to same sp at opposite side. Next Row: Ch 1, turn and work 1 sc in each sc. Repeat last row once, fasten off. With wrong side of work toward you, attach White at side edge of Turn Back and work a row of single knot st pat around Turn Back only. Fasten off. Trim with ribbon ties as illustrated.

**Bootees.** With Pink ch 14, 3 sc in 2nd st from hook, 1 sc in each of the next 11 sts of ch, 3 sc in end st, working on other side of ch, 1 sc in each of the next 11 sts, do not join this or following rnds, place a marker at beg of each rnd. Rnd 2: 2 sc in each of the next 3 sc, 1 sc in each of the next 11 sc, 2 sc in each of the next 3 sc, 1 sc in each of the next 11 sc. Rnd 3: * 1 sc in next sc, 2 sc in next sc, repeat from * twice, 1 sc in each of the next 12 sc, 2 sc in next sc, * sc in next sc,

2 sc in next sc, repeat from * once, 1 sc in each of the next 11 sc. Rnds 4 and 5: 1 sc in each sc on sides inc 3 sc evenly spaced around each end in each rnd (52 sc in last rnd), sl st in next st to even rnd, turn. Rnd 6: 1 sc in each st picking up entire st by inserting hook around entire st, join, ch 1, turn. Rnd 7: 1 sc in each sc, do not join. Rnds 8 and 9: Repeat Rnd 7. Fold in half lengthwise and mark center for toe. Rnd 10: 1 sc in each sc dec 3 sts evenly spaced around toe. Next Row: 1 sc in each sc to within 3 sts from center st at toe, then working in back loop of sts only, work 1 sc in each of the next 7 sc. Working through both loops of sts, 1 sl st in each of the next 2 sts, ch 1, turn. Next Row: Skip the 2 sl sts and working in back loop of sts, 1 sc in each of the next 7 sc, working through both loops of sts, sl st in each of the next 2 sc on side of bootee, ch 1, turn. Repeat the last row 6 times. Next Row: Skip the 2 sl sts and working in back loop of sts, 1 sc in each of the next 7 sc, sl st in same st on side of bootee, do not turn. Next Rnd: Beading: Ch 3, skip 1 sc, hdc in next sc, * ch 1, skip 1 sc, hdc in next sc, repeat from * around, ch 1, join in 2nd st of ch. Next Rnd: 2 sc in each ch 1 mesh, join in 1st sc. Next Rnd: Single knot st, skip 1 sc, sc in next sc, * single knot st, skip 2 sc, sc in next sc, repeat from * around, sl st into next single knot st, turn. Next Rnd: * Single knot st, sc over the 2 loops of next single knot st, repeat from * around, sl st in next single knot st, turn. Repeat the last rnd 3 times, fasten off. Attach White and work a row of single knot st pat around top of bootee, fasten off. Lace ribbon through beading. Work other bootee in same manner.

**Mittens.** With Pink ch 25 (to measure about 4¾"), join, being careful not to twist ch, ch 1 and work 1 sc in each st of ch. Without joining rnds and working in sc, work even until piece measures 2" from beg. Next Rnd: 1 sc in each of the next 3 sc, dec in next 2 sts, repeat from beg 4 times. Work 1 rnd even. Next Rnd: * 1 sc in each of the next 2 sc, dec in next 2 sts, repeat from * 4 times. Work 1 rnd even. Work 2 sts tog until

7 sts remain, cut yarn leaving a 4" length. Thread into needle and draw tog, fasten off. Beading: Attach Pink on opposite side of starting ch, ch 3, skip 1 st, hdc in next st, * ch 1, skip 1 st, hdc in next st, repeat from * around, ch 1, join. Next Rnd: Ch 1 and work 2 sc in each ch 1 mesh, join in 1st sc. Next Rnd: * Single knot st, skip 1 sc, sc in next sc, repeat from * around. Next Rnd: Sl st in 1st single knot st, turn, * single knot st, sc in next single knot st, repeat from * around. Repeat the last rnd once, sl st in 1st single knot st, fasten off. Attach White and work a row of single knot st pat same as bootees. Lace ribbon through beading. Work other mitten in same manner.

## Woven Baby Blanket
## 36 × 54 inches

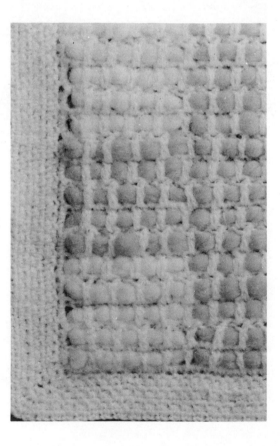

**Materials.** Fine Crochet Wool, 3 ply, 19 balls White; Jiffy Yarn, (2 oz. skeins) 3 skeins Bittersweet, 2 skeins Baby Pink, 1 skein Pearl Gray. Steel Crochet Hook No. 1.

**Gauge.** 7 dc—1"; 7 rows—2".

Starting at narrow edge with White, make a chain 45" long. Row 1: Dc in 4th ch from hook and in each ch across until there are 231 dc counting turning chain as 1 dc, cut off remaining ch 2 sts from last dc, ch 3, turn. Row 2: Skip first dc, dc in each dc across and in top of turning ch, ch 3, turn. Repeat Row 2 until there are 175 rows.

**Weaving.** First Block: Cut a strand of Baby Pink Jiffy Yarn 11" long. Row 1: Starting at one corner weave (under 1 dc, over 1 dc) 5 times (thread should be at back of work). Row 2: Working back in opposite direction, bring up strand directly above where needle was last inserted, weave (over 1 dc, under 1 dc) 5 times—these 5 sts should be in row directly above previous 5 sts. Weave next 3 rows to correspond. Weave ends neatly through wrong side of block. Using Bittersweet and Pink alternately, weave first row of blocks the same way, taking care to use 10 dc for each block. Starting with a block of Bittersweet, weave second row of blocks of Gray and Bittersweet alternately. Repeat Rows 1 and 2.

**Edging.** Rnd 1: Join White to any corner, 3 sc in same place, sc closely around, making 3 sc at each corner, join with sl st to first sc. Rnd 2: Sc in same place as sl st, ch 1, in next sc make sc, ch 1 and sc (corner); * ch 1, skip next sc, sc in next sc, repeat from * around, making sc, ch 1 and sc in center sc at each corner. Join. Rnds 3 through 8: Sl st in corner ch–1 sp, in same sp make sc, ch 1, and sc; * ch 1, sc in next sp, repeat from * around, working corners as before. Fasten off.

## Boy's Blazer Set

Directions are for Size 6 months. Changes for Sizes 1 and 2 are in parentheses.

**Materials.** Baby Wool, 3 ply (2 oz. Skeins), 3 Skeins White, Plastic Crochet Hook Size 3. 8 Buttons. 2½ yards Red Bias Binding. ½ yard Elastic, ¼" wide.

**Blocking measurements.** Chest: 18 (20–22)", Length from shoulder to lower edge: 9 (10–10½)", Length of sleeve seam: 6 (6½–6½)"; Pants: Waist: 18 (19½–20½)"; Length from top edge to crotch: 9½ (9¾–10)".

**Gauge.** 6 sts—1"; 6 rows—1".

**Jacket.** BACK: Starting at lower edge, ch 55 (61–67) to measure 10 (11–12)". Row 1: Sc in 2nd ch from hook, * hdc in next ch, sc in next ch, repeat from * across—54 (60–66) sts, ch 1, turn. Row 2: * Sc in next hdc, hdc in next sc, repeat from * across, ch 1, turn. Repeat Row 2 until piece measures 6 (6½–7)", ch 37 (41–41) for sleeve. Drop yarn. Join another ball at opposite end of last row and ch 36 (40–40) for other sleeve. Fasten off. Pick up dropped yarn and make sc in 2nd ch from hook, * hdc in next ch, sc in next ch, repeat from * across ch, then continue in pat across back and other ch. Ch 1, turn. Work in pat until piece measures 3 (3½–3½)" from first row of sleeve shaping. Fasten off.

RIGHT FRONT: Starting at lower edge, ch 33 (37–41) to measure 6 (7–7½)". Work in pat until there are 32 (36–40) sts on row. Work in pat as for back until piece measures 5 (5½–6)", ending at neck edge. Keeping pat, dec 1 st at neck edge on next row and every other row until 12 (13–13) sts in all have been dec; *at the same time*, when piece measures 1" from first row of neck shaping, ending at side edge, shape sleeve as follows: Ch 37 (41–41), turn. Next row: Sc in 2nd ch from hook, hdc in next ch. Continue to work in pat across ch and sts to end of row. Ch 1, turn. Continue in pat without dec at sleeve edge and continue to dec at neck edge as before, until piece measures 3 (3½–3½)" from first row of sleeve shaping. Fasten off. With pins, mark the position of 4 buttons on Right Front, having the first pin mark ½" up from lower edge and last pin mark 1" down from first row of neck shaping.

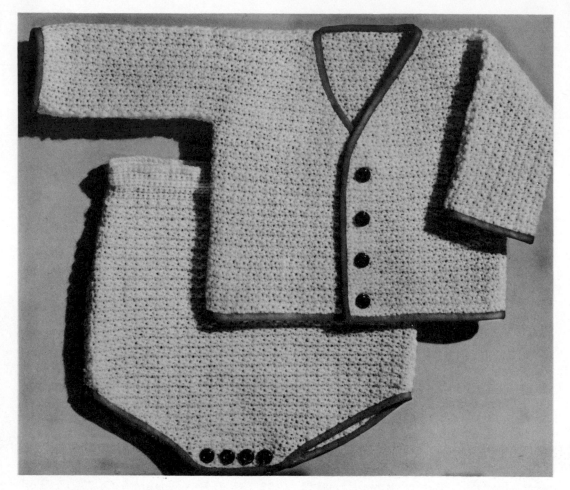

LEFT FRONT: Work exactly as for Right Front, making a buttonhole ½″ in from front edge opposite each pin mark. Make a buttonhole as follows: Row 1: Ch 2, skip 2 sts, work in pat across. Row 2: Work in pat across, including ch sts.

FINISHING: Block to measurements. Sew side, shoulder, and sleeve seams. Sew bias tape all around jacket and cuff edges. Sew buttons in place.

**Pants.** BACK: Row 1: Starting at top edge, make a ch to measure 9½ (10–10½)″. Row 2: Sc in 2nd ch from hook, sc in each ch across, having an even number of sc on row, ch 1, turn. Repeat Row 2 until piece measures 1¼″. Now work in pat, inc 1 st at both ends of row every inch 3 times, being careful to keep pat. Work even until piece measures 6¾″. To shape Crotch: Row 1:

Work in pat across, dec 2 sts at both ends, ch 1, turn. Row 2: Work in pat across, dec 1 st at both ends, ch 1, turn. Repeat Rows 1 and 2 9 (9–11) times more. Work even for ½″. Fasten off.

FRONT: Work as for Back until last dec row of crotch has been completed. Next row: Work in pat across, making 4 buttonholes evenly spaced. Now continue in pat for 2 rows more. Fasten off.

FINISHING: Block to measurements. Sew side seams. Beading: Join yarn to inside of Pants, 3 rows down from top edge, sc in same place, * ch 3, skip 2 sc, sc in next sc, 2 rows below, ch 3, skip 2 sc, sc in next sc 2 rows above. Repeat from * around. Join. Lace elastic through Beading and fasten securely. Sew bias binding all around lower edges of pants. Sew buttons in place.

## Child's Tyrolean Vest

Note the change in style in arrangement of instructions. This is done deliberately to familiarize you with the chart method of giving changes in instructions for the various sizes which is used in many crochet booklets.

|  | | Sizes | | | | | |
|---|---|---|---|---|---|---|---|
| **Materials.** Super Fingering | 6 mos. | 1 | 2 | 3 | 4 | 5 | 6 |
| (1 oz. Skeins); White . . . . . . | 2 | 2 | 2 | 3 | 3 | 4 | 4 |

For all sizes, 1 skein each of Scarlet and Emerald and small amount of brown and yellow yarn.
Afghan Hook Size 4. DP knitting needle.

| | 6 mos. | 1 | 2 | 3 | 4 | 5 | 6 |
|---|---|---|---|---|---|---|---|
| Buttons | 3 | 3 | 3 | 4 | 4 | 5 | 5 |

**Gauge.** 6 sts=1"; 4½ rows=1".

### Blocking Measurements

| | | 6 mos. | 1 | 2 | 3 | 4 | 5 | 6 |
|---|---|---|---|---|---|---|---|---|
| Body Chest Size . . . . . . . | Inches | 18 | 19 | 21 | 22 | 23 | 24 | 25 |

Actual Crocheting Measurements:

| | | 6 mos. | 1 | 2 | 3 | 4 | 5 | 6 |
|---|---|---|---|---|---|---|---|---|
| Chest (Vest buttoned) . . . . . | Inches | 19 | 20 | 22 | 23 | 24 | 25 | 26 |
| Width of back at underarm . . . | Inches | 9½ | 10 | 11 | 11½ | 12 | 12½ | 13 |
| Width of each front at underarm . | Inches | 5½ | 6 | 6½ | 6¾ | 7 | 7¼ | 8 |
| Length from back of neck to lower edge . . | | | | | | | | |
| . . . . . . . . . . . . | Inches | 9½ | 10¼ | 11 | 11¾ | 12½ | 13¼ | 14 |

### Directions

**Back.** Starting at lower edge with white .

| | | 6 mos. | 1 | 2 | 3 | 4 | 5 | 6 |
|---|---|---|---|---|---|---|---|---|
| Ch | | 57 | 60 | 66 | 69 | 72 | 75 | 78 |

Row 1: Retaining all loops on hook, pull up a loop in 2nd ch from hook and each ch across; work off loops as follows: yo and draw through first loop on hook, * yo and draw through next 2 loops on hook. Repeat from * until 1 loop remains on hook; this loop is first st of next row. Row 2: Skip first vertical bar, draw up a loop under next vertical bar and each bar across to within last bar, insert hook under last bar and the strand behind it and draw up a loop. Work off loops same as for Row 1. Repeat Row 2 for afghan st until piece measures .

| | | 6 mos. | 1 | 2 | 3 | 4 | 5 | 6 |
|---|---|---|---|---|---|---|---|---|
| . . . | Inches | 4 | 4½ | 5 | 5½ | 6 | 6½ | 7 |

TO SHAPE ARMHOLES: Row 1: Skip first vertical bar, sl st under next 3 vertical bars (3 decs at beg of row), work to last 3 vertical bars (3 decs at end of row); work off loops. Row 2: Insert hook under 2nd and 3rd bars and pull up 1 loop (1 dec), work to last 3 bars, insert hook under next 2 bars and pull up 1 loop (1 dec), pull up last loop as before, work off loops. Dec 1 st at both ends of every row in this way .

| | | 6 mos. | 1 | 2 | 3 | 4 | 5 | 6 |
|---|---|---|---|---|---|---|---|---|
| . . . . . . | Times | 2 | 2 | 4 | 4 | 5 | 5 | 5 |
| more. Work even on . . . . . . | Sts | 45 | 48 | 50 | 53 | 54 | 57 | 60 |
| until piece measures . . . . . . | Inches | 4 | 4½ | 4½ | 4¾ | 5 | 5¼ | 5½ |

above first row of armhole shaping.

| | Sizes | | | | | | |
|---|---|---|---|---|---|---|---|
| | 6 mos. | 1 | 2 | 3 | 4 | 5 | 6 |

TO SHAPE SHOULDERS: Work across until there are . . . . . . . . . Loops **15 16 17 18 18 19 20** on hook, work off loops. Dec 1 st at neck edge on every row 3 times. Sl st under remaining bars, decreasing 1 st at neck edge. Break off. Attach yarn to last bar worked in at base of shoulder, sl st under next . Loops **16 17 17 18 19 20 21** for back of neck, pull up loops under remaining . . . . . . . . . . Bars **14 15 16 17 17 18 19** Complete to correspond with other side. Sl st under free bars of left underarm.

**Left Front.** Starting at lower edge with white . . . . . . . . . . . . . . Ch **30 33 36 38 40 42 44** Work same as back to underarm, matching rows.

TO SHAPE ARMHOLE: Skip first bar, sl st under next . . . . . . . . . Bars **5 6 6 7 7 8 8** Complete row. Dec 1 st at armhole edge on next 2 rows.

TO SHAPE NECK: Dec 1 st at both ends of next . . . . . . . . . . Rows **4 4 5 5 6 6 6** Now dec 1 st at front edge only on next . . . . . . . . . . . . . Rows **4 5 5 5 5 5 6** Work even on . . . . . . . . . Sts **11 12 13 14 14 15 16** until armhole measures same as on back. Sl st under remaining bars.

**Right Front.** Work to correspond with left front, reversing shaping. Sl st under free bars of underarm. Block pieces to measurements. **Armbands.** Sew shoulder seams. Row 1: With emerald and right side facing, pull up a loop in each st of underarm, 3 loops in each 2 rows along decreased edges and 1 loop in end of each row along straight edge around entire armhole, work off loops. Break off. Row 2: Slip double-pointed needle under the vertical bars. Using scarlet, pull up a loop in each *back vertical bar, behind top of previous row,* dropping each bar off double-pointed needle as it is worked. Work off loops. Row 3: Slip double-pointed needle under vertical bars, skip first vertical bar, pull up a loop in each back vertical bar; work off loops. Row 4: Slip double-pointed needle under vertical bars, skip first bar, sl st in each back vertical bar across. Break off. Sew side seams.

**Bottom Border.** With emerald and right side facing, draw up a loop in each st of starting chain around lower edge. Work off loops. Break off. Repeat Rows 2, 3 and 4 of armbands.

**Neckband.** With emerald and right side facing, starting at base of neck shaping, pull up 3 loops in each 2 rows of neck decs, 1 loop in end of each row to shoulder seam, 1 loop in each st across back of neck and continue to base of neck shaping on opposite side in same way. Work off loops. Break off. Repeat Rows 2, 3 and 4 of armbands.

**Buttonhole Border.** With emerald and right side facing, pick up 1 loop in emerald row, 1 loop in end of each white row and 1 loop in emerald row on front edge. Work off loops. Break off. Row 2: With scarlet pick up 1 loop in each row of scarlet; slip double-pointed needle under vertical bars, pull up a loop in each back vertical bar, pull up a loop in end of each scarlet row. Work off loops. Row 3: Mark position of buttonholes evenly spaced on last row. Slip needle under bars, * pull up loops to within 1 st of next marker, sl st under next 2 vertical bars. Repeat from * across each marker, pull up loops under remainder of row; when working off loops,

ch 2 over each buttonhole. Row 4: Work as for Row 4 of armband, making a sl st in each ch st over buttonholes. Work other front border to correspond, omitting buttonholes.

**Embroidery.** Embroider spray on each front shoulder, working stem in outline stitch with brown, leaves in lazy daisy stitch with yellow and emerald alternately. Heart is worked with scarlet: first outlined with outline stitch, then filled in with vertical stitches. Press completed vest. Sew on buttons. With double strand of emerald, make a crocheted cord 13 inches longer than waist measure of vest. Run this cord in and out of crochet at waistline. Finish each end with a small tassel.

## Toy Monkey

**Materials.** Speed-cro-sheen, 3 balls White, 1 ball Mid Rose, and a few yards Aqua; Six-Strand Embroidery Floss, 1 skein Black, Steel Crochet Hook No. 2/0 (double zero). 2 Black Buttons for eyes. Scrap of Red Felt for mouth. ½ yard Blue Ribbon ¾ inch wide. Cotton Batting for stuffing.

**Gauge.** 6 sc—1"; 6 rows—1".

**Head. Starting at nose with Mid Rose,** ch 2. Rnd 1: 5 sc in 2nd ch from hook. Rnd 2: 2 sc in each sc around. Rnd 3: * Sc in next sc, 2 sc in next sc (1 sc inc). Repeat from * around. Rnds 4 to 7 incl: Sc in each sc around, inc 5 sc evenly around. Break off at end of Rnd 7. Rnd 8: Attach White to next sc, sc in each sc around, inc 6 sc evenly around. Work as for rnd 8 until there are 65 sc on rnd. Work without inc until piece measures 3 inches in all from center of nose. Next rnd: Sc in each sc around, dec 6 sc evenly around (to dec 1 sc, work off 2 sc as 1 sc). Repeat last rnd until there are 23 sc on rnd. Stuff head firmly and continue dec until all sc's have been worked off.

**Hand.** Starting at back of hand with White, ch 14. Row 1: Hdc in 3rd ch from hook and in each ch across. Ch 2, turn. Rows 2 to 11 incl: Hdc in each hdc across. Ch 2, turn. At end of Row 11, ch 12, sl st in first hdc at beg of row.

**Arm.** Rnd 1: Sc in each hdc and in each ch around. Rnd 2: Sc in each sc around. Repeat Rnd 2 until piece measures 4 inches from Rnd 1 at end of hand. Break off. Attach Mid Rose to base of first sc on opposite side of starting ch-12 of arm and work palm as follows: Row 1: Hdc in each ch across. Ch 2, turn. Rows 2 to 10 incl: Hdc in each hdc across. Ch 2, turn. Break off at end of row 10. Sew to back of hand around edge.

**Thumb.** With Mid Rose, ch 6. Work as for back of hand until 3 rows have been completed. Break off. Sew long edges together and sew to side of hand.

Make another arm and hand piece the same way. Place a pin as marker on last rnd of each arm on inner side.

**Body.** Rnd 1: Attach White to sc at marker on either arm, sc in each sc around arm, ch 4, sc in sc at marker on other arm, sc in each sc around second arm. Rnd 2: Sc in each ch of ch-4 between arms, sc in each sc around arm; working on opposite side of chain, sc in each ch across, sc in each sc around second arm. Rnd 3: Sc in each sc around. Repeat last rnd until body measures 3½ inches from end of arms. Next rnd: Sc in each sc around, inc 6 sc across back and dec 6 sc across stomach. Following rnd: Sc in each sc around. Repeat last rnd until body measures 4¾ inches in all. Next rnd: Dec 6 sc evenly around. Stuff arms and body firmly and continue dec 6 sc on each rnd until all sc's have been worked off. Break off. Sew head to body.

**Foot.** Work as for hand.

**Leg.** Work as for arm until piece measures 5¾ inches from Rnd 1 at end of foot. Break off. With Mid Rose work foot-pad same as for palm. Make a toe same as for thumb. Sew in place. Complete another leg the same way. Stuff legs firmly and sew to side of body.

**Tail.** Starting at tip with White, ch 2. Rnd 1: 6 sc in 2nd ch from hook. Rnd 2: Sc in each sc around, inc 3 sc evenly around. Repeat rnd 2 until there are 15 sc on rnd. Work without inc until piece measures 10 inches in all. Break off. Stuff firmly and sew in place.

**Ear (Make 2).** Starting at center with Mid Rose, ch 5. Row 1: Hdc in 3rd ch from hook, hdc in next ch, 5 hdc in last ch; working across opposite side of starting chain, make hdc in next 2 ch. Ch 2, turn. Row 2: Hdc in first 3 hdc, 3 hdc in next hdc, hdc in next hdc, 3 hdc in next hdc, hdc in last 3 hdc. Ch 2, turn. Row 3: Hdc in each st around, making 3 hdc in center st of each 3-hdc group at rounded end. Break off. With White make another piece the same way. Sew the 2 pieces tog. Sew straight edges of ears to head.

**Ball.** With Aqua, ch 2. Rnds 1 to 4 incl: Work as for head. Rnds 5 to 8 incl: Sc in each sc around. Rnd 9: Dec 5 sc evenly around. Stuff firmly and continue to dec 5 sc evenly on each rnd until all sc's have been worked off. Break off, leaving a 5-inch length of thread. Sew end of thread to palm of hand.

With black, embroider nostrils. With Mid Rose, embroider eyelashes at edge of nose. Sew buttons in place for eyes. Cut a mouth from red felt and sew in place. Tie ribbon around neck in a bow.

## CROCHETING FOR THE HOME

### Round Pot Holder

**Materials.** Mercerized Bedspread Crochet Cotton; 1 ball each White and Red. Steel Crochet Hook Size 7.

**Front Section.** With Red ch 5, join with a sl st to form ring, ch 1 and work 8 sc in ring, join in 1st sc. Rnd 2: Ch 1 and work 2 sc in each sc, join. Rnd 3: Ch 3 (always counts as part of 1st popcorn st), 4 dc in same space, drop loop from hook, insert in 3rd st of ch, pull loop through, 3 dc in next sc, * popcorn st in next sc (popcorn st: 5 dc in same space, drop loop from hook, insert in 1st dc, pick up loop and pull through), 3 dc in next sc, repeat from * around, join in 1st popcorn st. Rnd 4: Ch 3, 2 dc in same space, dc in next dc, drop Red, attach White, popcorn st in next st, drop White, * with Red dc in next dc, 3 dc in next dc, dc in next dc, drop Red, with White popcorn st in next st, repeat from * around, drop White, ending with Red dc in last dc, join in 3rd st of ch. Rnd 5: Ch 3, 2 dc in next dc, 1 dc in each

Rnds 7 and 8 once. Rnd 17: Work in same manner as Rnd 9, but repeat from * 40 times. Rnd 18: Ch 3, 1 dc in each dc, join, fasten off.

**Back Section.** With Red ch 6, join to form ring, ch 3, work 15 dc in ring, join all rounds. Rnd 2: Ch 3, dc in same space, 2 dc in each remaining dc. Rnd 3: Ch 3, 2 dc in next dc, * dc in next dc, 2 dc in next dc, repeat from * around. Rnd 4: Working in dc, inc 1 dc in every 3rd dc. Rnd 5: Inc in every 4th st, drop Red. Rnd 6: Attach White and work 1 sc in each dc, drop White. Rnd 7: With Red ch 3, and working in dc inc in every 5th st. Rnd 8: Inc in every 6th st. Rnd 9: Inc in every 8th st, drop Red. Rnd 10: With White work 1 sc in each dc, drop White. Rnd 11: With Red ch 3 and working in dc inc in every 6th st. Rnd 12: Inc in every 7th st. Rnd 13: Work even in dc, drop Red. Rnd 14: Same as Rnd 10, but cut White. Rnd 15: With Red and working in dc inc in every 8th st. Rnd 16: Inc in every 9th st, fasten off.

**Finishing.** With wrong side of both sections facing, with White, crochet the 2 sections tog with a row of sc, join, fasten off. With White, cover a bone ring with sc and sew to holder as illustrated.

of the next 2 dc, 2 dc in next popcorn st, * 1 dc in each of the next 2 dc, 2 dc in next dc, 1 dc in each of the next 2 dc, 2 dc in next popcorn st, repeat from * around, ending with dc in last dc, join in 3rd st of ch. Rnd 6: Ch 3, 1 dc in each of the next 2 dc, 2 dc in next dc, * 1 dc in each of the next 3 dc, 2 dc in next dc, repeat from * around, join, drop Red. Rnd 7: With White ch 1, work 1 sc in each dc, join, drop White. Rnd 8: With Red ch 3, work 1 dc in each sc, join. Rnd 9: Ch 3, drop Red, with White popcorn st in next dc, drop White, * with Red 1 dc in next dc, 2 dc in next dc, 1 dc in next dc, drop Red, with White popcorn st in next dc, drop White, repeat from * 18 times, with Red 1 dc in next dc, 2 dc in next dc, join. Rnd 10: Ch 3, 1 dc in next st, 2 dc in next st, * 1 dc in each of the next 2 sts, 2 dc in next st, repeat from * around ending with 1 dc in each of the last 4 dc, last inc is omitted (132 dc). Rnd 11: With White work 1 sc in each dc, join in 1st sc, drop White. Rnd 12: Ch 3, work 1 dc in each sc, join. Rnd 13: Ch 3, working in dc inc in every 11th st, join. Rnd 14: Ch 3, working in dc inc in every 6th st, join, drop Red. Repeat

## Petal Pot Holder

**Materials.** Cotton Rug Yarn, 4 ply: 2 Skeins; Plastic Crochet Hook Size 8.

**Gauge.** 5 dc—1″.

*Note:* Work into back loop only of each st throughout.

Row 1: Ch 9, turn. Row 2: Dc in third ch from hook, 1 dc in each of next 3 ch, 3 dc in next ch, 1 dc in each of last 3 ch, ch 2, turn. Row 3: Dc in each of next 4 sts, 3 dc in center st, dc in each st across, dc in top of ch-2 of previous row, ch 2, turn. Row 4: Dc in each dc to center dc, 3 dc in center dc, dc in each st across, dc in top of ch-2 of previous row, ch 2, turn. Repeat Row 4 until 13 rows have been worked in all. Fasten off. Make one more piece in same manner.

**Finishing.** Starting in center of top edge and holding pieces tog, join as follows: * Sl st into center of next rib, hdc in same place, repeat from * around, working 3 hdc in each corner st. Row 2: * Ch 3, sl st into sl st of previous row, repeat from * around. Fasten

off. Loop: With double strand of yarn, sl st into center top edge, ch 16, sl st into same st as first sl st, turn, sl st in each ch around, fasten off.

## Round Hairpin Lace Place Mat 14½″ diameter

**Materials.** Speed-cro-sheen Mercerized Cotton, 2 balls; Steel Crochet Hook Size 00. 2″ Hairpin Lace Loom.

**First Strip.** Make a strip of hairpin lace, having 35 loops on each side of loom. Fasten off. To Form Center: Keeping the twist in all loops, join thread through first 7 loops, make a sl st in same place, * make a sl st through next 7 loops, repeat from * around, join to first st made. Fasten off. Sew ends of hairpin lace together at center.

**Second Strip.** Make another strip having 70 loops on each side. To Join Strips: Keeping the twist in all loops, insert hook in first free loop on First Strip, insert hook through first 2 corresponding loops on Second Strip, draw the 2 loops from Second Strip through the single loop on First Strip (a sl st and an inc made), * insert hook in next loop on First Strip, draw loop through both loops on hook, insert hook through next 2 loops on Second Strip, draw both loops through loop on hook (another inc made), repeat from * around. Tack last loop on hook in place on wrong side. Make 3 more strips of hairpin lace, having 35 loops more than on each previous strip. Join as before, inc in every other loop on Third Strip, every 3rd loop on Fourth Strip and every 4th loop on Fifth Strip. Block to measurements.

## Irish Crochet Table Mat
## 14½" diameter

**Materials.** Six-Cord Mercerized Crochet Size 50, 5 balls White. Few yards White Pearl Cotton. ½ yard Linen, 36" wide. Steel Crochet Hook Size 12.

Cut a circular piece of linen, 4¾" in diameter. Make a narrow hem around linen and make 240 sc closely all around outer edge. Join with sl st.

**Shamrock Edge.** Rnd 1: Sc in same place as sl st, * (ch 2, picot) twice, ch 8, sl st in 6th ch from hook (this ch-6 loop is center of shamrock), turn, (ch 5, sc in center loop) 3 times, turn, in each of last 3 ch-5 loops make sc, 9 dc and sc, sc in ch-6 loop at center of shamrock, ch 2, picot, ch 1, sc between the first and second picots, ch 2, picot, ch 2, skip 4 sc, sc in next sc, (ch 2, picot) twice, ch 2, skip 4 sc, sc in next sc, repeat from * around (24 shamrocks). Fasten off. Rnd 2: Join thread to 7th dc of first petal (counting from stem), (ch 2, picot), 3 times, ch 2, sc in center of 2nd petal, * (ch 2, picot) 3 times, ch 2, sc in 3rd dc on 3rd

petal, ch 2, tr in next loop on center, ch 2, sc in 7th dc on first petal of next shamrock, ch 2, picot, ch 1, turn and work sc between first and second picots of last picot-chain, turn, (ch 2, picot) twice, ch 2, sc in center of 2nd petal. Repeat from * around. Do not fasten off.

**Edging—Rose.** With another ball of thread, work as follows: Starting at center, ch 7, join with sl st to form ring. Rnd 1: Ch 6, (dc in ring, ch 3) 6 times, join with sl st to 3rd ch of ch-6 (7 sps). Rnd 2: In each sp around make sc, 8 dc and sc. Rnd 3: * Ch 5, sc (from back of work) in next dc on first rnd, repeat from * around, ending with ch 5, sc in same place as sl st on rnd 1. Rnd 4: In each loop around, make sc, 10 dc, and sc. Rnd 5: * Ch 6, sc in the sc between next 2 petals on Rnd 3, repeat from * around, ending with sc between last and first petals. Rnd 6: In each loop around make sc, 12 dc and sc. Rnd 7: * Ch 7, sc in the sc between next 2 petals on Rnd 5, repeat from * around. Rnd 8: In each loop around make sc, 14 dc, and sc. Rnd 9: Sl st to 3rd dc of first petal, sc in same place, * (ch 6, sl st in 4th ch from hook—picot made—ch 2, picot, ch 2, skip 3 dc, sc in next dc) twice; (ch 2, picot) twice; ch 2, sc in 3rd dc of next petal, repeat from * around, ending with sl st in first sc. Rnds 10 and 11: Sl st to center of next loop, sc in same loop, * (ch 2, picot) twice; ch 2, sc in next loop, repeat from * around, ending with sl st in first sc. Fasten off at end of Rnd 11.

**Edging—Thistle.** Rnd 1: Wind thread 20 times around a match, slip off and make 21 sc in ring, join with sl st to first sc. Rnd 2: Ch 6, * tr in next sc, ch 2, repeat from * around, join last ch-2 with sl st to 4th ch of ch-6 (21 sps). Rnd 3: Working over 2 strands of Pearl Cotton make 4 sc in each sp around, join, fasten off the 2 strands. Rnd 4: Sc in same place as sl st, * ch 4, sc in front loop of next sc, repeat from * around, ending with sl st in first sc. Rnd 5: Sc in same place as sl st, * (ch 2, picot) twice; ch 2, skip 3 sc, sc in back of next sc, repeat from * around, join with sl st to first sc. Rnd

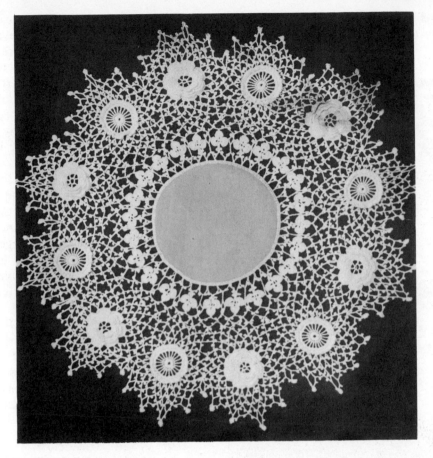

6: Repeat Rnd 10 of Rose. Rnd 7: Sl st to center of next loop, sc in same loop, ch 2, picot, ch 1, sl st in any loop on last rnd of Rose, ch 1, picot, ch 2, sc in any loop on Thistle and complete as for last rnd of Rose, joining 2nd and 3rd loops to corresponding loops of Rose as first loop was joined. Make 5 more Roses and 5 more Thistles, joining them in alternate order as shown in illustration as first Thistle was joined to Rose, and having 9 free loops on outer edge and 6 free loops on inner edge. Now work around inner edge as follows: Rnd 1: Attach thread to 2nd free loop on any flower, sc in same place, * (ch 2, picot) twice; ch 2, sc in next loop, repeat from * 3 more times, ch 2, picot, ch 2, sc in next free loop on next flower, turn, (ch 2, picot) twice; ch 2, sc in last loop on previous flower, turn, (ch 2, picot) twice; ch 2, sc in last loop made, ch 2, picot, ch 2, sc in next free

loop on flower, (ch 2, picot) twice; ch 2 and continue thus around, join and fasten off. Lay this piece aside.

Join Edging to center as follows: With thread from Shamrock Edge, sl st to center of first loop, ch 2, picot, ch 1, sc in a loop on Edging, * ch 2, picot, ch 2, sc in next loop on center, ch 2, picot, ch 1, sc in next loop on Edging, repeat from * around. Fasten off. Now work along outer edge of Centerpiece as follows: Attach thread to joining of flowers, * ch 2, picot, ch 2, tr in next loop, ch 2, picot, ch 6, insert hook in 2nd ch from hook and draw up loop (yo, insert hook under same ch and draw loop through) 10 times; yo and draw through all loops on hook, ch 1, sl st in next ch to hold strands tightly in place (clones knot made), ch 2, picot, ch 2, tr in same loop as last tr was made, ch 2, picot, ch 2, sc in next loop, repeat from * around, join and fasten off.

## Tweed Place Mat
### 12 × 20″, Including Fringe

previously. Work 4 more rows the same way. Next row: Continue weaving, working under sps that were worked over previously. Repeat last row to within last 6 rows, then weave last 6 rows same as first 6 rows. Stitch Fringe securely on each end. Trim ends evenly. Block.

**Glass Jacket.** Bottom: Starting at center with Purple, ch 2. Rnd 1: 6 sc in 2nd ch from hook. Rnd 2: 2 sc in each sc around. Rnd 3: * 2 sc in next sc (1 sc increased), sc in next sc, repeat from * around. Inc 6 sc evenly on each rnd until piece measures same as bottom of glass. Side Piece: Rnd 1: Ch 4, * skip 1 sc, dc in next sc, ch 1, repeat from * around, join. Rnd 2: Ch 4, * dc in next dc, ch 1, repeat from * around, join. Repeat Rnd 2 until 10 rnds have been completed. Fasten off.

**Weaving.** Cut 6 strands of Baby Pink, about 72″ long. Weave these strands through first rnd of sps, then through 2nd rnd, working spirally under sps that were worked over previously. Continue in this manner until all sps have been filled. Sew ends securely.

### Star Wheel Tablecloth
### 68 × 85″—16 × 20 Motifs
### (320)

**Materials.** Knit-cro-sheen, 2 balls Purple; Rayon Crochet, 2 balls Baby Pink. Steel Crochet Hook Size 7.

Starting at long side with Purple, make a chain 24″ long. Row 1: Dc in 6th ch from hook, * ch 1, skip 1 ch, dc in next ch, repeat from * across until row measures 18″, having an uneven number of dc. Cut off remaining ch, ch 4, turn. Row 2: Skip first dc, * dc in next dc, ch 1, repeat from * across, ending ch 1, skip 1 ch of turning ch, dc in next ch, ch 4, turn. Repeat Row 2 until piece measures 12″. Fasten off.

**Weaving.** Cut 6 strands of Baby Pink, 24″ long. Weave these strands through first row of sps on long side, leaving an even amount free on both ends for Fringe. Cut 6 more strands and weave through next row of sps, going over same sps that were worked over

**Materials.** Six-Cord Mercerized Crochet, Size 20, 37 balls White or Ecru. Steel Crochet Hook Size 9.

**Motif.** Ch 10, join with sl st to form ring. Rnd 1: Ch 3, 23 dc in ring, join with sl st to 3rd ch of ch-3 first made. Rnd 2: Ch 10, and complete a cross st as follows: yo twice, insert hook in 8th ch from hook, draw thread through (4 loops on hook), yo once, skip 1 dc and insert hook in next dc, draw thread through (6 loops on hook), yo and take off 2 loops at a time, 5 times; * ch 3, yo 4 times, insert hook in next dc and draw thread through (6 loops on hook), yo and take off 2 loops at a time twice, then yo, skip 1 dc, insert hook in next dc, draw thread through (6 loops on hook), yo and take off 2 loops at a time, 5 times; ch 3, dc in center point of the cross, thus completing the cross. Repeat from * until there are 8 cross sts around the circle. Join last ch-3 with sl st to 7th ch of ch-10 first made. Rnd 3: 5 sc in each sp. Rnds 4 through 7: Sc in each sc of previous rnd. Rnd 8: Ch 4, dc in first sc, * ch 1, dc in next sc, repeat from * around. Then ch 1 and join with sl st to 3rd ch of ch-4 first made. Rnd 9: Ch 10 and complete cross st as before, skipping 2 dc between each leg of cross st and inserting hook under ch-1 sp, ch 3, skip 2 dc, make a cross st as before, inserting hook in ch-1 sps and skipping 2 dc between each leg of cross st. Repeat thus around (20 cross sts), join last ch-3 with sl st to 7th ch of ch-10 first made.

Rnd 10: Sl st in first 2 sts of first sp, ch 5, * dc in same sp, ch 3, sc in next sp, ch 3, dc in next sp, ch 2, repeat from * around, join last ch-3 with sl st to 3rd ch of ch-5 first made. Rnd 11: Ch 6, dc in same sp, * ch 4, sc in next sc of previous rnd, ch 4, dc in next ch-2 sp, ch 3, dc in same sp, repeat from * around, joining with sl st to 3rd ch of ch-6 first made. Fasten off. Make necessary number of motifs and place in position. With neat over-and-over sts, sew 3 points of one motif to corresponding 3 points of the adjacent motif (thus leaving 2 points free on each motif).

**Fill-In-Lace.** Ch 4, join with **sl st to form** ring. ** Ch 15, sc at joining of 2 motifs, ch 15, sc in center ring, * ch 9, sc in point of next scallop, ch 9, sc in center ring. Repeat from * once more, then repeat from ** 3 times more. Fasten off. Starch lightly and press.

## Filet Monogram Sheet

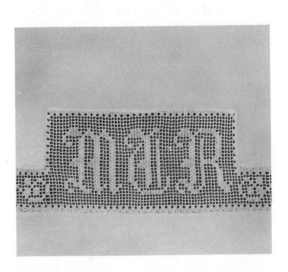

**Materials.** Six-Cord Mercerized Crochet, Size 50, 5 balls White. Steel Crochet Hook Size 12; a Sheet.

**Gauge.** 7 sps—1″; 7 rows—1″.

**Center.** Cut a piece of graph paper 27 × 61 sps (not including border). With a pencil draw your middle initial at center, then space the others evenly on each side (see illustration). Starting with center, ch 96. Row 1: Dc in 4th ch from hook and in next 59 ch (20 bls made), (ch 2, skip 2 ch, dc in next ch-sp made) 3 times, dc in next 9 ch, make 3 sps, dc in next 6 ch, ch 3, turn. Row 2: Skip first dc, dc in next 3 dc (bl made over bl), ch 2, skip 2 dc, dc in next dc (sp made over bl), ch 2, dc in next dc (sp made over sp), make 9 more sps, (1 bl, 1 sp) 9 times; 1 bl, ch 3, turn. Row 3: Make 1 bl, 2 dc in next sp, dc in next dc (bl made over sp), make 27 sps, 2 bl, ch 3, turn. Row 4: Make 1 bl, 29 sps and 1 bl, ch 3, turn. Repeat Rows 3 and 4, following chart for initials, ending with Row 3. Row 64: Repeat Row 2. Row 65: Make 20 bls, 3 sps, 3 bls, 3 sps, 2 bls, ch

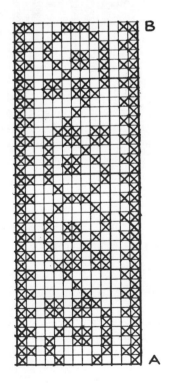

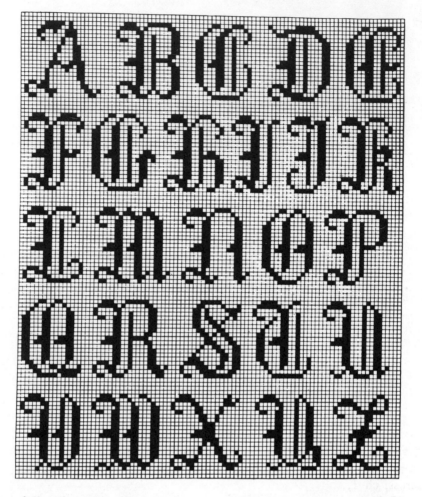

3, turn. Now follow insertion chart from A to B until piece is long enough to reach edge of sheet. Fasten off. Attach thread to opposite side of starting ch and complete to correspond. Pin insertion in place on sheet and cut away material in back, leaving ⅛″ for hem. Sew neatly in place.

## BATHROOM ACCESSORIES

### Curtain-Towel Edgings

Crochet is used to decorate the modern bathroom. In the photograph the towel and curtain edgings, bathmat, scrap basket cover, bench pad, and seat cover are all crocheted.

**Materials.** Six-Cord Mercerized Crochet, Size 30; 6 balls White; Knit-cro-sheen, 1 ball White. Steel Crochet Hook Size 10. Steel Crochet Hook Size 7. Hairpin Lace Loom, ½″ Wide. 2 Bath Towels.

Materials are sufficient for a pair of organdy ruffled curtains 36″×54″ long (not including ruffles).

Make a strip of hairpin lace slightly longer than side and bottom ruffle. Fasten off. Make another strip the same way, having the same number of loops on each strip. TO JOIN STRIPS: Keeping the twist in all loops, insert hook in first loop of First Strip, draw first loop on Second Strip through loop on hook, * draw next loop on First Strip through loop on hook, draw next loop on Second Strip through loop on hook, repeat from * across, fasten last loop securely.

**Heading.** Keeping all loops straight, attach thread to first loop on opposite side of First Strip, sc in same place, * ch 1, sc in next loop, repeat from * across, fasten off. SCALLOPED EDGE: Still keeping all loops straight, attach thread to first loop on opposite side of Second Strip, sc in same place, * ch 5, sc in 3rd ch from hook, (picot made), ch 2, sc in next loop, repeat from * across, fasten off. Sew edging to curtain. Make another piece to fit across top ruffle and a piece for tie-back. Sew in place. Complete other curtain the same way. Starch edging lightly and press. Make edgings for towels the same way.

## Toilet Seat Cover

**Materials.** Speed-cro-sheen Mercerized Cotton, 5 balls White. Steel Crochet Hook Size 00.

**Gauge.** 3 sc and 1 puff st—¾″; 4 rows—¾″.

Starting at back edge, ch 33. Row 1: Sc in 2nd ch from hook and in each ch across, ch 1, turn. Rows 2 and 3: Sc in each sc across, ch 1, turn. Row 4: Work in puff st pat, (see Bath Mat), ch 1, turn. Row 5: Sc in each st across, ch 1, turn. Row 6: Repeat Row 4. Row 7: Make dc, hdc and sc in first st (2 sts inc at beg of row) sc in each st across, making sc, hdc and dc in last sc (2 sts inc at end of row), ch 1, turn. Rows 8 through 14: Continue to work in pat, inc 2 sts at beg and end of each row (adding puff sts at both ends of puff st rows as needed to keep pat), 64 sts on Row 14. Row 15: 2 sc in first st, sc in each st across, 2 sc in last st, ch 1, turn (1 st inc at both ends of row). Row 16: Work in pat evenly. Rows 17 through 24: Repeat Rows 15 and 16 alternately, 4 more times (74 sts on Row 24). Work even until piece measures 9″ in all. Then dec 1 st at both ends of every sc row until piece measures 13½″. Now work off 3 sts as 1 st at both ends of every row until piece measures 15½″ in all. Fasten off.

**Border.** Rnd 1: Attach thread to opposite side of starting ch, sc in each ch across, sc closely around cover, join to first sc. Rnd 2: Ch 4, * skip 1 sc, dc in next sc, ch 1, repeat from * around, join to 3rd ch of ch-4. Fasten off.

**Cord.** Using thread double, make a ch 10″ longer than outer edge of cover. Starting at center back, lace through ch-1 sps.

## Bath Mat—Scrap Basket Cover

**Materials.** Speed-cro-sheen Mercerized Cotton, 24 balls White for Mat; 8 balls White for Scrap Basket. Steel Crochet Hook Size 00. Scrap Basket 8″ in diameter at top and bottom and 12½″ in depth.

**Gauge.** 3 sc and 1 puff st—¾″; 4 rows—¾″.

To start, ch 132 for Mat and ch 164 for Scrap Basket. Row 1: Sc in 2nd ch from hook and in each ch across, ch 1, turn. Row 2: Sc in each sc across, ch 1, turn. Row 3: * Sc in next 3 sc, yo, insert hook in next sc 2 rows below, draw loop through and up to height of row in work (yo, insert hook in same sc 2 rows below, draw loop through and up to height of row in work) 3 times, yo and draw through all loops on hook (puff st made), repeat from * across, ch 1, turn. Row 4: Sc in each st across, ch 1, turn. Row 5: Sc in first sc, * make a puff st in next sc 2 rows below, sc in next 3 sc, repeat from * across, ch 1, turn. Row 6: Sc in each sc across, ch 1, turn. Repeat Rows 3 through 6 until piece measures 34″ for Mat, or is long enough to cover depth for Basket, ending with 4th row.

**For Scrap Basket.** Sew narrow ends together and sl st closely around top and bottom.

**Border for Mat.** Rnd 1: Sc closely around, making 3 sc in each corner. Rnds 2 through 5: Sc in each sc around, making 3 sc in center sc, at each corner, join. Fasten off at end of Rnd 5. Block to measurements.

## Bathroom Bench Pad

**Materials.** Speed-cro-sheen Mercerized Cotton, 11 balls Yellow and 8 balls White. Steel Crochet Hook Size 00. A Foam Rubber Pillow, 22½″ × 15″ × 3″.

**Gauge.** 5 sts—1″; 2 stripes—2″.

Starting at long side with Yellow, make a ch slightly longer than pillow. Row 1: Sc in 2nd ch from hook, * dc in next ch, sc in next ch, repeat from * across until row measures same as pillow, ending with sc. Cut off

remaining ch, ch 1, turn. Row 2: Sc in each st across, ch 1, turn. Row 3: Sc in first sc, * dc around bar of dc 2 rows below (raised dc made), skip sc behind raised dc, sc in next sc, repeat from * across, ch 1, turn. Rows 4 through 7: Repeat Rows 2 and 3 alternately 2 more times. At end of Row 7, draw a loop of White through last loop on hook, thus changing color, turn. Rows 8 through 13: With White, repeat Rows 2 and 3, 3 times. Change color at end of Row 13. Rows 14 through 21: With Yellow repeat Rows 2 and 3, 4 times. Change color at end of Row 21. Repeat Rows 8 through 21 until piece measures same width as pillow, ending with Row 21. Fasten off, make another piece the same way.

**Gusset.** Starting at long side of piece, work as for cover until 3 stripes have been completed. Fasten off. Make another piece the same way. Then make 2 pieces the same width as narrow end of pillow.

**Finishing.** Sew narrow ends of Gusset pieces together, alternating long and short pieces. Holding Gusset and one side of pillow together and working through both thicknesses to join, attach Yellow to any corner and sc closely around. Join and fasten off. Insert pillow and join other side to Gusset the same way. Join and fasten off.

# Pineapple Popcorn Spread

**Materials.** Single Size: Knit-cro-sheen, 67 balls White or Ecru; Mercerized Bedspread Cotton, 120 balls any color. Double Size: Knit-cro-sheen, 79 balls White or Ecru; Mercerized Bedspread Cotton, 140 balls any color. Steel Crochet Hook Size 7.

*Note:* Each motif measures about 7″ from side to side, 8″ from point to point diagonally. For single-size spread, about 75″ × 108″ incl fringe, make 148 motifs. For double-size, about 90″ × 108″ incl fringe, make 175 motifs.

**Motif.** Starting at center, ch 8, join with sl st to form ring. Rnd 1: Ch 3, 17 dc in ring, sl st to top of ch 3. Rnd 2: Ch 3, 4 dc in same place as sl st, drop loop from hook, insert hook in top of ch-3 and draw dropped loop through (a starting pc st made), * ch 4, skip 2 dc, pc st in next dc (ch 1, 5 dc in same place, drop loop from hook, insert hook in ch preceding the 5 dc and draw dropped loop through), repeat from * around, ending with ch 4, sl st in tip of first pc st made. Rnd 3: Ch 3 and complete a starting pc st in same place as sl st, * ch 3, dc in next sp, ch 3, pc st in tip of next pc st, repeat from * around, ending with ch 3, sl st in tip of first pc st. Rnd 4: Ch 3 and complete a starting pc st in same place as sl st, * (ch 2, dc in next sp) twice, ch 2, pc st in tip of next pc st, repeat from * around, ending with ch 2, sl st in tip of first pc st. Rnd 5: Ch 3, 7 dc in same place as sl st (this is base of pineapple), * (ch 2, dc in next dc) twice, ch 2, 8 dc in tip of next pc st, repeat from * around, ending with ch 2, sl st in top of ch 3. Rnd 6: Ch 4, (dc in next dc, ch 1) 6 times, dc in next 2 dc, * ch 2, dc in next 2 dc, (ch 1, dc in next dc) 7 times, dc in next dc, repeat from * around, ending with sl st in 3rd st of ch-4. Rnd 7: Sl st in sp, ch 3 and complete a starting pc st in same place, (ch 1, pc st in next sp) 6 times, * ch 2, skip next dc, dc in next dc, ch 2, dc in next dc, ch 2, skip next dc, (pc st in next sp, ch 1) 6 times, pc st in next sp, repeat from * around, ending with ch 2, sl st in tip of first pc st made. Rnd 8: Sl st in sp, ch 3 and complete a starting pc st, (ch 2, pc st in next sp) 5 times (6 pc sts in pineapple), * (ch 2, dc in next sp) 3 times, (ch 2, pc st in the next sp) 6 times, repeat from * around (4 ch-2 sps between pineapples), ending with ch 2, sl st in tip of first pc st. Rnd 9: Work as for Rnd 8, having 5 pc sts in each pineapple, and 5 ch-2 sps between pineapples. Rnd 10: * Make 4 pc sts, (ch 2, dc in next sp) 3 times, ch 2 dc in same sp (inc sp made), ch 2, dc in next sp twice, ch 2, repeat from * around, join. Rnds 11, 12, and 13: Work as for Rnd 10, making 1 pc st less on each pineapple on each rnd, and working dc, ch 2 and dc in each inc sp, join. Rnd 14: Sl st in next ch, sc in sp, ch 5, * dc in next sp, ch 2, repeat from * to the inc sp, in inc sp make 3 dc, ch 2 and 3 dc, ch 2, dc in next sp. Continue in this manner around, join with sl st to 3rd st of ch-5. Fasten off. Make necessary number of motifs and sew together on wrong side with neat over-and-over sts.

**Fringe.** Make fringe in each sp around as follows: Cut 8 strands, each 12″ long. Double these strands, forming a loop. Pull loop through sp and draw loose ends through loop. Pull tight. Trim evenly.

## Fireside Afghan
## Approximately 49 × 68 inches

**Materials.** Knitting Worsted, 60 1 oz. balls Light Yellow; 8 balls Wood Brown for border and embroidery. Bone Afghan Hook No. 6.

**Gauge.** 5 sts—1"; 4 rows—1".

**Pattern.** Make a chain of 45 sts. Row 1: Insert hook in 2nd ch from hook and draw up a loop; retaining all loops on hook draw up a loop in each ch across—45 loops on hook—yo and draw through 1 loop, * yo and draw through 2 loops, repeat from * across. The loop which remains on hook always counts as the first st of next row. Row 2: Insert hook under 2nd vertical bar and draw loop through; retaining all loops on hook draw up a loop in each vertical bar across to within last vertical bar. Insert hook through the last vertical bar and the stitch directly behind it and draw a loop through—this gives a firm edge to this side—45 loops on hook. Repeat Row 2 as specified, for desired length.

To finish off, make a sl st in each vertical bar across. Fasten off.

**Block (Make 35):** With Yellow, ch 45 to measure 9¼" and work in Afghan stitch until piece is square—36 rows. Fasten off. Join Brown to corner st, make 3 sc in corner, * ch 1, skip 1 st, sc in next st, repeat from * around, making 3 sc in each corner. Fasten off.

**Embroidery.** Examine the diagram for making cross stitches over Afghan st. Placing design at center, embroider 18 Blocks according to chart.

**Finishing.** Sew Blocks neatly together on wrong side, alternating plain and embroidered Blocks.

**Border.** Rnd 1: Join Brown to corner, 3 sc in corner, sc in each st and in each ch-1 sp around, making 3 sc in each corner. Rnd 2: Sc in each sc around, making 3 sc in center sc of each corner. Row 3: Ch 3, sc in joining, sc in next sc, 3 sc in next sc, sc in next sc, * ch 3, sc in last sc, sc in next 5 sc, repeat from * around, making 3 sc in each corner. Fasten off.

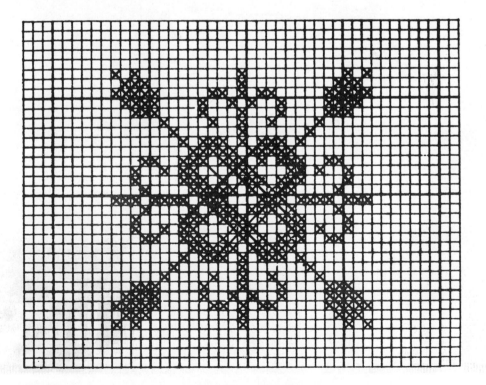

**2**

**3**

**4**

**6**

## Color Plate 10 — Hand-Woven Fabrics

A variety of textures and designs in weaving. Drafts and instructions for making are given in Chapter 10, Hand Weaving.

## CROCHETED FABRICS

This is a new slant on crochet. This technique results in colorful and interesting textures which can be made for various articles. It is especially suitable for pillows and chair seats. The color plate shows a chair pad and four additional patterns in this new type of crochet.

A simple background is made in a basic color after which various shades and weights of yarn are drawn or "woven" through to give the interesting textured effect.

## COLOR PLATE 8

### Woven Chair Seat

Chair Seat measures 17" across front, 14" across back, 15" deep.

**Materials.** Knit-cro-sheen, 5 balls Black for background; Cotton Rug Yarn, 1 skein each of Sea Green and Steel Blue; Knit-cro-sheen Metallic, 1 ball each of Hunter Green and Watermelon for weaving. Steel Crochet Hook No. 7. Padding (foam rubber is suitable).

**Gauge.** After weaving, 9 sts—1"; 3 rows—1".

**Background.** Starting at rear edge with Black, ch 129. Row 1: Dc in 4th ch from hook, dc in next ch, * ch 1, skip 1 ch, dc in next 3 ch, repeat from * across, ch 4, turn. Row 2: Skip first 2 dc, * dc in next dc, dc in next ch-1 sp, dc in next dc, ch 1, skip next dc, repeat from * across, ending ch 1, skip last dc, dc in top of turning ch, ch 3, turn. Row 3: Dc in first ch-1 sp, * dc in next dc, ch 1, skip next dc, dc in next dc, dc in next ch-1 sp, repeat from * across, ending with 2 dc in turning ch, ch 3 turn. Row 4: Dc in first dc (1 dc inc), * ch 1, skip next dc, dc in next dc, dc in next ch-1 sp, dc in next dc. Repeat from * across, ending with ch 1, skip last dc, 2 dc in top of turning ch (1 dc inc), ch 3, turn. Row 5: Skip first dc, * dc in next dc, dc in ch-1 sp, dc in next dc, ch 1, skip next dc, repeat from * across, end-ing with dc in last ch-1 sp, dc in last dc, dc in top of turning ch, ch 3, turn. Row 6: Skip first dc, * dc in next dc, ch 1, skip 1 dc, dc in next dc, dc in next sp, repeat from * across, ending with dc in last dc, dc in turn-ing ch, ch 4, turn. Row 7: Skip first dc, dc in next dc (1 sp inc), * dc in sp, dc in next dc, ch 1, skip next dc, dc in next dc, repeat from * across, ending with dc in last sp, dc in next dc, ch 1, dc in top of turning ch (1 sp inc), ch 3, turn. Row 8: Repeat Row 3, ch 4, turn. Row 9: Repeat Row 2. Keeping to pat, inc 1 st at both ends of the next row and every 3rd row until piece measures 15". Fasten off.

**Weaving.** Row 1: With 1 strand each of Steel Blue and Watermelon, weave up through first sp, * down through next sp, up through next sp. Repeat from * across. Row 2: With 1 strand each of Sea Green and Hunter Green, weave exactly as for Row 1. Row 3: With Steel Blue and Watermelon, weave down through first sp, * up through next sp, down through next sp. Repeat from * across. Row 4: With Sea Green and Hunter Green, work to correspond with Row 3, keeping continuity of pat and repeat these 4 rows to opposite edge. Now turn piece with side edge toward you. Row 1: With Steel Blue and Watermelon, weave up through sp at base of first st of same color, * down through next sp, up through next sp, repeat from * across. Row 2: With Sea Green and Hunter Green, work exactly as for Row 1. Repeat these 2 rows, forming a zigzag stripe of each color, to opposite edge.

**Reverse Side.** Starting at rear edge with Black, make a chain 4" longer than rear edge of woven piece. Row 1: Dc in 4th ch from hook and in each ch across until row measures same as woven row. Cut off excess chain, 2 sts beyond last dc, ch 3, turn. Rows 2 and 3: Skip first dc, dc in each remaining dc, dc in top of turning ch, ch 3, turn. Row 4: Dc in first dc (inc made), dc in each dc across, 2 dc in turning ch (inc made), ch 3, turn. Repeat Rows 2, 3, and 4 until piece measures 15". Fasten off.

**Finishing.** Block Pieces. Pin both pieces

tog, inserting padding. With Black, work 1 row sc through both thicknesses, thus joining edges, turn and sl st in each sc around.

## Woven Patterns

Directions are given for 1 square yard of woven fabric, but can be adapted to any size. This fabric may be treated as any loosely woven fabric. Before cutting, make 2 rows of stitching on each side of cutting line.

*Pattern 1*

**Materials for 1 Square Yard.** Knit-cro-sheen, 10 balls White for background; Knit-cro-sheen Metallic, 11 balls Spanish Red; Cotton Rug Yarn, 7 balls Black for weaving. Steel Crochet Hook No. 7.

**Gauge.** After weaving, 9 sts—1″; 2 rows—1¼″.

**Background.** With White, ch 9 for each 1″ of desired width, plus 5 chains. Row 1: D tr in 6th ch from hook, d tr in each ch across, ch 5, turn. Row 2: Skip first d tr, d tr in each remaining d tr across, d tr in top of turning ch, ch 5, turn. Repeat Row 2 for desired length. Fasten off.

**Weaving.** Cut single strands of Rug Yarn and 4 strands of Knit-cro-sheen about 4″ longer than row. Row 1: Step 1: With Spanish Red, weave under 1 d tr, * over 2 d tr, under 3 d tr, repeat from * across. Step 2: With Black, weave over 1 d tr, * under 2 d tr, over 3 d tr, repeat from * across. Step 3: With Spanish Red, weave under 2 d tr, * over 2 d tr, under 3 d tr, repeat from * across. Step 4: With Black, weave over 2 d tr, * under 2 d tr, over 3 d tr, repeat from * across. Step 5: With Spanish Red, weave * under 3 d tr, over 2 d tr, repeat from * across. Step 6: With Black, weave * over 3 d tr, under 2 d tr. Repeat from * across. Step 7: With Spanish Red, work through tops of d tr as follows: bring up needle in 4th d tr, * skip 1 d tr, insert needle through next d tr, skip 2 d tr, bring up needle in next d tr, repeat from * across. Row 2: Repeat steps 6, 5, 4, 3, 2, and 1 of Row 1, thus reversing order. Repeat Rows 1 and 2 until entire piece is woven.

*Pattern 2*

**Materials for 1 Square Yard.** Knit-cro-sheen, 15 balls Spanish Red for background; Cotton Rug Yarn, 4 skeins White; Knit-cro-sheen Metallic, 2 balls Black for weaving. Steel Crochet Hook No. 7.

**Gauge.** After weaving, 9 sts—1″; 7 rows—1½″.

**Background.** With Spanish Red, ch 18 for each 2″ of desired width, plus 3 sts. Row 1: Sc in 2nd ch from hook and in each ch across. The number of sc should be a multiple of 18, plus 2 sts, ch 3, turn. Row 2: Skip first sc, dc in next sc, * ch 1, skip 1 sc, dc in next 2 sc, repeat from * across, ch 3, turn. Rows 3 and 4: Skip first dc, dc in next dc, * ch 1, dc in next 2 dc, repeat from * across, ending with ch 1, dc in last dc, dc in top of turning ch, ch 3, turn. At end of 4th row, ch 1 to turn. Row 5: Sc in first 2 dc, * sc in next ch-1 sp, sc in next 2 dc. Repeat from * across, ending with sc in last dc, sc in turning ch, ch 3, turn. Repeat Rows 2 to 5 incl for desired length. Fasten off.

**Weaving.** Cut strands about 4″ longer than row to be woven. Row 1: With 2 strands of White, weave up through first sp, down through next sp, * up through next sp, down through next sp, repeat from * across. Row 2: With 2 strands of White, weave up through first sp, * skip 1 sp, down through next sp, up through next sp. Repeat from * across, ending down through last sp. Row 3: Repeat Row 1. Repeat these 3 rows to opposite edge. Turn piece sideways. With 4 strands of Black, weaving between the 2 dc of each Spanish Red stripe, weave under sc row, * over dc rows, under sc row. Repeat from * across. With 4 strands of Black, slip thread under the White sts half way between each Spanish Red stripe.

*Pattern 3*

**Materials for Making 1 Square Yard.** Knit-cro-sheen, 14 balls Yellow for background; Cotton Rug Yarn, 5 skeins Steel Blue and Knit-cro-sheen Metallic, 2 balls Spanish Red for weaving. Steel Crochet Hook No. 7.

**Gauge.** After weaving, 9 sts—1″; 2 rows measure 7/8″.

**Background.** Ch 9, for each 1 inch of desired width, having a multiple of 8, plus 3 sts. Row 1: Tr in 5th ch from hook, tr in each ch across, ch 4, turn. Row 2: Skip first tr, tr in each tr across, tr in top of turning ch, ch 4, turn. Repeat Row 2 for desired length. Fasten off.

**Weaving.** Cut strands about 4″ longer than row. Row 1: Step 1: With 1 strand of Steel Blue, weave under first tr, over 1 tr, * under next 4 tr, over next 4 tr. Repeat from * across, ending over 1 tr, under 1 tr. Step 2: With double strand of Steel Blue, weave under first 2 tr, * over 1 tr, under 2 tr, over 1 tr, under 1 tr, over 2 tr, under 1 tr. Repeat from * across, ending under last 2 tr. Step 3: Repeat Step 1. Step 4: With 4 strands of Spanish Red, working through center of Step 2, repeat Step 1. Row 2: Step 1: With 1 strand of Steel Blue, weave under first 2 tr, * over 4 tr, under 4 tr. Repeat from * across, ending under last 2 tr. Step 2: With 2 strands of Steel Blue weave under first tr, * over 1 tr, under 1 tr, over 2 tr, under 1 tr, over 1 tr, under 2 tr. Repeat from * across, ending under 1 tr. Step 3: Repeat Step 1. Step 4: With 4 strands of Spanish Red, working through center of Step 2, repeat Step 1. Repeat these 2 rows to opposite edge.
*Pattern 4*

**Materials to Make 1 Square Yard.** Knit-cro-sheen, 14 balls Purple for background; Cotton Rug Yarn, 2 skeins each of Dk. Rose, Flamingo, and Aqua for weaving. Steel Crochet Hook No. 7.

**Gauge.** After weaving, 9 sts—1″; 2 rows—1″.

**Background.** With Purple, ch 9 for each 1 inch of desired width, plus 4 sts. Row 1: Tr in 5th ch from hook and in each ch across, ch 4, turn. Row 2: Skip first tr, tr in each remaining tr across, tr in top of turning ch, ch 4, turn. Repeat Row 2 for desired length. Fasten off.

**Weaving.** Cut 3 strands for each row, about 4″ longer than row to be woven. Row 1: Use Dk. Rose. Step 1: Weave over first tr, * under next tr, over next tr. Repeat from * across. Step 2: Weave under first tr, * over next tr, under next tr. Repeat from * across. Step 3: Repeat Step 1. Weaving each row exactly the same way, use Flamingo for Row 2 and Aqua for Row 3, then repeat these 3 rows to opposite edge.

## CROCHETED APPAREL

### Crocheted Blouse

Directions are given for Size 12. Changes for Sizes 14, 16, and 18 are in parentheses.

**Materials.** Super Fingering Yarn, 3 ply, 1 oz. skeins, 12 (12–13–14). Plastic Crochet Hook No. 2. 8 Buttons. ¾ yard Grosgrain Ribbon ¾″ wide.

**Gauge.** 7 sts—1″; 7 rows—2″.

**Blocking Measurements.** Bust: 34 (36–38–40)″; Width across front at underarm: 17¼ (18¼–19¼–20¼)″; Length from shoulder at armhole to lower edge: 19½ (20½–21½–22½)″; Length of side seam: 12½ (13–13½–14)″; Sleeve width at underarm: 13 (13½–14–14)″; Underarm sleeve length: 11 (11½–12–12)″.

*Note:* Blouse is worked vertically.

**Left Back.** Starting at center back, ch 142 (150–156–164) to measure 20 (21–22–23)″. Row 1: Dc in 4th ch from hook and in each ch across, 140 (148–154–162) dc, counting turning ch as 1 dc, ch 4, turn. Place a marker in first dc of first row to indicate neck edge. Row 2: Skip first dc, * dc in next dc, ch 1, skip 1 dc, repeat from * across, ending with dc in top of turning ch. There are 70 (74–77–81) sps on row, ch 3, turn. Row 3: * Dc in next sp, dc in next dc, repeat from * across, ending with dc in turning ch, ch 4, turn. Repeat Rows 2 and 3 for pat. TO SHAPE NECK: Work in pat, inc 1 dc at neck edge on each dc row until there are 9 (9–10–10) rows in all. There are 143 (151–157–165) dc on row. TO SHAPE SHOULDER: Keeping pat, dec 1 dc on each dc row 7 (7–9–9) times in all. Work even until 24 (25–26–27) rows in all have been completed. Fasten off. TO SHAPE ARMHOLE AND SIDE SEAM: Place a marker 5 (5–5¼– 5½)″ above lower edge to indicate waist-line and another marker 6¼ (6¾–7¼– 7¾)″ below shoulder to indicate armhole. On Sizes 10 and 14, join yarn at armhole marker. On Sizes 12 and 16, join yarn at waistline marker. Keeping pat on all sizes, dec 1 st at armhole edge and 3 sts at waist-line each row 6 times in all. (To dec 1 st on an open space row, omit ch-1 and end with 2 dc. To dec 3 sts at waistline, draw up a loop in each of 4 sts, yo and draw through all loops on hook.) Continue in pat, keep armhole edge straight and dec 3 sts as be-fore at waistline for 1 (2–3–3) more rows. Fasten off. Join yarn ½″ below waistline marker and work 1 row in pat to lower edge. Fasten off.

**Right Back.** Work to correspond with Left Back, reversing shaping.

**Right Front.** Starting at center front, ch 128 (134–140–146) to measure 18 (19–20–20½)″. Rows 1 and 2: Work as for Left Back—63 (66–69–72) sps on Row 2. Row 3: Dc in first sp, * ch 4, skip next 2 sps, sl st at base of next dc, turn, make 6 sc over the ch-4, sl st in last dc made (scallop), turn, (dc in next dc, dc in next sp) 3 times, repeat from * across, making last dc in last scallop in top of turning ch, ch 4, turn. Row 4: Work as for Row 2 of Left Back. Rows 1 to 4 constitute the pat. TO SHAPE NECK: Work in pat, inc 1 st at neck edge on each dc row until there are 8 (8–9–9) rows in all. On Sizes 12 and 14 only: Ch 17 (19) at neck edge, turn. *On Sizes 16 and 18 only:* Join a strand of yarn at neck edge and ch 16 (18). Fasten off. *On all Sizes:* Pick up work-ing strand and work in pat across entire row, including ch. There are 143 (151–157–165) sts on row. Keeping pat on all sizes and starting at shoulder shaping, complete Right Front as for Left Back.

**Left Front.** Join yarn to first st at neck edge on Right Front. Row 1: Work-ing along starting ch, ch 4, * skip 1 dc, dc in base of next dc, ch 1, repeat from *

across, ending with dc in base of turning ch, ch 3, turn. Row 2: Dc in first sp, (dc in next dc, dc in next sp) twice,* ch 4, turn, skip the 3 sps just worked, sl st in base of next dc, turn, make 6 sc over the ch-4, sl st in last dc made (scallop), (dc in next dc, dc in next sp) 3 times, repeat from * across, ending with dc in turning ch, ch 4, turn. Row 3: Skip first 2 dc, * dc in next dc, ch 1, skip 1 dc, repeat from * across, ending with dc in top of turning ch, ch 3, turn. Row 4: Inc 1 dc in first sp, dc in each sp and in each dc across. Rows 1 through 4 constitute the pat. Work in pat to correspond with Right Front, reversing shapings.

**Sleeves.** FIRST HALF: Starting at center, ch 112 (118–122–126) to measure 16 (16¾–17½–17¾)″. Work in pat as for Left Back, even, for 6 rows. There are 110 (116–120–124) sts on row, including turning ch. Marker indicates top edge. To Shape Top: Work in pat, dec 1 st at top edge only on each row until there are 16 (18–18–20) rows. To Shape Side Seam and Complete Top: Row 1: Dec 1 st, work in pat to within 4 sps from lower edge, hdc in next sp, ch 1, sl st in next dc, turn. Row 2: Sl st in first 7 sts, sc in next dc, now work in pat, dec 1 st at top edge, ch 1, turn. Repeat Rows 1 and 2, 1 (1–2–2) time(s) more. Continue to dec at lower edge, omitting dec at top edge, until there are 23 (24–25–25) rows in all. Fasten off.

SECOND HALF: Attach yarn to starting ch at top edge and work as for First Half, reversing shapings.

**Collar (Make 2).** Starting at inner edge of Collar, ch 44 (44–48–48). Rows 1 and 2: Work in pat same as for Back. Row 3: Work in pat, inc 1 dc at both ends and 6 dc evenly spaced across row, ch 4, turn. Repeat Rows 2 and 3 once more. Fasten off.

**Finishing.** Block to measurements. Sew side and shoulder seams. Sew sleeve seams and sew in sleeves. Sew collar pieces in place, having center back edges extend ½″ beyond collar. With right side facing,

sl st around sleeve and collar edges. Face left back edge with grosgrain ribbon. Sew buttons in place. First space row on right back is used for buttonholes.

## Deep Cloche

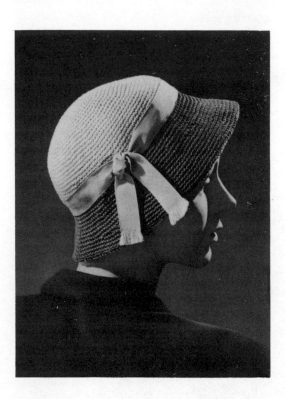

**Materials.** Knit-cro-sheen, 2 balls each of Kelly Green and Dark Gray. Steel Crochet Hook Size 0. 1 yard Gray Grosgrain Ribbon, 1″ wide.

**Gauge.** 6 sc—1″; 6 rnds—1″.

*Note:* Use thread double throughout.

Starting at center with Dk Gray, ch 2. Rnd 1: 6 sc in 2nd ch from hook, join. Rnd 2: 2 sc in each sc around, join. Rnd 3: * Sc in next sc, 2 sc in next sc—1 sc inc. Repeat from * around, join. Rnds 4 through 16: Sc in each sc around, inc 6 sc evenly on each rnd, join. Work even until piece measures 4½″. Fasten off. Next rnd: Attach Kelly Green and sc in back loop of each sc around, join. Continue working even until piece measures 5½″ in all.

**Brim.** Rnd 1: Sc in each sc, inc 10 sc evenly around, join. Rnd 2: Sc in each sc around, join. Rnd 3: Inc 10 sc evenly around, join, and fasten off. Mark joining for center back. Short Row 1: Attach Green to 20th st following center back, sc in same place, sc in each sc across to within 19 sc of center. Fasten off. Rnd 4: Attach thread at center back and sc in each sc around, join and fasten off. Short Row 2: Attach thread to 26th sc from center back, sc in same place, sc in each sc around to within 25 sc on other side of center, fasten off. Short Row 3: Skip 5 sc on last short row, attach thread and sc in each sc to within last 5 sc, fasten off. Rnd 5: Attach thread at center back and sc in each sc around, inc 10 sc evenly around, join. Rnd 6: Sc in each sc around, join and fasten off. Short Row 4: Attach thread to 16th sc from center back, sc in each sc, inc 8 sc evenly across to within last 16 sc, sl st in next sc, fasten off. Short Row 5: Attach thread to 11th st from joining, sc in each sc around to within last 11 sc, sl st in next sc, fasten off. Rnd 7: Attach thread to center back and sc in each sc around, join. Rnd 8: Inc 10 sc evenly around, join. Rnd 9: Sc in each sc around, join and fasten off.

**Underbrim.** Rnd 1: Attach Gray to center back and sc in back loop of each sc around, dec 10 sc evenly around. Rnd 2: Sc in each sc around, join. Rnd 3: Dec 10 sc evenly around, join. Rnds 4 through 7: Repeat Rnds 2 and 3 alternately 2 more times. Fasten off at end of Rnd 7. Sew Underbrim in place. Press hat. Tie ribbon around crown into a knot at side. Fringe ends of ribbon.

## Carry-All Bag

**Materials.** Speed-cro-sheen Mercerized Cotton, 3 balls Black, 2 balls each White and Aqua. 10 Metal Rings, ⅞″ diameter. Piece of Felt, 12″ in diameter. Steel Crochet Hook Size 0.

**Gauge.** 3 sps—1″; 5 rnds—2″.

**Base.** Starting at center with Black, ch 2. Rnd 1: 7 sc in 2nd ch from hook, do not join. Rnd 2: 2 sc in each sc around. Rnd 3: * 2 sc in next sc (1 sc inc), sc in next sc, repeat from * around. Rnd 4: Sc in each sc, inc 7 sc evenly around, repeat Rnd 4 until

**Finishing.** Cut a cardboard circle 10″ in diameter, cover with felt, stitching excess under cardboard. Sew to bag. Sew crocheted base in place. Sew rings around top of bag.

**Cord.** Cut 8 strands of Aqua and Black, each 54″ long; double Aqua strands; then draw Black strands through loop and double. Twist these strands tightly, then double and give them a twist in the opposite direction. Draw Cord through rings and knot ends together, leaving 2″ free for tassel. Make another Cord the same way.

## Crocheted Wool Boots

piece measures 10″ in diameter, sl st in next sc. Fasten off.

**Side—Background.** Starting at lower edge, make a chain 33″ long, join with sl st. Rnd 1: Ch 4, * skip 1 ch, dc in next ch, ch 1, repeat from * around, join to 3rd ch of ch-4. Rnd 2: Ch 4, * dc in next dc, ch 1, repeat from * around, join. Repeat Rnd 2 until 18 rnds have been completed. Fasten off.

**To Make Stripes.** 1st Stripe: Attach Aqua around bar of any dc on first rnd and working horizontally, hold thread on top of work, insert hook under first dc bar, * thread over and draw loop through, thread over and draw through both loops on hook, ch 1, insert hook under next dc bar, repeat from * around, working over starting ch as over dc's. Join last ch 1 to first sc. Work 2 more sc rnds of Aqua over same rnd of dc-sps (this completes one stripe—wrong side of work is right side of pat). Now work alternate stripes of White and Aqua across entire background to within last 2 rnds. Attach Black to any sp on top and sc closely around. Join and fasten off.

Directions are for Size 6½. For larger or smaller Sizes, inc or dec the number of rows over instep.

**Materials.** Knitting Worsted, 3 ozs. Navy, 1 oz. Red. 1 pair Slipper Soles. 5″ Zipper. Plastic Crochet Hook Size 5.

*Note:* Each boot is made in two parts.

Row 1: With Navy, starting at tip, ch 11, hdc in 3rd ch from hook and in each ch across, ch 2, turn. Row 2: Hdc in each st across, inc 1 st in last st, ch 2, turn. Row 3: 2 hdc in first st, 1 hdc in each st across. Rows 4 through 13: Repeat Rows 2 and 3. Row 14: 1 hdc in each st across, ch 14, turn. Row 15: Hdc in 3rd ch from hook and in each st to end of row. Work even for 9 rows. Fasten off. Make two parts alike. With Red, make 1 sc in each of the 9 hdc of the tip, ch 1, turn.

Work 5 more rows. With Navy, sew back of boot together; make a row of sc all around the top and down the front opening. With Red, make 2 rows of sc around top and 1″ of front opening. Cross red part of tip (see photograph). With Red, work 1 row sc around bottom part. For heel, work 2 rows sc for 15 sts on either side of back seam. Work another row sc all around bottom. Sew boot to sole, sew in zipper, join tassel to zipper tab.

# CHAPTER 9

# *Tatting*

Tatting is a knotting technique with which many lovely things can be made. The size of the shuttle and the thread determine the fineness or coarseness of the finished piece. Tatting has been used principally for trimmings on table linens, handkerchiefs, blouses, children's dresses, etc. By making small motifs and joining them as you work, it is also possible to make very beautiful all-over lace pieces suitable for place mats, table covers, etc.

Cotton thread with a hard twist is customarily employed for this craft but other types of thread and yarns can also be used. For example, the edging on the summer evening stole on the color plate was made of yarn. The effect was entirely different and the results very pleasing.

## SHUTTLES AND THREADS

Shuttles can be made of various materials such as bone, tortoise shell, steel, or plastic. The points should come together closely enough to prevent the thread from feeding too rapidly. Some shuttles are made with a hook

at the end but this tends to hinder the work. A crochet hook or pin can be used instead. Use larger shuttles for heavy thread and for wool yarn.

### Winding Shuttle

Fasten thread to shuttle by tying around the bar or through the hole in the bar if there is one. Wind thread evenly and not beyond the edge of the shuttle.

### Threads

There are threads especially made for tatting, fine and with a hard twist. Coarser threads may be used and even woolen yarn, but all must have a twist to work well.

## HOW TO TAT

### Holding Thread

With left hand grasp the free end of thread between thumb and forefinger. Spread the other fingers and bring the thread around them to make a circle. Hold securely with thumb and forefinger. Bend the little finger

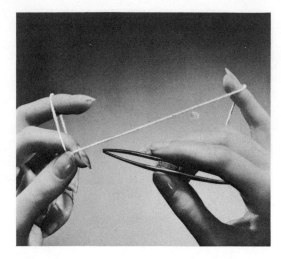

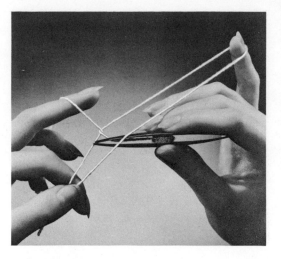

toward the palm to catch the thread and extend the middle finger to make the circle taut. This middle finger does most of the work of drawing up stitches or knots.

Without turning the shuttle, slide it first under, then over the thread held between middle and forefinger of left hand.

## Double Knot, First Half

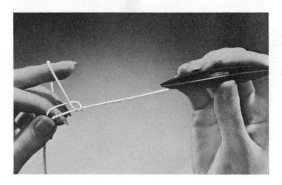

With right hand hold shuttle by flat sides, pointing to left hand and with thread coming from back of bobbin. Extend little finger of right hand to support the thread.

Drop middle finger of left hand. Draw shuttle thread taut; a loop will form with the thread around left hand.

Extend dropped finger of left hand sliding the stitch down the shuttle thread which is held taut, making a tight stitch between thumb and forefinger. This completes first half of a double stitch.

Practice this step until you do it with ease. The shuttle thread should slide easily through the stitches.

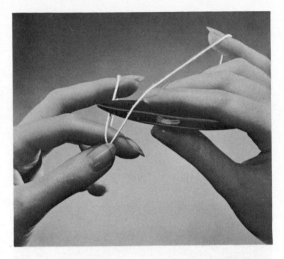

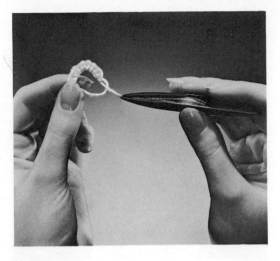

## Second Half of Double Stitch

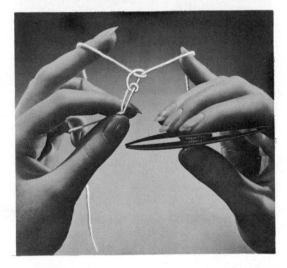

Hold shuttle in horizontal position. Slide shuttle first over, then under thread between middle and forefinger of left hand. Draw up as for first half of stitch. This completes double stitch.

## To Make a Ring

All tatting is made of rings, chains, and picots. The rings and chains are the basis

of the design and picots are used for decoration and for joining.

After making several double stitches, draw up the thread on the shuttle so the first and last stitches touch giving you a ring.

## To Make a Picot

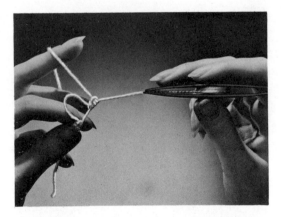

Make first half of a ds, but as you slide it into position, stop about ¼" (or less) from preceding ds. Make the second half of ds; then slide entire ds close to preceding ds. The resulting loop is the picot. A picot means only the loop and does not include the ds which fastens it.

382

## To Join Rings

When starting a second ring, leave a free space of about ¼ of the circumference of the first ring (this varies with the design).

For example: Make first ring of 3 ds, p, 3 ds, p, 3 ds, p, 3 ds, draw up. Make 3 ds of 2nd r about ¼″ away from first r. Insert pin through last p of first r, catch thread encircling left hand and draw a loop through. Slip shuttle through this loop and draw shuttle thread taut. This joins 2nd r to first r and counts as first half of next ds. Complete ring as for first r.

## Using Two Shuttles or a Ball and Shuttle to Make Chains

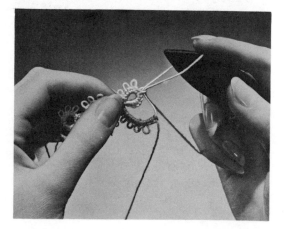

This is a way of covering the thread which passes from one ring to another. It also makes it possible to use two colors.

Rings can be made only with the shuttle thread wound completely around the left hand. Chains are made with the shuttle working on the ball (or second shuttle) thread.

Tie end of ball thread to end of shuttle thread. When making a ring use the shuttle thread in the regular manner.

When completed, turn it upside down so the base of the ring is held between the thumb and forefinger. Stretch the ball thread over the back of the fingers but instead of making a complete circle, wind it twice around the little finger to control the tension. Work over the ball thread with the shuttle as in making rings. (Picots and joinings are made in same way as on rings.) When chain is finished, pull stitches close together and put down ball thread. Pick up shuttle thread, turn work and make another ring.

## Reversing Work

The round part of the ring is at the top as you work. By reversing the work, a loop can be made on the opposite side. This allows for wider edgings and insertions. To do this, the ring you have just worked is turned so the base of the ring is at the top and the new ring is worked as usual with the loop side up. Then reverse and make another ring beside the first and so on.

## Joining Thread

When a new thread is required, make a square knot close to the base of the last ring or chain. Do not cut off ends as the strain of the work may loosen the knot. This is the only place to make knots, as they will not pass through the double stitches and therefore will prevent the ring from being drawn up if they occur on the thread encircling the hand. Cut off loose ends later.

## Josephine Knot

This is an ornamental ring consisting of the first half of a double stitch made a specific number of times.

## Long Picots

Make like regular picot but leave a longer space between ds.

## Using Two Shuttles

When working rings in two colors use two shuttles, one color in each. Alternate shuttles. Drop the shuttle which has made the first ring and pick up the second. When separated by a chain, hold thread of second shuttle like the ball thread.

## ABBREVIATIONS

r . . . . . . . . . . . . . . . . . . . . . . . . ring
lr . . . . . . . . . . . . . . . . . . . . large ring
sr or sm r . . . . . . . . . . . . . small ring
ds . . . . . . . . . . . . . . . . double stitch
p . . . . . . . . . . . . . . . . . . . . . . picot
lp . . . . . . . . . . . . . . . . . long picot
sp . . . . . . . . . . . . . . . small picot
sep . . . . . . . . . . . . . . . . separated
cl . . . . . . . . . . . . . . . . . . . . . close
rw . . . . . . . . . . . . . . . reverse work
sp . . . . . . . . . . . . . . . . . . . . . . space
ch . . . . . . . . . . . . . . . . . . . . . chain
*Repeat instructions following asterisks as many times as specified.

## TATTING DESIGNS

### Tatted Appliqué Corner and Edging

**Materials.** 1 ball each of Green and White Tatting Cotton, Size 70.

A Rolled-edge Handkerchief, and Shuttle.

**Edging.** Tie ball and shuttle threads together. (R of 6 ds, p and 6 ds) 5 times. * Rw, ch of 6 ds, 3 p's sep by 3 ds, 6 ds, p, 6 ds; skip one r of the 5-r group, join to p of next r, 4 ds. Rw, lr of 3 ds, 5 p's sep by 3 ds, 3 ds, cl. Rw, ch of 4 ds, p and 6 ds, join to p of previous ch, 6 ds, 3 p's sep by 3 ds, 6 ds. Rw, of 6 ds, p and 6 ds, cl r of 6 ds, join to free p of previous ch, 6 ds, cl, (r of ds, p and 6 ds, cl) 3 times. Repeat from * for length desired. Tie and cut.

**Corner Spray.** Flower (make 6): With White make (r of 15 ds, cl) 4 times. Tie and cut.

**Leaf (make 5).** With Green make (r of 6 ds, p and 6 ds, cl) twice. Tie and cut. Form branches of spray with Green thread and tack in place. Place flowers and leaves in position and sew in place. Sew edging to handkerchief.

## Narrow Insertion with Rickrack

**Materials.** 1 ball White Mercerized Crochet Cotton, size 30. Shuttle and Rickrack.

R, 6 ds, join in base between points of rickrack, 6 ds, cl r, turn. * Ch, 3 ds, p, 3 ds, join

in next point of rickrack, 3 ds, p, 3 ds, turn. R, 6 ds, join in next base between points of rickrack, 6 ds, cl r, turn, repeat from * for length desired. Work across opposite side in same manner.

## Narrow Edging with Rickrack

**Materials.** 1 ball White Mercerized Crochet Cotton, size 30. Shuttle and Rickrack.

Join thread in point of rickrack, ch, 5 ds, turn. * R, 1 ds, 5 p sep by 1 ds, 1 ds, cl r, turn. Ch, 5 ds, join to next point of rickrack, 5 ds, turn. Repeat from * for desired length. Working across opposite side, join thread in first point of rickrack, ch, 1 ds, p, 5 ds, turn. * R, 1 ds, 2 p sep by 1 ds, 1 ds, join to base between points of rickrack, 1 ds, 2 p sep by 1 ds, 1 ds, cl r, turn. Ch, 5 ds, p, 1 ds, join to next point of rickrack, 1 ds, p, 5 ds, turn. Repeat from * for length desired.

## Wide Edging with Rickrack

**Materials.** 1 ball White Mercerized Crochet Cotton, size 30. Shuttle and Rickrack.

Row 1: R, 6 ds, p, 6 ds, cl r, turn. Ch, 6 ds, join to point of rickrack, 6 ds, turn. R, 6 ds, join to p of first r, 6 ds, cl r. * R, 6 ds, p, 6 ds, cl r, turn. Ch, 6 ds, join to next point of rickrack, 6 ds, turn. R, 6 ds, join to p of last r made, 6 ds, cl r. Repeat from * for length desired. Working across opposite side of rickrack, r, 6 ds, join on side of rickrack near point, 6 ds, cl r. R, 6 ds, join on opposite side near next point of rickrack, 6 ds, cl r, turn. Ch, 6 ds, p, 6 ds, turn. Repeat from beginning across row.

Row 2: R, 6 ds, join to p of ch of previous row, 6 ds, cl r, turn. * Ch, 6 ds, p, 6 ds, turn. R, 6 ds, join to picot of same ch, 6 ds, cl r. R, 6 ds, join to p of next ch, 6 ds, cl r, turn. Repeat from * across row.

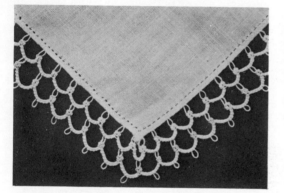

## Wide Insertion with Rickrack

**Materials.** 1 ball White Mercerized Crochet Cotton, size 30. Shuttle and Rickrack.

R, 2 ds, p, 3 ds, join to point of rickrack, 3 ds, p, 2 ds, cl r. * R, 2 ds, join to last p of last r made, 3 ds, join in base between points of rickrack, 3 ds, p, 2 ds, cl r. R, 2 ds, join to last r made, 3 ds, join to next point of rickrack, 3 ds, p, 2 ds, cl r, turn. Ch, 3 ds, 5 p sep by 3 ds, 3 ds, turn. R, 2 ds, p, 3 ds, join to same point of rickrack as last r made, 3 ds, p, 2 ds, cl r. Repeat from * for desired length. Work other side in same manner.

## Tatted Edging

**Materials.** Tatting-Crochet Thread, Size 70, 1 ball of No. 1 White. 1 Linen Handkerchief, 11 inches square. Tatting Shuttle.

**Edging.** 1st row: With ball and shuttle threads, r of 2 ds, lp, 2 ds, cl. Rw, ch of 4 ds, lp, 4 ds. Rw, r as before. Rw, ch as before. Continue to work this way for necessary length. Tie and cut. 2nd row: Tie ball and shuttle threads together. R of 2 ds, join to lp of *1st* ch of previous row, 2 ds, cl. Rw, ch of 4 ds, lp, 4 ds. * Rw, r of 2 ds, join to lp of next ch, 2 ds, cl. Rw, ch as before. Repeat from * across. Tie and cut. Sew edging to handkerchief.

## Tatted Edging

**Materials.** Tatting-Crochet Thread, Size 70, 1 ball of No. 1 White. 1 Linen Handkerchief, 11 inches square. Tatting Shuttle.

**Edging.** R of 5 ds, lp, 5 ds, cl. Sp of ⅛ inch. Rw, r of 5 ds, lp, 5 ds, cl. Sp, as before. Rw, r as before. Continue to work this way for necessary length. Tie and cut. Sew·edging to handkerchief.

## Tatted Edging

**Materials.** Tatting-Crochet Thread, Size 70, 1 ball of No. 1 White. 1 Linen Handkerchief, 11 inches square. Tatting Shuttle.

## Tatted Luncheon Cloth
## 36 Inches Square

**Materials.** Six-Cord Mercerized Crochet Thread, Size 30, White. Tatting Shuttle.
1 large and 1 small motif measure 2 inches.

**Edging.** * R of 1 ds, 8 lp's sep by 1 ds, 1 ds, half cl. Sp of ½ inch, r as before. Sp as before. Repeat from * for necessary length. Tie and cut. Sew edging to handkerchief.

**First Motif.** *1st row: 1st rnd:* Center r of 1 ds, 8 lp's sep by 3 ds, 2 ds, cl. Tie and cut. *2nd rnd:* Tie ball and shuttle threads together. * R of 7 ds, p, 7 ds, cl. Rw, ch of 7 ds, join to first lp of center r, 7 ds, Rw, r of 7 ds, join to p of previous r, (joint p), 7ds, cl. Repeat from * around, joining next ch to next lp and last ch at base of first r. Tie and cut. (Large motif made.)

**Second Motif.** (R of 7 ds, p, 7 ds, cl) 3 times. R of 7 ds, join to first joint p of previous motif, 7 ds, cl. Tie and cut. (Small motif made.)

**Third Motif.** *1st rnd:* Work exactly as for First Motif. *2nd rnd:* R of 7 ds, join to p of 2nd r of previous motif, 7 ds, cl. Rw, ch of 7 ds, join to first lp of center r, 7 ds. Complete as for First Motif, no more joinings.

## Tatted Edging

**Materials.** Tatting-Crochet Thread, Size 70, 1 ball of No. 1 White. 1 Linen Handkerchief, 11 inches square. Tatting Shuttle.

**Edging.** With ball and shuttle threads, r of 2 ds, 3 lp's sep by 2 ds, 2 ds, cl. Rw, ch of 2 ds, 3 lp's sep by 2 ds, 2 ds. * Rw, r of 2 ds, join to last lp of previous r, 2 ds, 2 lp's sep by 2 ds, 2 ds, cl. Rw, ch as before. Repeat from * for necessary length. Tie and cut. Sew edging to handkerchief.

**Fourth Motif.** Work exactly as for Second Motif, joining to a joint p of previous motif directly opposite previous joining of motifs. Continue to work in this way until 18 large motifs have been completed. *2nd row:* Make a small motif as before, skip 1 joint p of First Motif and join to next joint p of same motif. Make a large motif as follows: *1st rnd:* Work exactly as for First Motif. *2nd rnd:* R of 7 ds, join to p of 3rd r of previous motif, 7 ds, cl. Rw, ch of 7 ds, join to first lp of center r, 7 ds. Rw, r of 7 ds, join to same p of previous motif, 7 ds cl. R of 7 ds, join to joint p of First Motif (between small motifs), 7 ds, cl. Rw, ch as before, joining to next lp of center r. Rw, r as before, joining to same p of First Motif. R as before, joining to free p of adjacent r of Second Motif. Rw, ch as before, joining to next lp. Rw, r as before,

joining to same p of Second Motif. R as before, joining to adjacent joint p of Third Motif. Rw, ch, joining to next lp. Rw, r, joining to same joint p. Complete as First Motif, no more joinings. Make another small motif as follows: (R of 7 ds, p. 7 ds, cl) twice. R of 7 ds, join to next joint p of previous motif, 7 ds, cl. R as before, joining to next joint p of Third Motif. Tie and cut. Continue in this way, making small and large motifs alternately and joining to adjacent motifs until 17 large motifs have been completed.

*3rd row:* Make a large motif as follows: *1st rnd:* Work exactly as for First Motif. *2nd rnd:* R of 7 ds, join to p of 2nd r of first small motif of previous row, 7 ds, cl. Rw, ch as before, joining to first lp of center r. Rw, r as before, joining to same p of small motif.

R as before, joining to adjacent joint p of next motif of previous row. Rw, ch as before, joining to next lp. Rw, r as before, joining to same joint p of large motif. Complete as before, no more joinings. Now make a small motif, joining to adjacent large motifs as before. Continue as before until 18 large motifs have been completed. Repeat last 2 rows until piece is a square.

**Edging.** Tie ball and shuttle threads together. ** R of 7 ds, join to joint p (joining First Motif of 1st row and First Motif of 2nd row), 7 ds, cl. R as before, joining to free p of small motif. Rw, ch of 15 ds. Rw, r, joining to same p of small motif. R, joining to joint p (joining First Motif of 2nd row and First Motif of 3rd row). * Rw, ch as before. Rw, r as before, joining to same p. (R as before, joining to next joint p. Rw, ch. Rw, r, joining to same p. Rw, ch. Rw, r, joining to same p) 3 times. R, joining to next joint p between motifs. Rw, ch. Rw, r, joining to same p. Join to free p of small motif. R, joining to next joint p between motifs. Repeat from * across to within joining of last small motif. R, joining to joint p between motifs. Rw, ch. Rw, r, join to same p. R, joining to free p of small motif. Rw, ch. Rw, r, join to same p. R, joining to next joint p between motifs. Rw, ch. Rw, r, joining to same p. (R, joining to next joint p. Rw, ch. Rw, r, joining to same p. Rw, ch. Rw, r, joining to same p) 5 times. Repeat from ** around, joining at base of 1st r. Tie and cut.

## COLOR PLATE 9

### Summer Evening Scarf

To make the evening scarf shown on Color Plate 9: With selvages removed, cut a 40″ square of permanent finish organdy. Fold opposite corners together to make a triangle and pin along straight edges. Stitch close to the edge. Trim very close to the stitching. Turn this edge twice to make a very narrow hem. Slip-stitch by hand.

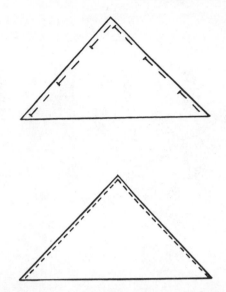

Make the tatted edge according to directions given. Lay the tatted edging to edge of the organdy on the right side so loops of inside row of rings just cover the hem. Pin carefully arranging "fullness" evenly. Sew on securely by catching each ring and running needle inside the hem between rings.

**Bow.** Cut organdy 3″ wide on the true bias. Turn in edges ⅛″ and crease. Fold down the center with raw edges to the inside and baste together, edges even. Be sure to fold so opposite edges meet exactly or strip will buckle. Slip-stitch edges together and press. Tie a permanent bow and tack it to the right side of scarf. Sew hook and eye or snap fasteners underneath to hold points together.

### Tatted Edging for Summer Evening Scarf

**Materials.** Nylon & Wool Yarn, 3 Ply, 1 oz. skein of Bittersweet. Tatting Shuttle.

**Edging.** *1st row:* Starting at one end with shuttle and yarn, make r of (1 ds, lp) 10 times, 1 ds, cl. Ch of 5 ds. * Rw, r as before. Ch as before. Repeat from * across until strip measures 25 inches—place rings in zigzag manner—ending with ch (center of corner chain). Reversing curve of chain make ch as before and repeat from * until strip measures 25 inches from center of corner chain, ending with r. Tie and cut.

*2nd row:* R of (1 ds, lp) 10 times, 1 ds, cl, ch of 5 ds. Rw, r of (1 ds, lp) 3 times, 1 ds, join to 7th lp of 1st r of 1st row, (1 ds, lp) twice, 1 ds, join to 4th lp of 3rd r of 1st row, (1 ds, lp) 3 times, 1 ds, cl. Ch as before. Rw, r as before. Rw, ch as before. R of (1 ds, lp) 3 times, 1 ds, join to 7th lp of 3rd r of 1st row, (1 ds, lp) twice, 1 ds, join to 4th lp of 5th r of 1st row, (1 ds, lp) 3 times, 1 ds, cl. This constitutes the pattern. Continue to work in pattern across until 4th lp of r preceding corner chain has been joined.

*To make corner, work as follows:* Ch as before. Rw, r as before. Rw, ch as before. R of (1 ds, lp) 3 times, 1 ds, join to 7th lp of same r of 1st row, (1 ds, lp) twice, 1 ds, join to 4th lp of r following corner chain, (1 ds, lp) 3 times, 1 ds, cl. Ch as before. Rw, r as before. Rw, ch as before. R of (1 ds, lp) 4 times, 1 ds, join to 8th lp of joined r of 2nd row, 1 ds, join to next lp of joined r of 1st row, (1 ds, lp) 4 times, 1 ds, cl. Ch as before. Rw, r as before. Rw, ch as before. R of (1 ds, lp) 3 times, 1 ds, join to next lp of same joined r of 2nd row, 1 ds, join to next lp of same joined r of 1st row, (1 ds, lp) 5 times, 1 ds, cl. Ch as before. Rw, r as before. Rw, ch as before. R of (1 ds, lp) 3 times, 1 ds, join to 7th lp of same joined r of 2nd row, 1 ds, lp, 1 ds, join to next lp of same joined r

of 1st row, 1 ds, join to 4th lp of 3rd r following corner chain, (1 ds, lp) 3 times, 1 ds, cl. Continue to work in pattern across, ending to correspond. Tie and cut.

## NETTING

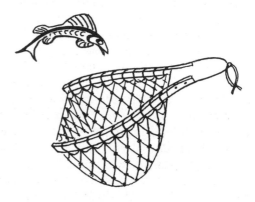

Netting is an ancient handicraft of unknown origin. It is a simple technique once you have mastered the fundamentals. Tying the knots and drawing up uniform loops is the only skill required. Netting can be exceedingly fine and delicate or bold and coarse; the size of needle, gauge and thread determine the result. It can be done with or without a gauge depending upon the skill acquired. Experienced fishermen never use a gauge. A netting needle and a gauge can be purchased or whittled from any thin wood.

Netting consists of loops secured to one another by knots. It is begun on a foundation loop of strong twine or thread. This must be firmly attached to something so one can pull against it while working. The loop can be tied to a chair or otherwise secured.

### Materials Needed

Netting needle, mesh sticks (gauge), and thread or yarn. Foundation cord. Two types of netting needles are shown as well as the gauge.

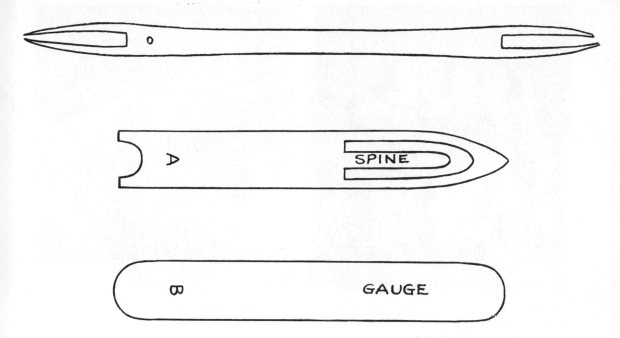

The foundation cord should be from 4″ to 12″ long. Tie ends of this cord together to make a loop and anchor the loop to some object.

## To Thread Needle

Fasten thread to the spine. Wind down over end A (see diagram) and up over spine on opposite side. Then down over end A and up over spine on first side. Alternate from side to side turning the needle. Fill the needle leaving ¼″ at tip of spine free.

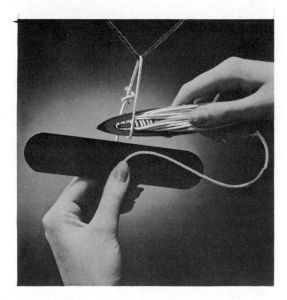

## How To Net

On end of thread coming from needle make a loop twice the width of the gauge tying it around anchor loop. Place this knot in middle of left side and hold gauge in left hand in position shown. With needle in right hand, pass it through loop from right to left. Use gauge to measure space of mesh.

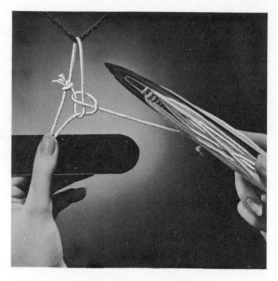

Pull thread to position and hold it firmly to the gauge with thumb.

Pull knot hard and tight.

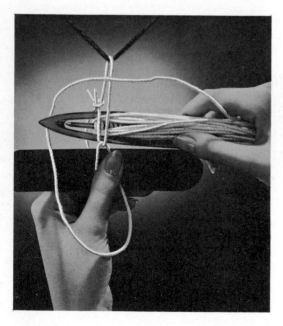

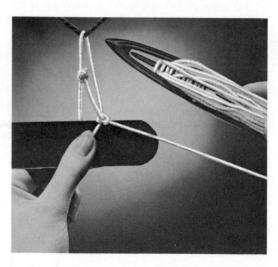

Loop twine down at right of first loop and hold with thumb. Pass needle under first two strands and over third and fourth strands above gauge.

Do not remove thumb from below knot until the knot has been made tight by pulling toward right.

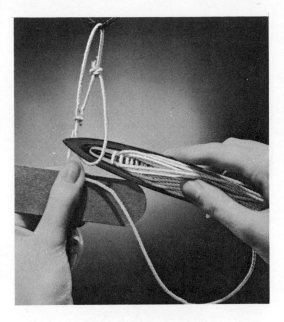

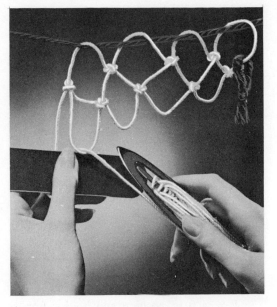

Remove gauge and place the new knot on the left and repeat until desired number of meshes have been made. This first row is a string of knotted loops the length of which depends upon the width of the article being made.

Now work across instead of down. Starting a knot at the first mesh to the left; continue working across to right until row is completed.

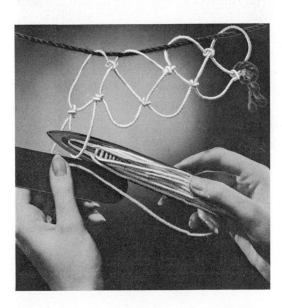

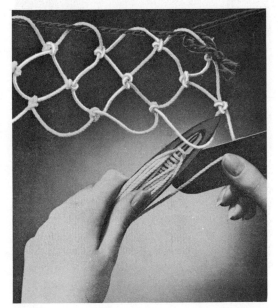

Now thread a heavy cord through the first row of meshes. This is the new anchor loop. Shorten the first anchor loop and leave tied on to locate starting mesh.

When row is completed change needle to left hand and gauge to the right hand. Work this row from right to left starting as shown.

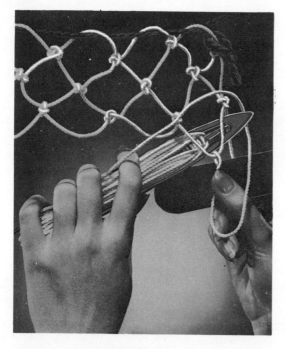

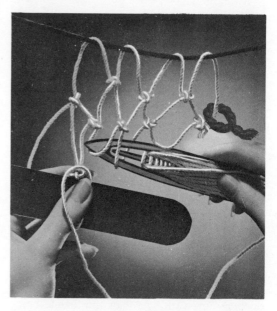

tinue working to left across row. Repeat alternate right and left rows for desired length.

**To Reduce a Mesh at End of Row.** Do not net last mesh.

Hold thread firmly with thumb at bottom of loop and reverse steps as shown. Con-

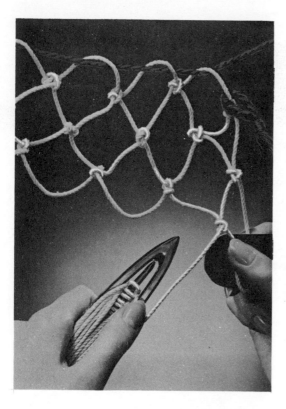

**To Reduce a Mesh in the Middle of a Row.** Net 2 meshes at one time by sliding needle through two loops instead of one and complete the knot.

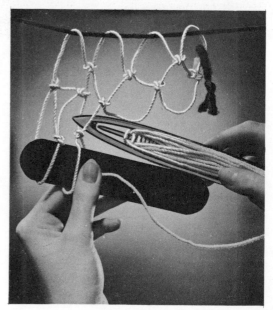

**To Increase a Mesh.** Make 2 knots in the same loop.

**To Make a Triangle.** Cast on required number of stitches. Decrease down to one stitch by joining the last two loops of every row with one knot.

## Net Embroidery

Motifs and borders can be embroidered or woven on hand-made or machine-made net. Since net is the foundation upon which you work, its construction influences the planning of the design and choice of thread to be used.

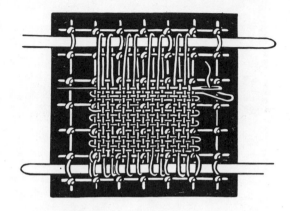

## Darning Stitch

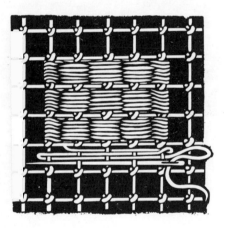

This is the simplest stitch. Weave back and forth through the net, filling the space but not crowding enough to bulge. Various sizes of thread may be used.

## Linen Stitch

This is the one most often used. Weave over and under the net but fill the space loosely (back and forth, 2 times, will usually be enough). Turn and weave or darn over and under the threads just laid as well as those of the net. The result should be "plain weave." A knitting needle placed at the first and last row will prevent the stitches from slipping when second darning is done.

## Simple Loop Stitch

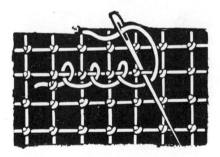

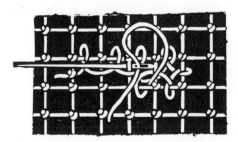

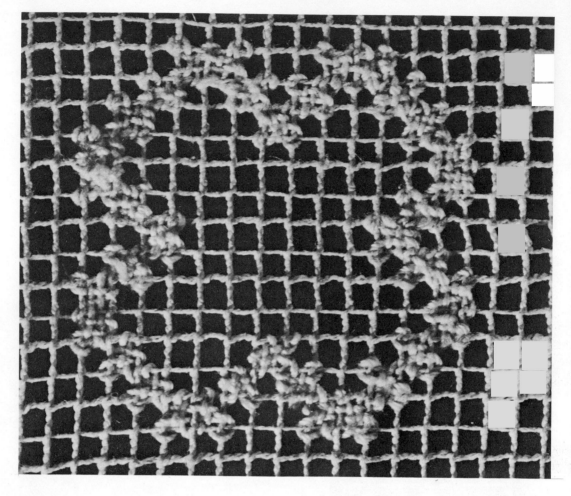

Basically a blanket stitch. Keep the loop at least half the height of the bars of the net. On return row, make a stitch over the vertical bar of the net as shown in diagram.

CHAPTER 10     # Hand Weaving

Like many of the other handcrafts, weaving was at one time a very practical and necessary occupation in the home. In the early days, weaving by the housewife or by the itinerant or village weaver was a matter of regular occurrence. In spite of the limitations as to threads, colors, etc., many early examples of this craft are still cherished for their beauty, ingenuity, and fine workmanship. Because of the introduction of power looms, weaving as a hand art was for a time almost lost in this country. However, it survived and in late years has enjoyed a thorough and enthusiastic revival among craftsmen over the country.

Weaving by hand is no longer a necessity but it has become a very practical and delightful hobby. After a glimpse at some of the exquisite designs, colors, and textures in fabrics it is possible to produce in hand weaving, it is easy to understand the urge to buy a loom and try one's hand at this lovely craft. Weaving is fun. It is a sensible and practical hobby, and although it is not a cheap hobby, it is not necessarily an expensive one. Many women and men as well have made it a money-making hobby. There is, furthermore, much that could be said for its therapeutic value in this modern fast-moving life of ours. It is the most widely used of all the crafts by occupational therapists in restoring the physical and mental balance of their patients. The rhythmic movements of weaving have a definite curative effect.

This chapter cannot possibly be a full course in weaving. It is, rather, a bird's-eye view of the craft to give you some idea of the equipment needed, what must be learned, and some of the possibilities it offers.

For the procedure of setting up a loom it is strongly urged that you have personal help from someone who knows the craft thoroughly. After you have learned this you can proceed on your own.

## BUYING A LOOM

This takes much careful consideration. Do not buy the first loom you see. Before buying, consider your needs: what kind of things do you want to weave? Will you be doing large things such as drapery and upholstery fabrics, possibly tweeds, or will you be making small things such as table mats, runners, babywear, etc.?

Also, fit the loom to your physical build. Are you short or tall? Try the loom to find out if you are comfortable working at it. Even if the first one seems to be right, try several other models. How much will the budget allow? This is a big investment, so choose wisely. A cheap, unsuitable loom is not an economy, but it is possible to find an adequate one for a price you can pay. Also many successful looms are made at home and it is possible to get good working drawings for them. How much space do you have for a loom? If you are fortunate enough to have the space for a wide loom, keep in mind that it is possible to weave narrow fabrics on a wide loom but not possible to weave wide things on a narrow loom. Probably the most practical width for a loom is the greatest width that a shuttle can be thrown by hand with ease. This is 42″ for some and 50″ for others. Try before you buy.

Choose a loom made of well-seasoned wood that will not warp and with hard wood in the parts that get the wear. Ratchets should be made of metal and easy to release. Heddles may be of metal (with fairly large eyes) or string and the reed should be metal.

Whether to use a sectional or plain warp is a matter of personal preference.

Another question that will arise is the number of harnesses in the loom. On a two-harness loom only tabby (or plain weave) can be woven. However, many lovely fabrics can be made by variations in thread and coloring and this may be all that you care to do. For pattern weaving you will need four harnesses, and here the possibilities are endless. Naturally, more harnesses allow for still more variation.

Extra shuttles and perhaps a flat pick-up shuttle.

Reed hook.

As you proceed you will find you may need other small tools such as paddle, scissors, pliers, etc.

## KNOW YOUR LOOM

1. Warp beam.
2. Rachet and paul.
3. Back beam.
4. Top castle.
5. Horses.
6. Heddle frames.
7. Heddles.
8. Heddle eyes.
9. Lamms.
10. Treadles.
11. Part of beater.
12. Reed.
13. Beater bar.
14. Dents.
15. Breast beam.
16. Cape.
17. Cloth beam.
18. Shuttle race.

*Note:* There are many kinds of looms; not every one will look exactly like this one. This is generally representative of looms which are all basically the same. They vary in the way of working the harnesses.

## WEAVING EQUIPMENT

In addition to the loom you will need:
Some sort of warping device.
A bobbin winder.
Skein holder.
Spool rack.

## HOW TO SET UP A LOOM

The whole process from making the warp to putting it on the loom ready for weaving is called "setting up a loom" or "dressing a loom."

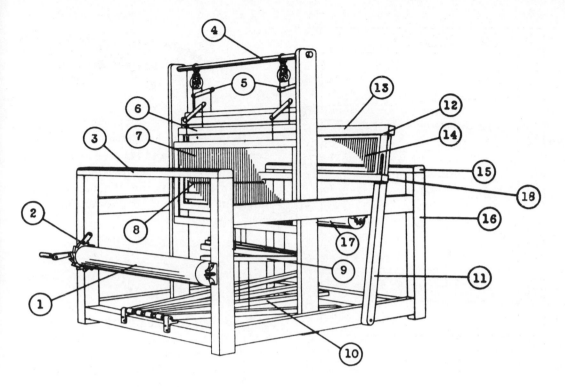

## How to Make a Warp

The first process in all weaving is the process of warping. This is done in the same manner regardless of the material chosen.

The warp is made by winding on a frame the threads which will run lengthwise on the loom. After winding, these threads are taken from the frame and finger crocheted (use the fingers as a crochet hook pulling one loop through another) into a long chain called the warp chain.

Warping may be done on a frame which limits the length of the warp but takes up little space. Or it may be done on a reel which allows for longer warp but takes up more space.

The most important single step in weaving is making the warp—it is the foundation for the whole thing. Therefore, learn to make a good warp.

Although a warping board limits the length of warp, it is still used in many cases, and a brief explanation on how to use one may be helpful.

A warp may be wound using a single thread but this is an unnecessarily long procedure. Two strands (not more) can be wound at one time and not get tangled, if the yarn is not the kind that will twist back on itself. It is, therefore, customary to use a number of threads at a time with a paddle. Any number of threads up to 20 can be used in this way.

The following procedure is for using 2 threads of a kind that has little or no tendency to twist. In order for the spools to unwind freely use a spool rack or place each spool in a separate receptacle.

Tie the ends together and loop them over peg A. Guide threads under B and over C, then follow the dotted line as shown passing threads around the outside pegs, back and forth and then under peg D, over and around E and back over D, then back in the same course to the top of the board where they go under C, over B, under and around A and then repeat from the beginning as many times as necessary for the number of threads

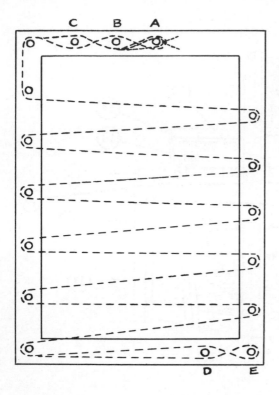

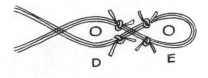

Tie the crosses as shown in the diagrams between C and B and between D and E. The threads may all be tied together at loop A.

The cross at the top of the board is the threading cross and the lower one is the counting cross.

## Taking Off the Warp

If you are beaming first, (fastening warp ends to warp beam), cut all threads at A and chain from that end. If threading first, chain from D, E end which may or may not be cut. At end of the chain cut all warp threads at dead center at A.

**To chain.** Hold with the left hand and make a big loose chain with the right hand (like chain stitch in crocheting using the hands instead of a hook).

needed in the warp. This forms a cross between B and C and another between D and E, which are the important ones. Whether they cross between A and B is unimportant.

Securing the crosses is very important and if not done the warp will be spoiled when removed from the board.

The warp is wound with a cross in order to prevent the threads from twisting around each other. Whether made on a frame or on a reel, the warp threads are placed one after the other. This position is held by a cross near the end. It is important that when the warp goes onto the loom the threads do not have a chance to twist and tangle. This is the function of the cross.

## Putting the Warp on the Loom

After making a good warp, the next most important step is putting the warp on the loom. Even the best weavers cannot get good results with a poorly warped loom.

There are various methods of doing this depending upon the kind of yarn being used and the type of fabric to be woven.

1. The warp may be wound onto the warp beam and then threaded through the heddles and reed.

2. Or the warp may be threaded through the reed and heddles and then wound onto the beam.

3. Or the warp may be tied onto a "dummy" or short warp already on the loom and then pulled through the heddles.

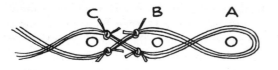

## Beaming

If the beaming is done first, the loops are put through a raddle or spreader (a reed may be used for a spreader); the loops are then slipped over a stick which is fastened securely to the warp apron. (The apron is a length of cloth or tapes fastened to the warp beam or the cloth beam and to which the warp ends are fastened in order to save length of warp.)

The warp must be wound very tightly onto the beam; every end must be under equal tension. Laying sticks on the beam as you

The rows of squares from front to back represent the harnesses. The rows of squares from right to left represent the heddles.

For convenience in threading we start at the right. One black square represents 1 thread through 1 heddle eye on a single harness.

Following the draft given here, this means that the first warp thread is pulled through the eye of a heddle on number 1 harness, the second through the heddle eye of number 2, etc., as shown on the numbered squares. Finish threading across row, repeating the black squares.

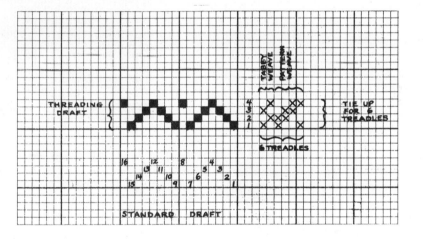

**Standard Threading Draft**

wind the warp is the old tried and true way of keeping the warp threads at an even tension. In recent years, however, many weavers have found that heavy brown paper wound with the warp is more efficient.

## Threading Warp Through the Heddles and Sleying

The directions for threading are called a "draft."

The most usual way of writing a draft is given here.

## Tie-Up

The group of x's at the side of the draft is called the "tie-up," which is a short way of saying "combination of harnesses used." The one given here is standard or most often used.

1 and 3 harnesses are used together alternating with 2 and 4 to produce tabby or plain weave.

If a loom has 6 treadles, harnesses 1 and 3 may be tied to one treadle and 2 and 4 to another for tabby. For pattern weaving, harnesses 1 and 2 are tied to treadle ⚹3, 2 and 3 to ⚹4 and 3 and 4 to ⚹5, and·1 and 4 to ⚹6.

On larger looms with more harnesses and more treadles and using other patterns, the tie-up will be different.

### Sleying

After the threads are through the heddles in the proper order, they must be brought through the reed. This is known as sleying. The purpose of the reed is to spread and to determine how close the warp threads will be in the finished cloth. A reed may be threaded 1 or more threads to a dent (opening). Reeds come in various sizes (different number of dents to the inch). Fifteen dents to the inch is most often used.

Now the ends of the warp are tied (keeping the tension uniform) to the apron of the cloth beam.

The loom is now dressed and you are ready to weave.

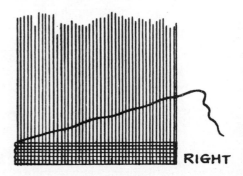

WRONG

RIGHT

## WEAVING

Developing a good rhythm in weaving is the secret of good finished fabric.

First weave in a few strands of coarse wool for a "buffer", then proceed as follows:

Open the shed (treadling), throw shuttle through with shed open, pull beater toward you. With beater in this position change to the next shed and push the beater back (away from you); throw shuttle. Repeat until you develop a rhythm.

To simplify:—tramp (open shed), back (beater back), throw, and beat. When the rhythm becomes even, the weaving will be even and the selvages good.

The beat must be regular or the fabric will show bands of close and loose weaving.

The thread left behind by the shuttle should lie close to the edge warp thread but not tight enough to draw it in. It should lie at a slant across the warp, not close to the fabric. In fact the weft should be allowed to lie as loosely as it will without making loops. If pulled too tightly the edges will

be drawn in, resulting in broken warp threads.

Before proceeding very far examine the fabric for possible mistakes in sleying or threading. Correct any mistakes.

A streak where the fabric appears to be thin probably means a mistake in sleying. Re-sley. Sleying is a simple process but like every other step in weaving must be done with great accuracy. Avoid or correct crossed threads, missed dents, or dents with too few or too many threads. If 2 or 3 threads fail to tabby there is a mistake in the threading.

No two weavers have the same touch; therefore, as in knitting, it is not advisable for two people to work on the same piece.

After practicing several inches of tabby, try other treadlings (pattern combinations of harnesses) in various sequences. All variations in weaving are obtained by changing the order in which the combinations of harnesses are used.

The pattern given is a point twill known as "Rosepath."

There are more than 200 variations pos-

**Color Plate 11 — Sewing for the Home**

Typical draperies and slipcovers which may be made at home. Step-by-step instructions are given in Chapter 11, Sewing for the Home for similar ones.

sible with this pattern when using only one shuttle.

When two shuttles are used, one shuttle using the pattern combination and each shot or "pick" followed by a tabby shot (second shuttle), the possibilities are endless.

Remember that the most fun and satisfaction to be had from weaving a pattern are in following one's own ideas and imagination rather than the directions written by someone who has woven it before.

## TYPES OF WEAVING

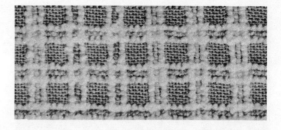

Twills open a large field of pattern variation. A direct twill is one in which the slant is in one direction only (serge). A point twill has the slant going in both directions to

Tabby is the simplest type of weaving. However, it may be varied in use of color—stripes, checks, and plaids—or it may be varied in texture by the use of different kinds of yarn. The possibilities are very great with this one simple weave.

make chevrons (herringbone and irregular twill). A broken twill is a point twill with the draft arranged so there is never a skip of more than 2 warps. Plain tabby cannot be woven on a broken twill threading. The twills may be varied in color and texture indefinitely. We need not know any more about weaving than twills in order to keep ourselves busy for a very long time.

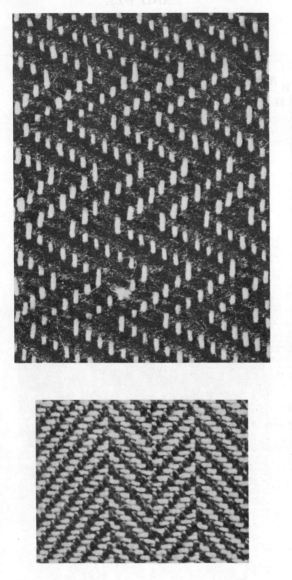

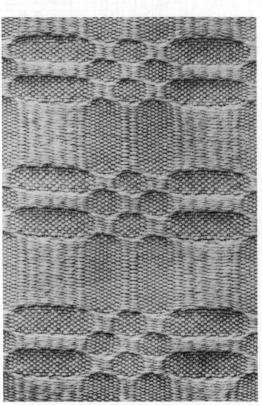

If you wish to go to other types of weaving, they are divided according to structures. To name a few:

M's and O's is a development of twill often used in Colonial times for linens.

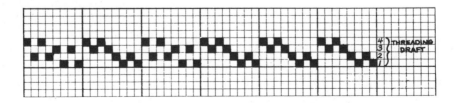

**M's and O's Threading Draft**

## Spot Bronson Threading Draft

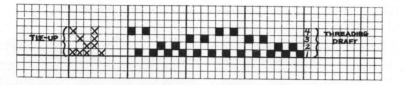

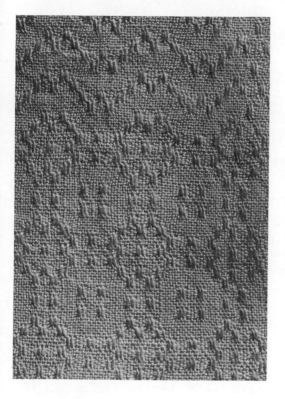

Huck can be elaborated to become Spot Bronson or rearranged to become a lace weave.

Summer and Winter is the only truly American type of weave. It was popular from about 1775 to 1825.

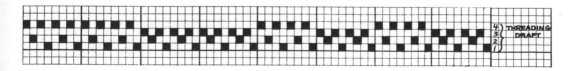

## Summer and Winter Threading Draft

## Crackle Threading Draft

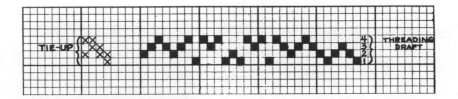

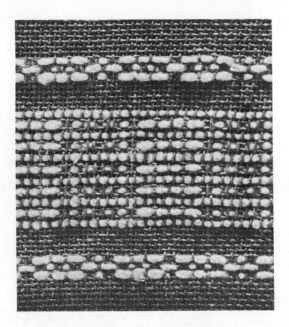

Crackle is an American name for a Swedish weave.

This example is linen with a silk border

*Narrow band*

Treadle 3 – 4

        1 – 2 (white)

        3 – 4

With 1 rose tabby between

6 rose tabby shots

*Wide band*

  1 white tabby

  1 rose tabby

  2 – 3 white (repeat 5 times)

  1 rose tabby

  6 rose tabby shots

Repeat narrow band.

Colonial Overshot is probably the most familiar of the pattern weaves and was used on the old coverlets.

Also there are many finger-controlled weaves which may be done on any tabby draft, and these allow for more freedom of design than the so-called pattern weaves.

Some examples of these are Spanish Lace Borders, Leno Weave, Brooks Bouquet, Danish Medallion.

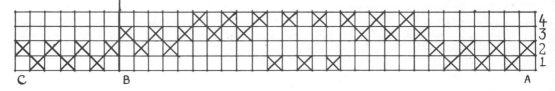

## Colonial Overshot Threading Draft

## Spanish Lace

## Leno

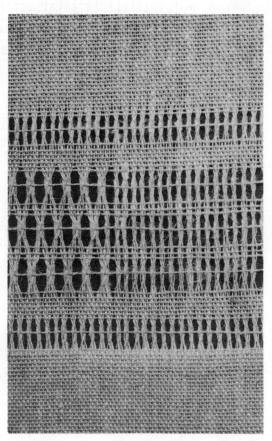

Spanish is one of the easiest kinds of lace weaves and has many variations. It is merely a tabby that weaves back and forth over a few warps at a time instead of completely across the web.

In all types of Spanish, the most important single factor is the tension; the weft must be pulled just the right amount and always the same amount. This is a matter of practice. Borders are effective and not really slow for usually they are woven with a very heavy weft and so grow rapidly. The effectiveness of all types of Spanish depends on balance of warp and weft and on tension.

Leno is a general term for any type of weaving where the warp threads cross each other. There are hundreds of variations.

When making the twists, it is usually easier to work from right to left. A knitting needle can be used to cross the threads and a shed stick inserted as the work progresses; or, if the cloth is narrow, a smooth pointed stick can serve as both pick-up and shed stick. When the shed is opened for the first row of twists and the passage of the shuttle from right to left, the first warp thread *must* be a *top shed* thread. This is important. If the first thread is on the bottom shed, no twist will result. Also it is much easier to work if the tension is not too tight.

Proceed as follows:

Open the shed. Insert the forefinger of the

left hand into the shed a couple of inches from the edge; with the thumb and forefinger of the left hand, pull the top shed threads a little to the left to make the work easier. With the pick-up stick, pick up the first thread from the bottom shed and pass the stick *over* the first thread of the top shed, dropping it from the fingers of the left hand. This is the fundamental principle of all Leno handweaving. Continue across the web in the same way to pick up one and drop one, moving the left hand as needed. When the pick-up stick has been taken across the width of the loom, look carefully to see that there are no mistakes in the crossing of the warps. It is easier to make corrections before the weft is put through. Turn the stick on edge to make a shed and pass the shuttle from right to left. Leno has a tendency to pull in and be narrow, so do not pull the weft thread too tightly. Beat the weft well back, but *do not* tighten the weft at the left edge. Because of

the twist, the weft will not go completely back to the plain weave; if it did there would be no lace effect. But it does need a good beat or it will be too loose and too much open lace is not attractive. Change the shed and pass the shuttle back to the right edge of the web. This will untwist the warps and return them to their proper sequence.

**Simple Rules for Weaving Leno.**

1. The first warp thread *must* be a top shed thread.

2. Begin at the right edge, pick up a lower warp and drop a top warp.

3. Pass the shuttle through the shed made by (2) from right to left.

4. Change the shed and pass the shuttle from left to right.

5. Beat well, but not excessively after each weft.

## Brooks Bouquet

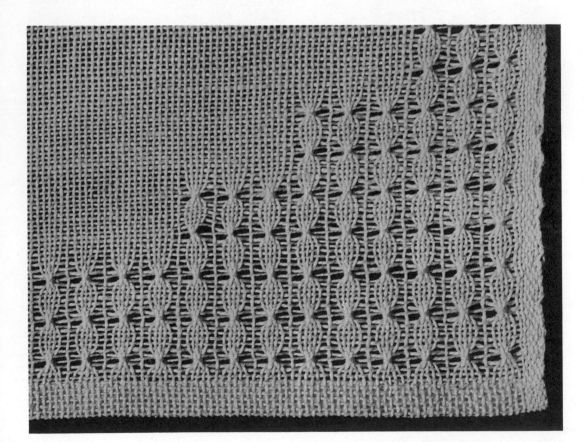

Square. Enter the shuttle at the right edge and bring it out of the shed to the top about one inch from the edge. Count three warp threads to the right and enter the shuttle into the shed at this point. Bring the shuttle to the top three top warps to the left of where it came out before. This is essentially "back-stitching" over three warp threads and progressing three warps—all on the top shed. The weft should be drawn tightly enough to pull the three warps together but not so tightly that the weft cannot be beaten back. Weave *three* tabbies. On the next row, back-stitch over the same warp threads as before. In square Brooks you may back-stitch over an even or an odd number of warps; but there must be an *odd* number of tabbies between the rows of "bouquets" and the back-stitching is always done from right to left. The lace can follow a pattern or it can be a straight band.

## Danish Medallion

This may be varied indefinitely, but only the basic principles will be given here. The regular weft thread may be used to make the "medallions" or an extra weft may be added. If the extra weft is added, it should be a heavier weight, or a color—there is no point in adding the extra weft if it does not contrast with the one being used. Medallions may be used as a border or groups can be used as surface decoration.

Without cutting the original weft, splice in a heavier colored weft at the right selvage and weave to the left. With the regular weft, weave four or six tabbies. After the fourth or sixth tabby, change the shed as usual. Enter the heavy pattern weft into the shed, weave far enough into the shed to bring the shuttle out of the shed and on top between the sixth and seventh warp thread of the top shed. At this point and with a crochet hook, go *under* the heavy weft previously woven; pick up a loop of the pattern weft and bring it to the top of the web. Pass the shuttle through the loop to form a slip knot; then pull the weft to tighten it.

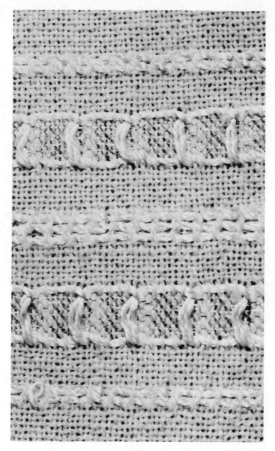

## COLOR PLATE 10

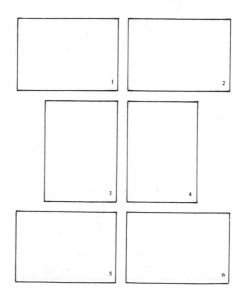

410

1. Tabby weave using plain and nubby threads.
2. Tabby weave in plaid arrangement.
3. Light weight woolen shawl. Draft as follows:

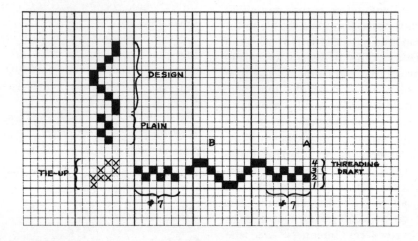

4. Rich texture with a variety of threads. Draft as follows:

5. Stripes in tweed wool yarn suitable for upholstery fabric. Draft as follows:

6. Striped drapery fabric using light weight and heavy yarns in an interesting effect. Draft as follows:

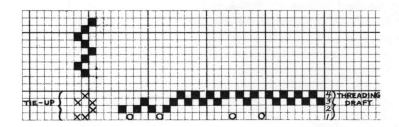

## TAPESTRY WEAVING

Tapestry weaving is an old technique which is enjoying a revival. The term is often misused because it actually means a certain type of weaving and not "picture making."

One characteristic of tapestry weaving is that the warp is completely hidden by the weft and plays no part in the design.

In regular weaving the weft extends across the entire width of the warp; in tapestry weaving the color may change at any point and a color is carried across only as far as it is wanted. It is then turned back and therefore a whole section of color may be woven separately.

When colors meet they may interlock over the same warp thread. This makes a fairly smooth surface. Or they may turn back over adjacent warp threads, which leaves a "slit." Both are old techniques. The first is the Aubusson method and the second is the Gobelin way of working. In the ancient "slit" tapestries the slits were left open but later they were more often sewed together.

**Gobelin Tapestry**

412

**Aubusson Tapestry**

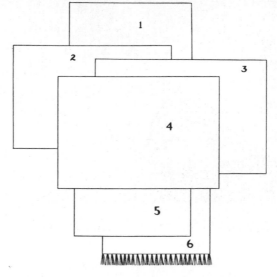

## HAND-WOVEN MATS

1. Tabby weave using linen with bouclé type yarn.
2. Tabby weave of linen with Leno border.
3. Tabby weave with Danish medallion border, linen and rayon yarns.
4. Tabby weave using linen, Crackle border in novelty yarn. See Types of Weaving for draft and instructions for border.
5. Tabby weave of linen with stripes of heavier yarn.
6. A colonial overshot pattern. Jute plus pearl cotton. Draft is available.

## SIMPLE LOOMS

Small "looms" are available for teaching the fundamentals of weaving to children. They are also useful for those who like to work on something small which can be carried about. These come in various sizes. The 2- and 4-inch square weave is the most widely used. Several patterns can be made and the small squares set together in various ways to make many lovely things such as babywear, afghans, etc. Full instructions and needle come with the looms.

Some patterns which **can be made on a weave-it** loom.

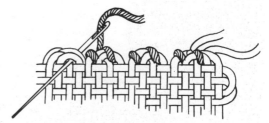

Sewing squares to-gether.

# CHAPTER 11

# Sewing for the Home

One of the most satisfying occupations for a woman is furnishing and decorating or "redoing" her home. New draperies, slipcovers, curtains, and bedspreads can lift the spirits of family and house alike and become an exciting project.

This type of sewing is not at all difficult although it does take care and accuracy, and many women prefer it to making wearing apparel. There is a wealth of beautiful and practical decorator fabrics now available. The many new fibers and blends plus the special finishes on all types of fabrics which make them easy to care for are a great incentive to all of us to plunge in and turn decorator.

There are many good methods of making draperies and slipcovers. We have chosen to give you those methods which are quickly done and which give a custom look. In general, the more hand work, the more "custom-made." However, in the interest of durability and keeping the shape it is advisable to do certain things by machine.

## MAKING A SLIPCOVER

Each chair, settee, or sofa is a problem in itself but there are certain general rules and procedures for making a slipcover which apply to all of them.

### General Hints

Although slipcovers are not difficult to make it might be advisable, if you are a beginner, to choose a chair with simple lines for your first project.

For the same reason choose a plain fabric or one with a small pattern which does not require much matching on your first try. Keep in mind that stripes are the most difficult.

Straighten one end of the fabric before you start cutting. Pull a thread (if it is a plain color or a woven design), or draw a straight line at right angles to the selvage with yardstick or T-square if it is a printed fabric.

Unless the chair is old and badly out of shape or the piece of furniture is not symmetrical (such as certain styles of settees and chaise longues), the fabric may be placed and fitted wrong side out, which saves turning the seams later. This is especially helpful when welting or fringe is used in the seam.

The pieces must be cut and pinned so that the lengthwise grain of the fabric runs up and down on the chair and the crosswise grain is parallel with the floor as nearly as possible, even when a panel slants.

Do not try to work with one long piece of fabric. Measure and cut a section for each part of the chair in the order given in the measuring instructions. Allow for tuck-in and seams plus a little more (2″ or 3″). Choose pre-shrunk fabric if at all possible. If necessary, and the material is washable, you can shrink it yourself. Do not try to get around this step by allowing for shrinkage as you make the slipcover. They will not fit right and will always look sad and droopy. Choose washable trimmings also if you plan to launder your slipcovers.

After cutting each section, lay it wrong side out and stay-pin to the part of the chair where it will be used. In this way you will know which pieces have been cut.

## If Your Fabric Has a Center Motif

Center the motif on the inside back of chair with cushion in place. Center the motif on the outside back of chair and match both inside arms placing motif with heavy part at top (depending upon the design). Center the pattern on the cushion top and make both sides alike so it will be reversible. Center the pattern on the border (boxing) of the cushion and on the front border of the chair (apron).

If fabric is printed with a large amount of white (or other background color) at sides, trim off part of it before cutting sections or you will have wide areas of plain color and no pattern (this happens especially when piecing the fabric).

## Measuring Fabric for Chair

1. Decide how deep the flounce is to be, measuring from the floor up. This depends somewhat on the style of the chair, whether it has a cushion, and whether legs are straight or curved. Flounces vary in depth from 8″ to 12″ on average-sized chairs and usually start at lower edge of front border. If a chair has a cushion remove it before measuring. The "platform" is the part beneath the cushion. If chair has no loose cushion this area is called the "seat."

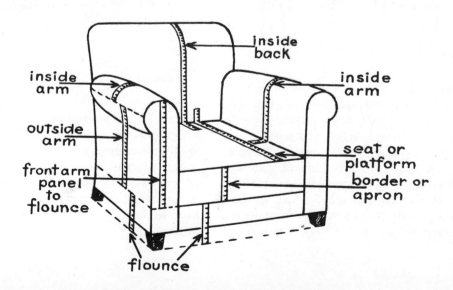

2. Measure:

*Front border,* from top of flounce to platform or seat. It reaches all the way across the front of the chair on some styles (T-cushion) and as far as the arms on others.

*Seat* or *platform,* from front edge to the back allowing 4″ tuck-in at the back.

*Inside back,* from top of chair to platform or seat, allowing 4″ tuck-in at the lower edge.

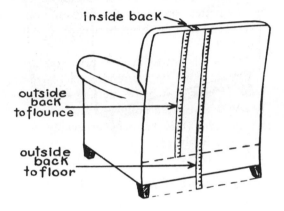

*Outside back,* from top of chair to top of flounce.

*Outside arms,* from farthest point of curve at outside to top of flounce.

*Inside arms,* from outside of curve over arm and down to seat or platform plus 4″ for tuck-in.

*Front arm panel,* from top of arm to top of border or to flounce as the case may be. These pieces can usually be cut alongside other pieces, but make sure they are accounted for.

*Flounce,* should be made on up-and-down (lengthwise grain) of the fabric; it will have to be pieced at intervals. Allow for a 2½″ hem and seam at top. In length, allow for kick pleats or shirring as desired. Allow double the length for shirring and 3 times for all-around pleating. Kick pleats (at corners) vary in size: allow 12″ to 16″ for each pleat (24″ to 32″ for each corner).

Allow at least 3″ on each piece for leeway in fitting and add sufficient allowance if pattern must be matched or centered (this depends upon the pattern; a yard or two perhaps).

Keep these various measurements handy to be used when cutting.

## Cutting

Following the same order as in measuring the fabric; measure and cut each rectangular piece which will cover the portion of the chair for which it is intended (no shaping at this point). Be sure to make adequate allowance to more than cover the area. The only exceptions to this are the front border and the flounce. (Also top border and side panel, if any, see diagram under Pinning Outside Back.) The front border is a straight piece and can be cut exactly to avoid trimming later when it is difficult to get at. The flounce is left to the last and can also be cut exactly.

**If the Fabric Is Printed.** Plan as you go as to placement of motifs, centering on cushion (from right to left and front to back), inside back above cushion, outside back, front border, and arms. The arrangement of the motifs should be as symmetrical as the pattern allows. If the fabric has a small all-over design, the problem of centering and matching is not so difficult but must be taken into consideration.

As you cut each piece lay it wrong side up on the place where it is to be used. Hold with a pin. This reminds you of what you have cut and keeps pieces from getting mixed up.

**Piecing.** On a settee or love seat, piecing will have to be done on seat, cushion, and inside and outside back if you are using 36″ fabric. Match or arrange motifs when doing this. These piecing seams should be pinned, stitched, and pressed open as soon as sections are cut.

418

## Pinning and Fitting, General Directions

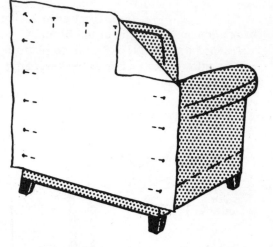

Start with seat or platform. Smooth out the piece, centering and adjusting. Stay-pin to chair near edge all around the piece with pins pointing inward. Be sure tuck-in allowance comes at back and sides.

Do the inside back next, smoothing, centering, and fitting as before and stay-pin to chair around outside edge. Cut away any large corners to within 2 or 3″ of seam.

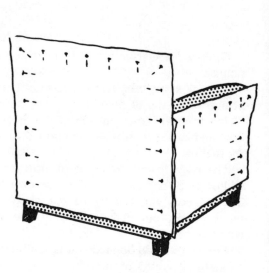

The outside back is next; then the outside arms and inside arms, front arm panel and front border. In each case this general pinning is done 2 or 3″ away from the seam line and not on it. Cut away any large corners which will not be needed so the remainder can be grasped in the hand.

## Final Pinning

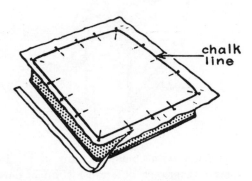

chalk line

flounce

**Cushion.** Lay the cushion on a table. Place fabric piece on it wrong side up, centering the pattern. Smooth fabric over the cushion and pin near the edge. With white chalk (do not use wax crayon), mark exactly over the welting or seam beneath. Trim one half the piece just outside the chalk line allowing for seam and rounding the corners a little.

Fold this cut half over, matching as nearly as possible to the chalk lines on the underneath piece. Cut remaining half. This makes the two sides symmetrical. Cut another piece like this one. Measure width of side border (boxing) from seam to seam (or welting), add seam allowances and cut a strip long enough to go half way around the cushion plus seam allowance at each end. Arrange so that pattern is centered in the front. Cut two more strips like this. These strips should be cut crosswise of the fabric and may have to be pieced.

**Chair.** As on the cushion, the final pinning is done exactly on the seam line. If the covering underneath has welting it can be used as a guide. Start at center front border where it meets the platform or seat. Pick up fabric each side of seam line and pin on the seam line fitting snugly as you go. Measure from the floor up to the lower edge of border from time to time as this distance

must be kept even for the flounce. You can trim the seam to the desired width as you go or do it all at one time later. (See "Trimming Seams.") Pin across top of border along edge of seat. Pin ends of border to front arm panel or outside arm piece if arm panel stops at platform.

Keep measuring from the floor up so lower edge is straight and the correct distance from the floor.

Pin the seat cover or platform to the inside back. Line up the tuck-in on the seat with the one on the inside back and pin along seam line. Leave the sides until you come to the inside of the arms.

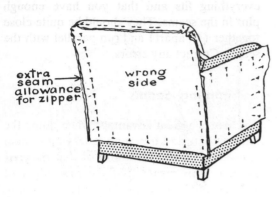

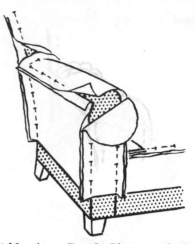

**Outside Back.** Work from the floor up. Since you know the width of the flounce, you know where the back must end (same as on front border). Allow for seam. Find the lower center and pin to the chair; pull the lower sides taut and pin to the chair. Smooth up and pin the top edge along seam line to the inside back. This is a hard edge and anchors the line of the back. Fit and pin top corners.

**Outside Arm Panel.** If arm of chair is curved, determine outermost point of curve. This is where the outside arm piece starts. Pin along this line to the inside arm panel. Adjust and pin to outside back leaving wide seam for zipper on right side of chair.

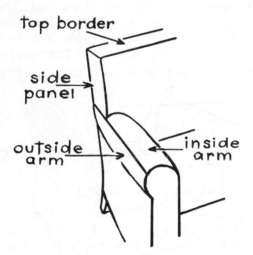

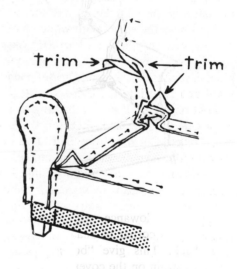

*Note:* If there is a top border and side panel on your chair (see diagram), you are pinning to this instead of to the inside back. The top border is a straight piece and has been measured and cut accurately with seams allowed, so trim the back and front but not this border.

Fit and pin at sides to outside arm pieces. Leave wide seam at right side for zipper.

**Inside Arm Panel.** Smooth the fabric over the arm and down the inside. Match the tuck-in piece to that of the platform piece. Trim evenly and pin along seam line.

On some chairs the tuck-in allowance is not needed toward the front, in which case it can be tapered off. On the curve at the back where the arm meets the back of the chair, trim to fit allowing for tuck-in. Pin to inside back. If no tuck-in is needed here (see dia-

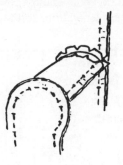

Go over the chair carefully to see that everything fits and that you have enough pins in the seams. They should be quite close together (1″ apart) and run parallel with the seams. Correct any errors.

## Trimming Seams

There is a great advantage when doing the final pinning and trimming in leaving a seam allowance exactly the width of that on your welting. This means that the raw edges of welting and seams can be matched as you baste and sew in the welting. If you make your own welting you can decide the width of the seam yourself (½″ is a good width; many professionals leave only ⅜″ on closely woven fabrics).

If you are using purchased welting, trim the seams of the slipcover to match it unless it is very narrow and the slipcover fabric loosely woven.

There is one seam which should be trimmed wider than the others and that is the seam at the right side of the back. The opening for zipper or snap tape is left here. Trim this seam 1″ wide or wider if desired, but mark on the seam line. The opening should extend several inches above the arm. Zippers for slipcovers come in 24″, 27″, 30″, and 36″ lengths.

gram) pin a curved seam and clip on curve.

The back corner of the seat is probably the most difficult spot on the chair. This is where side and back tuck-ins meet. Leave

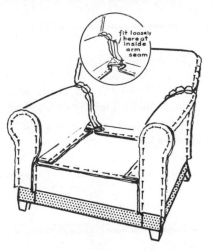

fit loosely here at inside arm seam

plenty of allowance which is eventually pushed into corner of chair as well as sides and back. This give "bounce" room and relieves strain on the cover when it is in use.

**Front Arm Panel.** See diagrams above. Keeping grain of the fabric vertical, pin this section to the outside and the inside arm pieces. If chintz is used, the top of the inside arm piece may be pulled and stretched for a closer fit over the front curve of the arm. Do this when pinning the front arm panel. Not all fabrics will stretch.

The lower right side is pinned to the front border unless the border reaches all the way across the front.

## Removing and Sewing

Unpin the seams to be used for the opening. Slip off the cover and stitch all inside seams where there is to be no welting. Baste the welting in the remaining seams and stitch using a cording or zipper foot.

Piece the flounce and hem it. If flounce is to be gathered, measure and mark with pins into eighths. Mark lower edge of slipcover at center sides. Adjust gathers, start at back opening, and pin flounce to the cover fitting each section (⅛ of the length) into ½ of each side of the cover.

If flounce is box-pleated all around, arrange pleats so the center of a pleat will come in the center front and so the others are evenly spaced.

If kick pleats are used, pin around making a deep inverted box pleat at each corner (6″ or 8″ pleat each side of corner). Pin and baste in welting and stitch.

## Inserting Zipper in a Welted Seam

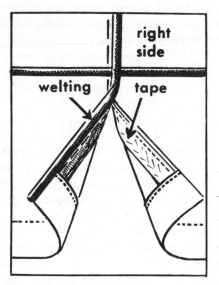

**1.** Prepare the opening as follows: Baste and stitch welting in place on one side and face the opposite side with twill tape (unless you have left a wide enough seam). Fold hem of flounce over welting and tape.

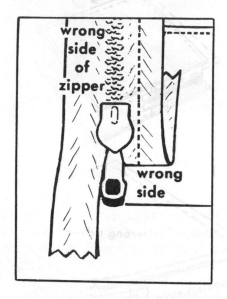

**2.** Pin welted edge over the zipper tape with the stitching line close to the teeth of the zipper and with the tab a little above hem edge. Fold under the ends of zipper tape. Baste and stitch on right side using cording or zipper foot.

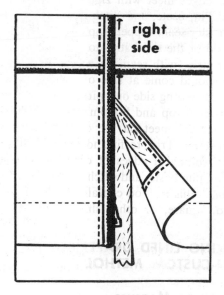

**3.** Pin opposite side to zipper tape so edges of opening meet. Baste, open zipper, and stitch.

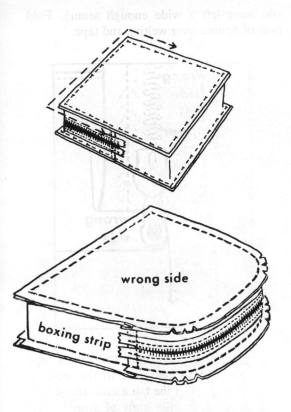

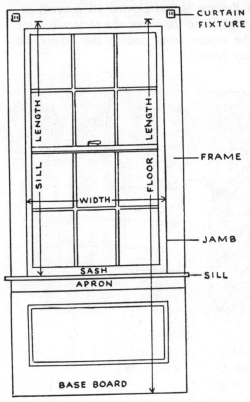

**Cushion.** Fold two boxing strips in half lengthwise and press on fold. Place so that folded edges meet with zipper centered beneath. Pin, baste, and stitch down each side as for slot-seam zipper application. Attach one end of the third strip to one end of the zipper strip, with seam on wrong side. This seam should come at side of cushion. With all pieces wrong side out, pin and baste boxing strip to top and bottom cushion pieces. They should meet on the opposite side of the cushion. Trim to fit and seam together. Insert welting at edges of cushion top and bottom, pin, baste, and stitch.

*Note:* This method can also be used on a round, square, or other shape of cushion.

## MAKING LINED DRAPERIES—A SEMI-CUSTOM METHOD

### How to Measure

Decide on the length of your draperies. Depending upon your furnishings and dec-orative scheme, they may come to the sill, lower edge of apron, or to the floor.

Have the fixtures in place or know where they are to go before measuring. Usually the fixture is placed so the heading of the drapery covers the frame of the window at the top. Also the top of drapery or heading should cover the metal part of the fixture. It is well to measure each window separately as they may vary slightly.

Allow 4″ for top hem and 8″ for a 4″ double hem at bottom on each panel (3″ at top and a 3″ double hem at bottom will do if draperies are not long and heavy). On very long panels 5″ to 10″ double hems at the bottom are more suitable. The top hem is not usually wider than 4″.

### Width

Draperies as a rule are made with 100% fullness; that is, twice the width of the space they are to cover. If fabric is sheer, 150% is better (3 times the width).

## Linings

Linings are used to give more body to draperies and cause them to hang better. They also protect from dust and sunlight which cause wear and fading. Cream or beige is a good choice although stronger colors are sometimes suitable. On draperies with a white background to be used where light will come through, a white lining is desirable so the colors will be more clear.

You will not need as much lining as drapery fabric since each lining piece is cut approximately 9" shorter than the outside panel (depending upon width of hem).

## Cutting

Since no housewife is likely to have a table large enough to accommodate a length of drapery, the best place to cut is on the floor. If the fabric is a plain color or has a woven pattern, straighten ends by pulling a thread and stretch into shape (see Fabric Preparation in Sewing section). If the fabric is printed, cut without pulling threads; cut by pattern, not by weave.

If you are using a repeat pattern arrange it so that a motif will come above the hem. It does not matter what happens to the pattern at the top because of the fullness. When cutting the panels be sure that the motif placement is the same on every panel. Cut off selvage edges.

## Making

Make a 2" machine hem at bottom of lining, press, and lay aside.

Hem lower edge of panels with a 4 inch double hem as follows:

An easy way to make a 4" double hem is to turn 8" to wrong side at lower edge of drapery panel and press on fold.

Bring the raw edge back to the pressed fold and press again on the new fold. Pick up double hem and turn again on the first fold and pin. This makes a double 4" hem. Pin, press, and blind-hem by hand or machine (some machines do blind-hemming).

## Making Front Edge Hem

*Note:* On side panel draperies the front edge and outside edge are made differently because the outside edge on a side panel usually ends against the wall (due to the "return" on the rod) and does not show. Very often a ring is sewed to the lower corner of the outside panel and this slips over a hook on the baseboard or wall.

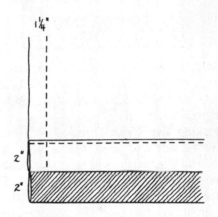

**To Make Front Edge on Panel.** With right sides together and edges even on one long side, lay the lining to the panel so that hem of lining comes 2" above lower edge of hemmed panel. Top edges will not meet. Pin a 1¼" seam down the side and stitch by machine.

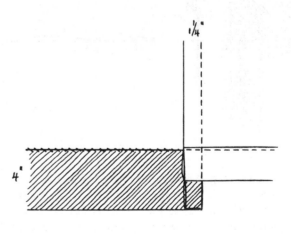

Open out lining and press this wide seam toward the center of the panel.

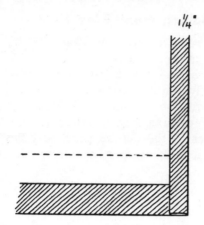

Fold lining into position, turning far enough so outside fabric shows 1¼". Seam should lie inside this edge. Press and pin along seam.

**Making Top Hem.** Turn top of panel 4" to wrong side and press. Cut a piece of 4" wide crinoline (permanent finish) long enough to reach across top of panel plus 1". Turn under 1" at one end and press. With this end at the seamed side, slip crinoline under the 4" top hem and press. The crinoline is "tacky" and will cling to most fabrics.

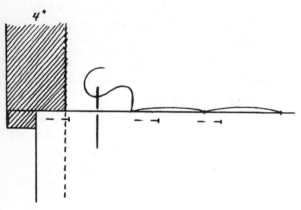

**Working Again on Edge of Panel.** Fold lining back (wrong side out) to the seam and tack the lining the full length of the outside seam edge with long stitches and needle pointed toward you as shown. Pick up a few threads only on needle. Stitches should not show on outside.

**Weighting Lower Hem.** Slip a covered weight inside lower hem of the panel at the corner and tack with a few stitches through the center.

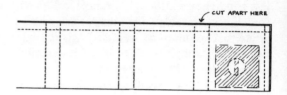

**To cover weights.** Cut a piece of muslin wide enough to fold double plus a seam and enclose weights. Stitch a pocket for each weight, stitching 2 rows between pockets with space for cutting apart. Slip in weights and stitch along top of pockets. Cut apart.

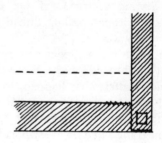

Fold lining back to wrong side. Hand-hem open edges of corner and also hem edge of lining for about 1½".

At top of lining press seam allowance to wrong side. If measuring has been accurate, top of lining and panel will match. Turn and press 1¼" seam allowance to wrong side on remaining long side of panel.

*Note:* On wide panels where more than one width of fabric has been used, fold lining back at piecing seams and tack the full length of the seam with long stitches as done on front edge. Also insert a weight in the lower hem at each seam.

When ready to finish the last side, turn raw edges of both lining and outside fabric to wrong side 1¼″ and press. Pin folded edges together. Turn this whole edge to the wrong side 1¼″. Pin and slip-stitch by hand catching both edges.

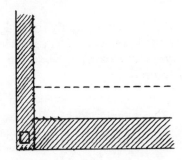

Fold lining to wrong side and smooth out. Pin across top, keeping folded edge of lining even with top of panel hem. Also pin down side turning in edge of lining even with turned edge of panel.

Edge-stitch across top and down side. This is the outside edge of the panel and goes against the wall. Make another panel with sides reversed so there will be a right and a left hand panel. The top edges may be secured with blind-hemming done by hand for a finish which looks more custom-made.

*Note:* If the panel is to be used in the center instead of at the side, both sides are finished to look like the front edge with a 1¼″ of the outside fabric turned to the wrong side.

Proceed in this fashion:

Finish lower corner like the first with weight and hemming of corner. Panels are now ready for pinch pleats or other finish at top.

**Making Pinch Pleats.** Measure the panel and arrange to have pleats approximately 4″ apart and 4″ in from each side. Allow four inches for each pleat.

Fold and stitch the pleat 2″ from the fold and the length desired (depth of crinoline).

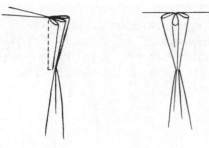

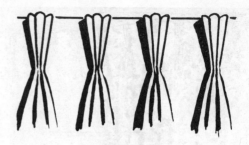

Divide each pleat evenly into 3 small pleats at the lower end of the stitching and stitch across by machine or sew by hand to hold securely.

Pinch pleats may be made in a great variety of sizes and spacings. They may be made extra deep and closely spaced.

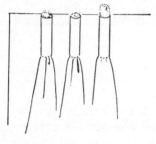

Cartridge Pleats. Make smaller pleats (stitch about 1″ from fold) and stuff with cotton or cord. They can be made extra large for long heavy draperies.

Or widely spaced and shallow.

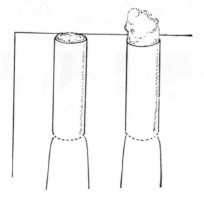

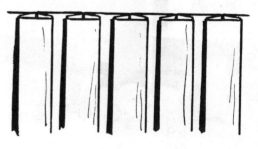

Insert drapery pins on back of panels on pleat seams and at each end. Place pins so that panel covers rod.

In place of pinch pleats, box pleats are now very widely used. Fold and stitch the pleat (see first step of pinch pleat), then press flat with seam down the center. These may also

be made in any size desired.

For the youngest member of the family: Pinch-pleated traverse curtains with a quaint air on the newest of windows—the clerestory or shoulder-high window. Highly suitable for the nursery.

# CAFE CURTAINS

Cafe curtains are now used on practically every type of window. They may be long or short, formal or informal, depending upon the fabric used, and almost any type of fabric *can* be used. It must be remembered that on cafe curtains the rod is exposed, and this must be taken into consideration in the final effect. Brass rods and black rods are available, or the rod can be painted to match the woodwork if there is not too much wear on it. Buy good quality rods that will not sag.

Cafe curtains may have scallops or V-points at the top with rings or clips for hanging, or they may be made straight across with straps or pinch pleats.

Sometimes they appear on one-half the window only, and sometimes two or three tiers will cover the window. There are many variations and arrangements.

Cafe curtains are easily made and have many possibilities for decorative effects.

Several ways of finishing the tops are given here.

## General Directions

**Width.** The width of the curtain should be at least twice the width of the window and may be fuller.

**Length.** Where straps or rings are used the curtain starts just below the rod. Some finishes require a facing and others do not.

## Scalloped Top No. 1

This makes its own loop.

1. Measure and cut panels the required length, allowing 6″ for top facing, plus 2 to 3½″ for lower hem.
2. Make narrow hems on the side edges (see step No. 6 for panels wider than 35″).
3. Turn top edge ¼″ to wrong side and stitch.

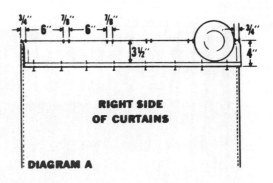

DIAGRAM A

4. Fold top edge 4″ to the right side. Pin and press.
5. For a finished 35″ panel use a 6″ saucer or plate and mark as shown.
6. On wider panels continue across in same way leaving 1¼″ beyond last scallop and trim off excess. Hem side edge.

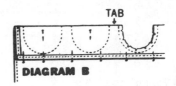

DIAGRAM B

7. After marking scallops, pin near fold. Stitch scallops on marked line. Cut ¼″ away from stitching and clip on curves.

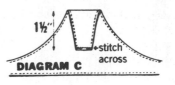

DIAGRAM C

8. Turn to right side, pulling out corners sharply. Top-stitch along edge.
9. Fold tabs 1½″ to wrong side to form a loop and stitch end of tab.
10. Hem panel.

## Scalloped Top No. 2

Follow directions for Scalloped Top No. 1 through step no. 8. Then, instead of folding the tab over and stitching to make a loop, attach metal clips at top of each one. This makes a deeper scallop suitable for a longer panel.

## Scalloped Top No. 3

This is without facing.

1. Measure and cut panels allowing ½″ at top and hem of desired width at bottom. Hem the sides.

2. Using a 6″ plate or cardboard circle mark scallops 2″ deep leaving 1¼″ between scallops and at ends.

3. Turn a ¼″ hem to wrong side along scalloped edge and baste, being careful not to stretch fabric on curves. Clip curves before turning if necessary.

4. Pin medium-sized rickrack on top of hem and stitch down center of rickrack.

5. Sew plastic or metal rings at points.

*Note:* This may be made *with* facing by cutting panels 4″ longer, then turn ¼″ to wrong side and stitch. Turn 3¾″ to right side before measuring with plate. Stitch on curved lines, cut ¼″ away. Clip on curves and turn.

## V-Point Tops

1. Measure and cut curtains allowing for ¼″ seam at top and for hem at bottom (desired width). Hem the sides.

2. Turn top edge ¼″ to right side and baste without stretching.

3. Pin narrow fancy braid over turned edge and stitch on both edges of the braid. Pin metallic rickrack (gold or silver) just below the braid and stitch down center. Use metal clip-on rings at points.

## Straight Top with Straps

1. Measure and cut curtains allowing ¼″ seam at top and desired hem at bottom.

2. Strips for making straps can all be cut and sewed at the same time. Allow about 3½″ for each strap (depending upon length desired and size of rod). Cut strips 2½″

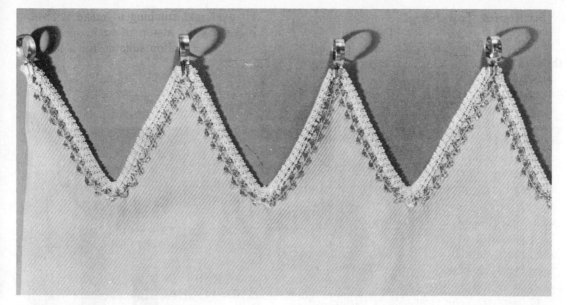

**V-Point Tops**

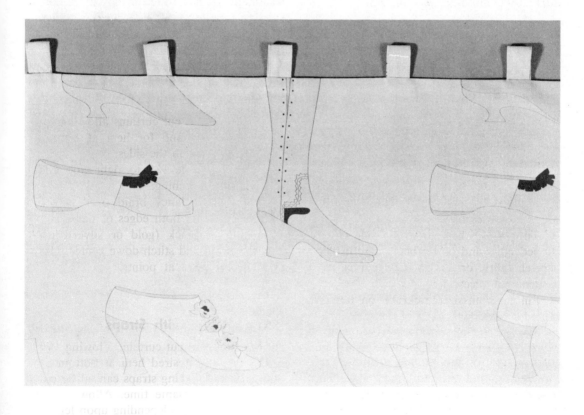

**Straight Top with Straps**

wide unless curtains are long and heavy, in which case they should be wider.

3. Fold strip down the center right side out. Turn raw edges ¼" to inside and baste together, edges even. Match grain when basting or strip will buckle. Edge-stitch on both sides of the strip. Pin sample length to the curtain and try over the rod before cutting into lengths. Adjust as necessary before marking off and cutting remaining straps.

4. Turn top edge of curtain ¼" to wrong side and press. Fold strips in half and pin to wrong side of curtain (3½" to 4" apart) matching raw edges to those of curtain top. Have a strap at each end of panel. Cover raw edges with bias-fold tape with edge of tape even with top of curtain. Turn in ends of tape. Stitch on both edges of bias.

Or pin straps on right side of curtain with raw edges even with raw edge of top. Face with 3"-wide piece of the fabric (cut on same grain as the curtain). Turn edge of facing and stitch; then blind-hem to curtain.

### Ready-Scalloped Pleater Tape

There is available a ready-scalloped tape with "pockets" for hooks which makes scalloped cafe curtains with pinch pleats. This is done easily and quickly with no measuring and marking for scallops necessary.

Cut the tape to fit the top of the curtain being sure it is centered between the sides. Mark at ends and make side hems.

The right side of the tape is the one where the little pockets have an opening at the lower end (the end opposite the scallops).

Lay wrong side of tape to right side of fabric, edges even with scallops at the top. Stitch across top and around scallops. Trim, clip curves, and turn to wrong side. Turn edges neatly and press. Turn under ends of tape ¼". Sew across bottom of tape on woven line.

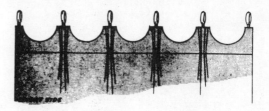

Insert ring pleaters and ring end hooks.

## AUSTRIAN SHADES

The elegant and graceful Austrian shade has come back into favor. This lovely window treatment is not too difficult to make if shirring tape available at trimming counters is used and directions are followed carefully.

The shades are made by sewing long strips together; the shirring is done at the seam line and on the outside edges. In order for the shades to hang properly the strips must be tapered in width being slightly narrower at the top than at the bottom.

There is no rule about the width of the strips but they average from 8 to 12". They may, of course, be narrower than this and would quite probably be wider on a shade used on a large picture window. The desired effect is the guide. On a 36"-wide shade, 3 strips would be sufficient to look well.

To measure and cut:

Measure the desired width of the finished shade.

Measure the desired length of the finished shade.

Decide how many strips (shirred spaces) you wish and divide the spaces to determine how wide each finished panel will be.

Each panel is cut 3 times the length of the finished shade.

**Color Plate 12 — Skirt Trimmed with Machine Embroidery**

A lavish use of decorative stitching which can be done on modern sewing machines. For other uses and general instructions, see Chapter 12, Machine Embroidery.

Each outside panel is cut 4½" wider than its finished width.

Each inside panel is cut 2½" wider than its finished width.

Cut the panels, centering on grain, and then trim each panel so that it tapers and is 1½" narrower at the top than at the bottom (take ¾" off each side so panel will remain centered on grain).

## Making

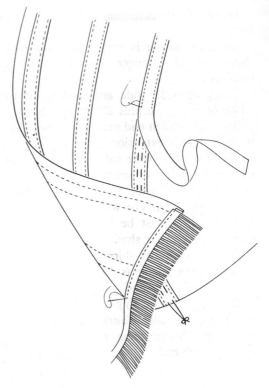

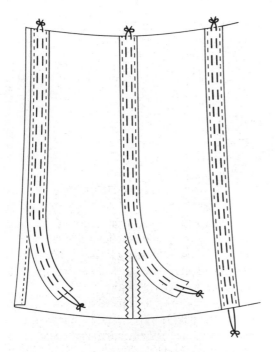

Sew a narrow facing over each length of shirring tape on the wrong side. Turn bottom edge of shade ⅜" to right side (leaving knotted cords free) and finish with 2" matching or contrasting fringe. A chainette fringe is the most authentic but other types are used. Small tassels may be attached at ends of shirring tapes.

Stitch strips together lengthwise with ½" seams, keeping narrow ends at top. Press seams open.

Cut shirring tape 4" longer than seams. Baste and edge-stitch shirring tape centered over seam on wrong side leaving 2" extending at top and bottom. Pull out cords a little inside edges of shade and knot at top and bottom. Trim ends of tape.

On outside strips turn 1" to wrong side and stitch. Baste and stitch shirring tape ¾" from edge covering raw edge of hem.

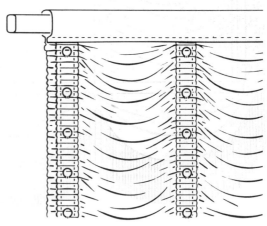

Make a fabric extension at top of shade as follows:

(If shade fabric is very sheer this piece should be of stronger material such as sateen.)

Cut a strip 3″ wide and as long as the width of the shade plus 2″ for end hems.

Turn 1″ at each end and hem. Right sides together, stitch extension along top edge of shade. Turn to wrong side, turn under raw edge and stitch over seam and knotted cord ends. Insert ½″-wide flat strip of wood in the finished hem. On windows wider than 36″ this strip must be heavier (and fabric extension wider) or shade will sag.

Pull up cords of shirring tape from the bottom, until shade is the desired length. Knot cords firmly and cut off ends.

Sew small plastic rings about 3″ apart on wrong side of each shirring row from top to bottom. Space them so one will come close to each end.

Cut a ¼″ brass rod the finished width of the shade and cover as follows:

Cut a strip of firm material 2″ longer than rod and 2″ wide. Seam lengthwise with ½″ seam. Turn right side out and insert rod. Turn in ends and finish by hand.

Pin covered rod at bottom of shade at shirring strips on the wrong side.

Tie one end of long lengths of No. 3 traverse cord firmly to rod at center of each shirring strip. Sew casing of rod firmly to each shirring strip where pinned.

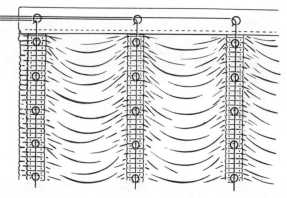

Fasten small screw-eyes to back of wooden strip at top of shade at center of each shirring strip. Carry traverse cords from rod at bottom up through screw-eyes at top. Carry all cords to right of window.

Attach shade to inside top of window frame with angle irons. Thread cords through eye-screw attached at upper right hand corner of window.

Pull and adjust cords until curtain rises and lowers evenly. Knot cords together and finish with heavy tassel.

## SHEER CURTAINS

Sheer fabrics are no longer reserved for glass curtains, sash and casement curtains, or cottage and ruffled curtains.

Many decorative treatments now call for long sheer curtains with no other drapery. They are usually made to draw, although this

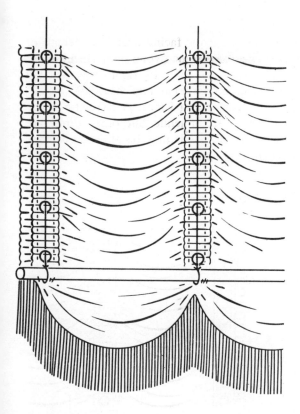

depends upon where they are used. They are, of course, made quite full—at least double and sometimes triple in width the space they cover.

They are treated at the top somewhat like lined draperies although, since they are not lined, the method of finishing is different.

This is the general procedure for long sheer curtains of the draw type:

1. Plan for 3, 4, or 5″ double hem at the top; 4″ double hem at the bottom. The inside edges should have 1¼″ double hems, the outside edges should have ½″ double hems.

2. Trim off selvage and make side hems.

3. Make bottom hem. See Making Draperies for directions on how to make a double hem.

4. Make top hem by inserting thin crinoline the full width of the hem on the first fold. Press, fold again, and stitch.

5. Make pinch pleats and use drapery hooks as on draperies.

Sheer curtains on large windows may also be made with shirred heading.

For glass, sash, and casement curtains several things must be kept in mind.

A 1″-wide rod will need a 1½″-wide casing. Round rods take a somewhat wider casing than flat ones.

5. Side hems are made first. One inch is a good width. This is stitched by machine.

6. The bottom hem is made next. 2½″, 3″, or 4″ double hems are used according to length of the curtains. Use a 4″ double hem on long curtains. They may be stitched by machine or by hand.

7. The top hems are made last. Turn under ½″ and press; then turn the hem, baste, stitch, and press. Stitch the casing line (if you have planned for a heading) above the hem line. Leave ends open for inserting rods.

8. Work on one pair of curtains at a time measuring them against each other for length, width of hems, etc.

Sash, casement, cottage, and ruffled curtains are made in a manner similar to that of making glass curtains.

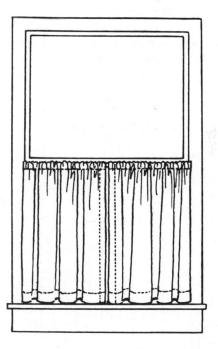

1. The size of the rod determines the width of the top hem. It must allow the rod to slide in and out easily.

2. Either a simple casing or a casing plus heading may be used.

3. A 1″ to 1¼″ (finished) heading is usually sufficient.

*Note:* A heading which is too wide on a sheer fabric will not stand up unless interfacing is used.

4. A ½″-wide rod will need a 1″-wide casing (finished).

Sash curtains cover the lower half of the window only and end at the sill.

Casement curtains are for windows which swing in and out instead of up and down. They may be attached to the windows with a rod at top and bottom or be hung in some other manner. It is well to investigate new types of curtain hardware.

Cottage or Dutch curtains are a combination of sash curtains and short curtains which may or not be trimmed with ruffles. The lower section may be drawn and the upper be left open to admit light.

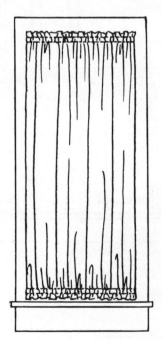

Ruffled curtains usually end at apron or floor. There is no hem at the bottom as the ruffle extends down the inside edge and across the bottom. Ruffles are usually 3 or 4″ wide and 1½ times should be allowed for fullness.

A ruffled valance may be used on a separate rod or a ruffle may be sewed to the curtain at the lower edge of the casing. It should be the same width as the ruffles on the curtain.

Ruffled curtains may cross at the top in which case two rods are used and the curtains are made extra wide and quite full. These are known as Priscilla curtains.

Printed fabrics may also be used for curtains made with casing or casing plus heading. Photograph shows double-tiered curtains with shirred valance.

## COLLECTION OF PILLOWS

### Quilted Pillow

**Materials.** ⅝ yard 48-inch shantung or other decorator fabric. Heavy-duty thread to match. 12 ounces kapok for stuffing.

**Cutting.** Cut two 20″ squares from fabric.

**Making.** Place front to back, right sides together, pin and stitch ½″ seam around four sides, leaving about 5″ opening for stuffing at center of last side. Turn right side out.

Measure in 5½″ from each side, and mark (lightly) to form center square. Machine-stitch square on three sides and part of fourth, leaving opening to correspond to opening on outside edge.

Stuff center square, firmly but not hard. Stitch opening by machine. Stuff outer square all around pillow. Slip-stitch opening by hand.

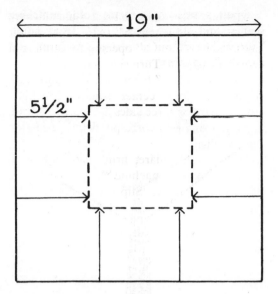

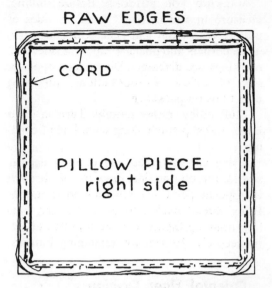

RAW EDGES

CORD

PILLOW PIECE
right side

## Tufted Pillow

**Materials.** ⅞ yard 48-inch-wide silk shantung or other decorator fabric. Heavy-duty thread to match. 2¼ yards ¼-inch-wide cording. 24 ⅝-inch-diameter button molds. 16 ounces kapok for stuffing, carpet thread. Darning needle.

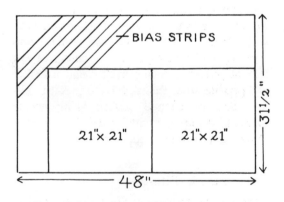

BIAS STRIPS

21"x 21"    21"x 21"

31½"

48"

**Cutting.** Cut two 21" squares from fabric. Cut 1½"-wide bias strips from remaining fabric; piece to make strip 85" long. Use remaining fabric to cover buttons.

**Making.** CORDING: Fold bias strip in half lengthwise, wrong sides together. Insert cord close to fold, and stitch (use cording foot) close to cord.

PILLOW: Beginning at the side and starting basting 1" from end of cording, baste cording with raw edges even to right side of one square of fabric all around, finishing ends as follows: Rip back and cut ¾" of cord out of first end, and fold in the bias strip ¼". Insert other end of cording. If too long, so cording does not lie flat, trim off raw end before inserting. Stitch all around (use cording foot) close to cord. Place the second square of fabric on top, right sides together, and stitch around same as first square, leaving 5" on center of one side open for stuffing. Turn right side out.

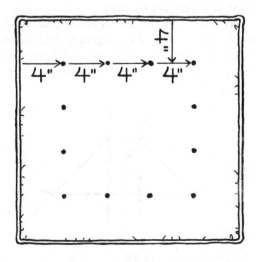

4"    4"    4"    4"    4"

MARKING FOR BUTTONS: Before stuffing, measure in and mark 4″ from all sides of pillow, both front and back. On this mark, mark corners and points 4″ apart at sides (12 markings; see diagram). Do same on opposite side of pillow. Cover buttons, following directions on package.

Stuff pillow rather loosely. Turn in open edge, and slip-stitch along seam line of cording.

Using carpet thread and darning needle, sew button on one side, draw thread through to opposite point, and sew on second button. Bring thread back through under first button; draw up tightly to make a puffed effect; tie securely. Repeat for remaining buttons.

## Oriental Floor Cushion

**Material.** ¾ yard 48-inch-wide heavy silk shantung or other decorator fabric; or 1½ yards 36-inch-wide fabric. Heavy-duty thread to match. ⅛ yard 4-inch-wide black rayon fringe. Two 1½-inch-diameter wooden buttons. Black Perlesheen. Small amount of carpet thread. 1½ yards muslin for pillow form. 2 pounds kapok for stuffing. Darning Needle.

**Making.** PILLOW FORM: Cut two 24″ squares from muslin. Pin together, matching edges, and stitch ½″ from edge around four sides, leaving an opening in center of one side for stuffing. Stuff firmly and evenly, but not hard. Sew opening by hand.

PILLOW: Cut two 24″ squares from shantung. With right sides together and edges matching, pin and stitch around four sides ½″ from edge, leaving 16″ opening at center of fourth side.

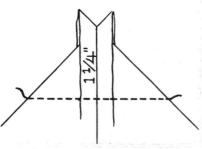

*Registered trademark.

Open seams at corners; fold, matching seams; and stitch across 1¼″ from point. Turn right side out. Insert pillow form, and slip-stitch opening.

Cut four 1″ lengths of fringe. Roll, sew, and tie to form tassels. With double-strand Perlesheen, take 1″-long stitches each side of corner on seam line. Do not pull tight. Bring needle out at corner, and sew on tassel. Repeat on other three corners.

BUTTONS: Cut two circles of fabric twice diameter of button. Gather edge, insert button, pull up thread, and sew at back of button. Measure and mark center of pillow on both sides. With carpet thread (use double) and darning needle, sew a button at center of one side of pillow, bringing needle out at center of opposite side. Pull tightly to puff the pillow. Sew on second button; bring needle through to opposite side under first button. Draw tightly, and tie securely.

## Fur-Fabric Pillow

**Materials.** ⅜ yard Orlon*-pile fur fabric. Heavy-duty thread to match. 12-inch dress zipper to match. Package single bias-fold tape to match. 13-inch-square pillow form.

**Making.** Cut two 13″ squares of the fur fabric (measure on wrong side). Place right sides together, and stitch around three sides ½″ from edge. Leave fourth side open for zipper.

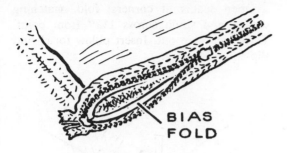

BIAS FOLD

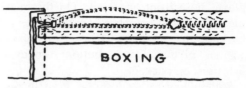

BOXING

Right sides together, sew bias tape ½" in from edge on both sides of opening. Center the zipper in the opening, pin, and sew in place by hand, using back-stitch.

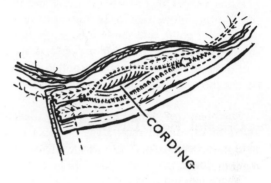

CORDING

## Boxed Round Pillow

**Materials.** ¾ yard 36-inch-wide fine ribbed corduroy. Heavy-duty thread to match. 10-inch dress-placket zipper. 2 yards ¼-inch-diameter cord. 11-inch round foam-rubber pillow form.

**Cutting.** Cut pillow, boxing strips, and bias strips, following diagram. Cut enough bias strips, 2¼" wide, to make two strips, each 36" long after piecing.

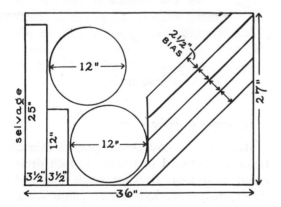

**Cording.** Fold bias strips in half lengthwise, right side out; insert cord, and stitch (use zipper or cording foot) close to cord.

**Making.** Right sides together and raw edges even, baste cording around each circle. See "Tufted Pillow" for how to end cording neatly. Stitch close to cording. Turn back ¾" on long side of shorter boxing strip, and press. Lay folded edge over metal part of zipper, centering ends. Baste and stitch to zipper tape ½" from folded edge.

Right sides together, pin and baste boxing strips together, end to end. Stitch one end only.

Right sides together and zipper closed, pin and baste boxing to one side of pillow around edge. If too long, adjust at basted end of boxing; then stitch this end, and stitch around. Baste and stitch other side of boxing to second pillow top. Turn right side out, and insert filler.

# CHAPTER 12  *Machine Embroidery*

Machines for home sewing have developed so rapidly in recent years that a new skill has been added for the woman who sews at home.

These modern machines

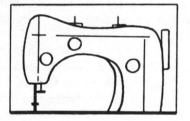

not only do straight sewing but perform miracles in machine embroidery. This is accomplished by the swing of the needle from side to side; for straight sewing it moves only up and down.

While straight sewing stitches look like this:

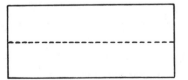

machine embroidery will look something like this:

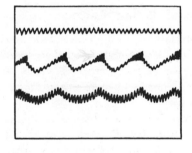

These are zigzag stitches which may lie close together:

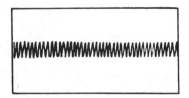

or be spread apart:

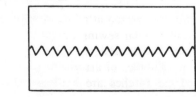

They may be of different widths of straight rows

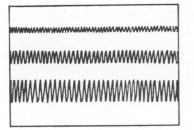

or varied in such a way as to make fancy patterns:

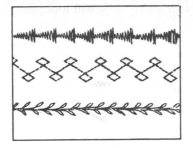

On the newest models it is possible to make many patterns automatically:

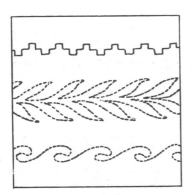

There are also zigzag attachments which can be used on regular sewing machines to make a number of stitch designs.

The possibilities of arrangement and variation of the stitches are endless. Also, the uses to which these new decorative stitches may be put are only limited by the imagination.

Sewing machines differ, and each woman should choose the one which suits her own needs best. She should also try out more than one model before making a decision.

Learn to use the machine you have purchased by having it thoroughly demonstrated and then practice on it yourself until you are skillful in using it.

The following pages are suggestions for using the decorative possibilities of your modern machine, with some reminders of its more practical points.

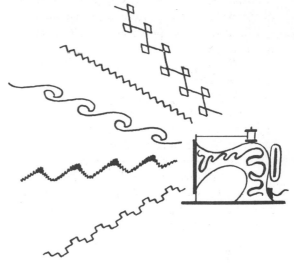

## GENERAL NOTES

Use a mercerized thread especially made for machine embroidery. It should be extra-fine and lustrous, which makes the stitches more attractive.

Use a fine needle.

Study carefully the book of instructions which comes with the particular machine or attachment you are using.

Learn to run the machine at an even speed and run it slowly if you are a beginner.

Do the embroidery before the article is sewed up and finished.

Embroidery with a zigzag machine is done on the right side of the fabric.

The design area should, in most cases, be backed with paper, organdy, or a nonwoven interfacing. The organdy or interfacing may remain if needed or be cut away after embroidery is completed. The paper of course is torn away.

Always make a practice swatch first. Work a part of the design on the fabric you are to use (with backing), and experiment with the stitches until they look right and you can execute them well.

Study the design. Where a line ends at another line, the latter should cover the former.

Keep bobbin case clean with a soft brush.

Adjust pressure on presser foot according to the weight of the fabric (see manual).

The three most important adjustments to be made are:

1. Needle position (center; left of center; right of center).

2. Width of stitch (known as bight).

3. Closeness of stitches. The lever that regulates the number of stitches to the inch for straight stitching regulates the closeness of the stitches in machine embroidery.

To fasten thread ends when making close satin stitch, start and end the work by taking a few stitches with bight lever at neutral; pull ends of thread to wrong side.

## DESIGNS FOR MACHINE EMBROIDERY

Some stamped goods patterns and hot-iron transfers are suitable for machine embroidery; these are available in needlework and pattern departments. Here are some suggestions for some simple uses of the decorative stitches which are not too difficult to accomplish.

## Double Needle on Zigzag Machines

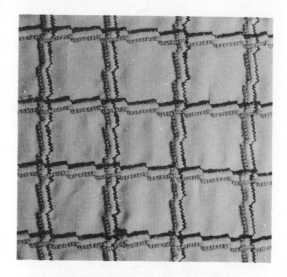

Two-color effects are possible when using the double needle, although the width of the stitches is somewhat limited. Trapunto effects and simulated tucks may be achieved.

## GENERAL TYPES OF MACHINE EMBROIDERY

### Borders and Bands

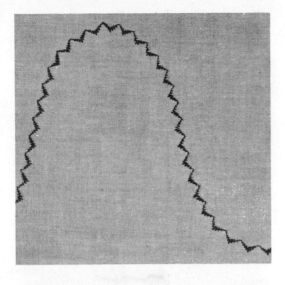

and blouses. Aprons, place mats, pillows, valances, and other suitable articles can also be decorated in this way.

Child's skating skirt trimmed with rows of bright stitching. Use a circular skirt pattern and work the embroidery before lining the skirt.

The decorative stitches, with many variations of design, can be worked in straight or curved lines.

These can be used in many ways and need not become monotonous. Done in bright colors on a dark fabric they produce a peasant effect (see color plate) on skirts

When worked in self-tone or monotone on organdy the effect is delicate and attractive and suitable for bridesmaids' and graduation dresses. With the addition of rows of lace, (applied with zigzag stitch), the result is even daintier.

### Appliqué

The possibilities with appliqué are limitless. Almost any shape, even quite intricate ones, can be applied with either satin stitch or open zigzag.

Transfer the design to the appliqué fabric (patch). When cutting out the design, leave a margin of about ½″ all around the outline. Baste the appliqué to the background fabric.

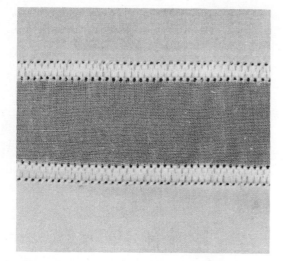

Stitch over the outline with either a close satin or open zigzag stitch. Trim away excess fabric.

It is possible also to find many attractive designs in printed fabrics which can be cut out and used for decoration in this manner. These are more often found on decorator fabrics.

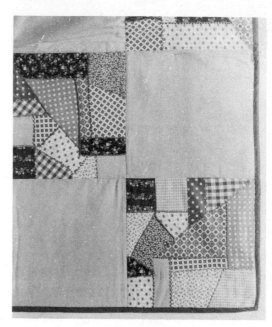

An old-fashioned "crazy quilt" can easily be made by machine using the decorative stitches for joining the pieces. Arrange, pin, and baste pieces on a foundation square. Use the same color thread throughout but vary the stitch design.

## Monograms and Lettering

A delicate transparent look may be accomplished by using organdy for the appliqué over a heavier fabric, then cutting away the fabric beneath.

Block letters or monograms are quite easily made by tracing the design onto the fabric and then using close satin stitch over it. The satin stitch may be any width which is suitable to the size of the letter being made.

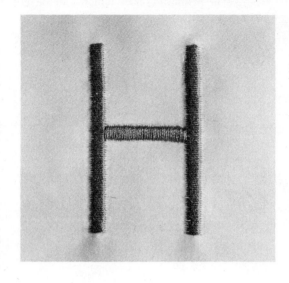

broidery hoop to get the best results. The fabric is moved freely as if the operator were writing or drawing on the fabric with the needle. Perfection depends upon moving with a steady hand. Almost any size or shape of design can be done in this way.

Some types of machines now have automatic devices for monogramming and doing small motifs. However, these limit the design in size and style.

### Fill-in and Large Designs

Script monograms or writing should be done with the fabric stretched in an em-

Fill-in designs can be done by using small motifs spaced at regular intervals. Also the

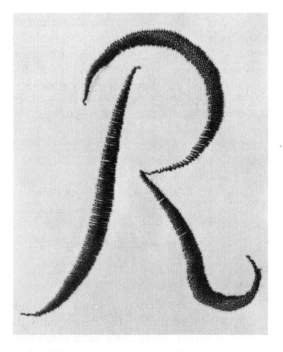

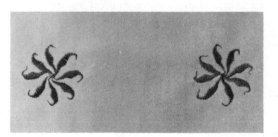

stitches may be used in rows or crossed over each other (see "Double Needle on Zigzag Machines").

When doing large line or scroll designs it is well to work in a hoop as described above.

A novel use for these machine embroidery stitches is for sewing on rickrack and other trimmings. Vary the stitches, the size of the rickrack, and the spacing as desired. A single row for edging may be all that is needed.

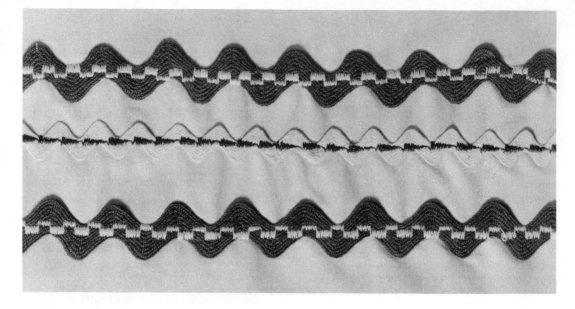

Rickrack may be set in as an insertion as follows:

1. Sew rickrack on top of fabric where wanted, catching points at each side.

2. Cut fabric underneath rickrack down the center. Press raw edges apart allowing openwork to show.

3. From right side stitch each folded edge of fabric using zigzag stitch. Clip away raw edges underneath.

Some machines make a narrow open-work embroidered scallop which is suitable for a trim on collars, blouses, children's wear, etc.

## Buttons and Buttonholes

Because of this same zigzag movement of the needle it is now also possible to sew on buttons and make buttonholes with these new machines. The needle can be set for various sizes of buttons and almost any length buttonhole can be made.

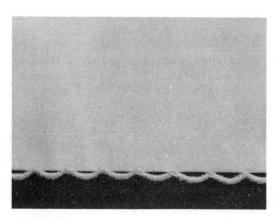

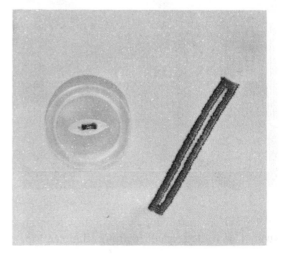

## Tucks

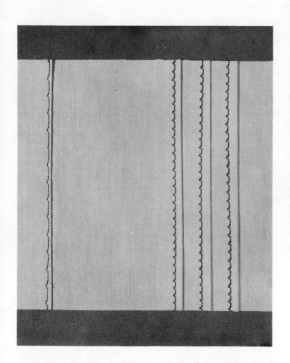

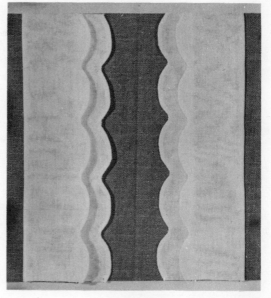

The wider scallops can be **used on tucks** or on hems. They are especially **attractive** on little girls' dresses.

Decorative tucks of various kinds and widths are easily and quickly made. Any of the daintier decorative stitches can be used to sew in the tuck. For the narrow scalloped **tucks the** blind-stitch is used.

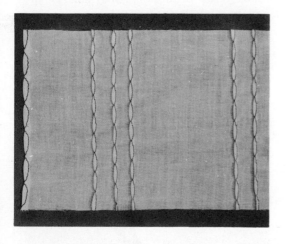

This is set so **the** sideways stitch will catch over the folded edge forming the scallop.

## Working in Circles

*Note:* This cannot be done if you are using a zigzag attachment on a regular machine.

You will need a thumbtack and a piece of Scotch tape about 2″ long. Push the tack through the center of the tape from the sticky side. Decide on the size of the circle you wish to make. Stick the tape and thumbtack to the bed of the machine to the right of the needle and as far away from the needle as ½ the diameter of the circle. Place fabric **over the** tack so the tack will be at the

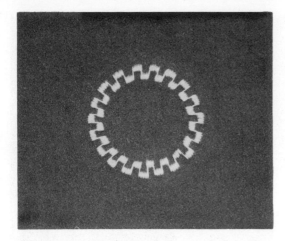

## PLACE MATS

A neat and attractive arrangement of stitches is shown here for place mats and napkins using narrow satin stitch and one of the decorative stitches.

Measure carefully and mark lightly with pencil where the lines should come on the mats, being sure they are all marked alike.

center of the circle you wish to make. Stitch, rotating fabric using the thumbtack as a center pivot. Some machines have an attachment for this purpose.

## LIVING ROOM

Appliqué bands on pillows and edge of valance add a neat tailored finish in a living room. The close-up shows the detail of the decorative stitching.

# PRACTICAL USES FOR ZIGZAG

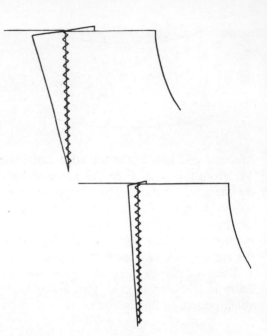

## Seam Finishes

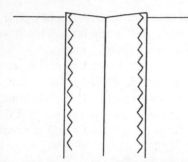

**Plain seams.** Zigzag stitch is excellent for seam edges on fabrics that ravel easily. Stitch near the edges and trim close to the stitching. Press seam open.

**Lapped seams.** Zigzag stitching is fine for closing a dart on interfacings. Cut the dart down the center all the way to the point. Lap dart so the seam markings match. Stitch on the seam line and a little beyond. Trim close to the stitching on both sides.

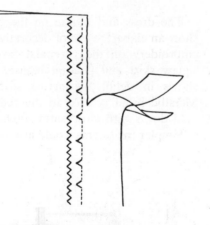

## Hems

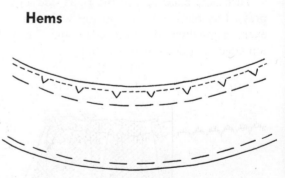

For seams in tricot lingerie, zigzag stitching is practical because it is flexible and will not break on stretching. Use light tensions and fine needle and thread. Do not press open. Finish if desired by stitching seam edges together with automatic blind stitch. Trim away the excess close to stitching.

The machine blind-stitch is a form of zigzag stitching. It saves time on simple hems and is especially good on soft spongy fabrics. Turn the hem and baste on the fold.

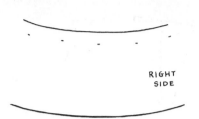

RIGHT
SIDE

Measure and turn in the top edge and baste ½″ from the edge. Fold the *garment* back leaving a fold at the basting line. Blind-stitch so the straight stitches come at the top of the hem and the sideward stitches into the garment fold. This makes a blind-stitch on the right side. Turn back and press.

Trim the narrow hem of a petticoat and finish it at the same time with a decorative stitch pattern in this manner:

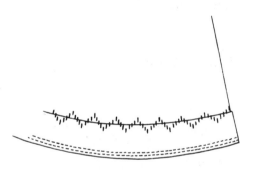

Turn hem edge ¼″ to the right side and press. Lay bias-fold tape on top with edges even. Top-stitch at lower edge and finish top edge with decorative stitching.

Baste ruffle at top of hem on wrong side of petticoat. Stitch ruffle to petticoat using a decorative stitch, working from the right side and using the basting as a guide. Trim top of ruffle.

## Other Uses for Zigzag Stitching

1. Sew elastic to waistlines of lingerie and pajamas with zigzag stitching. This is especially good for knitted fabrics.

2. To prevent breaking under normal strain, use zigzag stitching for seams and darts on knitted fabrics. It is also good for finishing the edge of facings on bulky fabrics instead of turning under and edge-stitching.

3. Use zigzag stitching to reinforce gussets at the underarm on kimono-type sleeves. Also at underarm on kimono sleeves where there is no gusset.

## COLOR PLATE 12

The dress and blouse on the color plate show an elaborate use of decorative machine embroidery on the perennial favorites, the squaw skirt and peasant blouse. The inset shows in detail the actual stitches used. Metallic braid is used in the center and is held down with close satin stitch.

Simpler treatments would also be effective.

CHAPTER 13 ## Mending and Care

## DARNING

Since the appearance of nylon, not as much sock and stocking darning is done as formerly. Even on children's socks the heels and toes are often reinforced with nylon, which prevents wear at these points.

However, there are other things which do wear out in spots so it is well to know how to darn. It may be done on almost any fabric.

Use thread as nearly the same color and weight of the fabric as possible. Sometimes threads can be pulled from the seam edges or from left-over fabric for darning.

Darning is a combination of running stitch over edges and thin parts and weaving over the hole itself. Do not use a knot. Work on the right side of the fabric. Start and end with running stitch beyond the hole. Do not pull threads tight.

### How to Darn

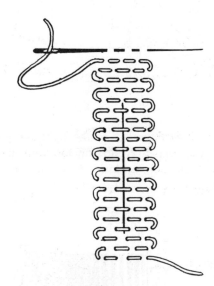

**Straight Tear.** Fit edges together and reinforce with fabric underneath if desired. Work back and forth with small running stitches covering a space wide enough so it will not pull out. For a quicker job use zigzag stitch with sewing machine.

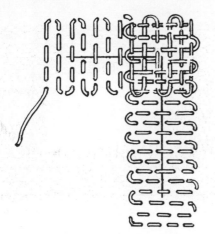

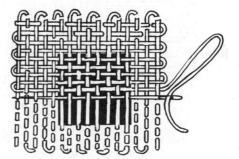

**Three-cornered Tear.** Darn as for straight tear in both directions lapping at the corner. This may also be done with zigzag stitch.

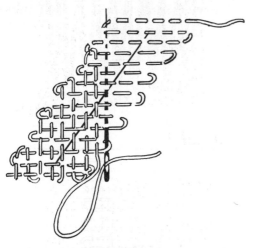

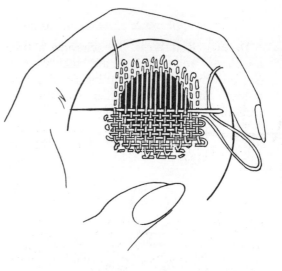

**Diagonal Tear.** Darn as shown covering a diagonal-shaped space. Turn and darn in the opposite direction to reinforce.

**Darning a Hole.** Trim the edges of the hole. Weave very closely over the hole. Follow the design of the fabric if possible.

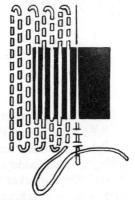

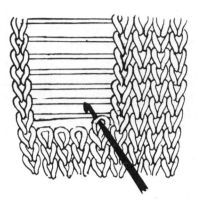

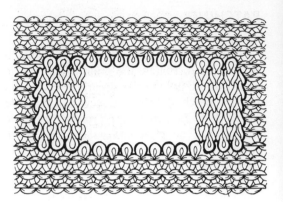

**Darning Knit Wear.** To reinforce a thin spot, work rows of duplicate stitch over it (see previous page and Knitting section). For weaving stockinette together see Knitting section.

To mend a run in knit wear, pick up stitches with a crochet hook. Fasten threads on wrong side.

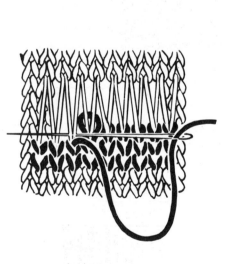

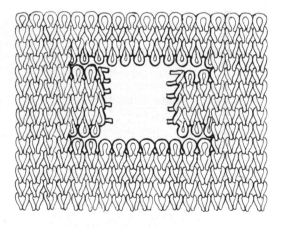

**To Weave a Hole in Knit Wear.** Unravel broken stitches to make a square or rectangle. Turn stitches along the sides to wrong side and hem. With needle and thread pick up the stitches (plus one beyond the hole on each side) working back and forth.

Fasten yarn on right side at lower right hand corner. Make stitches on the diagonal threads somewhat in the manner of duplicate stitch. Continue across row and work back in reverse. Keep stitches same size as those of the knitting.

# PATCHING

When a hole is large it is better to patch than to darn. Follow the grain of the fabric and trim the hole into a square or rectangle. Cut the patch ½″ to 1″ larger than the hole on all sides. Be sure to use pre-shrunk fabric for patches on garments which have been washed. Match stripes, prints, etc. as nearly as possible.

## How to Patch

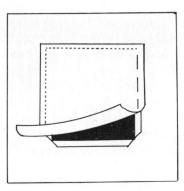

edges of patch on wrong side.

Or after hemming on the right side, press seams open and catch down on wrong side with herringbone stitch.

# MENDING NET OR LACE

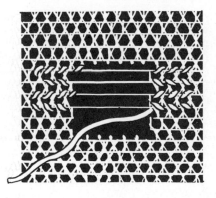

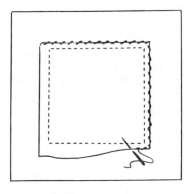

**Hemmed Patch.** This is suitable for many types of fabrics. Cut the patch 1″ larger than the hole all around. Clip the hole at corners ¼″ and turn edges under. Baste hole, centering it over patch. Hem the turned edges on the right side. Turn under and hem

Weave horizontal threads as for ordinary darning, starting and ending 3 or more meshes on each side of hole.

Now weave diagonally from upper right hand corner to lower left catching around the horizontal threads.

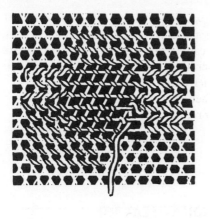

If it seems necessary, weave again from the opposite diagonal.

## RECLAIMING WOOL

Do not attempt to unravel knitting or crochet yarn which is matted. If yarn is worth reclaiming then rip the seams carefully by clipping and removing threads with which seams are sewed. Find the last bound-off stitch and unravel each piece separately. Wind the yarn around a piece of heavy cardboard, keeping ends free. Tie together in about 4 places. Remove from cardboard and dip in warm water. Let drip dry. The weight of the water will remove the kinks.

## CARE OF LACES

Fine lace should last indefinitely if properly cared for. The really fine laces were made in the 17th and 18th centuries and are mostly to be found in museums, but if you own some good lace of more modern vintage it is well to give it good care.

The enemies of lace are dampness, folding, and yellowing. Since dampness encourages mold keep laces in a dry place but avoid dry heat.

Never pack laces tightly; lay tissue paper in the folds to avoid creasing.

To delay yellowing, store in a cool dry dark place. Avoid chemically treated papers. Yellowed lace can be restored but it should be done by an expert. Handle lace as little as possible.

## CARE OF LINENS

Your good linens deserve careful treatment.

Wash linens in hot water with a mild soap or detergent; a water softener may be used if necessary. Linen yields dirt easily so one sudsing may be sufficient. Rinse thoroughly.

Where there are stains on white linen, a bleach may be used with care but it should be mixed with water in the washer or tub instead of being used on each spot. Rinse out thoroughly.

To give a light gloss to linen follow the directions on the package for "light starching" being sure it is well dissolved.

Straighten linen when hanging to dry. Dampen several hours before ironing. Use a hot iron, but be careful not to scorch. Do not press creases in with a hot iron as it may break the fibers. Fold by hand.

Fold large cloths down the center and roll on a mailing tube. Store unstarched to avoid attracting silverfish.

## CARE OF SYNTHETICS

None of the new so-called miracle fibers will take too much heat. They rate in heat sensitivity as follows: Dynel is most sensitive, acetates are next; Orlon and Dacron are medium and nylon is the least sensitive. Use a low temperature until you are sure how much they will stand.

Blends can be a problem if you do not know the fibers in the fabric. When you buy find out the fiber content and what the recommendations are for care. Keep labels for reference when laundering.

Always separate white from colors when laundering. This is especially important for synthetics because some fibers have a strong attraction for dye and soil.

Wash frequently and before garments become too soiled. Most of the new fibers give up soil readily if it has not become imbedded.

With the exception of some of the filmy, delicate fabrics, garments of synthetics if well made can be machine-washed. Use warm, not hot, water and add a water softener if necessary. Use a short washing cycle (4 to 6 minutes) and do not spin overlong. Avoid creasing with wringer or hand twisting. Hand wash delicate fabrics.

Grayed nylons can be whitened with a chlorine bleach following directions on the bottle. Rinse thoroughly. If this is not sufficient use a color remover.

In washing permanent pleats, do not use too-hot water. They were put in by heat and heat can take them out. Rinse at the same temperature and drip dry on a hanger. "Finger-press" if necessary.

When pressing synthetics, use low heat and press on the wrong side.

## MENDING LEATHER

Tears in leather articles (gloves, jackets, etc.) can be mended satisfactorily to extend their wearing period. Seams in gloves should be mended by using the same stitch as used in the construction of the glove—whipping, buttonholing, or saddle stitching.

To mend tears in leather, reinforce both edges with blanket stitches, drawing the tear together as you work. Use fine thread for thin leather and coarser thread for heavy leather.

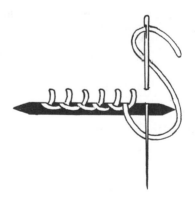

For small holes start in the same way with a row of blanket stitches around the edge of the hole. Fill in with rows of blanket stitch worked into the preceding row. Decrease the number of stitches (by skipping a stitch) toward the center.

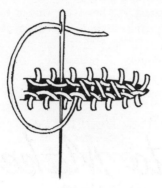 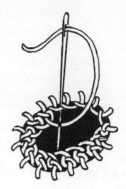

Large holes in leather will probably need to be patched. Cut a piece of leather, lay underneath the hole and attach with fine overhand stitches around edge of hole. Turn to wrong side, trim edges of patch and overhand edges of patch to the garment.

There are a number of products, such as press-on tape, mending tissue, and cement, available for doing quick jobs of mending and patching. For the most part they are satisfactory for certain jobs and withstand several washings and dry cleanings. Look for these at notion counters and follow directions which come with the package.

# CHAPTER 14

# Things to Make for Christmas

Here follow a collection of unique articles especially designed for Christmas. For holiday parties the jingle-bell stole or light-up skirt are fun to make and fun to wear.

Delight the children with a twinkling Christmas house or jumbo size (2-foot-high) dolls—gingerbread man and boy doll—which can be made quickly of felt.

A real conversation maker is a skirt with a Christmas tree that actually lights up. The skirt is made of a three-quarter circle of white felt with grosgrain-ribbon waistband. The tree is formed of rows of fringed green felt. The lap forms a pocket and the lights work on a tiny pocket battery. The skirt is decorated with tiny Christmas tree ornaments and is also lovely without the light-up feature.

## LIGHT UP HOLIDAY SKIRT

**Materials.** 2 yds 72″-wide white felt for skirt; ¼ yd green felt for tree; 1½″-wide green grosgrain ribbon for belt, twice the length of waist measure plus 2″ for lap and seams; small Christmas-tree decorations; large sequins; a string of eight lights; battery; switch; and tape. See: *"To attach battery."*

**To make pattern.** Fold a 72″×72″ piece of paper in quarters. For a 27″ waist measure, set compass at 5⅝″ and draw ¼ of a circle at folded corner. Measure out 29″ (or desired length of skirt) from this line around; mark. Cut ¼″ (dotted line) inside small circle. For other waist measurements, set compass: 5⅜″ for 25½″ waist; 5⅞″ for 28″; 6½″ for 29″ (always allow ¼″ for seam at waistline when cutting pattern). Open up pattern and cut away ¼ of it. Using pattern, cut skirt of white felt. From white felt, also cut a strip 1″ wide and length of skirt, and cut a triangle, following diagram. Divide triangle crosswise into nine sections and mark lightly. Cut strips of green felt 2¾″ wide to make nine rows across tree. Fringe strips by slashing ⅛″ apart to within ¼″ of top edge. Cut green base for tree 2½″ square with "trunk" ¾″ wide by about 2″ long.

**Making.** Bring straight edges of skirt together, centering over felt strip, edges meeting. Edge-stitch, leaving left side free 7″ from top for placket. Attach belt of double grosgrain. Sew on fasteners. Beginning at bottom, pin rows of green fringe to triangle. Edge-stitch at top of each row. If lights are used, arrange on wrong side of "tree" with end of string at bottom and loose wires at top near pocket, where battery will be placed. Make small holes in felt and push lights through.

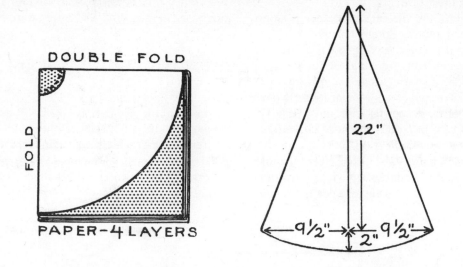

DOUBLE FOLD

FOLD

PAPER-4 LAYERS

22"

9½"    2"    9½"

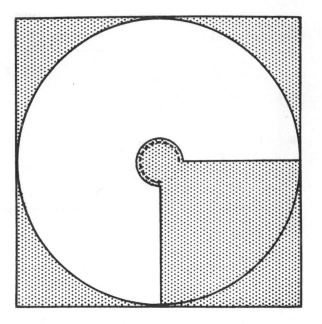

**Connection.** Cut insulation away about 1" from end of wires on switch and lights. When making connection, twist exposed ends together tightly. Cover with tape to prevent short circuit. Connect one end of switch (wire) to one of the terminals at end of battery (either terminal), the other end of switch (wire) to string of lights (either wire), the other end of lights to other side of battery terminal. (Wrap exposed end around terminal; cover with tape for good connection.) For compactness and to keep connection secure, wrap around with adhesive tape. If lights do not work, check for loose connections. If lights dim, let battery "rest."

Try on skirt and pin tree in proper position (see photograph). Stitch triangle to skirt around outer edge, leaving open above top three rows of fringe on left side. Stitch across at this point to form pocket. Apply base below tree. Arrange and sew decorations to tree. Use star or large snowflake sequin at top. By cutting a hole in centers, large round sequins may be used as reflectors on lights.

**To attach battery.** We used a 9-volt radio battery, ✕246 Neda 1602, which measures about 2″ long by 1″ wide and deep; a minia- ture rotary on-and-off switch, which can be purchased in radio and TV supply stores.

## TWINKLING CHRISTMAS HOUSE

The twinkling Christmas house will delight the whole family, but especially the children. It is fashioned of white and bright colored felt glued to cardboard. The string of lights can be on a transformer which causes them to blink on and off.

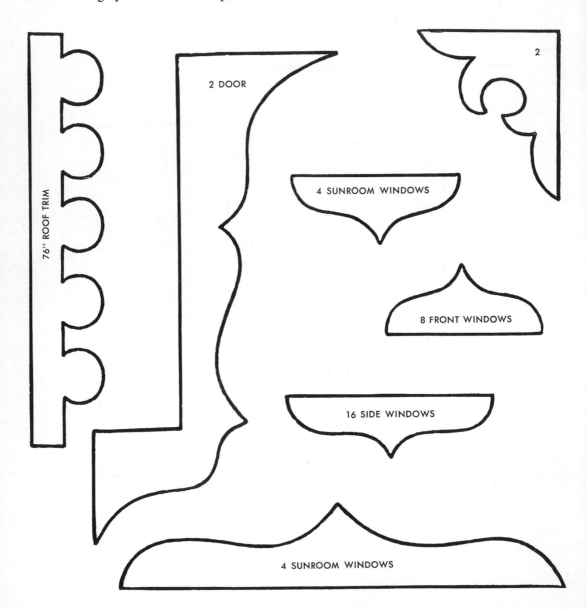

76″ ROOF TRIM

2 DOOR

2

4 SUNROOM WINDOWS

8 FRONT WINDOWS

16 SIDE WINDOWS

4 SUNROOM WINDOWS

**Materials.** Mediumweight cardboard; 72"-wide wool felt as follows—½ yd white, ⅛ yd pine green, piece of red 10"×20", piece of yellow 2"×10"; 2 small Christmas trees, a wreath, and a small angel; 16 gold rosette sequins ⅜" diameter; 4 large green sequins 1¼" diameter; 1 sun-burst red sequin ⅝" diameter; ice-cream stick; 1 soda straw; casein-plastic glue; heavy black paper; red plastic tape 1½" wide; yellow cellophane.

**Making.** Cut cardboard and white felt as follows: For *sunroom,* 2 pieces 4½"×7¼" (sides); 1 piece 6½"×7½" (end; measure up 4½" at sides, and draw lines from these points to center top). For *main house,* 2 pieces 5¾"×8½" (sides); 2 pieces 9½"×10½" (ends; measure up 5¾" at sides and draw lines to center top). Cut out front *windows* 1½" square; side windows (house) 2" square; side windows (sunroom) 1⅜" square—3 windows ¼" apart. Divide spaces evenly, and center windows. Lay cardboard on felt pieces, and mark and cut windows in felt. Line windows with yellow cellophane. For *yard,* 1 piece white felt and 1 piece cardboard 18"×25". For *turret,* cut 1 piece white felt 3¾"×5½"; slash deep V's at top. Cut cardboard and red felt as follows: For sunroom *roof,* 2 pieces cardboard 5¼"×8"; 1 piece felt 8"×10½". For *house roof,* 2 pieces cardboard 7½"× 9½"; 1 piece felt 9½"×15". Cut yellow felt for *door* 2"×3¾" and several *"flagstones."* Cardboard for *chimney*—4 pieces 2⅛"×3"; 1 piece 2½" square with center hole 1⅛" square.

**Decorations.** Cut 2 chimney curlicues (pattern given) and arrowhead and feather of black paper; cut window and door trimmings of green felt like patterns (number to cut given on patterns) and scalloped edging for roof.

**Building the house.** Assemble cardboard pieces of house, roof, and chimney with cellophane tape. Glue white felt to house and red felt to roof. Glue yellow felt door to center front of house. Glue green trimmings around door and windows and along edge of roof. Glue felt yard to cardboard base. Cut a V in two sides of chimney to fit roof. Cover chimney and top with plastic tape, and draw bricks on with white ink. Glue on top; glue chimney to roof and curlicues to each side of chimney. Roll white felt piece for turret into cylinder, and sew together. Insert soda straw, bring points together, and sew. Cut curve at bottom to fit roof. Glue to roof. Make weathervane cross (3½"×5") of narrow strips from ice-cream stick. Paint with black ink. Glue arrow and feather to cross piece. Glue gold sequins as shown in picture, red sequin over door. Place house on felt "yard." Attach wreath to door; set trees in front. Glue flagstones in front of door. If lights are used, cellophane tape holds them in place.

For source of where to purchase the string of lights, battery etc., for the Christmas articles, write to Needlework & Sewing Center, Good Housekeeping, 57th Street and Eighth Avenue, New York 19, N.Y.

## JINGLE-BELL STOLE

A jingling Christmas stole is easily made from a square of dress-weight wool jersey folded and stitched into a triangle and edged with white-wool fringe. Small Christmas bells are scattered on the outside, each attached to a large silver sequin on the inside.

**Materials.** 1⅜ yd of red wool jersey; a 2-oz skein of white knitting worsted or 2½ yd of 4" white fringe; 28 bells; 28 large (1") silver sequins and beads for sewing on.

Trim the jersey to make a 46" square. Fold diagonally to make a triangle. Pin together carefully along fold and at edges and round off lower corner. Turn raw edges to inside and baste. Stitch ready-made fringe along curved edge; or make fringe by winding yarn over two layers of 4"-wide brown paper and stitching ¼" from one edge. Remove paper; cut loops. On outside of stole, sew bells 6" apart in five rows. On wrong side of stole, sew a sequin (with bead in center) underneath each bell.

## GINGERBREAD MAN AND BOY DOLL

### Gingerbread Man

**Materials.** ½ yard 72″-wide medium-brown felt. Dacron fiber or kapok for stuffing. ⅜ yard featherboning. Scraps of white felt. 4 small pink pompons from ball fringe. 1 package white rickrack. Brown and white mercerized sewing thread. Black six strand embroidery floss, 1 skein. 1″ graph paper. Tracing paper.

**Patterns.** Make whole pattern for doll body (each square on diagrams equals 1″ on graph); fold graph paper in half; copy pattern (Fig. 1). Be sure to mark dots indicated on diagram. Cut pattern. Make pattern for arms in the same manner, using one thickness of paper. Patterns for eyes and mouth are given in actual size; trace Figs. 2 and 3.

**Cutting.** Cut two body and four arm sections from brown felt. Cut two eyes and one mouth from white felt.

**Sewing.** 1. Place boning along center of one body section, with one end 1″ from top of head as shown (Fig. 4). Sew in place by hand along both edges of boning, being careful that stitches do not come through to right side of felt.

2. With wrong sides together, stitch body sections ⅛″ from edges, leaving openings between dots as shown (Fig. 5). Stuff doll through openings, leaving doll rather flat. Stitch all opening edges except those for arms.

3. Stitch two arm sections together ⅛″ from edges, leaving straight end open. Stuff arms. Baste opening edges together. Insert arms about ¼″ into body (Fig. 6). Baste through all thicknesses. Stitch ⅛″ from edge of body. Stitch along neck as shown.

4. Sew rickrack in place by hand. Sew eyes in place 2″ from top of head and 3″ apart. Using three strands of black embroidery floss, take several stitches at centers of eyes. Attach a pompon for nose 3″ from top of head. Sew mouth in place. Sew remaining pompons to body (see photograph) 1¾″ apart.

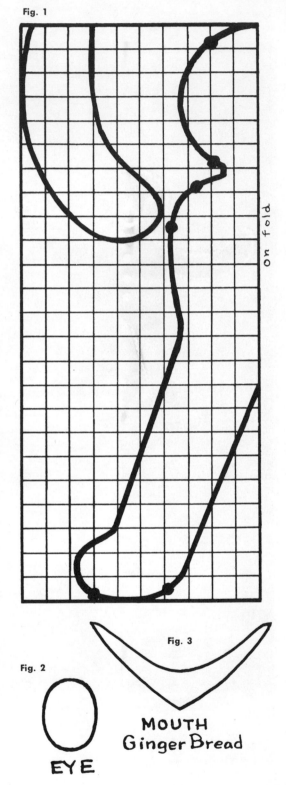

Fig. 1

on fold

Fig. 2

EYE

Fig. 3

MOUTH
GingerBread

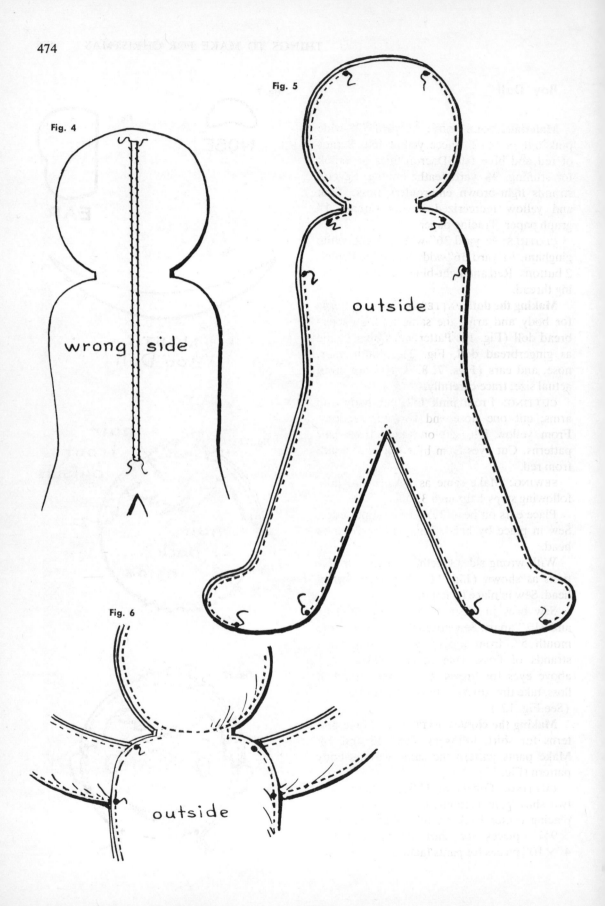

**Fig. 4**

wrong side

**Fig. 5**

outside

**Fig. 6**

outside

## Boy Doll

**Materials.** DOLL BODY: ½ yard 72″-wide pink felt, 8″×12″ piece yellow felt. Scraps of red and blue felt. Dacron fiber or kapok for stuffing. ⅜ yard featherboning. Several strands light-brown embroidery floss. Pink and yellow mercerized sewing thread. 1″ graph paper. Tracing paper.

CLOTHES: ¾ yard 36″-wide red-and-white gingham. ½ yard 36″-wide light-blue denim. 2 buttons. Red and light-blue mercerized sewing thread.

**Making the doll.** PATTERNS: Make patterns for body and arms the same as for gingerbread doll (Fig. 1). Patterns for eyes (same as gingerbread doll, Fig. 2), mouth, hair, nose, and ears (Figs. 7, 8, 9, 10) are given actual size; trace carefully.

CUTTING: From pink felt, cut body and arms; cut one nose and two ear sections. From yellow felt, cut one each from hair patterns. Cut eyes from blue felt and mouth from red.

SEWING: Make same as gingerbread doll, following steps 1 through 3.

Place ears on head 3½″ from upper edge. Sew in place by hand. This will be back of head.

With wrong sides together, stitch hair sections as shown (Fig. 11). Slip over top of head. Sew in place by hand.

Sew eyes in place 3″ from top of head and 3½″ apart. Sew nose in place 3¾″, and mouth 5″, from top of head. Using three strands of floss, take several stitches ¾″ above eyes for brows. Using one strand of floss, take tiny stitches above nose for freckles. (See Fig. 12.)

**Making the clothes.** PATTERNS: Make patterns for shirt, following Figs. 13 and 14. Make pants pattern the same way as body pattern (Fig. 15).

CUTTING: Gingham: Using patterns, cut two shirt-front sections; cut one shirt back, placing center back on fold. Cut two 3½″×9¾″ pieces for shirt facing. Cut two 4″×10″ pieces for pants facing.

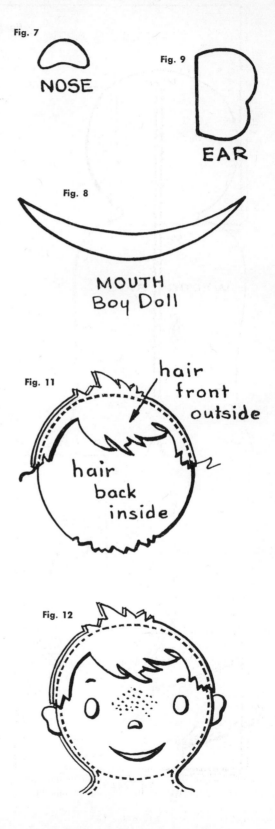

Fig. 7

NOSE

Fig. 9

EAR

Fig. 8

MOUTH
Boy Doll

Fig. 11

hair
front
outside

hair
back
inside

Fig. 12

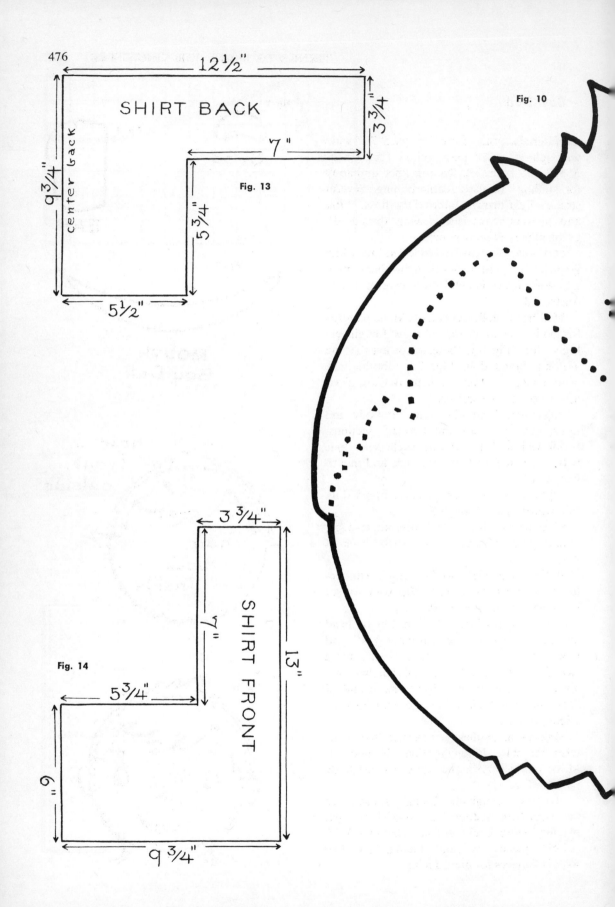

476

12½"

SHIRT BACK

3 ¾"

9¾"

center back

7 "

Fig. 13

5 ¾"

5½"

Fig. 10

3 ¾"

Fig. 14

7"

5¾"

SHIRT FRONT

13"

9"

9 ¾"

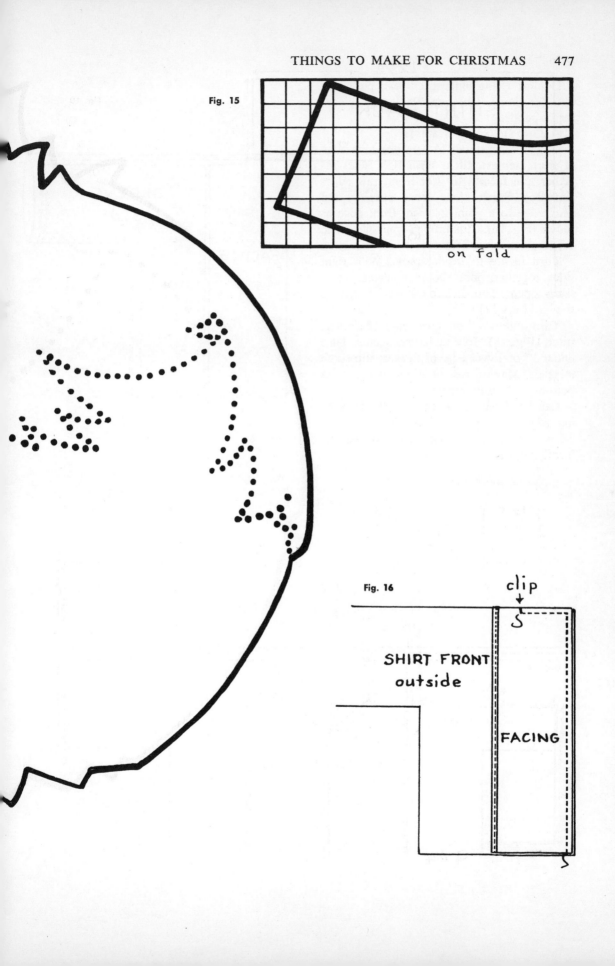

Fig. 15

on fold

Fig. 16

clip

SHIRT FRONT
outside

FACING

478

Denim: Using pattern, cut two pieces on fold for pants. Cut two 3½″×13″ pieces for suspenders.

SEWING (make ½″ seams).

SHIRT: Turn under ¼″ on one long edge of shirt facings; stitch. With right sides together, pin facings to shirt front, raw edges matching. Stitch along front opening and neck edge to a point 2″ from front edge as shown (Fig. 16). Clip through seam allowance at end of stitching. Trim seam.

Turn facing to inside; press. With right sides together, join shoulder seams. Press seam open. Topstitch back neck edge as shown (Fig. 17).

Turn under ¼″ on lower edge of sleeves; stitch (Fig. 18). Join underarm seams. Turn under 1″ on lower edge of sleeves; slip-stitch in place. Make a row of stitching ½″ from bottom of shirt. Pink edge.

Lap left front ½″ over right. Tack opening edges to a point 2″ below neck edge. Turn remaining opening edges to outside, forming lapels; press.

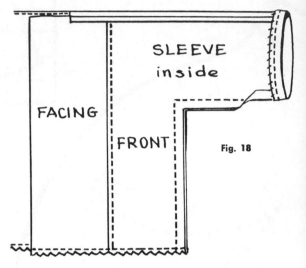

SLEEVE inside

FACING

FRONT

Fig. 18

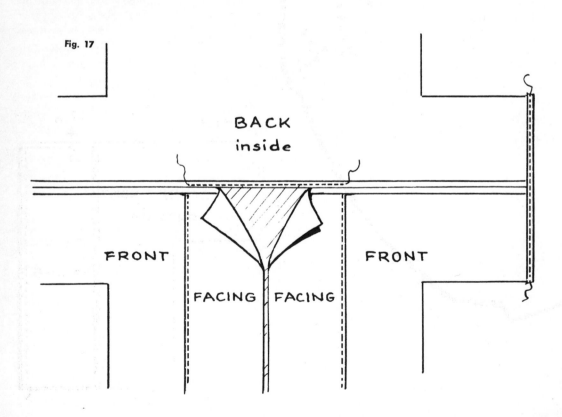

Fig. 17

BACK inside

FRONT

FRONT

FACING   FACING

Fig. 19

PANTS
inside

Fig. 20

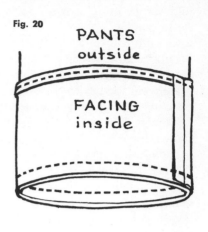

PANTS
outside

FACING
inside

PANTS: With right sides together, join pants sections along side and inner-leg seams (Fig. 19). Slash to point of stitching. Turn under ¼″ on upper edge; stitch. Turn stitched edge 1″ to inside; slip-stitch in place.

Turn under ¼″ on one long edge of pants-facing sections; stitch. Join ends of facing. (Crease seam open.) With right sides together, pin facings to lower edge of pants, matching seams at inner leg (Fig. 20). Stitch, and trim seam. Turn facing to inside; press. Slip-stitch in place. Turn lower edge of pants to outside, forming cuffs.

Fold shoulder straps in half lengthwise, right sides together. Stitch long edges. Trim seam. Turn right side out. Place one end of straps under pants front at upper edge 1½″ from side seam. Tack in place. Sew buttons on outside. Dress doll. Cross straps at center back. Adjust length. Sew straps in place.

# Index